SOUL SCHOOL

The Purpose of Life Revealed

By

Dan Lux

Soul School

b

For information contact Dan Lux at dlux@soulschool4me.com

Cataloging-in-Publication Data on file with the Library of Congress

First Printing: March 2019
Printed in the United States of America

ISBN: 978-1-7338074-0-1
ISBN: 978-1-7338074-1-8 (eBook)

d

Table of Contents

Table of Contents i

Introduction 1

Ch. 1: In the Beginning..6

- Ask Away! 6
- The Original Question 8
- Tiny Miracles of Life 9
- Scientific Theory of Life 16
- Irreducible Complexity 18
- Life from the Ether 24
- Who's Got Your Back?...29

Ch. 2: Universal Intelligence 35

- A Different Perspective 35
- The Atomic Operating Manual 38
- The Flight of Multiple Lifetimes 45
- Comparing Apples to Oranges..50
- Nature's Divine Ratio 55

Ch. 3: Energy 65

- Our Brick and Mortar World 65
- A Matter of Energy..67
- It Takes All Types 71
- The Emptiness Within 75
- It All Leads to the Beginning...79

Ch. 4: What Are You Made Of? 83

- Are You Different from a Rock? 83
- Life on the Dark Side 84

Energy of You 88
The Magnificent 7 93
Think About It..102
Putting It All Together 112
Ch. 5: Body and Mind 115
The Bridge to the Other Side..115
Making Sense of the Senses..120
Shhhh.... A Tree Is Falling..123
Are You Otta Your Mind!..135
Who Are YOU? 141
Ch. 6: The Soul..145
The Gift That Keeps Giving 145
Me, Myself, and I..149
Bonding with Your Soul 159
The 3 R's for the Soul 171
Cramming for Finals 179
Ch. 7: Life on the Other Side 183
Dying to be Born..183
Kicking the Bucket 185
Rebirth of a Soul..188
Hell on Earth..198
Life Between Lives..202
Ch. 8: Come Here Often?..215
Reincarnation 215
A Passport Through Time 220
Past Life Cases 228
Connected Souls..252
Ch. 9: Bound by Laws 257

Throw the Book At 'Em! 257
Law of Attraction 265
Law of Karma 287
Ch. 10: Fine Tuning the Mind 301
The Rock in Your Head 301
By All Stretches of the Imagination 307
A Clean Slate 326
The Mind-Body Refresher 335
Instruments of the Mind 347
I Can't Believe That Just Happened! 360
Ch. 11: Singularity 365
Worlds United 365
Inner Evolution 371
Soul Contracts 390
Dreamtime 396
Ch. 12: Your Purpose Revealed 406
Closing Arguments 406
The Divinity 411
INDEX 417

Introduction

"There are only two ways to live your life: One is as though nothing is a miracle. The other is as if everything is. I believe in the latter." -- Albert Einstein (attributed, but unconfirmed)

Have you ever wondered about life…why we are here? What's our direction? I mean, what IS the purpose of life anyway? Is there a reason why billions of people struggle to earn a living, provide for their families, or simply fight to survive? What's the point to all the toil, pain, and suffering? Is life really only about trying to achieve a hopeful balance between the good and the bad? Are we here to cram as much into one lifetime as possible, to experience all the world has to offer, to laugh, cry, love, and inspire without ever really knowing how much time we have? Then, in the end, do all our accomplishments and experiences simply vanish? And what if we fail to achieve some of our desires and ambitions, does that mean we blew our only chance?

When you look around and see a planet filled with enormous diversity and incredible marvels, do you question how it all came about? After all, billions of years ago the planet was just a giant ball of lifeless rock fused together from primordial space dust. How did all the majestic lifeforms develop? Is the entire planet - with its vast assortment of people, animals, vegetation, intelligence, culture, technology, and natural resources – all just the end result of random chemical reactions? Or, is there more to it? Is there a reason behind the physical world in which we live? Does life go far beyond the scientific theories of evolution that strain to ignore how a world filled with near-infinite life can develop by random chance?

These are all lofty questions, but questions I've been chewing on since I was very young, and questions I committed to take on in this book. Life's purpose is a mystery we'll investigate. We'll search for evidence, clues, and facts, and then examine our findings, piece together the evidence, and derive a conclusion based on logic and reason. Each chapter acts like a piece of a grand puzzle that provides a completer and more focused picture of the whole. We'll explore some rather advanced spiritual concepts, and to maintain credibility it's important to first build a firm scientific foundation. The first few chapters are more heavily weighted in science to help establish this base, which will allow us to explore some incredible spiritual insights in the later chapters.

Viewing the world in unusual ways has allowed me to ask questions and seek answers that many have never considered. In writing this book, I want to challenge you to also alter your perspective of reality. Together, we'll consider how the spark of life began and question if it was influenced by a higher intelligence. We'll investigate the building blocks of physical matter and the underlying energies holding it all together. We'll delve into the spiritual realm, open the possibility that your body contains an immortal soul, and discuss the spiritual laws that govern it. We'll explore the phenomenon of reincarnation and learn how to attract the life of your desires. All this is done with the aim of providing a framework to explain the function and purpose of life, delivered in a fascinating blend of science and spirituality.

You'll be introduced to some provocative, non-traditional concepts. Ideas and thoughts backed with science and deep understandings that date back thousands of years. We live in a physical world and conduct our lives in accordance with the laws of the physical world. Gravity acts on all of us whether we understand and acknowledge it or not. You don't have to believe in gravity to get hit in the head by a falling apple. We also live in a spiritual world. And whether we understand, acknowledge, and believe it or not, we are also bound by the laws of the spiritual world. Our physical lives are inseparable from our spiritual lives and vice versa.

Despite this, there is little recognition or discussion of spirituality in Western science, politics, business, academia, and many other aspects of Western society. In the West, we often seek to discover and understand how the universe functions, yet there's an inherent societal norm rejecting anything 'spiritual' as crack-pot theories. The predominant thought among many in the leading-edge sciences is ancient cultures are the least intellectually 'civilized,' creating an ironic paradox. In reality, ancient cultures have the closest understanding of the truths behind how the universe operates. These truths go ignored by some of the most public minds because they come from sources perceived as a primitive intelligence. It's an unfortunate bias. Contemporary science has blinded itself to the spiritual dimension, focusing its attention instead on only the study of the physical world. It's my belief Einstein's search for a unifying theory will not be discovered until modern science opens its mind to the spiritual realm and the influence consciousness has over the material world. Consciousness is the bridge connecting Newtonian physics (or classical mechanics) with the quantum world. The blending of the physical realm with the spiritual realm is where true unity exists.

My hope in writing this book is to play a small part in changing the public perception of the spiritual realm. To provide a simplified understanding of the how's and the why's of life from both a scientific and spiritual perspective. A resource that connects the dots of life's purpose for the ordinary person to understand and appreciate. Concepts in this book will encourage you to accept topics that are commonly mocked and ridiculed. They'll arouse your imagination with questions and awareness, and open minds' of even the fiercest skeptics just enough to allow the light of alternative possibilities to shine in.

When you have a basic understanding of how the physical and spiritual worlds interact, you'll be armed with powerful tools to shape and control your life and its purpose. But for all this to work, I need to ask that you read and digest the contents of this book with an open mind. Read with openness and desire, and your understanding of the world will transform. Ask questions that take you to the fringes of lunacy… and you'll discover you're not so crazy after all. Consider answers that may defy conventional thought and you'll recognize that conventional thinking can often be rather unconventional.

You deserve health, happiness, and fulfillment in your life. You can create it. You can learn, step by step, the process to change your life and make it full. Whether you have a life-threatening illness, relationship difficulties, financial issues, or are struggling with a difficult situation, you can start changing now. You can realign yourself with your deepest longing and your greatest good. Simply ask. Your requests will be answered. But you must believe with unrelenting conviction in what you are asking and in the source from which it will come. For that to occur you'll need evidence and proof. This book will arm you with that proof and allow you to understand how your thoughts and actions create your reality, for better and for worse. You'll discover that you have the power to change the things you dislike and attract the things you desire.

It's an honor to share these understandings to help you appreciate your purpose and guide your journey through life. By sharing what I've discovered, I'm not seeking to discredit or dismantle your belief system. Instead, my desire is to build upon your existing beliefs to enhance your cradle-to-grave journey. Whether you are driven to unravel life's mysteries, or you simply accept them as they are, understanding these profound realities is an invaluable gift. Over time, society has blinded us to the realities of the world, I'm about to restore your vision!

As quoted in the opening, "*There are only two ways to live your life: One is as though nothing is a miracle. The other is as if everything is. I believe in the latter.*" This is a mantra we should all live by. So, let's start now by exploring some of life's miracles…

Everything in life is a miracle.

Ch. 1: In the Beginning...

"He who asks is a fool for five minutes, but he who does not ask remains a fool forever." – Mark Twain

Ask Away!

One of the many things I've learned in life is not to be afraid to ask questions. Growing up I was often intimidated to ask about things I didn't understand. It didn't matter if I was at school, in public, or even in the company of family. I thought by asking questions it would reveal my ignorance. I'd be laughed at, ridiculed, and viewed as the only dumb person in the room. But as I grew older, I discovered I wasn't the only uninformed person - most of the time NOBODY knew the answers to my questions. All the people I feared that would mock and tease me were just as clueless as I was. Then, as my confidence grew, I became more courage about asking questions and would ask more and more. Through my inquisitive nature, I came to realize by asking questions I was the smart one! I mean, how else are you supposed to learn?

At every turn and conversation, I'd riddle people with questions. I questioned my way through college and into the business world. I would ask hundreds of questions a day. How does this work? What happens when you do that? Explain how you achieved these results? Why can't it operate this way? I was like a five-year-old asking questions and following the answers with more mind-numbing questions. It turned into a way of life for me. Meeting new people became an adventure. I'd learn so much about them, their background, and their aspirations. I could carry on a conversation for hours just by asking questions. But it wasn't a game or means to entertain myself during dull conversations, I was genuinely interested in learning the answers.

Being overtly inquisitive also opened me up to another level of human behavior - most people are far more confident in what they think they know than what they actually know. It's a nature desire to want to be perceived as intelligent, and henceforth respected. The general opinion is you will carry more credibility the greater your perceived knowledge of a particular subject. However, the flip side is also true. Knowledge can be a priceless gift, but the false impression of knowledge can be more dangerous than ignorance itself. Socrates defined wisdom as "*...knowing you know nothing*." Or to restate, a wise person is a person who knows what they don't know. Today, there seems to be an unlimited ability to ignore our ignorance. Many don't act out of Socratic wisdom, but rather Socratic irony. Instead of admitting they don't truly understand something, they'll mask their ignorance by parroting headlines and news sound bites to create the illusion of credibility. But, it's just an illusion. It seems like the hardest 3 words for people to say today is "I don't know."

So, don't be afraid to ask questions, it'll only make you smarter and see through the illusion. Don't be afraid to confess when you don't know something. Admitting you are aware of what you don't know makes you wiser... at least in the eyes of Socrates!

This is the philosophy that I'd like to set as the bedrock of the book. Strive to understand what you don't know. Through this you'll be encouraged to identify what to learn and what to ask. In all aspects of life, nature, society, politics, journalism, business, family, and relationships. Ask away! By asking questions, you not only gain an enormous amount of knowledge, you begin to perceive life differently. Don't be afraid of a smirk or sarcastic comment by asking what you may believe to be a stupid question. Odds are those making the smirks and comments don't know the answer either. Get out there and ask, ask, ask, ask, ask, ask, ask...Questions are the lifeblood of knowledge, and knowledge is power. As the ancient Persian proverb goes, *"Embrace your ignorance for one breath so you do not remain ignorant until your last."*

The Original Question

Since I took on the challenge of writing a book about the purpose of life, I thought the first question I should ask is one that takes us to the very beginning. How did life start?

I'm not talking about the start of life back on that fateful night when your dad looked at your mom with a gleam in his eye as she radiated a glow of fertility. I'm referring to the start that took place more than 3 ½ billion years ago. Way back in earth's primordial beginning when the first lifeform appeared on the planet.

As we understand it, life on earth began as a simple single-celled organism that carries the distinction of being the matriarch to every lifeform on the planet. Far in the distant past, this single celled lifeform was completely unaware that after billions of years of evolution it would advance into a being whose primary survival instincts is ordering a Triple-Venti-Soy-No-Foam-Latte at a drive through during morning rush hour! My, we've come such a long way from unicellular bacteria. Let's dig in and search for an answer to one of mankind's greatest mysteries, the looming question of life's beginning.

There are many different theories circulating on the origins of life that tend to fall into one of two categories – science based, and everything else. It turns out mainstream science doesn't let much into their folds. We'll explore both sides of the life's origins coin, beginning first with the accepted scientific theories of life and evolution. The scientific approach gets more street credibility and people tend to accept it as irrefutable truth since it comes from advanced scientific minds. However, as you'll soon learn, the more you dig into these theories with penetrating questions, large gaping holes and leaps of unfathomable logic begin to surface.

To fully understand and critique the theories of how life began, we first need a basic understanding behind the principles of how life functions. So, let's take a brief biology detour down the path of cell structure and we'll come back to the spark that triggered life better equipped with the knowledge to understand the problems that scientific theory presents. Our brief biology tutorial will not only provide a fundamental understanding of how these rudimentary lifeforms function but will also give an appreciation of the incredible miracles these microscopic organisms are.

Tiny Miracles of Life

Look in the mirror and staring back at you are about 30 trillion cells. Each microscopic cell is responsible for a specific function that maintains life in your body. In addition to working together collectively to keep you alive, these tiny cells must maintain their own individual life. If you could spend a day at the cellular level, you'd find a fantastically complex and busy world providing structure to the body, absorbing nutrients from food and converting them to energy, providing oxygen throughout the body, fighting off germs and infection, and carrying out specialized functions for your bones, skin, lungs, blood, muscles, and internal organs. All life sustaining tasks occur at the cellular level. Each one of these tiny organisms is a miracle in and of itself. It's absolutely amazing how such an ostensibly simple lifeform can operate with remarkable precision and ability. Each cell has a function to serve, and a code of operation it adheres to with faithful diligence and never a murmur of a complaint. There's never an issue of being underpaid and overworked, needing holidays off, sick days, or other HR grievances. They're just microscopic workers that keep chugging along performing their duty on time and without error.

Cells know their role and how to go about doing it through genetic codes that are embedded in its DNA when the body first develops. The encoded genes inform the cell of its function and provide an operating manual with detailed instruction on how to accomplish its tasks. It's a complex and coordinated process with absolutely no room for error, a function that simply cannot be left to chance.

Most cells in a human body have a relatively short lifespan. For example, cells of the stomach lining have a lifespan of only 2 days. Think about that. All the cells that make up your stomach lining as you sit reading this book will be replaced in two days. In just two days you'll have an entirely new stomach lining. Isn't that amazing! Two days from now the lining of your stomach will be coated with functioning, coordinated cells that today are merely inert molecules. And it's not just the cells of your stomach that continuously need to be replaced. On average, 300,000,000 cells die in the human body every minute. Cells of the small intestines last only about a week, lung cells replace themselves every 8 days, skin cells are good for about 2-4 weeks, red blood cells last about 4 months, fat cells last about 8 years (Argh! hit the Stairmaster!), and bone and muscle cells have a much longer lifespan of about 10-11 years.

Now isn't that interesting. The person you see when you look in the mirror each morning will have a completely new cellular body in roughly 10 years. When you turn 90, nearly all of the 30 trillion cells in your body would not have even celebrated their 10th birthday. You'll have a body made of fresh, new, young cells! The only cells that don't replace themselves are the neurons of your cerebral cortex, your heart muscles, and the lens of your eyes. Everything else gets replaced. Which raises another fascinating question – if all the cells of the body get replaced regularly with new ones, then why do we age? How come our skin, bones, muscles, and hair don't remain as youthful and vibrant as that of a 10-year-old? Scientists have been trying to crack that Fountain of Youth question for centuries, and some immoralist and yogis claim they have, but that's not part of this biology lesson, so let's forge forward.

Given the frequency that cells need to replace themselves, it's easy to understand that the most important function to sustaining life of the entire human body is cell division. Unless of course you prefer a lifespan of a common house fly. Now, we've been talking about cells of a fully formed human being. However, when life first began, it didn't start in one magical swoop as a fully formed human, or animal, or sea urchin. We know cells are the most basic unit of life. If life were to begin on Earth from random chemical reactions, it would have begun as a simple unicellular organism. Science and logic tell us life would have begun in the simplest of form and evolved into new and divergent species over billions of years. To accurately analyze the origins of life, we'll need to analyze the simplest single-celled organism known to man – the bacteria.

Every cell is a complex structure with the ability to survive and reproduce on its own, even bacteria. In effect, a cell can be considered very much like a teeny-tiny person. And like a person with specific organs that provide specific life sustaining functions, the cell is also composed of smaller units called *'organelle'* that act like the cell's organs - for example, the cell's membrane, cytoplasm, Golgi apparatus, mitochondria, ribosomes, and the nucleus. And like your body's organs, each organelle is responsible for specific life sustaining functions, such as cell division, cell mobility, creating and processing energy, determining what enters and leaves through the cell membrane, creating proteins, etc. The most important organelle is the nucleus. The nucleus is the brains of the operation and controls all actions of the cell.

The nucleus gets its instructions from the cell's DNA. These long strands of DNA contain genetic information the cell needs to sustain life, function, and reproduce. DNA takes the form of a double-helix (Figure 1). Imagine a DNA molecule as an extremely long ladder with handrails made of sugar phosphate and rungs made of amino acids. Then twist the ladder down the middle to form the all-familiar double-stranded helix.

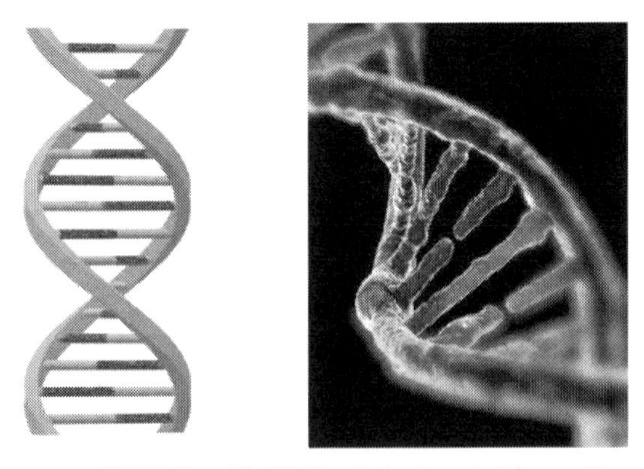

Figure 1 – DNA Double-Helix, 2 Amino Acids per Rung

Now, stay with me here, I know it's starting to get a little detailed and sounding like a high school biology class, but stick it out and you'll see the relevance shortly. Ultimately, we are going to examine the scientific theory of how life began on earth, and for life to continue today, the initial cell that formed life would have had to replicate itself many, many times. Generation after generation it would slowly add new functionality to where it eventually evolved into you! To critique the scientific theory of life, we'll need to get a more detailed understanding of the sheer level of complexity even the simplest of lifeforms present. So, back to the DNA structure…

We've discovered the DNA molecule resembles a very long ladder twisted down the middle. Each rung of the DNA ladder is called a '*nucleotide*' and is made of 2 amino acids. Let's build a DNA molecule starting from scratch to see how these little buggers form. To make our first rung we would connect 2 amino acids and attach them to the handrails. The second rung would require 2 more amino acids giving us a total of 4. We'd add two more to create our third rung giving a total of 6. We'd continue to add rung after rung of 2 amino acid combinations extending our DNA ladder higher and higher until it's fully complete.

When all the necessary rungs of amino acids are in place, we would have what is called a '*genome,*' or a complete set of all the biological instructions the cell needs to function. It gets even more impressive when you realize just how complex these DNA instruction codes are. The amount of information is staggering. To give an example, a typical bacteria cell, one of the simplest known cells in existence, has a DNA ladder with about 4 million rungs. In comparison, human DNA contains about 3 billion rungs! To put that into perspective, if you were to build a standard ladder with 3 billion rungs, then climb it, you would conk your head on the surface of moon before getting halfway up the ladder!

So, as you can see, the DNA molecule is a quite the impressive structure crammed into that teeny-tiny cell nucleus.

Now, for a cell to stay alive and carry out its functions, it needs to produce fuel in the form of proteins. The more complex the species, the more proteins are required. Humans have hundreds of thousands of different proteins, each requiring a separate set of instructions to produce. But exactly how does a cell know which type of protein to produce and how to assemble it? Well, this is where the genetic codes, or rungs of the DNA ladder, come into play.

The thing that makes these rungs so special is they combine to form a biological language the cell can understand. It uses this language to instruct itself on what to do and how to go about doing it. The language is written in an alphabet containing only four letters – A, C, G, and T. Each letter corresponds to a certain type of amino acid - **A**denine, **C**ytosine, **G**uanine, **T**hymine. There are hundreds of available amino acids, but these are the only 4 amino acids used to form the rungs of a DNA ladder. To create a complex instructional code using only 4 letters, you must combine a very long series of rungs, arranged in a very specific order, so their biological words will form the correct instructions telling the cell how to produce all the necessary foods to keep it alive. Each instructional message is called a gene, or a '*genetic code*' and acts as the cell's instruction guide.

As you go up and down this DNA ladder, each section of rungs corresponds to a different genetic code instructing the cell what to do. Some genetic codes are only about 100 rungs in length, while others in more complex species can be as long as 2 million rungs. All these genetic codes together make up the entire genome of that species. Now, here's an interesting little detail. When a cell builds proteins, it is only able to use 21 different amino acids. Why is this so interesting? Well, there are hundreds of amino acids, so the cell must be very careful which amino acids it selects!

Let's build a protein step-by-step to see how the cell uses genetic codes to function. Think of the cell nucleus as a tiny person who builds devices it needs to function out of Lego blocks. The Legos in this example represent amino acids. He's going to pull the Legos from bin containing 500 hundred different Lego shapes – some square, some flat, some round, some long, some short, etc. In total, there are tens of thousands of Lego pieces in this bin. But keep in mind, of the 500 different Lego shapes, you can only use 21. There are 479 Lego shapes that you cannot use mixed in the bin with the 21 shapes that you can use. Got it, you must be very careful which Lego you pull from the bin to make sure you don't accidentally grab one of the 479 unusable Lego shapes.

OK, now that you know what our Lego bin looks like, let's begin to make a protein that allows for cell division. The tiny person building this device begins to climb the DNA ladder until he reaches the section where the rungs provide the instructions on how to build the cell division device. He starts with the first rung, which tells him to take a square Lego from the bin. Then, he climbs up to the next rung which tells him to connect a rectangular Lego to the square one. Climbing up to the next rung, it instructs him to attach a circular Lego to the assembly. He continues to climb up the ladder reading instructions that tell him what specific Lego to connect to the assembly in a specific order until all the instructions in the sequence are completed. When finished, he's created the device using thousands of specific Legos connected in a specific order that can be used to divide the cell. (In the real world, this device is a protein, and the Legos are amino acids.)

Isn't that amazing! With all the possible combinations of Legos available in the bin containing tens of thousands of blocks, and 500 different shapes, only one very specific arrangement of very specific Legos will form this protein. One missed Lego, or one incorrectly shaped Lego, or one Lego out of place, and the entire protein fails. It's simply a miracle that these tiny cellular lifeforms have such precision and intellect. Think about that for a moment. How is it possible that a nucleus of a microscopic organism, with no formal brain or nervous system, no ability to form thoughts, no means of communication, no structured system of intelligence, can execute a task requiring such an enormity of precision? How is that possible?

Imagine if I asked you to take that Lego bin filled with thousands of assorted pieces and toss all them into the air. What do you suppose the odds are that when they land, the Legos you need to form this protein would land in precisely the right order? And that you could do this miraculous Lego toss repeatedly, over and over again, each and every time getting the thousands of Legos to randomly land in precisely the exact order. Hmmm, now we're starting to get into the land of fanciful thinking but hold this thought as we move forward.

Alright, we're now done with the biology 101 lesson! Let's get back to our initial subject, the almighty question of how life began. What do the scientists have to say about this?

Scientific Theory of Life

Now that we know what amino acids are, and how they combine in the millions and billions within the simplest single-celled organisms, it's time to explore what science has to say about how these organic compounds came together to form life.

To get a good frame of reference, let's step into our time machine and set the dial back to when the planet was still in diapers. Three to four billion years ago Earth was a lifeless rock of turbulent oceans, with vast reservoirs of minerals and elements swirling around like a giant bowl of chemical soup. This giant soup caldron contained all the vital components of life – carbon, hydrogen, oxygen, and nitrogen. As static electricity formed in the clouds, earth was repeatedly zapped with violent electrical storms that acted as catalysts fusing particles of different elements together to form exotic new compounds called amino acids, which are the most rudimentary building blocks of life. Once the amino acids were formed, eventually, they arranged themselves in certain patterns to create a simple life-forming thread of DNA (or RNA). Inevitably, over time, the DNA threads would spark the first primitive lifeform. In general terms, that is the theory science presents of how life may have formed on earth.

Well, in the 1950s scientists put this theory to test by recreating primordial earth conditions in the lab. They sealed various gases in an airtight container and exposed them to sparks of electricity to simulate lightning. After about a week, a substance developed on the walls of the container. When they examined the substance, they discovered it contained 11 of the 21 amino acids essential to all life on earth. Since then this type of experiment has been replicated many times and has gotten more and more sophisticated. It's very logical to theorize that all 21 essential amino acids could form naturally in the primordial earth conditions over millions of years when scientist were able to produce them in the lab in just a week. So, let's take the next step that brings us from creating amino acids to creating life. This is where science hits a wall. Scientists have not been able to replicate the formation of even the simplest organism, or anything that can self-replicate, as it raises an issue known as *"Irreducible Complexity."*

Irreducible Complexity

Irreducible complexity is a term used to describe a system that can only be reduced to a certain point before it loses its functionality. Take your smart phone for example. If you were to remove the battery cover, the phone would still function. You could also remove the entire case, set the internal components on a table and it would still work. You could remove the touchscreen and the phone would have some functionality. Calls could come in and you could answer them with voice commands. There are probably a few other non-critical components you could remove, and the phone would continue to have some functionality. So, a smart phone can be reduced in its complexity by removing certain components while still maintaining functionality; however, only to a certain point. Once you pull out the phone's microprocessor, the phone can no longer function, and you've reached its irreducible complexity.

It turns out biological forms also have irreducible complexity; whereby certain and specific components must be present for it to function. Even in the simplest lifeforms, which we know are bacteria cells, there requires an enormous amount of genetic information in the cell's DNA. And we've learned genetic codes must be arranged in precise sequences of millions of nucleotides for the cell to function (remember, nucleotides are the rungs on the DNA ladder). Without genetic codes instructing the cell how to operate and sustain life, the cell would simply die, much like the instruction set programmed into the microprocessor that controls your smart phone. Without that programming, the smartphone cannot function.

Let's now look at the importance of intelligent design vs. random chance. To do this, we can use something we're all familiar with – the very alphabet I'm using to write this book. Below are two different sequences of character arrangements. In the first sequence, the characters have been arranged with intelligent design, while in the second sequence the characters are strictly random.

1) These letters are arranged in a specific way to create a sentence.
2) Ahv oe aodhv eob wy fhpqzxl ncve tjqm znslg htek ky woff wnao dll.

Both sequences contain 67 characters from the same alphabet (including spaces), but since the first one had a little help from an intelligent designer (um, that would be me…) it's arranged in such a way that it can be decoded and understood. The second sequence is a random distribution of characters and as such cannot be decoded and has no meaning. So, how does this apply to the scientific theory of life?

For scientific theory to be credible, it must assume there was no intelligent design acting on the arrangement of amino acids that created the planet's first lifeform. And if that's the case, it must be left to random chance. With this pesky thing called irreducible complexity, we know that a cell cannot function, or divide to create new cells, without its genetic instruction set. We also know even the most basic genetic codes are extremely complex. So, let's see why making the leap from having the availability of amino acids to randomly creating a functioning lifeform is extraordinarily unlikely, so unlikely it renders it to be impossible.

Going back our biology 101 course, you'll remember that the DNA ladder is made of millions of rungs arranged in a very specific and complex pattern. If you recall, the simple bacteria DNA contains 4 million rungs. Now according to science, way back in our primordial soup bowl of organic chemicals, the newly formed amino acids would have to randomly collide to form a life-giving strand of DNA. Let's follow this process step-by-step to see just how unlikely it is this could happen by chance.

We'll examine the process of creating just a single gene, not the entire DNA genome. Each rung along the DNA ladder is made of 2 amino acids from a group of four possibilities – **A**denine, **C**ytosine, **G**uanine, and **T**hymine. Now if we build a DNA strand using random characters, we'll see how many possible combinations there are. Starting with the first rung, we would need a 2 amino acid combination. Since there are 4 possible amino acids to choose from, it gives us 16 different possible combinations:

A-A	C-A	T-A	G-A
A-C	C-C	T-C	G-C
A-T	C-T	T-T	G-T
A-G	C-G	T-G	G-G

Moving up the ladder we would build a second rung with two more amino acids and 16 more possible combinations. This is where the randomness builds exponentially, since in reading the genetic code, each rung is dependent on the other. Just like words in a sentence, they need to be in a specific order for the sentence to be legible. With only two DNA rungs, there are now a whopping 256 possible random combinations!

Following this pattern, by the time we reach the third rung the number of total possible combinations increases to 4,096. With each additional rung, the possible random combinations increase exponentially. Table 1 demonstrates the power of exponential factoring in each of the first ten rungs.

You can see that by rung 10 we've already exceeded 1 trillion possible combinations. To create a very simple genetic code of only 100 rungs, the total possible random combinations is a number followed by 120 zeroes! Putting it in perspective, a single cell in your body contains 100 trillion atoms, your entire body contains 10 octillion atoms (a 1 followed by 29 zeros). If you add up every atom of every planet in the entire Milky Way galaxy the number would be a 1 followed by 68 zeroes.

Genetic Position	Possible Amino Acid Combinations
Rung 1	16
Rung 2	256
Rung 3	4,096
Rung 4	65,536
Rung 5	1,048,576
Rung 6	16,777,216
Rung 7	268,435,456
Rung 8	4,294,967,296
Rung 9	68,719,476,736
Rung 10	1,099,511,627,776

Table 1 - Possible Amino Acid Combinations

So, if a simple gene of only 100 rungs were to be constructed purely by chance, the probability of producing a functioning gene is far greater than the total number of atoms in the entire Milky Way Galaxy! But wait, it gets even more improbable. That's just for one gene. A cell capable of functional life requires many, many more genetic codes than one, and contains sequences that far exceed 100 rungs. A DNA strand of the most basic genome corresponds to a number of random amino acid combinations so inordinately large that it has no relevance to the real world.

And just when you thought it couldn't possibly get any more improbably, it does! The calculation we've just stepped through only considers the 4 viable amino acids. There are hundreds of amino acids that are not feasible swimming around in that same primordial soup bowl adding impurities that would render the genetic code inoperable. When we add this to the equation, you can see the odds of creating just one functioning genome through random chance is so astronomically small that it can comfortably be considered impossible.

So, the mere presence of amino acids in earth's early beginnings does not explain the intelligent arrangement required for life to begin, and scientific theory hits a very big, impenetrable wall. The only way over this wall is through ignorance, denial, or fantasy.

A similar analogy to this scientific theory involves our old companion the smart phone. We all take these ubiquitous devices for granted. Every day people cling to their smart phones to navigate through life, never really taking into consideration the sheer complexity of its internal guts. And just like a biological cell, the more you understand how a microprocessor works, the more you will marvel at the scientific and engineering accomplishments behind them. A smart phone's microprocessor is smaller and thinner than a dime, yet contains billions of electronic components such as resistors, capacitors, diodes, and transistors designed and engineered in a very specific arrangement that help you do everything from video calling your mom to dictating a grocery list. It's comparable to the DNA instructional codes of a cell.

We know what microprocessors are made from, after all, we make billions of them every year. The elemental compounds consist of silicon, arsenic, boron, phosphorous, and copper. The process to create a silicon chip is so precise it almost defies belief. For example, the silicon used in microchips must be so pure that only one out of every ten billion atoms can be an impurity. This is the equivalent of one grain of sand in ten buckets of sugar. Every one of the transistors, diodes, capacitors, and resistors need to be in a specific order and location for the processor to work, even the slightest flaw will render the chip useless.

Now, imagine that we take all these basic elements - silicon, arsenic, boron, phosphorous, and copper - and place them in a large chemical soup bowl with a whole bunch of other chemicals diluting the soup's purity, like the one that was present in earth's beginnings. Then we subject our chemical stew to lightning bolts of electricity to stimulate the particles to bind and fuse. Now, if we follow the same rationale as the scientific theory of life, then we would assume that since all the elemental particles of a smart phone's microprocessor are present in our chemical soup, that eventually with enough electricity and enough time, the atoms would arrange themselves by random chance to form a perfectly functioning smart phone microprocessor. One that we could pluck from the swirling oceans, insert into our smart phone and start posting selfies on Instagram!

The odds of such an event happening is so infinitely small that it is simply considered impossible. It's like picking the winning lottery numbers not once, not twice in a row, not 20 times in a row, but 100 trillion times in a row without ever missing one drawing. Then chalking it up to 'chance,' reasoning that every day in America someone somewhere is winning the lottery so why couldn't someone pick the correct numbers 100 trillion times in a row?

The only possible way a microchip of this complexity could be made is through the help and guidance of an intelligent designer. It is simply impossible if left to random chance. It's such a ridiculous notion that it's laughable. However, we must take seriously the similar notion made with amino acids randomly arranging themselves in just as complex a form to create a functioning genome. The only reason science gets away with it is because most people don't truly understand the complexities of DNA. Welcome to the group of the informed.

Hopefully I've raised your eyebrow at the enormous leap of faith it requires to accept that even rudimentary forms of life began on earth by random chance. Which leaves us to ask, "*If science isn't able to explain life's beginnings without making a fanciful leap of faith, what possible theory could spiritualists have?*" Good question. Let's dive into that.

Life from the Ether

Up to now we've looked only at the scientific theory of how life developed on Earth. Let's now journey to the other end of the spectrum and get our feet wet with spiritual theory.

I'd like to first raise a point I recognized when exploring the differences and similarities between science and spirituality. Theories and findings in science tend to change and get adjusted as technology advances. For instance, there was a time when science believed Earth was the center of the Universe, as science advanced the sun was believed to be the center, now as we're further along scientifically we believe the Universe is infinitely expanding and according to the cosmological principle everywhere is the center of the Universe…or is it? An atom was theorized to be the smallest particle of matter by an ancient Greek philosopher named Democritus, and then in 1897 J.J. Thomson discovered the electron and it became the smallest elementary particle, and then it was leapfrogged by the discovery of quarks and leptons. The planet Pluto was discovered in 1930 and for decades we grew up memorizing the list of nine planets, then along came sophisticated imaging satellites and Pluto lost its planetary status sending us down to eight planets. (I felt bad for the little guy when that happened.)

Spirituality on the other hand, draws much of its knowledge and practices from ancient cultures dating back thousands of years. It has fundamentally remained consistent since spiritual findings are rooted in consciousness, not laboratory equipment. It's a common cultural phenomenon that the more advanced and cosmopolitan a society becomes, the more it separates from nature, and the further distant it becomes from spiritual connectivity. So, it makes sense that ancient societies were more in tune with the spiritual dimension than we are today. When societies and cultures don't teach nor recognize the spirit, it can foster disbelief in spiritual ideas, almost to a point where the spirit or soul takes on fairy tale-like qualities. This lack of spiritual awareness can result in long-standing teachings and beliefs in spirituality to be met with skepticism and ridicule. There are spiritual teachings that have been accepted throughout the world for centuries that can sound incredulous to a person hearing them for the first time. I assure you, if you maintain an open mind and conduct thorough research, spiritual concepts that may seem fanciful will begin to transform into accepted realities.

The core belief central to spiritual philosophy is that all things are energy based – including thought. I dedicate a couple chapters to explore the depths of energy, evaluating both the scientific and spiritual perspectives, so hang in there, before the book is over, you'll be as knowledgeable about energy as you now are about DNA!

A spiritualist believes the essential building blocks of all matter are tiny little packets of swirling energy, not tiny little particles of material. Shaman, yogis, ancient philosophers, and monks have taught this belief for centuries, yet it's only been in recent history that quantum physicists have caught up and proven it to be true. Now it's commonly accepted in particle physics that matter doesn't actually exist until it is measured by some form of conscious awareness. The cars you drive, the furniture you lounge on, the clothes you wear, the homes you live in, and the physical body you occupy – everything in the material world is not composed of tiny little building blocks of matter, but rather tiny little fragments of energy.

In addition to matter being energy based, thoughts are also believed to be energy. When a person focuses their attention on something, thought energy is generated. We've begun to see proof of this through the development of electronic devices that are operated by the mind. Today, there are off-the-shelf gadgets and headsets that translate brain waves (the mind's energy) into digital information and use it to control computers and other apparatus. The technology is used in devices that range from video games all the way up to controls in fighter jets. It's no longer debatable - the human brain emits measurable energy. Brain wave energy has even been categorized. Sleep produces *delta* waves that are below 4 hertz, deep relaxation or meditation creates *theta* waves in the 4 – 7.5 hertz range, light meditation and daydreaming produced *alpha* waves in the 7.5 – 14 hertz range, problem solving produces *beta* waves in the 14 - 40 frequency cycle, and high mental activity produces *gamma* waves in the 40 - 100 hertz range.

So, what does all this have to do with how life on earth began? From a spiritual point of view, the energy that makes up all matter is believed to have originated from thought of a higher intelligence. Tiny packets of energy that quantum physicists say make up the sub-atomic particles of all atoms, originated from thought waves of the Creator. For centuries in many cultures and societies, it has been part of spiritual teaching that life began with the consciousness of God. This pure thought energy, or Universal consciousness, bent inward and created a tremendous explosion of light through which the Universe was born. Some say this is what scientists refer to as the "Big Bang." This is the energy that is said to be the fabric of the Universe that connects everything. It is referred to in some scientific circles as zero-point energy, or quantum vacuum energy, which is the energy that exists in what was once thought to be the vacuum of space.

The individual fragments of energy created from the Big Bang contain all the love, power, and wisdom of the Creator. The whole is within every fragment, much like a hologram. If you divide a holographic image in two, both pieces will contain the entire image of the original. No matter how many times you divide the holographic image, each part will always contain the totality of the original. DNA is the same. Each strand of DNA within every cell contains the genetic code for the entire species. Since this holographic concept is present in many aspects of life, so why can it not be present in the spirit?

These energy fragments, which some believe are the original forms of a soul, lowered the frequency of this thought energy to create particles of matter that formed into the planets and suns throughout the physical universe. After the planets cooled and became suitable for life, the same spiritual intelligence introduced the cell with life-giving genetic codes. Complex genes and their collective genomes became the physical manifestation of this intelligent consciousness, which guided cells to evolve into vast varieties of plants and animals. Over time, each intelligent thought manifestation built upon the other. Minerals supplied sustenance for plants, which made it possible for herbivores, which became food for carnivores, which returned as minerals creating a balance of life. It's a perfectly balanced physical manifestation achieved through intelligent design. While natural mutations and natural selection have occurred and account for many of evolution's diversity, the genesis of life and the vast diversity of species has been guided and shaped by energy-based intelligence, or a universal consciousness.

I recognize hearing this for the first time may sound a bit zany and you're probably wondering if I'm out to lunch, but I ask you to keep an open and objective mind and see where it leads. We've studied amino acids and know the assembly of life-producing genetic codes within a DNA strand is far too complex for random chance. It's a level of structure and order that cannot be explained through arbitrary collisions of particles and must have some form of intelligence involved. Quantum physicists have demonstrated that all matter in the physical world is made of energy. We've been able to not only prove that thought is energy, but we are actually using mind energy in real world applications. Connect the dots and you can see a pattern leading to a creditable case providing validity to the spiritual theory of life. The atoms which formed the original strand of life-giving amino acids on earth were not created by happenstance, but by thought energy of a higher consciousness.

Now if I've just rocked your belief system and you're thinking all this is just insane metaphysical ramblings of a crazy person, well you're not alone. There are many people throughout Western culture who share your sentiments. We live in a society where thoughts of intelligent design are frowned upon, mocked and ridiculed as being religious fanaticism. The entire concept of intelligent design has been wrongfully equated with creationism and all but banned and rejected in Western society. Only 2 states out of 50 allow it to be taught in the public-school systems. I'm not referring to the religious or biblical interpretation of creation, but a common-sense scientific approach – like the version of intelligent design we're exploring and discussing in this book. Here's where it starts to get really crazy. What do you suppose the response would be if you pose the silly and irrational theory of intelligent design to leading scientists who study quantum physics for a living? Well, let's see…

Who's Got Your Back?

One of the greatest minds in contemporary theoretical physics is Dr. Michio Kaku, the co-founder of String Field Theory, bestselling author, acclaimed professor and public speaker. Dr. Kaku has made it one of his life's ambitions to carry on Einstein's quest for a unifying theory. Recently, Dr. Kaku went public discussing particles known as *'primitive semi-radius tachyone'* that he says are physical evidence the Universe was created by a higher intelligence. After analyzing the behavior of these sub-atomic particles, Dr. Kaku concluded the Universe is a "Matrix" governed by laws and principles that could only have been designed by an intelligent being, *"We are in a world made by rules created by intelligence. To me it is clear that we exist in a plan which is governed by rules that were created and shaped by a universal intelligence and not by chance."*

That's a pretty strong endorsement from a mind that knows a thing or two about particle physics. But, let's face it, he's only one person. Perhaps all the chalk dust he's inhaled working through complex mathematical formulas has somehow affected his mind. What do others believe? Well, it turns out that he's not the only one in the intelligent design camp, many prominent scientists also agree the mechanics of cellular design and function can only be so due to a higher intelligence, and who are they…

Let's start with the patriarch of physics himself – Albert Einstein, probably the best known and most highly revered scientist of the twentieth century. What did Einstein believe about intelligent design? Well, here's what he had to say, *"Everyone who is seriously involved in the pursuit of science becomes convinced that a spirit is manifest in the laws of the Universe - a spirit vastly superior to that of man, and one in the face of which we with our modest powers must feel humble."* – *Albert Einstein*

Einstein recognized that the mathematical probability of random selection simply could not account for the vast complexity of even the simplest lifeform, atomic structure, and the delicate balance of nature. There are others who share this belief:

Max Planck - recipient of the Nobel Prize in Physics and known as the father of quantum theory who revolutionized our understanding of the atomic and sub-atomic worlds. *"As a physicist, that is, a man who had devoted his whole life to a wholly prosaic science, the exploration of matter, no one would surely suspect me of being a fantast. And so, having studied the atom, I am telling you that there is no matter as such! All matter arises and persists only due to a force that causes the atomic particles to vibrate, holding them together in the tiniest of solar systems, the atom. Yet in the whole of the universe there is no force that is either intelligent or eternal, and we must therefore assume that behind this force there is a conscious, intelligent Mind or Spirit. This is the very origin of all matter."*

Theoretical molecular biophysicist, Sir Francis Crick, was jointly awarded the Nobel Prize for co-discovering DNA, concluded that the formation of DNA by random natural processes was impossible and life could not have evolved from non-living chemicals under any conceivable earth conditions. Crick is quoted as saying, *"An honest man, armed with all the knowledge available to us now, could only state that in some sense, the origin of life appears at the moment to be almost a miracle, so many are the conditions which would have had to have been satisfied to get it going."*

Dr. Brian Josephson - Nobel Laureate for Physics (1973) said in a lecture he delivered to the Cambridge Physics Society on March 5, 2008, entitled, A Critical Point for Science? *"I can imagine intelligent design is real. Intelligent Design is rejected just because it's part of the scientific culture that it cannot be true, you must not talk about it, but it's not actually disproved. I think it will turn out that there is a design and that the usual theories are wrong there as well."*

Dr. Richard Smalley - Nobel Laureate for Chemistry (1996), wrote in a letter to the Hope College Alumni Banquet in May 2005, *"God did create the universe about 13.7 billion years ago, and of necessity has involved Himself with His creation ever since. The purpose of this universe is something that only God knows for sure, but it is increasingly clear to modern science that the universe was exquisitely fine-tuned to enable human life. We are somehow critically involved in His purpose. Our job is to sense that purpose as best we can, love one another, and help Him get that job done."*

Sir John Carew Eccles – a neurophysiologist and Nobel Prize winner in Physiology / Medicine for his work on the synapse, when asked about the origin of humans stated that he concluded the evolution of life is an *"immensely improbable event"* and added that the origin of life and humans *"is in fact"* a result of *"design, a divine design."*

Sir Fred Hoyle - astronomer and mathematician who developed the Steady State Theory, and pioneer in the science of nucleosynthesis stated, *"If one proceeds directly and straightforwardly in this matter, without being deflected by a fear of incurring the wrath of scientific opinion, one arrives at the conclusion that biomaterials with their amazing measure or order must be the outcome of intelligent design. No other possibility I have been able to think of..."*

There are now scientific organizations whose principle missions are to provide awareness of intelligent design. The Biologic Institute, whose slogan is, *"The more we learn about life, the more clearly it reveals design,"* boasts an impressive list of experts in molecular biology, biophysics, biochemistry, genomics, and astrobiology that include brilliant minds such as; Douglas Axe (PhD Caltech), Stuart Burgess (Professor of Design and Nature), Ann Gauger (BS in Biology from MIT and PhD in Developmental Biology), Guillermo Gonzalez (PhD in Astronomy), David Keller (PhD from UC Berkeley and Postdoctoral Fellow at Stanford University), Matti Leisola (Professor of Bioprocess Technology), Philip Lu (Biotechnologist), Mariclair Reeves (BS in Animal Science and PhD in Cell and Molecular Biology), Richard Sternberg (PhD in Molecular Evolution), Jonathan Wells (PhD in Molecular and Cell Biology), Lisanne Winslow (BS, MS, and PhD in Biology), and the list goes on and on...

... But I think you get the point. Here are some of the deepest thinkers and most brilliant minds in all disciplines of science, who after enormous study have individually reached the conclusion that intelligent design has had a hand in the creation of life on this planet. Perhaps our ancestors were in possession of spiritual wisdom. If all these scientists and Nobel Laureates have concluded that life could not have occurred by random chance and intelligent design has played some role, wouldn't it make sense that high school students should have the benefit of learning what our greatest scientific minds have?

Now that you have the support of a robust list of exceptionally gifted scientists, do you feel you are in better company than those speaking from ignorance? Is it now less foolish and more prudent to believe in what may have initially sounded fanciful? Are you less likely to care if someone ridicules you for considering intelligent design with the understanding you now have and knowing there's a legion of sound-minded scientists behind you? Or perhaps it opens your mind just a crack to the objectivity of intelligent design.

Whatever the case may be, at least now you are better equipped to understand and dwell upon which theory of life's origins makes more logical sense. That life on earth began from a series of random chance collisions that are in such extraordinary violation of mathematical laws of probability that it renders them impossible, and that an octopus, elephant, bird, and human all evolved from the same single-celled organism through endless series of additional mathematically impossible random mutations… Or, that some form of guiding intelligence was involved in the creation and evolution of complex, specifically ordered and structured life systems. After much study, I have joined the list of the aforementioned scientists and placed my beliefs in intelligent design. Because once you understand the awesome and majestic complexity of life, from a logical and scientific perspective, the belief that all life occurred through random chance is what truly becomes the fairy tale.

Well, we've just been through an extensive comparison of life's origins. To understand the purpose of life, it's good to start by understanding life itself, which has been the intent of this chapter. We've seen that the information stored in living cells consist of specific sequences of extremely complex genetic codes that must be arranged in specific ways for the cell to function. There is no undirected physical nor chemical process that demonstrates the capacity to randomly produce a code of such specificity. No chemical evolutionary theory has been able to offer an adequate explanation. Intelligent design holds the most valid theory for the structured order of information in the form of genetic codes necessary to produce life.

Additionally, it is inherently implausible to think that the specificity necessary to coordinate the movements and arrangements of the trillions of cells that constitute a complex lifeform could be explained by the interactions of chemicals. So, if natural selection and random chance didn't create life on earth, and leading minds from many disciplines of science have joined ancient philosophers and shamans who taught the theory of intelligent design, what does it mean to have a higher intelligence infused in our physical world?

Ch. 2: Universal Intelligence

"All Matter originates and exists only by virtue of a force, which brings the particle of an atom to vibration and holds this most minute solar system of the atom together. We must assume behind this force the existence of a conscious and intelligent mind." – Max Planck, father of quantum theory

A Different Perspective

I hope you enjoyed the first leg of our investigation into of the genesis of life. The intent of the thorough analysis is to give a more complete understanding of the complexities involved in DNA genetic codes, how they defy explanation by random chance and necessitate some form of a higher intelligence to produce. As detectives, digging into the purpose of life, we now have a glimpse of the first piece of our mysterious puzzle - a higher intelligence. And like any good gumshoe worth their weight in donuts, having one piece of evidence only pulls us deeper into the case. Follow this lead takes our case in the direction of a higher intelligence.

We've seen that even the simplest unicellular lifeforms require highly structured and specifically arranged genetic codes to function and replicate. The genome capable of supporting life is so intricate and its arrangement so precise, that the probability of it occurring through random chance mathematical reduces to a number so infinitesimally small that in the real world it has no significance and boils down to zero.

For example, assume the arrangement of letters that form the words, sentences, paragraphs, pages, and chapters of this book are left to random chance. At this point in the book, a total of 63,380 characters (including spaces) have been used. Imagine you have a bucket filled with hundreds of thousands of characters from many different alphabets – Greek, Russian, Chinese, Polynesian, Sanskrit, Latin, etc. - and you tossed all of them into the air. What do you think the possibilities would be that the letters would land with only the English characters arranged in the precise order they appear in the preceding pages? You could comfortably say the probability in the real world is zero. It's foolish to even suggest such an experiment is possible. Yet this is only 64,000 characters, imagine the same outcome with 3,000,000 characters! Clearly, these characters could only arrange themselves in the specific order that appears in this book through the help of some type of intelligence acting on them.

Alright then, back to doing what I love, asking questions! There are many on the rigid side of the scientific spectrum who subscribe to the theory that we, and the Universe, exists for no other purpose than simply because it does. Well, that always struck me as odd. If the Universe has no purpose that would mean that each one of us gets to define what that purpose is. But how can each of us have a different definition of purpose if we're all composed of the same biological substances governed by the same unchanging laws of chemistry? Shouldn't that create a giant homogeneous population who all think and react the same? But we don't…why? Perhaps the Universe does have a purpose. In the last chapter we explored a 'higher intelligence' giving order to the construct of genic codes. Would this same higher intelligence also be responsible for providing purpose to the Universe? Let's dig into this further and see how a higher intelligence manifests in other ways. After all, if a Universal Intelligence is responsible for the foundations of life, it must have imprints in other parts of life...right?

To determine this, we'll need to reach back to the challenge I gave you to in the opening pages and look at the physical world differently. I want you to build a sense of intrigue for why things act the ways in which they do. It's fun to do and provides an alternative perspective through which you'll begin to recognize that nature is governed by certain rules and physical laws. There are laws of mechanics, laws of gravity, laws of relativity, laws of thermodynamics, laws of electromagnetism, laws of quantum mechanics, and laws of geophysics. Each of these laws have been hypothesized, experimented on, and proven by great scientific and mathematical minds throughout the centuries. These laws work collectively to keep a balance and order to the physical world. But how were these laws originally defined? Who came up with them and determined their rules of operation? How do they get enforced? And how do inorganic particles of matter, with no power of free thought nor consciousness, know about these laws and how to abide by them? Perhaps a higher intelligence plays a much larger role in the physical world than we could have imagined...

In this chapter, we will explore the physical world for indicators of a higher intelligence guiding its operation. I'll toss around a few atypical perspectives that may alter your views of reality, and hopefully open your eyes to the miracles of life and the balance of the universe that occurs in everything – from the smallest sub-atomic particle, to the largest galaxy. To appreciate them, we'll start small and work our way up. And you can't get much smaller than sub-atomic particles, so let's begin our super-sleuthing there and see if we can find fingerprints of a higher intelligence at the crime scene.

The Atomic Operating Manual

In order to conduct our investigation, we'll need to break out our electron-microscopes and beam ourselves down into the teeny-tiny sub-atomic world to examine the fundamental components that constitute all physical matter – atoms. The structure of an atom is rather simple. Each one resembles a tiny solar system with a sun at its center and a number of orbiting planets (Figure 2). In our miniaturized solar system, the sun is called the nucleus and the orbiting planets are called electrons. You've probably seen graphical representations that looks like a golf ball with a bunch of ping-pong balls swirling around it. There are other complexities and elementary particles such as quarks, gluons, hadrons, fermions, leptons, and bosons. Together, scientists have identified many elementary particles that constitute an atom. They each play a unique role, such as quarks make up protons and are held in place by gluons, but for now we'll look at the basic atomic structure that science has come to accept.

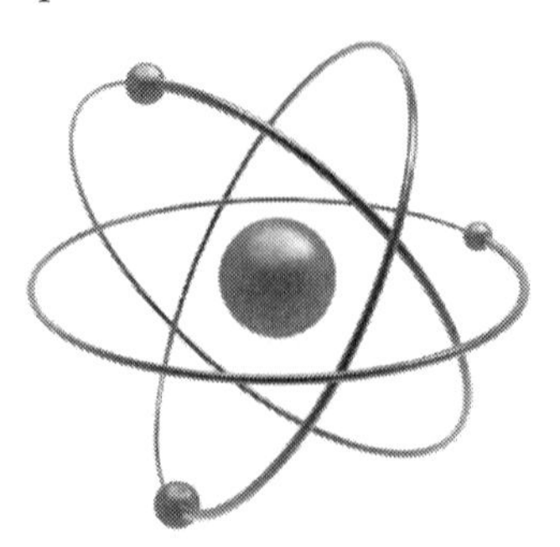

Figure 2 – Structure of an Atom

The nucleus of all atoms is formed by two types of particles – protons and neutrons. The number of protons in an atom is how we identify one element from another – zinc from gold, sodium from calcium, boron from hydrogen, sulfur from arsenic, etc. In total there are 118 different elements that have been discovered. Every element contains a different number of protons in its nucleus. The number of protons is what gives that element its atomic number. We've even created a Periodic Table to arrange the known elements by their atomic number. For example, carbon has an atomic number of 6, meaning it has 6 protons in its nucleus, while nitrogen has 7 protons in its nucleus giving it an atomic number of 7. It's straightforward stuff.

The number of protons in the nucleus in most elements is also equal to the number of electrons that orbit the nucleus. So, if an element has an atomic number of 12, it has 12 protons and 12 electrons. Essentially, that's how atoms are structured. All physical matter that you can see, feel, touch, taste, and smell is composed of trillions of these tiny little solar system-like entities we call atoms. All humans, all animals, all plants, all the oceans, mountains ranges, everything on the planet and throughout the galaxy is made from the same three basic components – electrons, neutrons, and protons. That's it. These three tiny particles arranged in different quantities make up all that we know. Isn't that amazing!

There's not one type of electron for iron and another type of electron for oxygen. Both are the same. The protons in the nucleus of a fluoride atom are not made of a different substance than the protons in the nucleus of a silver atom. It's all the same stuff! We don't think of our physical world in these terms. We see furniture made from wood, countertops made from marble, shoes made from leather, buildings made of brick and mortar, sidewalks made of concrete…yet all of these items, despite its shape, form, texture, density, pliability, viscosity, or state are all made from the same 3 particles. It's one of the most supreme wonders I can think of.

Can you imagine every meal you've ever eaten… every breakfast, every lunch, every dinner, every snack, every dessert, every dish prepared on the entire planet, using only 3 ingredients? Or imagine that every piece of music ever composed in the history of mankind used only 3 notes, or that all the great literary classics ever written used only 3 words. But yet, the entire universe with all its diversity is created from only 3 elementary particles – electrons, neutrons, and protons. It's simply fascinating!

Of the 118 elements in the Periodic Table, each one is constructed from the same 3 sub-atomic particles – electrons, neutrons, and protons. Despite all the physical and chemical differences in everything from hydrogen to iron, the only thing that differs among their constitution is the quantity of particles in each atom, not the different types of particles, but the amount of the same particles. Take a moment to contemplate this since it has such awesome implications. Simply by altering the number of particles, an entirely different element is created, each with entirely different characteristics.

To illustrate just how incredible this is, let's deconstruct an atom purely on a particle basis. When we take apart an atom and separate its parts, what we'll find are three components - electrons, neutrons, and protons - three inanimate components. There is no central nervous system, no brain, no heart pumping life-giving blood throughout the atom, there is no inherent form of intelligence, consciousness, nor ability to create thought or free-will, just inert, lifeless sub-atomic particles. People don't pick up a hunk of magnesium and say, *"wow, looking at this intelligent lifeform. It's alive with knowledge and free will!"* It's just a piece of mineral composed of trillions of atoms. Having this perspective begs the question, how does a group of tiny inanimate particles, combined in different quantities, know exactly and precisely how to differentiate themselves and exhibit the various traits and characteristics of every known element? How does a group of 19 electrons whirling around a nucleus of 19 protons, know that they are supposed to exhibit the specific characteristics of potassium? And then, a group of 20 of the very same electrons, neutrons and protons, know they should obey a completely different set of characteristics of an entirely different element known as calcium. Are you getting this? How is it possible?

It's such a mind-bending marvel. Can you imagine anything else in your life having this quality? Suppose you put two socks in a drawer and close it, knowing inside you have a pair of socks. Then imagine you add a third sock to the drawer, close it and suddenly it becomes a shirt! Add a fourth sock and it becomes shampoo. Add a fifth sock and it becomes Play-Doh®. Add a sixth sock and it turns into a helium balloon. Each time you add another sock, it turns into something completely different. You could do this 118 times and each time you tossed an additional sock into the drawer you'd discover something completely new. Well that's how it works with atoms.

Here's another way to look at this phenomenon. Suppose you put 3 cups of flour, 3 cups of water, and 3 cups of sugar into a bowl. When you mix it together it makes a bowl of dough. Then you decide to take 4 cups of the same flour, 4 cups of the same water, and 4 cups of the same sugar, and mix it together. This time it makes a rubber tire. You then take 5 cups of the same flour, water, and sugar mix it together and now it becomes lead. You are not changing the ingredients you put in the mixing bowl, but HOW MUCH of the ingredients you put in.

Now, I know this all sounds a bit strange, and that's because it is! As we step through the comparison of two specific elements it may help gain some sense of it all. Remember, we're looking for examples throughout the physical world that point to a higher intelligence acting in ways to guide or control the process. Let's look more closely at the characteristics of neon and sodium to see how an ostensibly insignificant difference can make a substantial change.

Looking at Table 2, we can see that the element neon has 10 protons, 10 neutrons, and 10 electrons in its mini-solar system, while the element sodium has 11 protons, 12 neutrons, and 11 electrons.

<table>
<tr><th>Characteristic</th><th>Neon</th><th>Sodium</th></tr>
<tr><td>Atomic Number</td><td>10</td><td>11</td></tr>
<tr><td>Protons</td><td>10</td><td>11</td></tr>
<tr><td>Electrons</td><td>10</td><td>11</td></tr>
<tr><td>Neutrons</td><td>10</td><td>12</td></tr>
<tr><td>Atomic Weight</td><td>20.180 amu</td><td>22.989 amu</td></tr>
<tr><td>Melting Point</td><td>-248 ^{C} (-415 F)</td><td>98 ^{C} (208 F)</td></tr>
<tr><td>Boiling Point</td><td>-246 ^{C} (-411 F)</td><td>883 ^{C} (1621 F)</td></tr>
<tr><td>Density</td><td>0.0009 g/cm^3</td><td>0.971 g/cm3</td></tr>
<tr><td>State</td><td>Gas</td><td>Solid</td></tr>
<tr><td>Classification</td><td>Noble Gas
(nonmetal)</td><td>Alkali Metal</td></tr>
<tr><td>Color</td><td>Colorless</td><td>Silvery-White</td></tr>
<tr><td colspan="3">Other Qualities</td></tr>
<tr><td colspan="2">Neon
• Not known to be toxic
• Glows a reddish-orange in a vacuum discharge tube
• Forms no known stable compounds</td><td>Sodium
• Humans need for cellular fluid balance
• Burns with a brilliant yellow flame
• Reacts violently with water</td></tr>
</table>

Table 2: Characteristics of Neon and Sodium

In terms of the building blocks that comprise these two elements, the only difference between them is 1 electron, 1 proton, and 2 neutrons. Deconstructing each atom and arranging the particles on a table we'd have one pile containing 10 protons, 10 electrons, and 10 neutrons, and another pile containing 11 protons, 11 electrons, and 12 neutrons. That's it. Otherwise they are identical. The insignificant difference between the two is 1 electron, 1 proton, and 2 neutrons. Now, let's look at what happens to their characteristics when you simply add 4 sub-atomic particles to the pile of neon particles.

The pile containing 10 protons, 10 electrons, and 10 neutrons forms together to become a colorless gas (neon), while the pile containing 11 protons, 11 electrons, and 12 neutrons would form together to become a solid silver-white metal (sodium) with a density 1,000 times that of neon. Table 2 also shows us that neon boils at -411 F and sodium boils at 1621 F. That's a difference of 2,032 degrees!

Think about that, simply by adding 1 proton, 1 electron, and 2 neutrons, the element changes from a gas to a solid, and its boiling point changes by over two thousand degrees. How is this possible? How do these tiny particles know the rules and characteristics of the respective element they're supposed to obey simply by the number in their group? How can inert particles even discriminate between a quantity of 10 and a quantity of 11? Are we to assume electrons, protons and neutrons have the ability to count? Where is the instruction manual telling them that when 11 of you are present you become a metal at room temperature, but if there are only 10 of you then you'll turn into a gas at room temperature? How do we make sense of this phenomenon?

One way to look at this wonder is to simply assume these whirling bits of sub-atomic particles somehow have the ability to comprehend, acknowledge, and rationally discriminate between all the rules and characteristics of the 118 elements in the Periodic Table. Another way is to recognize that for this phenomenon to occur these whirling bits of sub-atomic particles need to be acted upon by some external form of intelligence that provides the specific properties for each of the 118 elemental states. Without a higher intelligence acting on these particles, they would all exhibit the same characteristics and properties regardless of their quantity. For sub-atomic particles to alter their properties, an intelligence governing the rules and order of the elements in the Periodic Table is necessary.

Now, the sub-atomic world is not one that we live in and can readily relate to, so grasping these miracles takes a touch of imagination. None-the-less, we can see, touch, and hold physical objects, which have mass and are made of matter composed of atoms. Atoms that quantum physicists tell us have no mass nor substance - are merely energy. It's a paradox that really deserves some thought. Your perceptions of the world can simply be that everything in the physical world exists purely because it does, or you can look at the building blocks that make up all we see, feel, and touch, and strive for an explanation of its existence. Let's step back from the sub-atomic world now and look at the world that is a bit more familiar.

Coming back to the environment we experience in our daily lives, we'll explore some of the other ways a higher intelligence shows its influence. As you become more in tune with nature and begin to study your surroundings, you'll start to recognize miracles popping up all around you. This next miracle comes in the form of a commonplace and colorful flying insect…

The Flight of Multiple Lifetimes

It's funny how the fluttering beauty of a butterfly has a way of grabbing your attention. They're like flying bits of confetti that make you want to jump up and give chase with childlike enthusiasm. Adding to their wonder is an event that is one of the most incredible spectacles of nature - the Monarch Butterfly migration. Unlike other butterflies that can survive winters as larvae, Monarchs can't. Instead, the North American Monarch embarks on an amazing 2,500-mile migration each year to the Sierra Madre Mountains in central Mexico. Researchers consider it to be the most unique and amazing migration in nature. Most Monarchs' have a lifespan of about 6 to 8 weeks, meaning no single Monarch butterfly will complete the round-trip journey itself. The migration actually becomes multi-generational where each leg of the trip gets passed on to the next of kin. How'd you like that kind of pressure for keeping the family bloodline alive! Let's fly along and follow the annual migration and see why I call them the 'Monarch Miracles.'

Each year as summer gives way to fall a new generation of Monarch butterflies from Northern United States and Southern Canada begins a cross-continental flight to the warm mountains of central Mexico. It's not the fact that some will travel over 200 miles in one day that makes the migration so amazing, but rather that the butterflies making the journey have never even been to the Sierra Madre Mountains in central Mexico! They are four generations removed from the last colony of butterflies that made this migration. In fact, the closest affinity they have to the Sierra Madres is great-great-grandparents who once spent the winter there. It's a mystery how the Monarch butterfly can have an awareness of a migratory destination some 2,500 miles away they've never been to, but somehow, they do.

This epic journey begins in the Northeast United States and Southern Canada when millions of Monarch butterflies head south for winter hibernation. For months a colony of tiny polychromatic insects flap and flutter their way from one state to the next, into Texas and across the Mexican border, stopping only for a traditional Tequila shooter in Nuevo Laredo (Yee-Ha!). After making the long 2,500-mile flight, the Monarchs finally reach their winter home in the Sierra Madres. Colonies return not only to the same mountain as their great-great-grandparents, but often to the very same tree! Now that astounding feat alone has got to boggle your mind, but it only gets more remarkable.

Once the Monarch colony reaches the predestined tree in which their ancestors hibernated, they prepare to overwinter by clustering together for warmth and going into a hibernation-like state. This allows them to live off stored fat and survive the winter. When spring arrives and temperatures warm, the butterflies awaken from their diapause state, flap the sleep from their wings and begin travelling the 2,500 miles back north.

However, this generation will not make it back, so along the way they breed and lay eggs throughout Texas. Shortly after laying eggs, the first-generation butterflies die off leaving their offspring to pick-up and take over their North American journey. The second-generation larvae take about 40 - 50 days to develop, and then in late April they'll emerge from their Texan chrysalis and continue their parents' northern migration. Somehow the second-generation Monarchs intuitively know the precise direction and location to travel. Unlike their parents, this generation of Monarchs is heading to a north-eastern location to which they've never been.

During their northern flight, the second-generation Monarch mates and lays eggs throughout much of eastern North America. Eventually the second generation lives out their 8-week lifespan and gives rise to a third generation of Monarchs, the grandchildren of the Monarchs that overwintered in Mexico. The third generation hatches and continues the flight originated by their grandparents. They'll arrive in the Northern US and Southern Canada in June and July.

Once the third-generation flutter returns to its North American homes (yes, a group of butterflies is actually called a 'flutter'), they too mate and lay offspring throughout the Northern US and Southern Canada. These offspring become the fourth generation. Finally, a fifth generation is hatched, becoming the great-great-grandchildren of the Monarch that overwintered in Mexico. As the seasons come and go, spring gives way to winter, temperatures drop, and after five generations of Monarch butterflies the migratory cycle repeats.

The fifth generation is different from the prior generations in that it will live up to 8 months, while generations two, three, and four survive for only a couple months. In addition, this is the generation that will make the 2,500-mile flight back to Mexico for the winter. Their flight will take them back to the precise location where their great-great-grandparents spent winter the previous year. This incredible multi-generational migratory journey is a phenomenon of nature I like to call 'The Monarch Miracle.' So, now that you know the amazing excursion this species of butterfly endures to survive, let's break this migration down from a logical and inquisitive perspective.

We'll start with the generation of Monarch that begins its life as a tiny egg laid on the leaf of a milkweed plant somewhere in Texas. Its mother hibernated the winter in Mexico and now lays the egg and moves on. It doesn't stay behind to protect the eggs and raise the hatching larvae. It doesn't provide any support nor guidance once the caterpillar emerges. It simply lays an egg on a leaf and lets it hatch on its own. When it does hatch, the caterpillar typically remains on the same plant eating its way into adulthood. As far as this caterpillar is concerned, the world around it doesn't exist beyond the plant it is munching for dinner. It's not aware of a nest of birds in an adjacent tree, nor a family of rabbits burrowed in the ground below, nor a school of fish in a nearby pond, let alone a range of mountains hundreds of miles away! All this caterpillar knows is, *"I gotta keep eating!"*

Once the caterpillar reaches its full size, it'll form a chrysalis around itself and go through a multi-week metamorphosis into a butterfly. During these weeks, the insect shelters itself even further from the outside world within a cocoon-like structure. The insect's awareness of the outside world becomes further restricted within the tiny sarcophagus it has entombed itself. Yet, when a butterfly emerges, it pumps its wings full of blood, and with no instruction, no guidance, no teaching, no Google maps, the darn things flaps its wings and heads precisely to a location hundreds of miles away that it's never seen, been to, nor heard of.

Think of how remarkable that is. Here we are, as humans, the most intelligent and sophisticated species on the planet, and we get lost going to a place just a few blocks away after being given detailed directions and having signs and GPS showing us the way! But this little insect, with a brain the size of the ball at the tip of a pen, and no form of written or verbal language, no use of pre-charted maps, no sonar or echolocation abilities to pick up signals from other butterflies, this tiny insect with extremely limited intelligence somehow intuitively knows exactly where to fly. And, if that isn't enough, the precise location of their winter sanctuary is passed on through four generations, with each generation beginning just as this one – as an isolated egg on a milkweed plant! It's truly fascinating how the more you know about nature, the more amazing it becomes.

Now, scientists have come along and cracked the butterfly's internal guidance systems, learning that it uses the earth's magnetic field in combination with the sun's positioning as directional aids. However, they haven't been able to explain HOW the butterfly is preprogrammed to know the precise coordinates of 19° 36′ 23″ N latitude and 100° 14′ 30″ W longitude in central Mexico that is home to its winter migration. How do these tiny colorful creatures know about its migratory locations – both southern and northern - with pinpoint accuracy? How are they even aware that this relatively small area of forest some 2,500 miles away in Michoacan Mexico even exists? How is it possible that after hatching on a leaf in a tree somewhere in New England, they inherently know this distant forest will serve as their roosting sanctuary? They haven't been taught this in butterfly school. They don't stop along the way and ask where they can find a verdant forest full of lush pine and oyamel trees. They aren't aware of other natural resource like the Great Lakes, the Grand Canyon, the Gannett Glacier, the Everglades, or the Giant Redwoods, but somehow, they know about the Michoacan forest in Mexico.

Not only are they aware of this winter retreat, but they also know precisely how to get there. What provides them the instinct to fly in a south-west direction instead of north, or west, or east? How are the geographic coordinates programmed into their DNA, so that each year, without failure, their flight pinpoints them precisely in the Sierra Madre Mountains? They don't end up in a Louisiana swamp, or Colorado ski resort, but the very same tree of their great-great-grandparents. They've never been to this location. They don't have a description of it. There's no smartphone app giving them voice-command directions in a sultry British accent. They don't take Uber, catch a train, or even follow migratory routes of other animals. So, how do they know? What causes entire colonies of Monarch butterflies to embark on a flight of such remarkable precision, going to destinations they've never been too and couldn't know exist, year after year? This is simply a phenomenon that requires some type of external intelligence beyond that of the Monarch butterfly itself.

You can understand now why I call them the Monarch Miracles. It's certainly an amazing migration to say the least. We've now seen how universal intelligence is present in the quantum of an atom and the flight of a butterfly, but does it ever show itself in obvious ways that are so ubiquitous that it literally takes its roots across the planet? I have a hunch you're about to find out...

Comparing Apples to Oranges

It's time to conduct a little experiment. For this one, I'd like you to take a moment from reading and observe the great outdoors. When you reach the end of this paragraph, take a short break. If you can, step outside, otherwise a nice window should do the trick. Look around and locate a good-sized tree, one that's been around for a while. Examine the tree from top to bottom. Study its intricate branches, its leaves, and its root system. Recognize its growth patterns, its majestic beauty. Try to imagine water and minerals being absorbed through its roots and traveling throughout its labyrinth structure. Acknowledge that year after year the tree grows in height, girth, and size. Notice how it seems to mature in wisdom as it develops in age. Lose yourself in visualizing the cool shade it provides, the animal life it supports, the carbon dioxide it inhales and life-giving oxygen it exhales. Marvel at its ability to convert sunlight to energy through photosynthesis and how this energy travels within its complex network of branches. Cherish these objects of nature that are so full of life, acknowledge the enduring role they've had in sustaining and sheltering mankind, and then admit to how trees tend to simply blend into the background in our everyday frantic lives. Notice how easy it is to take for granted these miracles of life that breathe out the oxygen needed to sustain your own life. When you're done appreciating these magnificent pillars of nature, come back and we'll step through another impressive display of universal intelligence that stares you in the face every day…

Welcome back. Hope you've enjoyed your moment of bonding with nature and appreciating its glory. This little experiment was a bit of a trick. I really did want you to take some time to appreciate the gifts of nature, but as far as our next example of universal intelligence goes, all you really need to do is acknowledge that trees exist. That's all. Simply admit that out there in your yard, in the park, in the forest, and around the globe, growing out of the ground is physical matter in the form of a tree - nothing to disagree with so far, right? Trees have been around for nearly 400 million years, and there are roughly 3 trillion of them in the world today (that's trillion with a 'T'). There's even a pine tree that's been growing in northern Greece for more than 1,075 years! And we complain about stiff joints in our 60's.

Getting back to the acknowledgment that trees exist, the next thing to recognize is that trees are physical objects made of matter. Again, this shouldn't create much dispute since so much of what we use in daily life comes from a tree - fruit, nuts, wood, paper, furniture, rayon fabric, nail polish, rocket fuel, cleaning compounds, deodorants, flavorings, medicines, cosmetics, dyes, varnish, tires, photographic film, cork, adhesives, turpentine, oils, syrup, mulch, menthol, and much, much more. So, it should be rather easy to acknowledge that trees do exist and that trees have mass. Now, let's notch the challenge up a bit...

When you look at a tree growing equally large above ground as it does below ground, where does all the matter that makes up a tree come from? Think about it. They begin as a small sapling and each year become larger and larger until eventually, they're a massive towering structure with a thick supportive trunk, strong twisting branches, thousands of veined leaves, and a deeply entwined root system. So where does all that matter making up this towering structure come from? I'll give you a minute to think about this one.

If you said trees are made from the minerals and water in the soil, which they absorb through their roots, you'd be in the majority since that's what most people answer. However, you along with the majority would be wrong. If this were true, there'd be giant gaping holes in the earth from where the trees sucked up all the minerals and relocated them into its branches, but there's not. So, where does a tree come from?

Alright, are you stumped? (I couldn't resist that one! Ha!) Here's a little clue, 95% of a tree is made from carbon dioxide. Wait a minute that sounds like I'm telling you trees come from thin air. Well, I am. Trees do come from air! Trees get most of its mass from air and water. It absorbs airborne carbon dioxide, and then uses the sun's energy through photosynthesis to separate out the oxygen and breathe it back into the atmosphere, leaving behind carbon and water that mix with an assortment of nutrients to build its mighty branches. These towering pillars materialize out of thin air. Now that we know where trees come from, let's take this exercise one final step to demonstrate how universal intelligence has a hand in these great carbon structures.

To begin, we'll need to grow a couple of imaginary trees, an apple tree and an orange tree. To do this we're going to need some seeds. So, imagine in your left hand you hold an apple seed and in your right hand you have an orange seed. Now, let's take these two seeds and find some nice fertile soil to plant them. We'll dig two holes about 10 feet apart. In one hole we'll plant the apple seed, and in the other hole we'll plant the orange seed. Assuming they both get adequate sunlight and water, each should begin to grow, one as an apple tree and one as an orange tree. Over time, each will absorb carbon dioxide from the air, water and minerals from the ground, and produce solid structures of nature bearing fruit, one producing apples and one producing oranges. Since we've learned trees get their mass from air, soil, water and the sun, in our hypothetical experiment we have two different trees that grew from the same soil, sunlight, air, water, and minerals. Now, let's introduce our friend universal intelligence. With everything being the same, how does one seed know how to arrange all the available atoms and molecules in such a way that they form an apple and the other seed know how to arrange the very same atoms and molecules in such a way that they form an orange? Well now, you didn't think I'd spring something like that on you did ya!

I told you at the beginning I'd challenge you to look at the world with a different perspective, and this is one of those times. Let's go back to step 1 of this experiment when you were holding an apple seed and an oranges seed in each of your hands. Now look down and analyze them. What do you see? An intelligent lifeform? Is there some form of consciousness beneath the seed's coat? Is there some internal ability these seeds possess to create thought? Do they have the capacity to make coherent decisions? Somewhere immersed inside is there a tiny brain that acts as a central command center to instruct the plant how to assemble its fruit? Do these seeds possess a mental process that allows them to manipulate information to solve problems, to reason, and carry out a logical set of operations?

There is nothing within those seeds that contains any of the abilities mentioned above. So, ask yourself, how is it possible? How is it that an apple seed has the brainpower and intellect to gather and collect trillions of necessary building blocks from its surroundings and arrange them to form a perfectly delicious apple, and do it over and over again? While in the very same soil, a different seed can collect trillions of the very same atomic and molecular building blocks from the very same surroundings and arrange them in a different order to form an orange. How is that possible? Where are their instruction manuals? If all the essential elements that constitute a tree – carbon, hydrogen, oxygen, potassium, calcium, magnesium, nitrogen, phosphorus, sulphur, iron, manganese, zinc, copper, molybdenum, boron and chlorine – are simply unconscious matter, there needs to be some form of intelligence guiding them into order. It's certainly not the end result of random chance. Perhaps the same universal intelligence that guides the butterfly and gives structure to an atom is providing an influential hand in the formation of our apple and orange trees.

In this example, we've compared apples to oranges, but this very same analysis can be applied to any plant, regardless if it bears fruit, flowers, nuts, or neither. Each plant species relies upon a higher intelligence to instruct the specific arrangement of the atoms and molecules in order to create the distinct lifeform of its species. And with over 1 million different plant species, and trillions of individual plants, it speaks to the awesome power of this universal intelligence. Try to imagine a force so knowing and omnipresent that it brings balance and order to every single plant life on the planet. It's a concept that is difficult to grasp, but one we experience daily.

I'll end this chapter with a profound and ubiquitous example, that some call the divine blueprint of the creator. This miracle happens to come in the form of a ratio, a distinct proportion, which is found throughout nature and seems to be a constant in the design of the universe. The ratio is referred to as the Golden Ratio or the Divine Proportion and has a numerical equivalent of 1.618. But, enough with silly numbers, we want to hear about divinity!

Nature's Divine Ratio

The Golden Ratio was discovered by an Italian mathematician when he derived a series of numbers known as the Fibonacci Sequence. The Fibonacci Sequence has captivated mathematicians, artists, designers, and scientists for centuries. Many believe its ubiquity and astounding functionality in nature suggests the trademark of a universal designer and shows proof of a blueprint on the fundamental design and characteristics of the universe left by a creator. While others feel it's simply a coincidence. Let's see what you think about the divine ratio.

The Italian mathematician first introduced the omnipresent sequence in 1202 when Fibonacci developed a series of numbers that are extremely basic in concept but have profound uses still today in financial market algorithms, mathematics, architecture, design, computer programming, and yes, nature. The premise is straightforward. In the series, each number is the sum of the two previous numbers.

So, the Fibonacci Sequence would look like this:

0, 1, 1, 2, 3, 5, 8, 13, 21, 34, 55, 89 and so on…

Take any number along the sequence and it is derived by adding the 2 numbers that precede it:

0+1=1
1+1=2
1+2=3
2+3=5
3+5=8
5+8=13
8+13=21
13+21=34
21+34=55
34+55=89, etc.

The emergent pattern calculates to a ratio of 1.618... (also known as Phi, Φ). It's calculated by dividing any number along the Sequence by the previous number. That's all there is to it!

This pattern, mathematical in design, is hidden in plain sight virtually everywhere. You just have to know where to look. The ratio presents itself from the micro to the macro, as though it's a built-in mathematical design constant. Its applications are astounding and numerous. In fact, as people began to recognize how the Golden Ratio accounts for an underlying order in the physical world, they began to accept it as a mathematical secret of nature. Let's see how the Fibonacci Sequence manifests throughout the physical world.

Look at the center of a sunflower and you'll find an array of seeds. Study them and you'll notice a spiral pattern curving to the left, and another spiral pattern curving to the right – one clockwise and the other counter-clockwise (See Figure 3). Amazingly, if you count each spiral, you'll get two consecutive Fibonacci numbers – 55 going counter-clockwise, 34 going clockwise.

Figure 3 – The Golden Ratio within a Sunflower

If you examine the bottom of a pinecone, or the rind of a pineapple, you'll also find two sets of spirals, one going clockwise and one going counterclockwise. Mark and count the number of spirals going in each direction and again you will discover two consecutive Fibonacci numbers – 8 clockwise spirals and 13 counter-clockwise spirals (Figure 4). These same spiral patterns expressed by the Fibonacci sequence are found in a wide assortment of seed heads.

Figure 4 – Fibonacci Sequence within a Pinecone

Flowers also obey this Divine Series of numbers. When you count the number of petals in a flower, you'll discover they consistently equal one of the numbers in the Fibonacci sequence. Lilies and irises have three petals, buttercups and wild roses have five, delphiniums have eight petals, marigolds have thirteen petals, and so on.

Fibonacci Petals

3 petals - lily, iris
5 petals- buttercup, wild rose, larkspur, columbine
8 petals - delphiniums
13 petals - ragwort, corn marigold, cineraria
21 petals - aster, black-eyed Susan, chicory
34 petals - plantain, pyrethrum
55, 89 petals - michelmas daisies, the asteraceae family

Trees don't escape the Fibonacci sequence either. Scientists recognize the series in the formation of tree branches. The main trunk grows until it produces a branch, giving the tree two growth points. Then, the new stem will branch into two while the other continues to grow as one, creating three branches between the growth points. This pattern of branching continues for each new stem generated. Count the stems between each growth point and you'll find a surprising series of numbers – 1, 2, 3, 5, 8, 13, 21, etc. (see Figure 5) - a natural Fibonacci Sequence. This pattern also occurs in root systems and even algae.

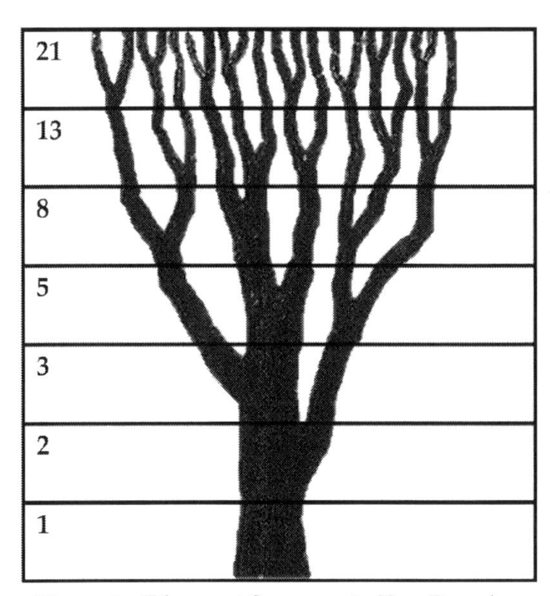

Figure 5 – Fibonacci Sequence in Tree Branches

But it's not just plants that show evidence of the Golden Ratio, it appears throughout the animal kingdom as well. There is a consistent design throughout nature known as a Fibonacci Spiral, that forms when you take squares whose sides are equal in length to the Fibonacci series and place them adjacent to one another (as shown in Figure 6). Drawing an arc through each of the squares forms the Fibonacci Spiral.

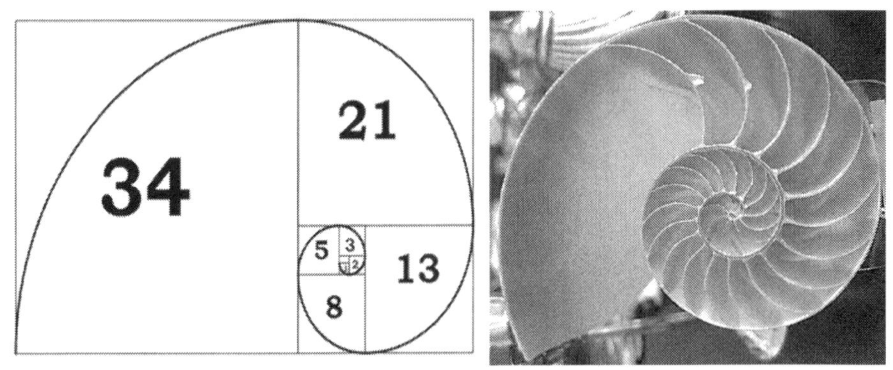

Figure 6 – Fibonacci Spiral

The Fibonacci Spiral is found in snail shells, nautilus shells, the cochlea of the inner ear, sand dollars, starfish, the horns of certain goats, the shape of certain spider's webs, hurricanes, the curls of an ocean's wave, and galaxies! All show this incredible blueprint.

Figure 7 – Fibonacci Spirals in Nature: Plants, Hurricanes, Galaxies

There's also a naturally occurring event called a "Hyperbolic Spiral of Falling Water," which occurs when you flush the toilet or drain a sink that also lends support to the Golden Ration and a divine blueprint. When viewed from above, a hyperbolic water spiral forms the same pattern as the spiral of hurricane or a nebula in space (Figure 8).

Figure 8 – Hyperbolic Water Spiral in Comparison to Hurricane and Nebula

Even more startling, if you view the spiral from the side, the stem takes the form of the pulsing double-helix of DNA (Figure 9).

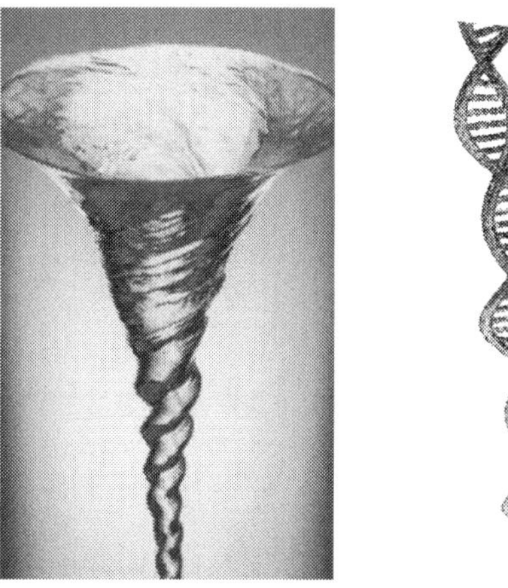

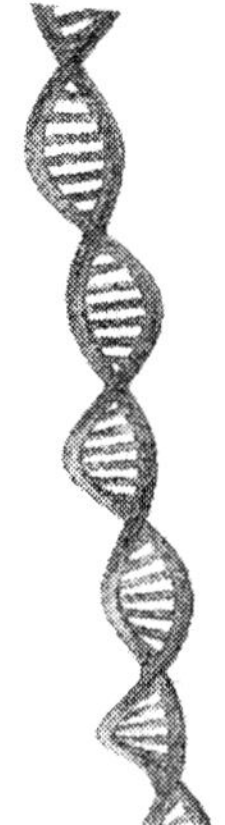

Figure 9 – Hyperbolic Water Spiral and DNA Double-Helix

Honeybees have an interesting way of following the Golden Ratio. Female honeybees always outnumber male honeybees in a bee colony. Interestingly, the ratio of the number of females to the number of males in a colony remarkably comes to 1.618 – the Golden Ratio.

The human body is brimming with examples of the Golden Ratio. It's astounding the number of times 1.618 in found in proportions and measurements of the human body. Figure 10 illustrates those found in the face.

- The distance from your eyes to your chin is 1.618 times the distance from the bottom of your nose to your chin.
- The width of your forehead is 1.618 times the length of your nose
- The distance from your eye to your mouth is 1.618 times the length of your nose
- The distance from the bottom of your nose to your chin is 1.618 times the distance from your mouth to you chin
- The distance between the pupils of your eyes is 1.618 times the width of your mouth
- The width of your mouth is 1.618 times the width of your nose
- The length of your face is 1.618 times its width
- Your front tooth is 1.618 times the width of the next tooth over

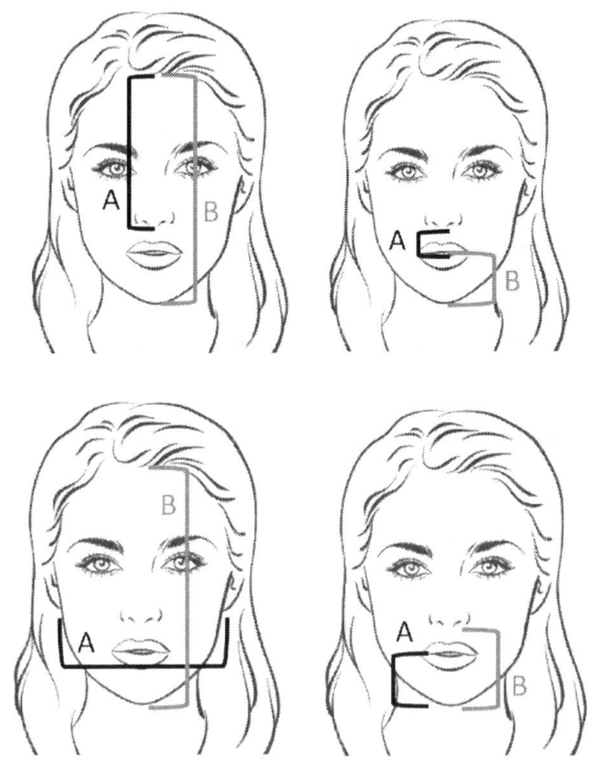

Figure 10 – Golden Ration in the Human Face

This ratio repeats in your body as well, as shown in Figure 11.

- Fingers are composed of 3 bones, the length of the bone closest to the knuckle is 1.618 times the length of middle bone
- The length of the middle bone is also 1.618 times the length of the bone at tip of finger
- The length of your forearm is 1.618 times the length from your wrist to your fingertip
- The length of your arm is 1.618 time the length of your upper arm
- The width of your shoulders is 1.618 times the length of your upper arm

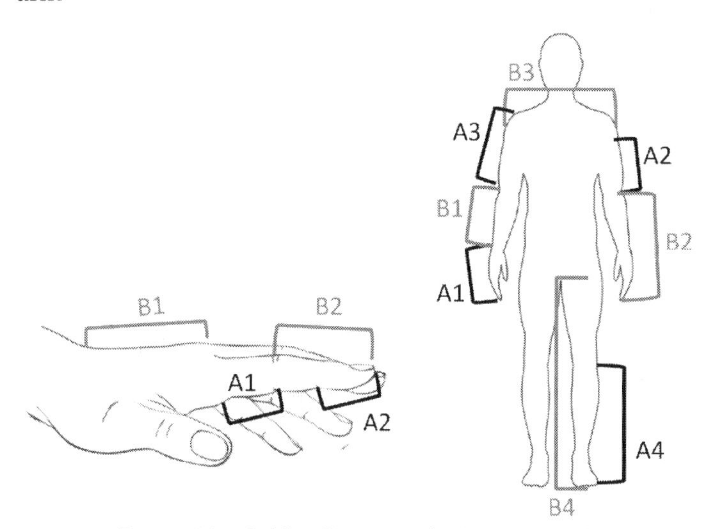

Figure 11 – Golden Ration in the Human Body

Even the microscopic realm is not immune to Fibonacci. DNA molecules measure 34 angstroms long by 21 angstroms wide for each full cycle of its double helix spiral giving it a ratio of 1.618!

The Fibonacci Sequence and its corresponding ratio leaves a universal fingerprint in Nature from the microscopic structure of DNA, to the bracts of a pinecone, to the formation of a shell, all the way to the awesome spiral of the Milky Way Galaxy and touches virtually everything in between. How is it that so many natural patterns reflect the Golden Ratio? Could it really be a Divine constant in the design of the universe? Scientists have pondered this for centuries. Some believe the ubiquitous correlation may just be coincidence, a *'pareidolia,'* or autosuggestion of the mind. It's like seeing a bunny rabbit in the clouds, just because a cloud happens to take the shape of a rabbit doesn't mean clouds are made of bunnies. However, there are many others who recognize the ratio as a sign of intelligent design left behind by the creator. What do you think?

In this chapter we've seen examples of a higher intelligence leaving its mark on sub-atomic particles, migratory patterns of the Monarch butterfly, the assembly manuals of apple and orange trees, and as a mathematical constant in the design of the universe. In fact, universal intelligence can be seen everywhere you look, you just need to know how to recognize it. The concept of a divinity or intelligence connected to all things throughout the universe is called *'Pantheism.'* Its Greek derivation of *'pan'* meaning 'all' and *'theos'* meaning 'God,' translates to 'All is God,' or 'All is One.' Essentially, pantheism states that all of nature and the entirety of the universe IS God. All things are linked by an interconnecting force or consciousness, which brings us to our next area of investigation...

If there is such an 'all-connecting' intelligence guiding everything in the physical world, providing rules for quantum particles, instruction manuals for Nature, and connecting all as one, then where does this intelligence reside? How does it interact with the physical world? Looks like our case is taking us in a new investigative direction...

Ch. 3: Energy

"Those who are not shocked when they first come across quantum theory cannot possibly have understood it." - Niels Bohr

Our Brick and Mortar World

We about to follow another clue down a new path as we continue our investigation into life's mysteries. From the start we knew this would be a lofty undertaking, but every clue helps to provide a more focused view of life's purpose. So far, the puzzle pieces we've uncovered connect to form a picture showing a higher intelligence behind life's formation, and a higher intelligence behind life's ongoing operations. There are still many more pieces to add to this puzzle, and hopefully each one will give more clarity to the whole.

As super-sleuths following a series of clues, the evidence presented in the first two chapters leads us down an investigative path of "Universal Intelligence." The next logical question to ask is, "If a higher consciousness does exist and somehow has influence over the physical world, where does it reside and how does it function?" Interesting questions…let's see if we can find some answers.

You may be wondering why I've spent so much time on a higher intelligence that is intangible and immaterial , when at the end of the day the lives we lead are very tangible and material. The challenges and hardship, the joys and whimsies, and the triumphs and defeats are all real things we face separate and apart from one another. How we react to and cope with these real-world experiences are a matter of free will that we each possess. We are the ones experiencing our lives, not some higher consciousness. We are the ones in control of our thoughts and reactions, not a Universal Intelligence. Right? It's our self-determination that guides our direction. Why lend such authority to an ethereal intelligence? After all, our world is a physical world, not a spiritual one.

Each day we wake up and go through our respective routines to face the physical world. For some, every day is an adventure eagerly welcomed with open arms, enjoying the excitement and challenges life has in store. For others, it's a repetitive grind meandering through life with little spirit or zeal. Regardless of your disposition, the simple, undeniable fact is we are immersed in a physical world that tests and engenders our temperament, not an ethereal world. The homes we live in are made of physical materials – bricks, wood, concrete, plaster, paint, etc. The cars we drive are constructed with metals, engines, tires, plastics, circuitry, and leather. They burn fossil fuels extracted from the ground and processed into fuel to get us from one place to the next. The roads and freeways we travel are made of asphalt and cement. Our workplaces are solid buildings. The schools that teach our children are real classrooms. The stores we buy food and products from are physical locations. It's all real. We can touch it, feel it, see it, smell it, and taste it. All our senses confirm the material world surrounding us is a physical certainty. It's not a fantasy. It's not illusion. It isn't a dream, nor complex holographic matrix of the mind. Everything is brick and mortar, flesh and blood, physical matter! …Or is it?

Is the world that surrounds you really what you believe it to be? Are the homes, cars, roads, buildings, schools, stores, and workplaces all made of physical matter? Hmmm, this is where you take a moment to ponder this brain twisting reality…It's quite a profound question to ask, but to ask is one thing, answering is another. To do so, we'll need to go on an equally profound investigation utilizing leads, facts, logic, and an open mind.

A Matter of Energy

To investigate the physical world, we'll need to begin with the basics - physical matter itself. What is matter anyway? I suppose this could be summed up elegantly in one word – *ENERGY*. Yes, energy. Believe it or not, we live in an energy-based world. Our senses that determine sight, sounds, smells, taste, and touch do so by tuning in and deciphering energy vibrations. There's even a mathematical equation correlating energy to matter:

$E=MC^2$

It's one of the most ubiquitous and profound scientific equations. I'm sure you've seen **$E=MC^2$** many times - on posters, in ads, in school, or heard in conversation. **$E=MC^2$** has taken on a pop-culture like status. While most people have seen this equation hundreds, if not thousands of times, the average person couldn't tell you what it means. So, what does **$E=MC^2$** mean?

Einstein derived this mathematical equation as a way of explaining the relationship between Mass and Energy. This simple formula with only two variables tells us the **Energy** of a system is equal to its **Mass** multiplied by the square of a constant, '**C**,' representing the speed of light in a vacuum. Mass is simply a measure of how much matter something contains, so if something has Mass, it's made of Matter. Since '**C**' is a very large number (984,251,968 feet per second), Einstein's equation tells us that even small amounts of matter contain large quantities of energy. With the help of Einstein's mind, we can see that Matter IS Energy.

But how can matter be energy when the solidity of the world seems to be so indisputable? A rock has solid shape and form, as does a meatball (which if you've ever tried my cooking is indistinguishable from a rock!). The vehicles you drive, your physical body, the mental asylum people will think you escaped from when you tell them the concepts in this book…these are all physical, tangible things that have shape, size, weight and structure. So how can they be energy? As we'll soon see, that's exactly what they are, big massive piles of vibrating energy!

Now, this may come as a surprise, but an energy-based world isn't a new concept. The notion of a primordial energy flowing throughout the universe has been studied and practiced by philosophers, monks, shaman, and aborigines for thousands of years. The view that all things have a conscious underpinning is known as *'Panpsychism,'* and dates back to pre-Socratics. Anaximenes was a 5th Century B.C. Greek philosopher who believed the ruling principle behind the entire universe was *pneuma,* which translates to breathe or spirit. Anaxagoras, another ancient Greek philosopher, spoke of the world being composed of primordial substances existing in infinitesimally small fragments that are ordered and regulated by a universal mind. Plato advanced the concept of *anima mundi,* or a world-soul. Socrates hypothesized that the universe was made of pure energy, and eventually after much debate, Aristotle concurred that a soul-like presence inherited all objects in the physical world.

This belief wasn't unique to the ancient Greeks, cultures from China, Japan, India, Indonesia, Korea, Malaysia, Mongolia, Philippines, Siberia, Hawaii, South and Central America, Africa, Australia, and Native

America all shared similar philosophies of an energy flowing through everything in creation. Shamans in every period of history around the globe, some dating back to over 20,000 years ago, hold a common belief in the existence of a vital force that pervades all things. And if you really want historical context, *"A long time ago in a galaxy far, far away...."* a little guy by the name of Yoda taught us all the power of the force!

The popular belief of an energy-based world from ancient times continued for many, many moons, until in the late seventeenth century when Sir Isaac Newton developed the laws of motion. This scientific breakthrough altered the view of the universe. Newton came up with mathematical formulas to calculate precisely how forces act on different bodies, which became the bedrock of classical mechanics. The age of Newtonian physics pulled science out of the energy mindset and into the physical. Centuries of Newtonian thought changed how societies and cultures viewed the world. Then in the early 1900's, with the dawning of quantum physics, Newtonian science began to shift when it hit a roadblock. As scientists delved deeper into the atom, they discovered that Newton's laws didn't apply at the atomic level. With this revelation, we've come full-circle and scientists have once again begun to embrace the ancient wisdom of an energy-based world.

It's become accepted doctrine that as you distill the tiny building blocks of matter down to their elementary components, you'll find that an atom is not made of little particles, but rather tiny packets of energy. Electrons have no mass. They're not made of some weird subatomic substance. They're not physical particles at all. They're just tiny bits of energy swirling around a nucleus that itself is nothing more than an energy wave. In fact, the more we learn about subatomic particles, the more mysterious they become.

For example, one of the unusual properties that has been discovered is that electrons can act as both a wave and a particle. It's known as the Double-Slit Experiment. What this means is the very same electron can act as two completely different things! What's even more amazing is they discovered that the factor determining if an electron would exhibit properties of a wave or properties of a particle is the state of mind of the individual conducting the experiment. That's quite a monumental discover. If the scientist was testing for wave-like characteristics the electron would exhibit wave functions. If the scientist tested for particle characteristics the electron exhibited particle functions. So, the electrons were actually influenced by the consciousness of the experimenter! These are the very same electrons that make up the matter of our day-to-day lives. This incredible discovery should have far more relevance in society. It should be taught throughout schools, and everyone should have a common awareness that there's scientific proof of consciousness having direct influence on the behavior of particles of matter. It should be as widely known as gravity, or at least the Kardashians' dating lives!

Another characteristic physicists have discovered that's difficult to wrap your mind around is *'Superposition,'* which states that quantum particles cannot actually be determined, they don't really exist, but rather they exist in multiple possible realities called superpositions. Another brain-rattling discovery is called *'Bi-location'*. This is a property exhibited by subatomic particles in which they exist in two different places at the same time. Wouldn't it be great if we could bi-locate in our daily schedules! Quantum physicists have also discovered a subatomic phenomenon called *'Quantum Entanglement.'* Physicists have found that actions performed on one particle are exactly and instantaneously mirrored on another particle that is quantum entangled, even if the particles are separated by a vast distance.

Now, I don't want to get too mired down in the complexities of quantum physics, and all the strange and freaky ways that subatomic particles act, BUT….since we do know that atoms are energy based, and they are the essential building blocks of all physical matter, and they can be influenced by consciousness, and they can be connected instantly at vast distances, it will probably do us some good to learn a little more about energy. At the very least, it'll give us a better understanding of the underlying ingredient that forms our physical world. And, as we apply this to our investigation of a higher intelligence, we may find that the energy at the base of our physical world may very well be the same residential address of our friend - Universal Intelligence.

It Takes All Types

I should probably begin with some disappointing news about energy… unfortunately, nobody really knows what energy is. I know, kind of a spoiler alert. So, how can we learn about energy if nobody knows what it is? Well, let me clarify the term 'energy.' When I talk of energy that forms physical matter, I'm not referring to the type of energy we think about in our day to day lives. For example, when you go to the gas station to '*Fill'er up*!" you get energy in the form of petroleum. When you flip on the light switch, energy in the form of electricity travels through the wires of your house and when it contacts the bulb it triggers energy in the form of a chemical reaction, and your room becomes illuminated with light energy. When you chug a Red Bull 12 ounce, you get walloped with energy in the form of caffeine. Drag your feet along the carpet and you're zapped with static electricity energy. Charge up your smartphone's battery and you get hours of electrochemical energy. There's solar energy, wind energy, gravitational energy, nuclear energy, sound energy, light energy, chemical energy, mechanical, and thermal energy. There are so many forms of energy bombarding us, how could I possibly say nobody really knows what energy is?

While we may not know what the energy of matter is or how it originated, we do have ways to determine its power and describe its characteristics. There are two fundamental forms of energy - Potential Energy and Kinetic Energy. Potential Energy is used to describe any type of energy that is in a stored form. For example, if you hold a brick over your head, the brick would have 'potential' gravitational energy because once you let it go it'll drop and clunk you on the noggin. Gasoline has stored 'potential' chemical energy since when it reacts with a spark or flame it'll release energy in the form of a chemical reaction. Other forms of potential energy include mechanical, nuclear, and elastic.

Kinetic Energy describes energy that is in motion. If that same brick is instead tossed at a window, while in flight it'll have kinetic energy or energy in motion that will cause the window to shatter on contact. This energy is used to describe movements of celestial bodies down to vibrating atoms. Different forms of kinetic energy would include, thermal energy, sound waves, electricity (the flow of electrons between atoms), and light energy.

Now, let's peek at some of the properties of energy. It's important to have a fundamental understanding of energy's characteristics since later we'll see how these characteristics apply to you. After all, if matter is nothing more than energy and your physical body is made of matter that means you too are nothing more than a massive pile of vibrating energy! So, an understanding of energy provides an understanding of yourself.

One of the most important properties of energy is that it never stops moving. It's in constant vibration. It never rests. Energy is constantly and perpetually vibrating. And since everything is made of energy, everything vibrates. Next time you need a steady hand and you can't stop shaking, just blame it on your vibrating energy!

The rate that something vibrates is called its 'Frequency.' Everything also has a frequency. All material objects, every person, all animals and plants, and all the physical matter of the Universe vibrate at different frequencies. Even your thoughts and emotions are energy with distinctive frequencies. (We'll get into this more later.) Simply put frequency is the number of times something occurs in a given unit of time. The most common measure of frequency is called a hertz (Hz), named after the German physicist Heinrich Hertz. One hertz = one cycle per second. So, if you can do two jumping jacks per second, you would say you have a jumping jack frequency of 2 hertz. If you're grinding out a cycling class at the gym, and the wheel of your stationary bike is spinning at 10 rotations per second, you could say you are peddling at 10 hertz. A frequency of 60 hertz means that there are 60 things occurring in one second. When we talk about energy, the frequency is extremely high, like a million or a billion cycles per second. You'll burn a whole lot of calories if you can peddle your lifecycle 1 megahertz! You'll often hear of Megahertz (MHz) or Gigahertz (GHz) in reference to computers, which are one million and one billion cycles per second respectively.

Over the years, physicists have learned that as the frequency of energy changes, so does its function. When we step through the energy frequency range, starting from a low frequency and moving towards higher frequencies, we'll transition through different functional purposes. At the lower end are radio waves, as we move towards higher frequencies we'll bump into microwaves, infrared radiation, visible light, ultraviolent radiation, X-rays and gamma rays.

Radio waves are used for television, radio, mobile phones, MRI's, and wireless networks. Microwaves power those amazing box-like ovens that can cook a potato in minutes, all the way to powering Wi-Fi devices. Infrared frequencies are used in night vision and thermal imaging technologies, and visible light frequencies extend from the color of red through the full spectrum ending with violet. Moving up to the next level of frequencies we'll stumble into the ultraviolent spectrum, which gives us ultra-high energy frequencies that can break chemical bonds. Moving further along we hit X-rays that as you know are so small, they can pass through most substances and are used in medical applications. Finally, we find gamma frequencies, which is a frequency produced by subatomic particles. As you can see, the movement of atoms and their energy components are some of the fastest frequencies known to man.

Just as atoms have energy frequencies, so do cells in the human body. Every organ and tissue in the human body has a natural frequency. This even extends to brainwaves, which are also measured in frequencies that range from a low of about 1 Hz (relating to deep sleep) to a high of up to 30 Hz (an awaken state of deep concentration). In addition to brainwaves, emotions have a vibratory frequency too. Fear, hate, and negativity have slower frequencies than love and positivity which have high frequencies. You'll hear these being referred to as low or high frequency thoughts and emotions.

The last quality of energy we'll look at is energy density. All elements can exist in three different states – solid, liquid, and gas – depending on the temperature and pressure. Water is a nice familiar compound to illustrate this. Everyone has seen all three of its glorious forms, solid (ice), liquid (water), and gas (steam). The molecules are most tightly packed in the solid form, and then as it changes to liquid and gas the molecules' density loosens up. As things heat up, the molecules increase their vibration, giving them a higher frequency. This means that the same compound can have different densities depending on its vibrational frequency. This is an important energy concept to keep in mind as we'll revisit this in Chapter 4 when we discuss the densities of spiritual energy.

The Emptiness Within

I hope you're not too shocked by the revelation that matter is not matter at all, but energy because this next concept is really going to blow your mind. In addition to atoms being made of energy, the entirety of an atom is virtually nothing but empty space. That's right, they are virtually non-existent! Imagine that. The physical world is composed of energy and the solidity of all things is primarily empty space. If you need a little more convincing, then let's take a closer look…

To put this into context, let's go back to the diagram of an atom from Chapter 2 (Figure 12) and create an atomic model in its proper proportion. Starting with the atom's nucleus, we'll build a model where the nucleus is represented by a standard marble that you find in a child's marble set. If this were the case, the electrons orbiting this nucleus would not resemble a smaller marble only a few inches away as shown in illustrations of an atom, but rather they would be a sphere roughly the diameter of a human hair and positioned about 2 miles away! Think about this for a moment. If you placed a marble representing the nucleus of an atom on the floor, you'd have to walk two miles before coming into contact with the closest electron that's a tiny spec the diameter of a human hair. Everything in between would be nothing but empty space. And that's the CLOSEST electron.

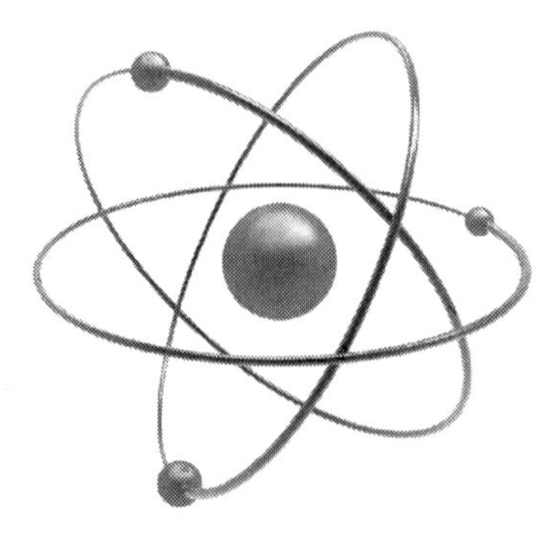

Figure 12 – Atomic Structure

The reason all the diagrams you've seen of atoms are not drawn to scale is you'd need a piece of paper over 10,000 feet wide to illustrate it (that's close to 2 miles). Since we've all grown up learning and seeing this condensed pictorial representation of an atom, we've come to believe that atoms are tightly packed objects. Most atoms have electrons orbiting in 'shells' at varying distances from the nucleus, similar to how we have planets orbiting the sun at various distances. In our scale model, these outer orbital shells would extend some 15 - 20 miles from the nucleus. That's a whole lot of empty space you'd have to traverse just to find an electron the size of a human hair.

To better understand this proportional scale, let's duplicate this process for the neon atom we examined in Chapter 2. This little experiment will help illuminate just how much of an atom is empty space. If you remember, neon contains 10 electrons that orbit the nucleus in two different orbital shells. When we convert this atom into a scale model, we'll get some astonishing results.

First, imagine a circle 8 miles in diameter that is completely empty. In the center of this enormous circle place a child's marble representing the nucleus. Then walk out two miles, or 10,560 feet. That'll be about 40 minutes of walking if you walk at the average speed of 3 miles per hour. Once you've reached the 2-mile point, place a smaller marble with a diameter equal to that of a human hair, about one one-thousandth of an inch (1/1000). Do this again for the 2nd electron in this orbital. When you're finished with that, you'll have to continue walking to the second orbital shell. So, keep going a couple more miles - a total of 4 miles from the marble at the center. Once there, place eight more tiny human hair sized marbles evenly along the edge of this outer circle. We now have our neon atom constructed to scale...well almost. We'll have to take it from 2-D to 3-D. To do this, you'll need to stand way back and envision the flat circle as an enormous sphere, like a giant 8-mile-wide beach ball containing a child's marble in the center and 10 human hair sized marbles 1/1000th of an inch orbiting inside it. With this image locked in your imagination, try to describe how much of the volume of this giant beach ball is occupied by marbles, and how much is empty space. That gives you an understanding of how little 'substance' an atom actually contains.

I recognize some have more vivid imaginations than others and imagining an 8-mile diameter beach ball may not be all that easy. So, let's put this into a numerical equivalent. When we calculate the volume of a sphere 8 miles in diameter, we get a spherical volume of:

68,190,000,000,000,000 cubic inches!

That's 68 quadrillion, or 68,000 trillion cubic inches! We've all heard how massive our National Debt is, and that's only 20 trillion. So, you can see, there are a whole lot of cubic inches in this atomic model. Now, let's figure out how much space the combined volumes of the nucleus and all the orbiting electrons take up. Collectively they will combine into a sphere of about 1 inch in diameter. Calculating their volume gives us:

.524 cubic inches

Comparing the two volumes gives a sphere with a volume of 68,190,000,000,000,000 cubic inches, and atomic particles with a combined volume of only 0.5 cubic inches! The rest is nothing but empty space. That means 68,189,999,999,999,999.5 cubic inches are empty. To give you a visual comparison, imagine an Olympic swimming pool 1 mile long and 1 mile wide filled with water. Now, drop a grain of sand into this ginormous pool and you have a rough representation of the volume of an atom. The sand is equivalent to the sum total of all the atomic particles, the rest is empty space.

As you can see, it's virtually nothing but emptiness. The more we learn about physical matter, the more we recognize that matter is almost ENTIRELY empty space. It is as empty as the free space between the planets. When you look into the night sky, you don't see giant orbs blocking out the sky. The planets are merely tiny specks in the sky, only five are visible to the human eye. These 8 or 9 planets (depending what planetary school you come from) represent the entire solar system of over 3.7 billion miles wide. And just like an atom, there's a whole lot of empty space between these planets.

Another example to illustrate the concept of emptiness is that crazy challenge of how many people can fit into a Volkswagen Beetle. Well, on November 8, 2009 in Dade City, Florida, the world record was set when 17 people crammed themselves into a 1971 Volkswagen Beetle. Seventeen people is pretty amazing, but what's even more amazing is you could fit the entire population of Earth, all 7+ billion people, into that same 1971 Volkswagen Beetle. Here's how. If you were to remove all the empty space from the atoms of every human on the planet, the actual mass would become exceedingly small, so small that you wouldn't even need a container the size of a Volkswagen Beetle. In fact, by removing the empty space of the atoms, the entire human population could fit into a container the size of a sugar cube!

By now I hope you've gotten a better understanding of the assertion that an atom is effectively empty, and physically they are virtually non-existent. Here's where the conundrum comes in. When you perceive atoms from our vantage point, and not from the atomic level, physical matter appears much different. We see that it does have form, shape, and size. We don't see empty space but rather solidity. But, how in the world can this be possible? How can something that has no substance just energy, and contains so much free space, appear to us as solid?

Well don't try to run through walls just yet, we've just uncovered another puzzle piece to investigate! Hang in there, we're about to explore this phenomenon in Chapter 4, but for now there's one last bit of energy to sink our teeth into.

It All Leads to the Beginning

Now that we know physical matter is not very physical at all and contains virtually no matter whatsoever, you must be wondering what other conundrums of the physical world I have up my sleeve…Well, there's just one more for now. It's a commonly cited theorem that you may have heard once or twice in your life – *Energy can neither be created nor destroyed.* This little theorem is known as the law of Conservation of Energy and dates back hundreds of years. Many scientists have circled this wagon, from Galileo to Newton to Joule, with each providing more clarity, but Einstein gets the credit for the famous line *"Energy cannot be created nor destroyed, it can only be changed from one form to another."*

While this may be simple to read and recite, for many it's a concept that goes in one ear and follows an empty tunnel straight through to the other side without ever making a stop in between. So, let's get on the Law of Conservation of Energy bus and make a short stop in our brains to analyze what it's all about.

What does it really mean to say energy cannot be created nor destroyed? All day long we seem to be destroying energy by burning fuel in our cars, cooking meals on a gas stove, or burning oil to heat our homes. And isn't energy being created when decomposing trash forms methane gas? Or what about solar panels, don't they create energy? Actually, we'll see that in all these instances Einstein and other scientists are correct, we really don't create nor destroy these forms of energy, the energy simply transitions from one form to another.

When we start our cars or flip on a light switch the energy released is not 'created' in that moment, it merely shifts from one form of energy to another. For example, when you get in your car, the gasoline in the tank is in the form of potential energy. Once you turn the key the gas injected into the engine's cylinder is ignited. It explodes converting from potential energy to chemical energy, which shifts to thermal energy forcing the pistons to move upwards within the cylinder. That in turn changes to mechanical energy that turns the drive shaft attached to the axel which powers your vehicle forward. Once in motion it now has kinetic energy. As you can see, the energy isn't actually created, but rather it shifts from one form to another.

If we trace the potential energy of the petroleum back to its origins, we'll find it originally came from ancient plants that decomposed over billions of years and in the process became fossil fuels. Those plants absorbed their energy from the sun, captured through photosynthesis.

Going one step further leads us to the sun. But where did the sun's energy originate? And where did all the energy of all the stars in all the galaxies of the Universe originate? The search for the original form of source energy is the unanswered question of energy I spoke of earlier. By the end of the book, you'll have a diverse enough understanding of these concepts to form your own ideas of this original source energy ...so stay tuned!

OK, it's time to take inventory of our energy investigation and see how our puzzle is shaping up. We've seen that energy comes in various forms, and we've been able to come up with ways to describe its characteristics and formulas to calculate its force. We've learned that the whirling atomic particles making up our physical world are nothing more than energy. We know this energy never stops vibrating and does so at an infinite range of frequencies. We've discovered that atoms are nearly all empty space and the physical matter we thought was composed of tightly packed atoms giving it form and solidity is virtually 100% empty. We also learned some crazy things about sub-atomic energy, like they can be in 2 places at precisely the same time (bi-locate) and can instantaneously behave identically even when separated by extraordinary distances (quantum entanglement). Finally, we know that energy can neither be created nor destroyed, but rather transitions from one form of energy to another.

So, if all that we can see, feel, and touch is nothing more than tiny bits of energy amongst extraordinary amounts of empty space, and if the energy forming all that we can see, feel, and touch can never be created nor destroyed, where did all this energy come from in the first place? What is the original source of the energy that makes up the physical universe? Think about that for a moment. An energy that is omnipresent, connects everything, and exists everywhere simultaneously…what else have you heard that fits this description? Can you think of something that is said to be embodied with these very same properties? You may want to make a mental note of this question as I'm certain we'll revisit this omnipresent force before the end of this book. But, let's not get ahead of ourselves.

Before we move on, there's one last question I'd like to raise. If matter is nothing more than energy and our flesh, bones, and organs are also made of matter, does that mean we are nothing more than energy? Think about it. Are you nothing more than a gigantic bundle of swirling bits of energy like all the other matter in the physical universe? When you're done chewing on this, turn the page cause that's what we'll be exploring in Chapter 4!

Ch. 4: What Are You Made Of?

"Man lives only as long as he has vital energy in his body. If he lacks vital energy, he dies." – *Hatha Yoga Pradipika*

Are You Different from a Rock?

We're coming off a chapter that put our magnifying glass to energy and discovered many fascinating aspects about how energy works; how it's quantified and calculated; how it makes up the basis of our universe; and how it can never be created nor destroyed. The interesting thing about energy is it's a force we're not able to see. We can feel it and measure its presence, but we can't see the bugger. From time to time we're able to appreciate its effects, for instance watching waves crash to shore on the beach. The ocean's waters take the shape of the energy flowing through it in the form of a wave, giving us a front row seat of its power. However, energy itself is like the wind, while our senses detect its presence, the force itself is invisible to our sense of sight.

While I'm on the subject of invisible forces, it's important to point out that we spent the first two chapters investigating and uncovering evidence that supports the notion of a higher intelligence permeating all things, from the genetic codes of life, to the atomic building blocks of matter, to spiral galaxies trillions of miles in width. Perhaps we should consider if a connection exists between the unseen force of a higher consciousness permeating the universe and the underlying energy permeating the physical world. Could these two forces be one and the same? And, if energy can never be created nor destroyed, is this higher consciousness also the original source of energy for the physical world? Interesting thoughts to dwell upon, aren't they?

Here's where things really start to get interesting. The first few chapters have been heavily weighted in science. It's critical to our investigation to have a solid scientific foundation to support our findings. I thank you for sticking around through the seemingly interminable science and math lectures. However, for those of you expecting a frolicking stroll down a path of spirituality, your journey is about to begin!

We've spent quite a bit of time analyzing the energy that makes up the elements and materials of the physical world, but these are all inanimate objects without free thought or consciousness. What about the energy that makes up lifeforms? What makes living creatures different from the minerals in the ground? If all matter is composed of the same subatomic energy particles – electrons, neutron, and protons – how are we able to have life, consciousness, free will, and independent thought? How can we express emotions and personalities if we're made from all the same stuff as a pile of coal or slab of iron? Hmmm…this seems like another interesting hunch to investigate. So, let's get right to it!

Life on the Dark Side

We've learned that matter is virtually 100% empty space, and since YOU are also made of matter your physical body should be no different…and it isn't. Just like all other matter in the universe, your physical body is composed of trillions of atoms. And like all other matter in the universe, those trillions of atoms are virtually nothing but empty space! I know it's a bizarre concept, but it's true. Remember if we collapse all the free space from the atoms in a human body, the entire human population could fit into a box the size of a sugar cube. So, imagine how microscopic the box would be to hold just your atomic particles. The physical area that your body occupies is overwhelmingly lots and lots of empty space. So next time someone calls you an airhead, you can assure them they're right!

I have a confession to make. There's a bit of a twist I haven't told you…yet. All this time I've been talking about the free space that exists within atoms, I haven't quite been giving you the whole truth. In reality, the empty space between the energy particles of an atom is not a pure vacuum. It's filled with a mysterious energy that has only recently caught the attention of the scientific community. This mysterious energy was initially suspected when astrophysicists were faced with a baffling conundrum involving the expanding universe. Scientist knew that gravitational forces should be pulling the space-time fabric of the universe together causing it to compress, but it isn't. The universe is expanding. Not only is it expanding, it's expanding at an accelerated rate. No matter how much scientists crunched their numbers, they were unable to account for the universe's expansion. The numbers just didn't add up. The only way astrophysicists can account for this contradiction is to theorize the universe must be filled with a uniform force that counters the pull of gravity and pushes the universe apart. They call this invisible force '*dark energy.*' In other words, rather than the energy particles of atoms whirling around in an empty vacuum of space, they're actually immersed in a sea of energy…dark energy.

The understanding of dark energy is in its infancy and scientists are still at a loss as to what dark energy consists of, where it comes from, and the effect it has on humans. They have been able to determine dark energy is an antigravity force that contributes to the expansion of the universe. They also believe it accounts for over 70% of the total volume of the universe. The theory of dark energy has been recorded in the annals of science as a revolutionary discovery, and it is. But, hold onto your Nobel Prizes, it may not be such a new theory.

We've seen other instances of ancient knowledge being 'rediscovered' by contemporary science, and this may be another example. The belief in a primordial energy permeating the universe dates back thousands of years and is referenced in many different cultures. In India it is called *Prana* or the breath of life, China calls it *Chi,* Jewish Kabbalists refer to this energy as *Astral Light,* yogis call it *Shakti,* in Japan its known as *Ki,* Polynesians call it *Mana,* in Hebrew it's called *Ruach,* Islam refers to it as *Baraka,* the Navajo and the Lakota Indians call it *Nilch'i* and *Ni* respectively, Hawaiians call it *Ha* or *Tane,* ancient Egyptians referred it is as *Ka* or *Ankh*, the ancient Greeks named it *Pneuma,* the Aboriginals of Australia call it *Maban,* Taoists refer to it as *Qi,* and if you're a Jedi Knight you call it *The Force*!

The name is irrelevant, regardless of the name it's the same energy. All these cultures throughout time, across the globe, and even from galaxies far, far, away, reference an omnipresent, ubiquitous, unseen primordial energy that expands the depths of the Universe. It is not air, nor is it the empty space of a vacuum, but rather an energy of higher consciousness that permeates and animates the entire Universe. It is recognized as the energy of life itself. It's been referenced and debated by philosophers like Aristotle, Socrates, and Cicero, and the debate leads right up to present day.

Many practices study the flow of this Vital Life Energy and have been doing so for thousands of years. Some lay claim to being able to strengthen and enhance their physical bodies through the enrichment of this energy, such as yoga and tai chi, while other practices develop the ability to control and redirection it, like acupuncture, reiki, or qui gong.

Vital life energy has become the foundation of many health and fitness practices that have been providing significant benefits to billions throughout recorded time. Westerners have been slow to the table incorporating these beliefs and practices into their daily routines, but we're quickly catching up and are now accepting the benefits of these ancient systems. Just go to any metropolitan city and try to find a block that doesn't have yoga studio!

However, despite all the history, practice, and study of Vital Life Energy, there are still millions and millions of people, perhaps billions, who are not even aware of it, and many who outright deny its existence. Fortunately, we're at a privileged time where we no longer need to rely on the village oracle, tribal shaman, or local philosopher for insight into the power and benefits of Vital Life Energy. There are so many resources available to anyone willing to do the research and learn about it. All you need is a little push to engage your curiosity and the desire to understand what makes you as a human being tick. So, consider this my little kick in the pants to get you curious enough to do some outside research of Vital Life Energy. For the sake of simplicity, from this point forward, I'll refer to this Vital Life Energy as 'Chi,' which is one of the most commonly used terms.

Your body can absorb Chi from three major sources – the sun, the air, and the earth. Solar Chi is derived from sunlight, invigorating the body and promoting positive health. You can absorb solar Chi simply by exposing yourself to sunlight, or by drinking water that has been sitting in the sun. Chi that comes from the air is sometimes called '*ozone Chi*.' It is absorbed by the lungs and can be most effectively acquired through slow and deep rhythmic breathing. When you practice diaphragmatic breathing, it's not only oxygen that you are absorbing into your body, Chi energy get absorbed as well. The third source of Chi is the earth.

'*Ground Chi*" enters through the soles of your fee and can be absorbed automatically simply by walking barefoot.

Ground Chi has spawned a recent phenomenon in the West called *Grounding* or *Earthing*. While ancient in its origins, people are now discovering the healing powers of ground Chi by walking barefoot through nature. And just like us, plants, animals, and even water can absorb Chi from sunlight, air, and the ground. Did you know that in addition to releasing life-giving oxygen into the atmosphere, trees also release a lot of excess Chi? In fact, trees can be a nice source of Chi energy to keep you in tip-top condition. Next time you're feeling tired or sickly, try lying down, resting, or meditating beneath a majestic old tree. By absorbing its excess Chi energy you'll find many positive benefits and a quick pick-me-up!

This brings us to another pivotal point. Whenever mainstream science and ancient knowledge seems to be in mutual agreement on a belief, it acts as a sign of another clue to investigate – how Vital Life Energy (Chi) of the universe interacts with the human body.

Energy of You

From our exploration of matter, we've come to understand that atoms are the building blocks of the physical world, and the subatomic particles forming atoms are nothing more than energy. However, we can't deny that material objects like a fire hydrant, bathtub, or shovel, don't have the same free will and consciousness that humans share. They don't express emotion. They don't exhibit personality traits, thought, consciousness, awareness, mental breakdowns, or temper tantrums. They don't require therapy, need time-outs, or a moment to collect themselves…they're all just inert matter. However, we as human beings DO require all these things. So how can that be? If the building blocks of our bodies are made from the very same particles as inanimate matter what makes us different?

The simple answer is your body has two fundamental components, the physical matter that makes up the biological you, and the energy force that makes up the spiritual you. There's a physical you and a spiritual you together in the same body. Going back to our study of energy, we learned that energy comes in different forms. Well, it's no different with our bodies. They are composed of energy in different forms. Your body is not just trillions of atoms forming billions of cells that make up your organs, bones, muscles, and skin. You also contain an energy that's different and apart from the physical cells of your body. They are two separate entities infused into one being. One is mortal flesh and bones matter. The other is an immortal spiritual being.

Now, everyone is quite familiar with their physical body, but not too many know about their spiritual body. So, let's introduce you to the other part of yourself. The individual cells of your body are surrounded and interpenetrated by a form of energy referred to as the '*human energy field*.' Science has made great strides in identifying and confirming the existence of the human energy field. Roughly 50 years ago, Soviet scientists conducted experiments that led to their discovery of an energy field infusing and surrounding the body of all living organisms – humans, animals, and plants. They concluded all lifeforms emit an energy vibrating at a frequency ranging between 300 and 2,000 nanometers, which they called the '*biofield* or *bio-plasma*.' As scientists studied it further, they noticed the human energy field exhibited nodes of intensity throughout the body that corresponded exactly to the 700 acupuncture points on ancient Chinese charts. Again, science catching up to ancient knowledge!

Today, there's highly sensitive equipment that can detect the human energy field. Science now fully acknowledges the human body is infused and surrounded by an energy field extending outwards up to 4 - 5 feet from the body's surface. You've probably heard it referred to as an *'aura'* or *'etheric body.'* Your energy field is very powerful and can influence the physical tissue of your body (more on this later). When the human energy field becomes stagnant, out of balance, or depleted for extended periods of time, illness and disease will begin to manifest in the physical body.

None of this is new to traditional Chinese medicine. For centuries they have asserted the body has a natural flow of energy in channels called *meridians*. These meridians are precise pathways in the body that guide the flow of energy to your vital organs. Over 3,000 years ago, Chinese sages began mapping the energy meridians and the juncture points in the body. Three centuries later, modern science confirmed these energy meridians. Today, acupuncturists commonly treat illnesses and relieve pain merely by controlling and redirecting the flow of energy. In fact, many symptoms of illness are believed to be the byproduct of blocked or disrupted energy flow. In addition to acupuncture, there are other therapeutic techniques, exercises, practices, and meditations developed throughout the world to relieve energy imbalances. Since I've dedicated this book towards solving the purpose of life, and not a Reiki, Tai Chi, or acupuncture manual, I'll assume that you have many outlets at your disposal to learn more about the health benefits of maintaining and strengthening your energy field in ways that suit you and your lifestyle. For the purposes of this book, know that I HIGHLY recommend you engage in one or more of these practices.

Now, how does the human energy field interact with the physical body? The human energy field is different from Chi energy in that it is an independent energy that draws sustenance from Chi. You can think of it this way. Your physical body contains blood vessels that carry nutrients throughout it. The cells of your body draw strength and energy from the blood flow. Without the flow of blood, the cells could not survive. In a similar way, the energy body draws strength and energy from the flow of Chi. Without the flow of Chi, your energy body could not survive.

Your energy body also contains channels or meridians which Chi flows through to nourish and invigorate the spiritual body, much like the network of veins and arteries of your circulatory system. The flow of Chi throughout your spiritual body is like an 'energy blood' providing life-giving sustenance. While each cell is independent from the others, with different functions and responsibilities, collectively they combine to form a person, like you. Likewise, each human energy body is separate and apart from each other, but collectively they combine to form a Universal Consciousness. It's how we are all connected. Everyone has an energy field.

The strength and vibrancy of your energy field has a direct correlation to many physical conditions including your physical and emotional wellbeing. When a person is healthy, their energy field radiates with a balanced flow of bright, colorful energy. In contrast, when a person is unhealthy, the illness or disease will become evident in their energy field. Most diseases initiate in the energy field and through time manifest in the corresponding cells of the body to form illness.

We've now learned of energy forming physical matter, energy of the spiritual body, and Chi or Vital Life Energy. To illustrate how the spiritual energy is separate from the energy of physical matter, let's do a little imaginative exercise. It's a bit on the macabre side, but it will help illustrate the difference. Think of how a human body appears when someone dies quietly in their sleep. In the final moments of life, the body contains all its biological parts – its cells, organs, muscles, bones, etc. – all working together to sustain life. The precise moment after the individual is pronounced dead, the physical body still contains all the same biological parts that were present moments before when the individual was still alive. Now ask, what differentiates the mass of 'living' cells from the mass of 'dead' cells?

Answer: the spiritual energy body. Once the spiritual energy leaves the body, the flesh and tissue become a lifeless mass of matter with no consciousness, no different from any other lifeless mass of matter. In this instance the body no longer contains its two different forms of energy, but only the singular energy of physical matter. Without the spiritual body the cells, tissues, and organs of the body become as inert as any other elemental substance. It's the spiritual body that brings life to the physical body. It animates the body and gives you free will, emotion, personality, thought, consciousness, and awareness.

Now, we've heard about meridians, nodes, and channels that allow Chi to flow through the body providing life-giving energy. They're like the circulatory system pumping blood throughout the body. Chinese acupuncturists have even mapped and defined the energy meridians. But our circulatory system has a physical heart responsible for pumping blood through the veins and arteries. How does Chi energy get pumped throughout the energy body? What serves as the pumping station of Chi? Well, you've heard of the Seven Wonders of the World, well I'm about to introduce you to the Seven Wonders of the Human Body...the Chakras!

The Magnificent 7

There are many things that come in groups of 7. We have 7 days of the week, 7 deadly sins, 7 seas, 7 continents, 7 Wonders of the Ancient world, 7 colors of the rainbow, 7 games in the World Series, 7 stars in the Big Dipper, 7 dwarfs with Snow White, 7 books in the Harry Potter series, 7 years of bad luck if you break a mirror, 7 words you can't say on television, 7 Swans a swimming, 7 Samurai…there are even 7 castaways on Gilligan's Island! But, probably the most important group of 7 influencing your life is the 7 chakras, and you don't have to journey far and wide to find them. They're located smack dab in your body (Figure 13).

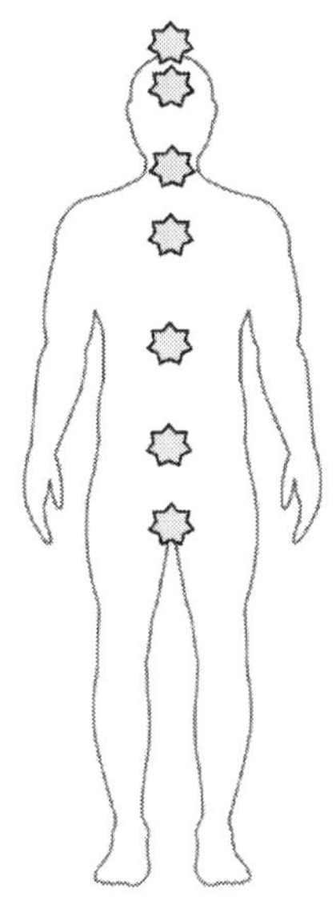

Figure 13 – The Locations of the Body's 7 Major Energy Centers

What makes them so important is Chi energy (Vital Life Energy) flows in and through your body via these energy vortexes. Each chakra controls the flow of Chi through your system and becomes part of your internal spiritual guidance system. The chakras correspond to physiological attributes involving your body's health, emotions, and spirit. We've seen how energy is an invisible force and since your chakras are energy vortexes it stands to reason that they too are invisible.

These energy centers are funnel-like vortexes extending from the surface of your body. Visualize a chakra as a mini-tornado of energy spinning on the surface of your body. Of the seven chakras, two are standalone tornadoes, one at the top of the body and one at the bottom. The other five chakras are double-sided tornados with one extending outwards from the front of the body and the other extending outwards from the back of the body. The chakras located at the top of your head and at the tip of your tailbone are vertical energy centers that point straight up and straight down respectively. The remaining five chakras are positioned along the body extending horizontally outwards as though they're two mini-tornados whose tails are touching (see Figure 14).

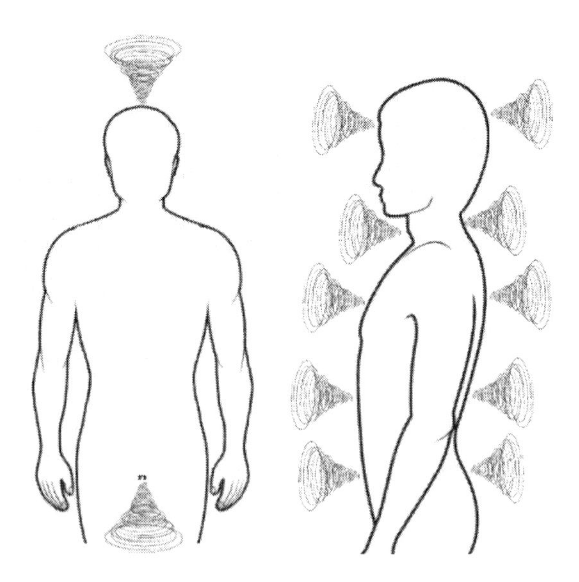

Figure 14 – Chakras are Tornado-like Vortexes Extending from the Body

If you're hearing about these swirling energy centers scattered across your body like tornado alley for the first time, I'm sure you're thinking, '*We're not in Kansas anymore!*" But I assure you we are still operating very much in the real world. We're about to uncover the mysteries of the Magnificent 7 and don't worry, you don't have to travel somewhere over a rainbow to explore these energy tornados, all you have to do is click your heels together three times and say, '*There's no place like home*'... Just don't get disappointed if we don't encounter any Munchkins, heartless tinmen, brainless scarecrows, cowardly lions, evil witches, or flying monkeys!

To learn about the tiny tornados of energy swirling about your body we'll begin at the bottom and working our way up, examining how each chakra impacts and influences your physical body, your emotional body, and your spiritual body. When I say starting at the bottom, I really mean YOUR bottom. The first chakra is located right there at the base of your booty, between the tip of your tailbone and your genitals. It's commonly known as the '*First Chakra*,' or '*Root Chakra*.' This energy meridian acts as the distribution center for Chi energy supplied to the cells of your spinal column, legs, bones, feet, and immune system. Envision it as a mini-tornado whose tail touches the base of your spine and points downward.

On a spiritual level, the root chakra ties you to the material world, grounds you, forms your identity, and is the foundation of your emotional and mental health. The energies of the first chakra get called upon when you need to deal with emotional issues involving survival, order and structure, logic, and the five senses. Socially, it provides energy associated with bonding, honor, loyalty, and justice. Any anxiety or discord you face with these issues will disrupt the energy of the root chakra. For instance, when you mock or ridicule someone less fortunate than you, you'll be able to sense the disharmony in the seat of your pants! Those with a developed sensitivity to their body's energy can recognize the disturbance right away and connect the sensation with its cause. This is one of the ways that your chakras become an internal guidance system for you.

Here's a little experiment you can do to get a sense of this energy. Close your eyes, still your mind, and relax your body. After a few relaxing moments, focus your attention on something that makes you feel part of a group or organization, or gives you a sense of patriotism or family. Concentrate strongly on that experience and let it really trigger an emotional response. The thing that works for me is Whitney Houston singing the National Anthem during Super Bowl XXV. To me it's the greatest rendition of the 'Star Spangled Banner' since Francis Scott Key wrote it. No matter how many times I hear it I get chills racing up my spine. But find something that works for you. Perhaps it's that powerful rendition of the National Anthem, or a memorable Olympic victory, or maybe there's a child named after you. As you focus on this experience and allow it to take an emotional effect on you, bring your awareness down to your root chakra and see if you can detect this area of your body responding to your emotional experience. You'll be able to feel a slight tingle or energy sensation in that area. That is your root chakra reacting to your emotional identity to family or honor.

Working our way up the body we'll bump into the second chakra about 3 inches below the navel. This chakra is known as the '*Belly Chakra,*' or '*Sacral Chakra.*' With this one you'll want to envision one mini-tornado extending outwards from the front of your body just below your navel, and a second mini-tornado on the opposite side extending outward from your back. Physically this chakra acts as the distribution center of Chi energy to the cells of your sexual organs, large intestines, lower vertebrae, pelvis, hip, appendix, and bladder. It regulates emotional issues relating to honor and power, loss of control, addiction, and abandonment. All attachments to the physical world are associated with this chakra. There are many different types of seductive powers in the physical world that get regulated by the belly chakra - sexual, material, physical desires, addictions, etc. A strong and vibrant second chakra helps provide stamina to survive hardships, the confidence to take risks, strong decision-making abilities, and the ability to overcome external temptations and desires. A healthy second chakra enables you to generate a sense of identity and negotiate the physical world without falling prey to its seductive forces, giving you the strength to act with integrity and honor in all your relationships – from marriage to friendship to business. When you violate issues of honor and integrity, you'll feel the discord in the second chakra.

Continuing our voyage upwards we'll find the third chakra known as the *Solar Plexus Chakra.* The name itself is a bit of a spoiler since it pretty much lets you know this chakra is located above the solar plexus, which is the top of your abdomen just below the sternum. Like the previous chakra, this one also has mini-tornados extending on both the front and back of your body. This chakra is your personal power center and core of your personality and ego. It is most closely associated with intuition of the physical world and contains your survival instincts protecting you from physical danger. When you feel a sense of danger emanating in your belly, it's your third chakra at work. This is the fellow behind your 'gut instincts.' The third chakra also involves emotional issues of honoring yourself, your ego, self-esteem, rejection, criticism, embarrassment, and fear of physical appearance (aging, balding, weight, etc.). Physically this chakra acts as the distribution center of Chi energy to the cells of the stomach, pancreas, upper intestines, gallbladder, liver, and the mid-section of the spine behind your solar plexus. A vibrant third chakra provides strength in self-esteem, ambition, the ability to handle crisis, generosity, and strength of character.

As we continue our energetic climb up the body, we'll run into the fourth chakra, which is the central powerhouse of the chakra system. Its primary association is with love. With that as a clue, I'll let you use your refined super-sleuthing skills to guess where this chakra is located…If you guessed, *"the heart,"* you've proven yourself worthy! While it's often referred to as the *'Heart Chakra,'* it's not actually located above the heart. You'll find this mighty energy center on the same plane as your heart, but positioned directly in the center of the chest in line with all the other chakras. Emotionally the fourth chakra relates to issues involving lessons in love, forgiveness, loneliness, commitment, betrayal, inspiration, trust, and compassion. A robust fourth chakra provides strength in all these areas. You've heard the expression, *'follow your heart,'* well, that has to do with the heart chakra. A weak or poorly energized forth chakra can give rise to jealousy, bitterness, anger, hatred, and an inability to forgive. Physically the fourth chakra is the distribution center of Chi energy to the cells of the heart, circulatory system, ribs, breasts, lungs, shoulders, arms, hands, and diaphragm.

The reason the I refer to the heart chakra as the central powerhouse is it's the interface between the physical realm and spiritual realm. The lower three chakras connect us with elements of the physical world, while the upper three chakras connect us with elements of the spiritual world. In the middle is the heart chakra, regulating the interaction between the physical and spiritual. This powerhouse is what gives rise to the expression *"the path to spiritual consciousness is through the heart."* The true motivator of the human body and spirit is love. Few will argue that love is one of the purest forms of power. You are attracted to love, intimidated by love, motivated by love, controlled by love, inspired by love, and can easily be destroyed by love. Love energy is the essence of the heart chakra, master it and mastery of the physical world will follow.

We climb further up the chakra ladder to find the fifth chakra lying right in the center of your throat. Due to its location this chakra is commonly called the *'Throat Charka'* or *'Communication Chakra.'* Physically this chakra distributes Chi energy to the cells of the throat, thyroid, esophagus, neck vertebrae, mouth, jaw, and teeth. This is the first chakra associated with the spiritual body. Emotionally, this chakra relates to issues involving personal willpower, self-expression, the power of choice, and faith. A fully energized throat chakra provides strength in faith, self-knowledge, and personal authority. When your fifth chakra is weakened you become susceptible to lying and deceit.

As we move farther upwards to the sixth chakra, we'll find ourselves in the center of your forehead, giving this energy center the distinctive name the *'Mind Chakra'* or the *'Third Eye.'* This is the second spiritual center in which the interaction of mind and psyche can lead to intuitive sight and wisdom. Physically it distributes Chi energy to the cells of the brain, neurological system, pituitary and pineal glands, the eyes, ears, and nose. The sixth chakra is involved with emotional issues relating to the mind, spiritual intuition, insight, and wisdom. A fully energized sixth chakra will help you receive spiritual answers to questions and challenges you encounter in life. As you master the Third Eye chakra, you'll develop the ability to detach yourself from the influences of the physical world and become more in-tune with your internal spiritual guidance. This chakra is very powerful as the path to understanding 'thought' is the precursor to 'form,' and the physical reality you create begins in the spiritual realm. (This will become more defined in later chapters.)

And topping off the list is the chakra that also tops off your body, the '*Crown Chakra.*' This seventh energy center is positioned at the very top of your head and is the most spiritual chakra of all. To envision this chakra, imagine a mini-tornado whose tail sits at the top of your head, and extends upwards swirling around in a vortex of energy. (Don't worry, regardless how energized your crown chakra is, it's not going to mess up your hair!) The seventh energy center is associated with all issues relating to spirituality, spiritual abandonment, loss of identity, and loss of connection with life and people around you. It is your connection to the spiritual realm. Strengthening this energy center will strengthen your inner guidance, insights into the spiritual realm, and a quality of trust that extends beyond normal human fears. It contains the energy that generates inspirational and prophetic thoughts, transcendent ideas, and mystical connections. Physically the crown chakra distributes Chi energy to the cells of the central nervous system, muscular system, and the skin. Vital life energy flows into your body through the seventh chakra, and surges endlessly throughout your body.

As you can see, each chakra serves a specific purpose in the context of your physical, emotional, and spiritual bodies, but they also function collectively as a whole. The first three chakras – root, sacral, and solar plexus – all relate to issues of the physical or external world, while the top three chakras – crown, third eye, and throat - relate to issues of the non-physical or internal, and the magical interface between the physical and non-physical lies at your heart in the fourth chakra (see Figure 15).

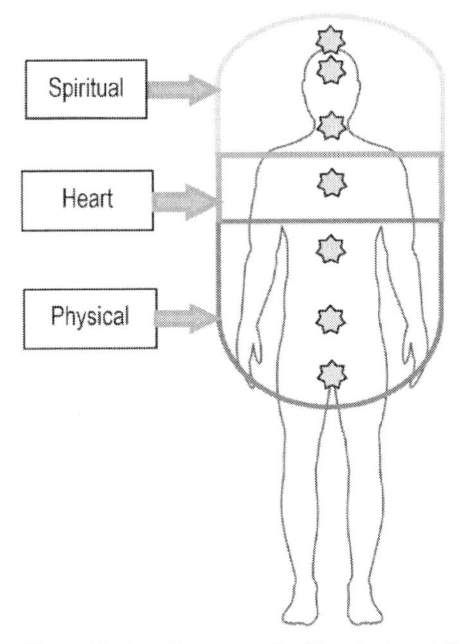

Figure 15 – The Heart Chakra Connects the Physical and Spiritual Realms

Now, here's something you'll find intriguing. Your human energy field, or aura, is composed of seven different concentric energy bodies each extending beyond the prior and all occupying the same space. It would be like having a large balloon containing a smaller balloon, which in turn contains a smaller balloon, which in turn contains a smaller balloon, all the way down through six levels. Or, similar to a set of wooden Russian nesting dolls placed one inside another. That's exactly how your aura is structured, seven energy bodies each within one another.

It's no coincident there happens to be seven layers of the aura and seven chakras. Each layer of the aura is associated with one of the chakras. As the chakras absorb Chi energy, they also radiate energy outward. This radiated energy is what forms your aura. We are like sponges in the sea of Chi energy absorbing the energy needed to sustain life. Your aura is just as real, alive, and functioning in your spiritual body as your circulatory system is functioning in your physical body.

Now that you know why I call these incredible energy centers "*The Magnificent 7.*" They truly are magnificent in what they do for you physically, emotionally, and spiritually. Think of the power you can have over your own life, your physical health, your emotional wellbeing, and your spiritual growth, when you understand, master, and control your energy bodies. And as I leave you in deep thought over that, it brings us to our next topic of energy exploration…Thoughts!

Think About It

As we investigate new and unusual concepts, some will build to a "*Eureka!*" moment. In my humble opinion, this section will be one of those moments. But, for you to jump out of your chair and scream "*Eureka!*" you'll need to pay particularly close attention. The revelation we're about to extrapolate is truly grand in scope. So, if at any point this section becomes confusing, I encourage you to reread and digest each concept in order to grasp its full weight. What makes this section so important is we get to bridge science with spirituality in a way that illuminates the mysteries behind our thoughts.

I've asked you to dwell on certain thought-provoking questions and perspectives, and during those times I'm sure you've had unique thoughts racing through your head – big thoughts, profound thoughts, and some out of the box thoughts. With all these thoughts whirling around, it brings us to the next subject to explore…what are thoughts? How are thoughts created? Everything we do, feel, and act upon occur because of our thoughts. How does something with no tangible form become such an integral part of our very tangible world? Are thoughts nothing more than biochemical reactions and synapses firing in the brain? Or, is it possible that thoughts arise from somewhere beyond the physical brain?

Neurological researchers from traditional schools of cognition tell us thoughts are a function of the brain. The body uses its senses to collect information, which are communicated to the brain through a network of neurotransmitters. The brain in turn, uses this data to do the actual thinking. With over 100 billion *neurons* connected through trillions of *synapses,* each capable of transmitting up to 1,000 signals per second, the brain uses the combination of these bio-electrical pulses to produce thought. So, essentially thought is an electrical signal generated by billions of brain cells. Nothing more than a big bunch of bio-chemical reactions. All the amazing advancements in human history, innovation, creativity, the great works of literature, music, art, expression, architectural wonders, and everything that you've ever considered, solved, or achieved are all the results of random, arbitrary bio-chemical reactions. Hmmm, to me this seems to be a fancy neuroscience way of saying, *"We don't really know how thoughts originate."*

To be fair to neuroscientists, many do admit to not knowing the answer to the enigma of where thoughts originate. They have made tremendous strides in mapping the brain and associating certain bodily functions with different areas of the brain. For example, they've found the *brainstem* controls autonomic functions like breathing, digestion, and heart rate, the *cerebellum* coordinates motor skills, the *temporal lobe* is involved with the senses, the *hippocampus* is essential for memory function, and the right hemisphere generally controls the left side of the body, and vice versa. However, in the same way that mapping the human genome doesn't explain how life began, mapping the human brain doesn't explain how thoughts begin.

While researchers are busy trying to figure out the origin of thoughts, let us consider the possibility that perhaps they've been putting the cart before the horse. What if we flip the premise around and approach it from a different perspective...an energy perspective? Let's assume the brain is not the birthing place of thoughts, but rather a physical transmitter of them. With our newfound understanding that the body contains both a physical component and an energy component, could it be that thoughts arise from beyond the biological matter of the brain? Is it possible the spiritual body, your consciousness, is the true creator of thoughts?

Let's explore this notion. If thoughts really are born from the energy body and not a bio-chemical reaction, how are they able to interact with your physical body? Your energy thoughts would have to stimulate the brain's synaptic network to transmit them to your physical body. How can something as ethereal as a thought interact and control the solid cells of your body? Well this is certainly something we'll need to look into.

When you consider thoughts as an energy with the ability to manipulate the physical body, it can sound a bit paranormal. Pop culture portrays mind-control and psychokinesis as superhuman or a freakish oddity - from Jedi mastery of the Force to the horrors of "*Carrie*." But what if we were to learn that there's nothing freakish about psychokinesis. In fact, EVERYONE has psychokinetic abilities to some degree. You'll see what I mean as we immerse ourselves deeper into thoughts and the brain...

Humans have been fascinated with the internal workings of the mind for centuries. Philosophers, scientists, psychologist and neuro-researchers throughout time have been baffled by this enigma. However, cognitive research took a giant leap forward about 100 years ago when a German scientist named Hans Berger produced the first *electroencephalography* recording, which is just the fancy-pants name for an EEG. Berger recognized the brain as an electrochemical organ that generates electrical pulses called *'brain waves.'* He then went on to develop equipment to measure and record these brain pulses. This breakthrough led to decades of study and advancements that provided neuroscientists the ability to quantify and associate brain wave frequencies with different types of brain activity. For instance, we now know that higher frequency brain waves are generated during alert states when your brain is aroused and engaged in mental activity. The more intense the activity – fear, shock, anger, hunger, and surprise – the higher the brain wave frequency. During tranquil states, such as meditation, creative visualization, and pre-sleep state, the brain produces lower frequency brain waves. During sleep and deep levels of hypnosis, the brain wave frequency becomes even lower.

As we come to better understand the waves emitted by the brain, we're able to utilize them in innovative ways. Currently, thought-control technology is being developed and put to use using just the focused intensity of the mind. You can input information into your computer, control your smart phone, navigate a wheelchair, move prosthetic limbs, play Angry Birds®, fly a toy helicopter, or wear furry ears that stand up when you're upset and a tail that wags when you're excited! This is real technology that exists today, not something from a Philip K. Dick sci-fi novel. There are thought-control applications for doctors, the military, teachers, gamers, and many, many others. Theses telekinesis-like technologies are all possible because thoughts ARE energy. The human brain does emit a measurable energy via thought, and science has developed technology to capture this energy and use it to control physical items. So, how does this work with you? How does your body use the energy of your thoughts to control the physical muscles, organs, and cells of your body?

Let's look at some of the evidence we've uncovered. We know thoughts are energy operating at different frequencies. And frequency is simply the number of instances something occurs during a given time frame – miles per hour, jumping jacks per minute, cycles per second, etc. A characteristic intrinsic with frequencies is the higher the frequency becomes the more difficult it is to detect. When a frequency becomes too high it can move outside the range of detection by our physical senses.

Take a hummingbird for example. It's amazing to watch them hover around plants and flowers. All you see is a tiny torso floating freely in space as if they're defying gravity. But we all know hummingbirds have wings, it's just that they flap at an extraordinary high frequency of about 30 - 40 beats per second. This 'flapping frequency' is so fast it can exceed the rate a normal human eye can detect. The same holds true with sound. Certain sounds waves are emitted at such a high pitch the human ear is incapable of detecting them, like a dog whistle. Likewise, the vibrational frequency of atoms can affect our sense of touch. If you immerse your hand in a bucket of liquid your sense of touch can detect it, but when you speed the atoms up to a gas it's no longer so easy to detect. Insert your hand in a balloon filled with helium and you won't feel a thing.

So, when we speed up the frequency of something, it can exceed human senses. Conversely, when the frequency is lowered, the rate of movement is slowed. Place a liquid in the freezer, the atoms vibrate at a lower frequency and it becomes a solid. Now, let's apply these common examples of frequency change to thoughts and see what happens.

We typically think of things existing in three different forms – gas, liquid, solid – because we see and live it all day long, from the plume of steam rising off a boiling pot of pasta, to giant icebergs breaking off the Artic shelf. When you add heat, atoms vibrate faster, and solids turn to liquids and then into gas. When atoms are cooled, they vibrate slower and gas turns to liquid and then to solid. But what happens when we alter the frequency of energy? We experience very similar results.

The sea of energy permeating the universe has a very high frequency, appreciably greater than the wings of a hummingbird. Due to its extraordinarily high frequency, it is extremely difficult for our senses to detect, whereas the energy of matter vibrates at a much lower frequency making it considerably more detectable. This range of frequencies defines an energy spectrum. On the high-frequency side of the spectrum we have Universal energy and on the low-frequency side of the spectrum we have energy of physical matter. Given these two ends, we're left to wonder what lies in the middle.

Here's where things get very interesting. There's a type of matter that physicists call '*plasma.*' A common misconception is to assume there are only three states of matter - solid, liquid, and gas - but there are actually four, plasma being the fourth. We get to experience a nice big glowing gob of plasma each day - the sun. The sun and stars are all real-world examples of plasma. Scientists define plasma as a state that exists between energy and matter. Interesting isn't it? Think about this, a scientific state that exists between physical matter and energy known as plasma.

Where have you heard the term '*plasma*' before? If you reflect back to earlier in this chapter, we learned that Soviet scientists discovered an energy field, or an aura, that exists within and around all living organisms (including you). Do you remember what the Soviet scientists called this energy field? Bio-***Plasma***! So, scientists refer to a property that exists between energy and matter as *plasma*, and scientists also refer to the aura as *bio-plasma*. If you also recall, earlier in this section we set out to find an interface between the physical body (matter) and the source of your thoughts (energy or consciousness). Consider the possibility that your body's aura, or bio-plasma, IS the interface that allows your non-physical thoughts to interact with your physical body. How about that! Your thoughts are born in the non-physical spiritual dimension of your energy body and get transmitted to the brain's neurotransmitters through your bio-plasma. Isn't that an eye-opening revelation!

Now that we've made the connection that the human energy field is the interface between thoughts born from the spiritual dimension and the physical body, how does it make us Jedi Masters with psychokinetic abilities? We've seen that physical matter is nothing more than energy, operating at a certain frequency. We also know energy can neither be created nor destroyed, meaning the energy of physical matter must have originated along with all energies of the Universe, which includes the energy of your physical and spiritual bodies. All these things – physical matter, your spiritual body, your physical body, your bio-plasma - are offshoots of the same energy source operating at different frequencies. It's all the same stuff!

Since you have the capacity to control your thoughts and your thoughts derive from the same energy source as all matter, then you also have the potential to influence the energy of physical matter through intense focused thought. It's all part of the same energy spectrum! You simply need to be brought to this understanding, so it becomes an accepted belief, and then trained on how to use this inherent gift.

"Nonsense!" you say, *"psychokinesis is a fabrication of fiction!"* Well, look at it like this. Every human has the ability to throw a football, but only the most skilled, well-practiced athletes have a shot at becoming the starting quarterback in the Super Bowl. The same holds true with psychokinesis. There are Qi Gong, Tai Chi, and Shaolin masters who have developed abilities to control Chi energy that makes Tom Brady's abilities to control a football look like the Pee-Wee league. Through years and years of applied practice, truly superhuman feats can be achieved with the energies of the mind.

Let me share a first-hand experience I had with a Qi Gong master that really opened my eyes to this phenomenon. I was working at a major production company in Hollywood at the time, and the head of business affairs was a woman who always suffered from some type of discomfort - her neck, her lower back, shoulder, carpel-tunnel, etc. Each day was a mystery as to what pain she'd be afflicted by. One day, I witnessed her skipping down the hall singing *"Zipity-Do-Da!"* It was so unusual I had to stop her and find out why she was so giddy. She went on to tell me she had just gotten back from her 'energy therapist'! All I could think was, *"Energy therapist! What the heck?"* So, I grilled her for answers in my usual fashion and learned there was a Qi Gong Master from China, named Master Zhou, whose office was just around the corner.

Imagine that! I had always wanted to experience an energy healer, now one of the foremost energy specialists in the world was only a few blocks away. You have no idea how fast I was on the phone scheduling an appointment! Within a couple weeks I was in to see the Qi Gong, Tai Chi, and Kung Fu Master. I snuck away during a lunch break for my first appointment and it couldn't have arrived fast enough. I was both excited and skeptical at the same time.

When I first met Master Zhou, I was taken aback. I had expected there to be a radiant glow about him. That he'd have some sort of energy field I'd be able to feel in his presence. When I shook his hand, I hesitated, anticipating getting zapped like one of those hand-buzzer pranks you see in a joke shop. But, none of that happened. He was just an ordinary man in his mid-70's from China. Small in stature, Master Zhou barely pushed 5'3" and only spoke a couple words of English. We worked through an interpreter and my first session began with Master Zhou asking why I was there. "*Oh Crap*!" In all my excitement I overlooked the fact that didn't have anything wrong, no pains, no aches, no reason to be there! I was really just there out of curiosity. So, acting quickly I came up with an ailment... I told him I had a stiff knee from a long run I recently went on and asked if he could also give me an overall energy cleansing.

His interpreter asked that I lay face down on a massage table and Master Zhou would work on me. So, I climbed onto the table fully dressed in my office clothes waiting to be mesmerized by the energy healer. He began by rubbing various pressure points along my back and shoulders with his fingers and the palm of his hands. So far, no jolts of arcing energy...not even the shock of static electricity. After a few minutes, all I could think about was how much he was wrinkling up my dress shirt! Finally, he worked his way down to my stiff knee where his real healing power would emerge. Now, remember I'm face down and can't see what he's doing, but I could hear him rub his hands together and take a few deep, diaphragmatic breaths. Then he held his hands about two inches above the back of my knee and suddenly I began to feel a warm, intense heat. Not the heat of friction nor the warmth of another person's body, much hotter than that. My knee began to heat up almost to the point of being so hot I thought my skin would burn. The heat would go right up to that breaking point intensity, but never cross the line of 'too hot.' I was amazed at what was happening, but disappointed that I couldn't see for myself that there was no trickery involved.

Then, the great Master spoke the only words of English I ever heard him say, "*Turn Over*." Great! My chance to determine what type of gimmick he was up to. So over I go fully alert and on the lookout for a battery-pack hidden up his sleeve. Like before, he began rubbing pressure points along my chest, and again, wrinkled the heck out of my shirt. Finally, the moment arrived when he did the hand-rub and deep breaths to work on my knee. I watched diligently to see how he pulled this trick off. I peeked up his sleeves, nothing hiding up there. He then placed a piece of paper towel over my knee and held his hands about two inches above it. As he continued to breathe deeply, my knee again began heating up. I was riveted. There was some form of energy radiating from his hands that was interacting with my knee. There was no doubt in my mind. This wasn't trickery. There was no gimmick nor battery pack. This was without a doubt human energy interacting with my body. It was one of those defining moments in life that you never forget. I had to figure out how this worked. So, on the way out the door, I signed up for personal classes with Master Zhou to learn how he worked his energy magic. And before I left, I asked if those healing hands could take wrinkles out of a shirt!

During the following weeks, I'd dash away during lunch and take private lessons from Master Zhou. Through his interpreter he began to teach me the various body movements, stances, and routines that promoted energy flow. But for me, I was more curious about what he did. I didn't have as strong an interest in spending fifty years of intense practice to be able to replicate his abilities. After a couple lessons of Master Zhou getting frustrated by my constant interruption of questions, we decided to set aside the 'training' and instead have a sit-down discussion. He detected my innate curiosity, which somehow appealed to him, and at that point I became his 'Grasshopper.' He opened up and told me all about his fascinating life and abilities. It was such an honor to have spent that time with this incredible person. It made me recognize that there is a field of energy within and surrounding the human body. And with enough practice and training, anyone can learn to strengthen, control, and project it. I know. I met a real-life Jedi Master named Master Zhou.

Putting It All Together

Time to take a little breather and pull together all we've covered in this chapter. Our overall objective is to investigate the purpose of life. To accept our conclusions, we need to fully understand the supporting evidence. Living in a physical world that is entirely energy based is a pivotal pillar of support for the purpose of life. This is the reason I've spent so much time and effort on the topic of energy. Like any other subject, you need to first understand the basics before you can fully comprehend more advanced concepts. For instance, engineers can't use complex calculus to solve advanced equations of physics until they first learn basic arithmetic. In the same way, you won't truly believe and accept the purpose of life without first having a fundamental understanding of the physical world. Consider these first few chapters the basic arithmetic needed to use advanced calculus of life.

To summarize this chapter: You are an energy being living in a physical body, on a physical planet that is moving through a sea of energy. This sea of energy has been referenced throughout the centuries as Vital Life Energy, Chi, Prana, Ki, Mana, Ka, and the Force. This Vital Energy flows throughout the body via extensive energy channels and vortexes.

Acupuncturists have mapped and mastered the hundreds of nodes and meridians of the body's energy network. There are seven major energy centers called chakras that serve as the pumping stations of Chi throughout the energy body. These energy centers regulate everything about you physically, mentally, and emotionally. We've also discovered a human energy field which has been termed bio-plasma, or a state that exists between matter and energy. The human energy field is formed by multiple concentric fields radiating outwards, each with one of the seven chakras at its center. This energy field acts as the interface between spiritual energy and physical matter of the body. Thoughts are born in the spiritual dimension and are transmitted to the body's network of neurotransmitters via the human energy field. This is how your spiritual soul manifests and manipulates the physical world.

Your thoughts are quite powerful. Masters of Eastern philosophies believe thoughts have such a profound influence over life they are literally considered living things. These Masters believe thoughts have a reality in space, take on a certain form, last for a certain period of time, and have the power to control actions. If you master your thoughts, they can become a powerful guide. However, if you do not control and direct your thoughts, they will control and direct you, ensnare you, and lead you to misfortune. There's much more about this in later chapters.

Every human being has at their core an amazing spiritual energy. This energy stems from the same source that makes up the entirety of the Universe. As you evolve in your spiritual understandings and learn to balance the energies of your soul and body, your thoughts and actions, you will begin to gain a more powerful control of your purpose. Mastering the energy flowing into and throughout your body, gains you power, knowledge, and self-awareness. Over time it becomes integrated into the composition of the cells in your body. This physical change stimulated by controlled thought, provides a powerful tool to achieving your life's fulfillment.

We are energy in various forms – body, mind, and soul. The body's matter is physical energy, the soul is spiritual energy, and the mind is the bio-plasma interface between the two. As we follow one clues and answer questions, interestingly new questions are generated that pull us deeper into our case, and closer to solving our mystery. With this in mind, what new question will bring us further into our case? I'm curious how many have considered this question on their own?

If it's true that the physical world and the spiritual world interact with one another, how do they co-exist? What is the true structure of a world with such a multidimensional reality? That's something rather intriguing to think about. But let's do one better than just think about it, let's give it a full chapter of exploration!

Ch. 5: Body and Mind

"Infinite energy is at the disposal of everyone, if he only knows how to get it." -- Swami Vivekananda

The Bridge to the Other Side

After four chapters of exploring the physical world we've gotten a little more than our toes wet, you could say we're up to our necks in understanding the mechanics and functions of the physical world. We've gained a full understanding of its structure, its atomic make up, and its underlying energies. After all that work, you should have a fundamental grasp of the physical world. It's now time to shift the investigation to the spiritual dimension. So, let's dip our toes into the ether and splash around a bit.

Now, I've been describing a reality in which the physical world simultaneously co-exists with a spiritual dimension. Given this structure of reality, an important question comes to mind - how do they interact? If these two dimensions exist at the same time literally on top of one another, then what allows one to function within the other? How can a dimension made of solid physical form be capable of interacting with a dimension of intangible, ethereal composition?

Well, the answer is closer than you think. In fact, it's right at your fingertips. Go ahead. Look down at your fingertips, follow them up past your wrist, along your arm, past the elbow and up to your shoulder, you'll find they're attached to the very interface between the physical

and spiritual dimensions. That's right, it's YOU! Human beings are the bridge between these worlds. Now, I know what you're thinking…
"Hold on just a New York minute! How is that even possible!?!"

Well, your body is a marvelous vehicle that most people know very little about. All our lives we've been taught different features of our physical bodies. In school we've learned all about its many biological systems - the nervous system, the digestive system, the immune system, the circulatory system, respiratory system, skeletal system, muscular system, etc. We've learned how individual organs that make up these systems function and contribute to the process. We've been taught how each organ consists of many distinct cells, and how each cell is made of various components. We've been instructed on how to feed our bodies, how to exercise them, how to cure them when they're sick, how to treat them when injured, how to groom them, clean them, apply make-up to them, add hair to them, remove hair from them, laser treat them, wrap them in seaweed, stretch them, build muscle, and of course…how to accessorize them! However, only a rare few have been taught how the body is a tool for your spirit to experience the physical world. And for those who've never been given this significant use of the body, you're in for an eye-opening treat!

There may be some who still have lingering doubts whether your body even has a spiritual component. I'd like to take a slight detour and propose a premise that may help solidify the concept of the body's spiritual component. It'll give you a whole new way of looking at yourself. From all we've learned about the body there shouldn't be any argument that we are made of trillions of cells, about 30 trillion if you're counting. And it's self-evident that these 30 trillion cells collectively form together to create you. Just look in the mirror to verify this if there's any reservation. Each of the 30 trillion cells in your body is a separate and independent cell. They live, replicate, and die independently. In fact, you can remove individual cells from your body, place them in a petri dish, and under proper conditions keep them alive. These independent cells all serve a unique function, and when combined, they form a whole and complete individual known as you. You are the results of trillions of individual cells working in unison to carry out the functions of life. Each cell in your body intuitively knows exactly what it must do to keep you alive, and they go about performing their functions with precision, harmony, and balance so you as an individual can function in the real world…well most of us anyway.

Given this scenario, have you ever wondered how it's possible that all these individual cells know exactly what that common cause is? After all, you don't consciously direct each and every one your 30 trillion cells on what to do, when to do it, and how to get it done. In fact, most of these 30 trillion cells don't have the slightest clue about the existence of the other 29, 999, 999, 999, 999 cells. Take a muscle cell in your calf for instance. It may only come in contact with other muscle cells in its immediate surroundings and some passing blood cells for its entire lifespan. It's not aware that only a couple inches away are bone marrow cells in the tibia. Nor is it aware of lung cells only a couple feet away, nor nasal cells, nor lymph node cells, nor retinal cells, nor any of the other cells in the very same body. There's an amazing organized operation involving trillions of little workers all carrying out a purpose and function for a common goal. And what's truly miraculous is not one of the individual cells making up you, knows what that common goal is! They just go about their individual function. Only YOU know what the common goal of all these cells working together will be. Which leads us to ask, what exactly constitutes YOU, the CEO of 30 trillion workers?

That's a doozy to contemplate. So, while you noodle on that, let me remind you that way back in Chapter 1 we discovered that cells constantly die off and regenerate, so much so that your entire body regenerates itself every 11 years. Your physical body today contains cells that vary in age from newborn to elderly, but none are more than 11 years old. Let's put this concept through a little experiment. To do it I'll need to perform a little calculation. I'll use my body in the example, but as I step through the exercise, substitute your body into the calculation.

I was born in the wee morning hours in Woonsocket, Rhode Island back in 1963. I sprung into the world at a scale-tipping 5 ½ pounds! Since that time, I've grown to an adult and now check in at 5' 8," 160 pounds of flesh, muscle, and bone...and some tiny traces of love handles. Somewhere along the line, I went from a 5 ½ pound baby to a 160-pound adult, gaining 154 ½ pounds of physical matter. Now, run these numbers for yourself. Think about your physical size at birth and where you are today. Do the calculation. Whatever number you come up with represents the amount of physical matter you've gained since birth. Got it?

We should all be able to agree the size and density of your skeletal system, muscles, skin, blood, organs, etc., all the biological components you're made of are physical matter. Now, ask yourself, where did that 154 ½ pounds of physical matter that makes up you come from (or whatever your number is)? How did all the cells that make up the bones, muscles, organs, skin, hair, and body parts of you originate? Well, this one should be easy enough to answer – food!

The foods we ingest are broken down, digested, and used to provide the nutrients and minerals for your cells to reproduce and your body to grow. We've all heard the expression, *"You are what you eat."* There's nothing revolutionary about this. However, when you look down at the foods on your dinner plate, your breakfast bowl, or the snacks you're about to wolf down, what do you see? Do you see an intelligent being? When you scoop up a fork-full of mashed potatoes, do you see a substance capable of expressing thought and emotion? When you're about to toss a handful of trail mix in your mouth, do you look at it as a mixture complete with the power of free will and expression?

Or, do you see these things exactly as they are - a pile of mashed potatoes, a handful of trail mix, a Twinkie, an apple, or some vegetables. The foods on your plates, in your bowls, in your refrigerators, cupboards, and lunch boxes are not items you'd describe as intellectual consciousness. Despite the expression, *"You are what you eat,"* you would never look at a bowl of Fruit Loops and say, *"See those colorful circles of oats, sugar, and 7 essential vitamins and iron floating in milk, well THAT is the personification of me as an intelligent, conscious being!"* Of course not. We simply recognize food for what it is – molecular nutrients to keep our bodies alive. But food IS more than that. It's also the very stuff we are made of. The 154 ½ pounds I've gained since birth, all 30 trillion cells in my body, have all been formed from the foods I've ingested. All my physical mass has come from the foods I've put into my body. And the same holds true for you.

This is an important revelation, so don't let it zip by. If the entire body regenerates itself every 11 years, and it does so with food that has neither consciousness nor free will, then where does your consciousness and free will come from? Where does consciousness reside in an ever-changing physical body? If you are simply the rearranged atoms and molecules from the foods you eat, how can you have a continuous, complete personality, with thoughts and memories that last a lifetime, when the cells making up your body are formed from random, disconnected food sources originating from arbitrary locations throughout the world? What is the component of YOU that remains constant throughout the years as your body continually regenerates? Perhaps, just perhaps that constant is an energy-based consciousness…or your spiritual energy body.

As you let that thought settle, I'd like to get back to our original question: If two realms of reality exist – a physical universe and a spiritual universe - then how do they interact? Well, no spoiler-alert here, I've already told you the answer, it's you - Human Beings. And if the human body really is a vehicle for your spiritual being to interact with the physical world, then how does it all work? How does the body become an interface between a physical universe and a spiritual universe? This brings us to another part of the human body you've probably never been taught in a way I'm about to explain…your senses!

Making Sense of the Senses

We live in a world that's constantly competing for our attention. Every minute of every day in every aspect of our lives we're inundated with advertisers and businesses stumbling over themselves to grab our attention. Small mom and pop businesses to large multi-national conglomerates use print media, social media, television, film, billboards, emails, banner ads, telemarketers, newspapers, magazines, mailers, promotions, and everything in-between to capture your attention. Everywhere we look and turn our senses are being stimulated, knowingly and subliminally, to sights, sounds, smells, and sensations. They're all battling for you! All these external stimuli are being picked up and interpreted by our bodies. It's enough to give us sensory overload. And with our senses on overdrive, wouldn't it be nice to understand how our senses work, to really know how they function and help us detect the physical world around us?

Think about it. Do you really know what happens when your eyes project an image onto your retina? Or, how specific noises are determined when your ears pick up a sound wave? What makes homemade cookies smell so good and rotting garbage smell so bad? Unless of course they're my homemade cookies, in which case the rotting garbage has a slight smell advantage… Are all our senses merely electro-chemical reactions of the biological body? Or is there something beyond the physical that brings functionality to our senses?

There's a whole lot happening in the outside world that gets detected by your senses. You see, hear, smell, taste, and touch all day long giving you the full experience of your physical surroundings. Since our day-to-day lives are immersed in the physical world, we assume our senses are part of that same physical world. Just think about those delicious homemade cookies. When mom cooks some yummy chocolate-chip cookies, you can smell them throughout the house. You race to the kitchen and see them cooling on the counter. You hear your mom warning not to eat any before dinner, but you sneak one anyway and feel the warm cookie in your hand. And finally, the cookie meets your tongue and its mouthwatering taste makes it all worth defying your mom. All these things are as physical as the whooping you get when mom discovers a missing cookie! So, how can this experience NOT be physical? How does your energy body have anything to do with all this? And if it does, when exactly does this bridge to the spiritual dimension come into play during all these physical events?

What you may not be aware of is when you see, smell, hear, touch and taste that cookie it's not really happening in the physical world. *"What!"*

you say, *"Now you've really fallen off your rocker!"* We saw in Chapter 3 that things aren't always as they appear. Remember our very physical and solid world is nearly entirely empty space…likewise, our senses aren't exactly what they appear. When you experience the physical world, your senses draw in different frequencies of vibrating energies, those energies are then translated into biological data that gets transmitted via electrical nerve impulses to the brain, which interprets the bio-electrical signals in the mind. All the sights, sounds, tastes, sensations, and smells actually occur in the mind, not in the physical world. Now, I know this may seem like one of those esoteric concepts but give me a few minutes and it'll all become clear. I find one of the best ways to comprehend the senses is to analyze in detail the timeless philosophical question: *"If a tree falls in the forest and nobody is there to hear it, does it make a sound?"*

I remember being young and arrogant and hearing someone discussing this nonsensical question and I sarcastically thought, *"What kind of a fool would actually think a tree makes no sound when it falls, simply because nobody is there to hear it! Of course, it makes a sound! Period. End of discussion!"* Well, youthful ignorance is bliss, because one day while meditating, the true answer to this nonsensical question came to me in vivid clarity and I realized I was the fool. It was one of those defining moments I kept rethinking and re-analyzing over and over, each time I'd come to the same conclusion…*"The darn tree doesn't make a sound!"*

As I stepped through the process of how the body's sense of hearing works, moment by moment in ultra-slow motion, it occurred to me the falling tree did not create any noise, but instead it produced a wave of energy. At the time I thought I had cracked some secret code known only to the Gods. I realized I had fully comprehended the notion of duality, and I figured it out all by myself…little did I know this was a widely understood concept dating all the way back in the late 1500s! Rene Descartes gets the street credit for theorizing that matter and mind are separate calling it a mind-body duality. Just think, I came so close to owning 'dualism,' I was only half a millennium late!

Getting back to that soundless tree falling in a forest, I can't guarantee you'll have the same type of epiphany as I had, but I will do my best to explain the underlying concept so by the time we're through, you too will be saying, *"He's right! The darn tree doesn't make a sound when it falls!"*

But to get to that point, like so many other concepts in this book, we'll need to get some of the basics out of the way. In order to answer the philosophical question of a tree falling, we'll need to have a fundamental understanding of sound and your sense of hearing. So, listen up...

Shhhh.... A Tree Is Falling

What is sound? Simply put, sound is a series of *compression waves* (also called *pressure waves*) generated when something vibrates. The movements of the vibrating object cause a series of high and low pressures that 'compress' the surrounding medium – air, water, solids – creating waves of pressure. The most common medium is air, and depending on the temperature and humidity, a sound compression wave can travel through air around 750-770 miles per hour. That means it covers 1 mile in about 4 ½ seconds. Compression waves are recognized as sound waves when they are picked up and interpreted by a detector, like your eardrum. Confusion sets in by the terminology used to describe sound and compression waves. We commonly refer to compression waves as *'sound waves,'* and we also refer to the mind's interpretation of compression waves as *'sound.'* I don't mean to play a game of semantics, but a sound wave is different from a sound, or noise.

What we call a *'sound wave'* really isn't sound at all, but rather a compressed wave of energy.

To put it another way, compare a radio wave to the music generated by your speakers when you listen to the radio. Radio towers throughout the country send out radio signals 24/7. With more than 15,000 radio stations in the US there's always a plethora of radio waves being transmitted around you. Wherever you are, from the bathroom to an isolated country walk, there's no getting away from them. In fact, you're being bombarded with them at this very moment. However, despite hundreds of radio waves rippling past your ears, you're not inundated with the 'music' of hundreds of radio stations playing simultaneously. There is no music, nor sound, transmitted by the radio signal, only an electro-magnetic wave. It isn't until your radio intercepts and deciphers the electro-magnetic wave that music is generated. Think of sound waves and your ears in the same regard. While a compression wave is a different form of energy than an electro-magnetic wave, the principle behind the concept is the same. The compression wave of energy traveling through the air is similar to a radio signal traveling through the air. You don't refer to a radio signal as 'music.' You simply call it a radio signal. Similarly, the compression wave is not sound, it's simply a compression wave. In this example, your ears and mind act as the radio and speakers that decipher the signal. The music isn't generated until the radio converts the signal and feeds it through speakers. Likewise, sound isn't generated until your ears convert the compression wave and feeds it to your mind. Are you still a little unsure about this? Well, let's examine the ear in detail to really make you a believer.

When you hear a sound, what is really going on? Your sense of hearing is a complex process that requires various parts of the ear to work together to convert compression waves into information the brain can use to interpret. There are three main components providing you the gift of hearing - the outer ear, the middle ear, and the inner ear (Figure 16).

The outer ear consists of the external visible parts of the ear called the *pinna,* and the ear canal. The pinnas are those two flappy things on the sides of your head made of cartilage and soft tissue. They're shaped in such a way to funnel compression waves into the ear canal. They also help to determine the direction and source of sounds.

The middle ear begins where the ear canal ends - at the ear drum. The middle ear also includes three tiny bones connected to form what's known as the *ossicular chain*. The three tiny bones in this chain are called the Niña, Pinta, and Santa Maria! Just kidding, the ossicular chain didn't help Columbus sail the ocean blue... just wanted to make sure you're paying attention. The three bones in the ossicular chain are the *malleus, incus,* and *stapes*.

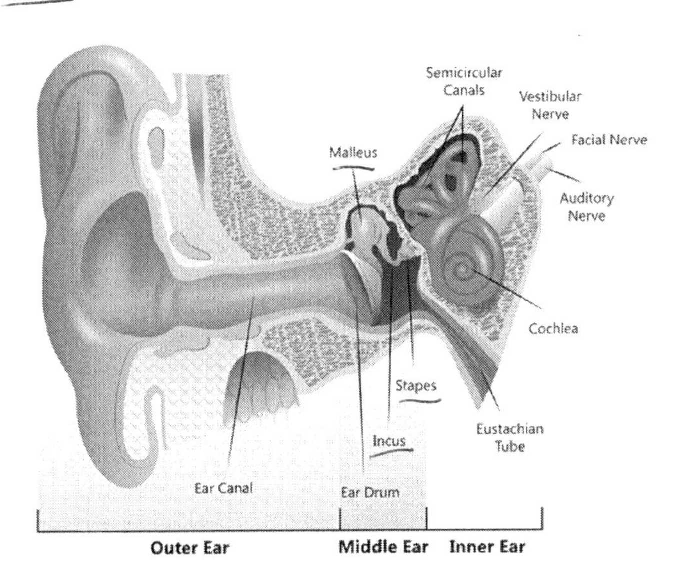

Figure 16 – Diagram of the Ear

The final part is the inner ear, which consists of the *cochlea* and the *auditory nerve* leading to the brain. The cochlea gets its name from Latin meaning 'snail.' Not to imply it moves slowly, but rather the cochlea has a distinctive coiled shape giving it the appearance of a snail. The cochlea is filled with fluid and nerve receptors that stimulate auditory nerves which in turn send signals to the brain.

Now that we have a rudimentary understanding of sound and the ear, let's put these two partners in auditory crime together and see what happens off in that empty forest. Will we discover 'noise' is generated when the tree impacts the ground, or will we learn 'noise' is generated internally…in our minds?

Let's set off into the verdant forest to find a large tree about to come crashing down. For the purposes of this exercise imagine you are in an isolated forest and by some stroke of luck, you happen upon an old tree about to call it quits. Imagine the tree's massive trunk gives way and the giant tower falls and smashes to the ground. Watch and wait for the moment when the heavy trunk slams onto the forest floor. Shortly after, you hear a booming 'crash' echoing throughout the hills. Now, your natural reaction is to say, "*See! There you have it. That crashing boom I heard is the sound created when the tree hit the ground. It doesn't matter whether I'm there to hear it or not, the sound echoes through the hills regardless. What's the argument?*"

Well, don't jump to conclusions so fast. Let's slow it down and step through this phenomenon in detail, keeping in mind our lessons on sound and the ear. When the giant tree hits the ground, its impact causes immense vibrations, which release large waves of compressed energy. This energy is known as a compression wave or sound wave. The compression wave radiates outwards in a symmetrical pattern as the energy travels in all directions. The further it travels from the source, the more the energy weakens. As you stand quietly observing the falling tree, the compression wave races towards your ears at 767 mph. Upon contact, your pinnas funnel the compression wave into the ear canal where it strikes the eardrum causing it to vibrate.

Now, pay attention since this is where the entire process takes an important shift. Once the compression wave created by the falling tree strikes the eardrum, the energy wave itself continues on at 767 mph looking for more eardrums to strike. But as far as your eardrum is concerned, from this point forward, the original compression wave is no longer part of your hearing process. Everything that occurs after the compression wave strikes the eardrum is completely separate from the wave of energy created when the tree hit the ground. The original sound compression wave no longer acts on any of the components of the middle or inner ear. As of now, no sound has been generated. There is only a vibrating eardrum.

The vibration of the eardrum causes the tiny chain of bones – remember the malleus, incus, and stapes - in the middle ear to move. The original 'sound wave' has been transformed into a mechanical process of three interconnected bones moving back and forth. It is no longer a compression wave. As those tiny bones move in response to the vibrating eardrum, they transmit the vibration to the cochlea. This is done when the last bone in the chain - the stapes - taps against the cochlea generating tiny vibrations in the cochlea's fluid. This process transforms the mechanical energy of the ossicular chain into a fluid transverse wave rippling within the cochlea, taking us one step further from the original sound wave. But we're not done yet!

The fluid movement within the cochlea stimulates tiny hair cells inside the cochlea creating neural signals. This transforms the fluid transverse wave into electro-chemical signals, which are picked up by the auditory nerve. This is now the fourth form of energy. We went from a compression wave, to mechanical energy, to fluid transverse wave, to an electro-chemical neural signal. At this point no noise has been generated, and we're STILL not done!

The auditory nerve carries the neural signal and begins the process of transmitting it to the brain. To do this, the signal must flow from one neuron to another neuron, crossing small gaps between them called *synapses*. It's important to note the neurons don't physically touch one another. The synaptic gaps are empty spaces between neurons. Since there is no direct contact between one neuron and another, when the electrical signal comes to the end of a neuron it is incapable of continuing to the next neuron. If there are any electricians in the room, this is what's known as an open circuit. The electrical signal can't jump the synaptic gap to reach the next neuron. In order for the signal to cross this gap the neuron has to convert the electrical signal to a chemical signal using specialized neurotransmitters.

The neuron uses its neurotransmitters to create the proper chemical signal in order to cross the synaptic gap, and then the upstream neuron detects the chemical signal with its receptor. This neuron must now convert the chemical signal back to an electrical signal so it can travel the length of its body. When the electrical signal reaches the end of this neuron, it must be converted again to a chemical signal in order to cross the next synaptic gap. With amazing speed and accuracy, the signal goes through the process of being converted from an electrical signal to a chemical signal and back to an electrical signal over and over through thousands of neurons and synapses on its way to the brain.

Alright, let's stop for a moment and look at where we are in the hearing process. What began as a compression wave from a tree falling in the forest is now an electro-chemical signal moving along a chain of thousands of neurons. Let's pluck just one of these neurons out of the chain and analyze it...how about we take the 3,428th neuron in the chain. When the receptor of this neuron gets dinged with a chemical signal by its neighbor, neuron 3,427, all it knows is it has a job to do, and that job is to transmit the signal through its cellular structure and onto neuron 3,429. Neuron 3,428 has no awareness of a tree falling, nor the compression wave it created when it hit the ground. The signal being transmitted is no longer a pressure wave and is about as different from the original sound wave as you can get. At this stage, we still have not reached the point in the hearing process where noise has been generated since the signal has not been deciphered yet. The mind has not received and interpreted the signal to know what type of 'sound' created the compression wave. No noise has been generated. It's still an electro-chemical signal traveling along a neuron chain.

Once the electro-chemical signal reaches the brain, the mind interprets and decodes the signals into a recognizable noise. This is the point in the hearing process where 'sound' is finally formed.

Now, ask yourself, "*Where does this occur*?" Does the interpretation of the compression wave to sound occur at the point when the tree hits the ground? Or, does it occur in the spirit-based mind after the compression wave is converted countless times into mechanical energy, transverse fluid energy, neural energy, electrical energy, and chemical energy?

The 'sound' is not generated from the pressure wave hitting your ear drum. It is not generated from the ear drum causing the tiny ossicular bones to vibrate. It is not generated from the stapes creating fluid vibrations in the cochlea. It isn't generated from the tiny hairs stimulating neural signals to the auditory nerve. And it's not generated when neurons transmit the neural signal by converting it from a chemical signal to an electrical signal and back again. It is not until the mind interprets and decodes the bio-chemical signal that your body 'hears' a sound. And the mind is part of the spiritual energy component of your body.

So, you see, the actual 'noise' of a large crash was not made by the tree hitting the ground, it occurs within the context of your mind. If no person is there with an accompanying mind to interpret the compression wave, then no sound is generated. The compression wave simply travels through the air looking for something to strike and decipher it.

That was quite a resounding journey, don't you think? Oh, aren't I so witty! It's fascinating to understand what goes on inside your body. It helps appreciate just how marvelous a creation the body truly is. Stepping through this process of hearing a basic sound really underscores the quote, *"There are only two ways to live your life. One is as though nothing is a miracle. The other is as if everything is. I believe in the latter."* When you break down what's required just for a simple noise to be heard, it truly is a miracle! Just imagine what goes on internally when listening to a 100-piece symphony orchestra. And now, you can join the great philosophical minds and answer the much-debated question of a tree falling in the forest with confidence. And like me, you too will be repeating, *"It's true, that darn tree doesn't make a sound when it falls!"*

The process of hearing is known as a dualistic process. Essentially, it's where two things, or a duo, are needed for something to occur, just like all the great duos, you know, Batman & Robin, Sonny & Cher, Beavis &

Butt-head, Macaroni & Cheese, Bonnie & Clyde, Peanut Butter & Jelly... In order to achieve a certain outcome, you need a duo. In the case of hearing you need a sender and a receiver. The tree is the sender, you are the receiver. Without you to receive and convert the pressure wave into sound there is no noise. There's only a wave of pressure moving through the air. That pressure wave can result in different outcomes depending on what it comes into contact with. Not all of them end with the generation of sound. For example, when a compression wave contacts a microphone, it produces an electrical signal in the form of a voltage or current, which is different from what your ears generate when struck by the same compression wave. That electrical signal can go to speakers to create sound, or it can go to an LED light system to create a really cool visual light display which has nothing to do with sound at all.

Let's take the concept of 'sound' occurring in the mind as an inner interpretation of an outer energy and apply that concept to all the senses and see what it does to your perspective of the physical world. You're about to discover as with hearing, so it is with your other senses. They too occur in your mind. While I won't go into the level of detail for each, it's important to recognize all your other senses merely detect energy vibrations, transform those vibrations into biological data, which gets sent to the brain to be interpreted by the mind. All we experience in the physical world through our senses takes place in the mind.

Vision is nothing more than the eye capturing photons of light (a form of energy), converting them to electro-chemical signals that travel along neurons to the brain, where they're interpreted into objects. Light rays enter the eye at the *cornea* and get refracted by the *lens* after passing through the *pupil* (Figure 17).

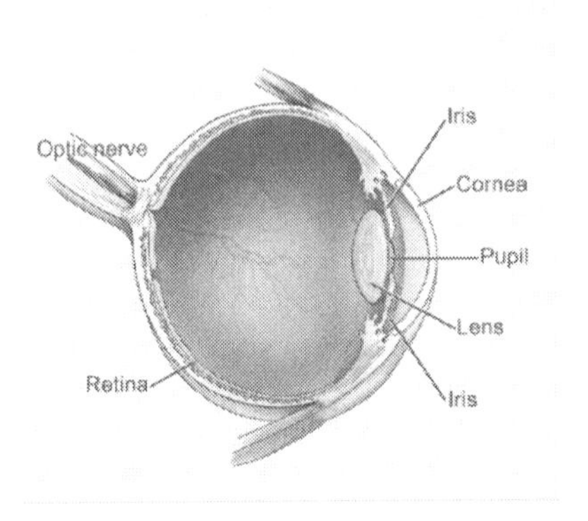

Figure 17 – Diagram of the Eye

The refracted light is then focused on the *retina* at the back of the eye. The retina contains millions of light-sensitive nerve cells called *rods* and *cones* that convert the light energy into electrical impulses, which are carried via the *optic nerve*. At this point, the photons of light no longer have any impact on the remaining process of vision. The electro-chemical signals traveling to the brain are completely independent of the originating photons of light. As we learned from the study of hearing, signals generated by the auditory nerve follow a long chain of neurons where they are repeatedly converted from electrical to chemical signals along the way. The same process occurs with signals created by the optic nerve. They go through a continual process of being converted from electrical to chemical signals as they journey along the neuron chain to the brain. Once again, it's the mind that interprets these signals into images.

Are you nosy about the other senses? Well, when you smell something, much like sight and hearing, the sense of smell also occurs in the mind. Your ability to smell originates from sensory cells called *olfactory neurons* found on the inside of the nose (see Figure 18). The olfactory neurons have *odor receptors* that connect directly to the brain. As microscopic molecules release substances into the air, like freshly brewed coffee or a silent-but-deadly fart, those microscopic particles enter the nasal cavity and stimulate olfactory neurons. It's here where the molecules are transformed into an electro-chemical signal. And we know the journey along neuron chains these signals take as they make their way to the brain where the mind identifies them as a smell. Once again, the mind is interpreting external energies.

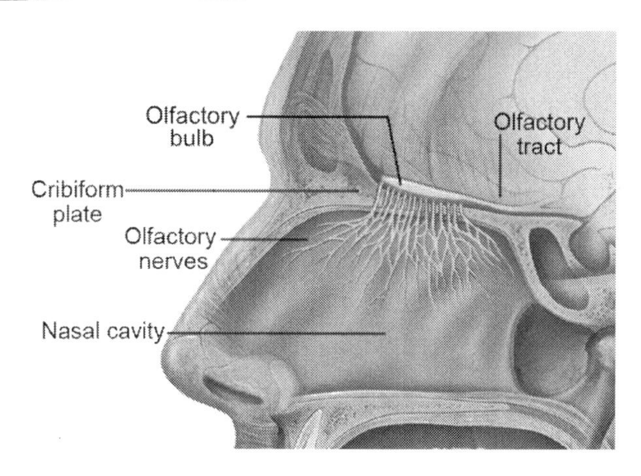

Figure 18 – Diagram of the Nose

Are you curious about your tongue with its thousands of taste buds? Are you wondering if all those mouthwatering flavors you've tasted all your life are merely a figment of your imagination? Well, yes they are! With all you've learned about the senses, this shouldn't be a bitter pill to swallow. All those savory tastes also occur in the mind. Your tongue is covered with 2,000 – 4,000 in tiny bumps called *taste buds* which are sensory cells connected to *nerve fibers*. The taste buds can decode five basic tastes – sweet, sour, salty, bitter, savory. When combined with different levels of intensity, the taste buds can produce over 100,000 different flavor possibilities. When substances come into contact with these sensory cells, they transform it into signals carried along the *cranial nerves* to the brain, where once again they're identified by the mind.

And of course, we can't forget about the sensation of touch. The body's nervous system is a complex labyrinth of nerves and receptors located beneath the skin's surface. When acted on by an outside stimulant – heat, cold, a sharp, rough, or soft object, etc. – these receptors send a signal to neurons in the central nervous system, which travel to the brain to be processed and understood by the mind.

Putting this all together, on one side we have the mind that's part of the non-physical energy or spiritual body, and on the other side we have the physical world brought to you by your senses in vivid colors, smells, tastes, sensations, and sounds. Having stepped through the process of our senses, we now understand how the non-physical mind uses the senses to experience the physical world. That's all there is to it. You now know how the senses bridge the physical with the non-physical, and how your body becomes the interface between the spiritual dimension and the physical dimension.

We are immersed in a sea of vibrating energies. All we see, hear, smell, touch, and taste are nothing more than pulsating energy interpreted by the mind. Everything we experience in the physical world plays out within the context of the mind. That's a strange concept to wrap your head around, isn't it? Viewing the world as a turbulent sea of energy with no mass or form, no sounds, no tastes, no smells, and all these real-world experiences occur only in the inner recesses of your mind, is quite a profound twist on reality. When you really stop and dwell on this it's enough to make you feel like you're living in a real-life version of "The Matrix." However, your mind is what brings form and shape to a world of vibrating energies. To truly believe this can be quite a challenge, especially since all we've learned and experienced is contrary to it. Perhaps it's why Leonard da Vinci said, *"The five senses are the ministers of the soul."*

The senses deliver external data to the mind for interpretation, allowing the spiritual body to experience the physical world. But what exactly IS the mind? This question leads to our next subject of investigation, the device that brings sense to the senses...your mind!

Are You Otta Your Mind!

As you digest the possibility of the world being merely vibrating forms of energy that play out in your head, I want to remind you of the importance of exploring and considering alternative perspectives to find one that conforms to your belief system. This is one that may take some time to seep in, but I encourage you to remain open and not dismiss it immediately. We've been bouncing around the idea that you are simultaneously physical matter and non-physical energy. At this point in our investigation, I hope you've uncovered enough evidence to accept this as truth. In the event you remain unconvinced, I hope there's a tiny crack in the veneer of skepticism that allows you to be open to its possibility. I say this because we're about to explore an element of the body that you can't get through an organ donation program – the mind.

We've considered the possibility that thoughts are energy which originate in the spiritual body and are transmitted to the physical brain through a network of neurotransmitters. The mind being the epicenter of thoughts, by extension, makes it part of the spiritual body as well. However, some hold the belief that the mind is merely a bio-chemical manifestation of the brain. So, let's investigate the mind further to see where the evidence leads.

The physical mass of cells that fills the cavity beneath the frontal, temporal, and parietal bones of your skull are what we refer to as the brain. The average adult has about 100 billion cells forming this three-pound organ that controls all functions of the body. We all have one…but at times it seems people are using theirs less and less! Since the brain itself is a physical organ, it stands to reason that its functions center on the physical operations of the body. For instance, voluntary and involuntary motor activity, processing sensory input, digestion, the circulatory system, respiration, the immune system, the release and balance of hormones, etc. These are actions and functions that can be connected to physical biological systems.

Traditional teachings inform us that non-physical activities such as memory, thought, emotions, imagination, and personality are also functions of the physical brain. The conventional belief is the left-brain controls things such as logic, analysis, memorization, speech, planning, etc., while the right brain is responsible for creativity, emotions, intuition, and imagination. While common theories give credit to the brain for these non-physical attributes, perhaps as with thoughts, the real credit should go to the mind, which is separate and apart from the brain. If we follow the chain of logic that the mind is part of the non-physical spiritual body, this would place it in the category of energy.

One of the important characteristics of energy we've come to understand is it comes in different frequencies, or vibrations. If the mind is non-physical energy, then based on what we know about energy, the mind should operate in different frequencies. Well, it does! When you are in a waking state of full consciousness it's called the *Beta State,* where the mind's frequencies ranges from 14 - 40 hertz. This range is considered the high end of the frequency scale for the mind. Beta activity is an important staple in the functioning of our minds, but too much Beta activity can lead to stress and anxiety. Unfortunately, many adults in the United States operate in a state of excessive Beta waves…which is one of the reasons you see so much road rage. I suppose you could call it Beta rage!

As you enter a state of light or medium meditation, hypnosis, or daydreaming you transition to the *Alpha State,* where mind frequency slows down to the 7.5 – 14 hertz range. In this state energy waves slow down making it ideal for visualizing, memorizing, and imagining. The Alpha state has been called the bridge between the conscious and the subconscious. Cross over that bridge and you enter the subconscious mind or the *Theta State.* This is a state of deep meditation or light sleep. It's the point just prior to losing consciousness or falling asleep. At the Theta State energy frequencies range between 4 – 7.5 hertz. It is here where you can tap into prolific inspirations, vivid creativity, powerful intuitions, and marvelous insights. Reduce mind frequencies even slower and you'll reach the next stage called the *Delta State.* Frequencies at this state are in the slowest range of ½ – 4 hertz. Here your body enters a state of deep sleep bridging the subconscious mind with the super-conscious mind. This is the final and deepest state you can achieve.

As frequency increases, energy vibrates faster making it less detectable to the human senses, like a dog whistle or ultraviolet light. It's the same with the mind. Since the mind is part of the spiritual energy body it has a natural frequency much higher than that of the physical body. When the mind operates at its natural high-frequency state, the body isn't able to interact with it. When you still your mind and lower its frequency through meditation, you bring it closer to the frequency of your physical body thus allowing an interaction to exist between the two.

Going through the frequencies of the mind we can see it operates at different levels of consciousness. As you go about life making decisions, taking actions, and having emotions, you call into action all stages of consciousness - the *conscious mind,* the *subconscious mind,* and the *super-conscious mind*. Think of them as concentric circles, with the super-conscious mind at the center, followed by the subconscious mind, and the conscious mind as you go outwards. To help illustrate how they work in unison, let's step through an ordinary action we've all done time and again…changing the TV channel.

To do this, plant your couch-potato butt on an imaginary sofa in front of a state-of-the-art 88-inch 8K Ultra-HD flat-screen TV streaming hundreds of programming options. As you stare apathetically at the screen you think, *"Oh God, can television get any worse than this! There must be something better on."* Now you've just made the decision to change the channel, which comes from your conscious mind. Armed with your remote, you instinctively point it at the television to begin your channel surfing session. You don't even have to think about it, pointing the remote at the TV is an instinct, a reflex, a repetitive action that's been branded into your subconscious mind. This action would be your subconscious mind at work.

You then direct your index finger to press the 'channel up' button on the remote. This simple action must be incredibly precise. If your finger is off by only a small fraction it'll mute the set, or change the TV's input, or power off the set. However, the incredible accuracy of your finger allows you to push the channel up button displaying the next show. This is more work of the subconscious mind working. You continue pressing the channel up button show after show, and while you are busily changing channels, your body is busy maintaining itself. Your heart beats blood through your veins, your lungs breathe in oxygen, your stomach digests the bag of chips you're munching, and the trillions of cells in your body are all carrying out their respective tasks, as you struggle between "Shark Week" and "Wheel of Fortune!" All these cellular and biological functions are controlled by your subconscious mind. When you finally stop on the show that grabs your attention, there's something deep within drawing you to that program. This is an example of your super-conscious mind kicking in.

Examining in detail a simple function like changing the channel demonstrates the marvels of the body and mind. It's another example of how the human body is a complex miracle…and an example of how often we underutilize this miracle! Given this simple task of changing the channel, ask yourself how is it that each individual cell knows what task the overall body is trying to accomplish? On a cellular level, a cell's primary function is to maintain its life and prepare to replicate. How is it supposed to assist YOU in changing the channel? How does a muscle cell in your finger that is unaware of a digestive cell in the lining of your stomach, work to sustain its own life, while at the same time work in perfect coordination with 30 trillion other cells to complete the function of changing the channel? Is your physical brain the manager that coordinates all 30 trillion cells? Perhaps, but if that were the case, then what controls the cells of the brain? This is where the non-physical mind comes in to play.

Your mind is the Top Dog, the Big Cheese, the CEO of Body Inc. Your body is merely a machine the mind operates using a highly complex controller called the brain. The conscious mind is where everyday reasoning and motor skills occurs. The subconscious mind is the body's autopilot controlling essential functions that keep you alive – digestion, respiration, nutrition, waste, circulation of blood, etc. It's also where memories are stored, emotions and imagination take place, creativity blossoms, and thoughts originate. When you experience a flash of genius, it's nothing more than energy from the subconscious mind flaring up into the conscious mind.

You can change, alter, and retrain the conscious mind rather easily simply by reading, listening, and educating yourself in ways you'd like to adjust. However, reprogramming the subconscious mind is not as easy. For most people, the subconscious mind learns through repetition. It's programmed through years and years of habits and repeated thoughts and behaviors. This holds true for both positive and negative behaviors. Reprogramming the subconscious mind requires concentration and meditation on a regular and repeated basis to alter negative patterns into positive ones.

The final level that lies deep within the center of the consciousness circle is the kingmaker known as the super-conscious mind. It is here where the essence of your spirit is housed. And just as the subconscious mind controls the conscious mind, the super-conscious mind is what influences the subconscious. The super-conscious mind is the powerhouse providing access to universal consciousness. It's like having high-speed fiber-optic Internet tapped into the Universe. The super-conscious mind gives access to all the stored knowledge for the existence of the entire Universe. These three layers of consciousness together form the entirety of your spiritual body. Combined they contain all the properties of Universal consciousness. Now that is powerful!

You can draw upon the super-conscious mind through deep meditation or hypnosis. Once reached it can reveal incredible depths of knowledge and inspiration that eventually leads to the state of enlightenment. Since consciousness is formed in concentric levels, you can also program the super-conscious mind by way of the subconscious mind, which can be reached through control of your conscious mind. Your conscious mind is the bouncer that lets in thoughts to the nightclub of your life. Checking the ID's of your thoughts carefully determines the success or failure of your establishment. Letting in positive, loving, compassionate, and desirable thoughts makes for an enjoyable experience rife with fun and great memories. But, by not checking ID's and letting in negative players, you set yourself up for negative, destructive, judgmental, and angry experiences, making a nightclub filled with conflict that's certain to be shut down before last call! Have a conscious awareness of what you think. Control your thoughts. Cast out negative and judgmental thoughts whenever they try to sneak in. Welcome and encourage positive, appreciative, and compassionate thoughts and over time it will percolate down to the core of your existence and result in positive transformation of your life.

Who Are YOU?

We're just about complete with this chapter and I want to congratulate you on getting this far without tossing the book through an open window…at least I hope you had the wherewithal to open the window if you did toss the book through it! This has been an important chapter as we've begun to shift our investigation into the spiritual dimension. We'll continue to study the spiritual realm to gain a better understanding of it.

The evidence we've uncovered in this chapter points heavily towards the existence of both a physical world and a spiritual dimension. We've learned that the bridge uniting them is you – the human body. We've seen how we're able to use the body to experience the physical world through our senses by picking up energy vibrations that get interpreted in the mind. Since the mind and thoughts have no physical form, they are attributed to the energy body, or the spiritual component. The mind is the CEO of the physical body consisting of different levels of consciousness, but who is in control of the mind?

The mind is amazing. It allows us to generate thoughts from the most complex to the truly trivial. It gives us the ability to navigate life, accomplish incredible physical feats, awesome displays of love, profoundly creative works of art, music, and written word, all the while, quietly in the background, maintaining a perfect balance of the body's biological functions. And it all happens automatically. Each of us experience our own unique reality making choices and decisions distinct to ourselves. You control your thoughts, actions, and emotions. You determine your destiny. It's your mind guiding your life, not mine, nor anyone else's. Others may influence your decisions, but ultimately, it's you, and your mind, that directs your body to follow through on those decisions. You determine what your mind will think. How to move and operate your body. What works of art, music, or literature you'll create. You have control over all these things. The ability for an individual to experience life through a first-person perspective comes from the mind…your mind. So, if you control your mind, are you and your mind two separate things?

Let's explore this concept. Having control over something implies the object being controlled is separate and apart from the controller. But how could that be with your mind? Aren't you and your mind one and the same? We don't make this assumption with other things we control. For instance, if you use a remote control to operate a drone, flying it where and when you like, you wouldn't say you and the drone and are one and the same. Of course not, you refer to them as two separate things. When you use the remote to change the TV channel, you don't say your fingers and the remote are both part of the same thing. So, why is it that we draw this conclusion with our minds? You can control your thoughts, change your mind, shift your attention, and regulate your emotions. So, how is it possible that you have control over your thoughts, emotions, and physical body if you and your mind are one and the same? Puzzling, isn't it?

The answer to this lies in the title of the previous section - *"Are You Otta Your Mind!"* I chose this as a fun way of planting a seed in your subconscious mind. So, are you otta your mind? It's a simple little expression used quite often. I could have used any of the other fan-favorites such as; *Are you crazy! You're not playing with a full deck! You're nuttier than a five-pound fruitcake! You've only got one oar in the water! Your elevator doesn't go to the top floor! The lights are on but no one's home! You're one taco short of a combination plate!* And of course, the beloved multi-generational darling; *You're off your rocker!*

However, I didn't choose any of them. I specifically went with *"Are You Otta Your Mind!"* I did so for a reason. This particular expression when perceived from a different context is wholly valid and true. It's not simply rhetorical. YOU are otta your mind! Examine the expression closely. Exactly who is 'You'? Are YOU the hyperactive voice in your head churning out thoughts and ideas? Or, are YOU the person who listens to and argues with that voice? Are YOU the 30 trillion cells making up your physical body, or are YOU the consciousness giving them direction? Are YOU the physical body with five senses detecting the sights, sounds, smells, tastes, and sensations of the physical world, or are YOU the energy body that interprets them?

These are all interesting concepts to contemplate. They can really make you wonder if YOU truly do exist… out of your mind? Well, it appears our case has just presented another fascinating lead to investigate…

Ch. 6: The Soul

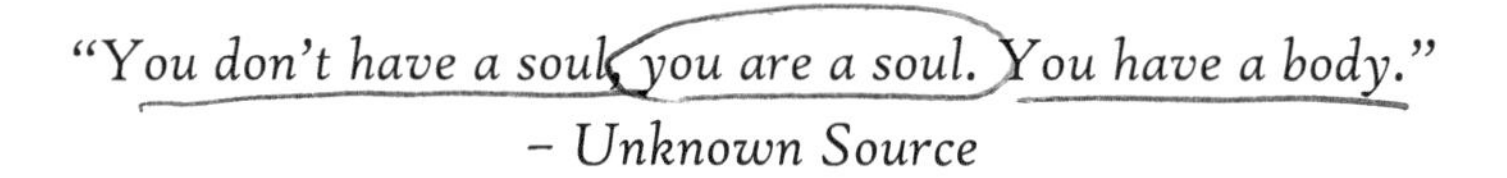

"You don't have a soul, you are a soul. You have a body."
– Unknown Source

The Gift That Keeps Giving

It's that time again to analyze the evidence we've amassed. In the first chapter we've uncovered evidence supporting a higher intelligence behind the creation of life. Chapter 2 revealed an assortment of examples where a universal consciousness governs the rules and operations of the physical world. We then examined the quantum science of the physical world in Chapter 3 and learned that it isn't very physical at all. In fact, the building blocks of matter are not tiny particles of substance, but tiny particles of energy that are nearly 100% empty space. We're immersed in a sea of Vital Life energy that permeates and brings life to the entire universe referred to as Prana or Chi. All this evidence paints the picture of an energy-based world, which Chapter 4 showed us extends to the human body. Within our bodies are energy centers called chakras that regulate energy flow to the physical and emotional bodies. Finally, in the previous chapter, we discovered the human body is a bridge uniting the spiritual and physical worlds through the senses. All we see, touch, taste, smell, and hear in the physical world plays out in the inner recesses of the mind. We've learned how the mind functions on different levels of consciousness – the conscious mind, the subconscious mind, and the super-conscious mind – with the deeper mind having control over the conscious mind. All this evidence of an energy-based reality provides support for the existence of a non-physical component of life. With our investigation leading us in the direction of a spiritual body, let's follow this path to see where it leads. For the spiritual enthusiasts, things are about to get real…or should I say unreal!

There's so much to learn about the spiritual dimension yet it's seldom discussed in any serious manner in Western society. Many prominent thinkers believe the spiritual realm is the essence of life. Anything that could potentially rise to this level of importance should engender a little more attention, but it hasn't. Wouldn't it be nice to have a class or two in grade school that introduces the fundamental concepts of the spirit, or advanced electives in colleges and universities that fully delineate spiritual realities, or even 'hard-hitting' questions in political debates about the beliefs and understandings of the soul?

Unfortunately, little recognition, acknowledgement, teachings, and public discussion of the spirit, soul, or the spiritual dimension occur in America. It's really a shame that American culture, touted as one of the most forward-thinking on the planet, not only ignores the spiritual aspects of life, but in many circumstances shuns it. The mention of spirituality or talk of the human soul can provoke ridicule in certain circles. Fortunate for you this is NOT one of those circles. Here we'll explore the spiritual dimension in all its glory and strive to have as complete an understanding of the functionality, rules, and laws of the spiritual dimension as we have of the physical dimension.

However, I will give you a cautionary note as you join the leading edge of spirituality. You'll find as you strive to learn more about the spiritual realm and prompt its discussion, many will refer to it as supernatural, paranormal, mystical, eerie, unearthly, or just plain foolish, but don't be discouraged. The more you learn about the spiritual dimension, the more confidence you'll have in your beliefs, and compassion for those who doubt its existence. Knowledge and understanding of the spirit are the quintessential conduit to enlightenment. However, getting there may come with a verbal battle or two, so here's a little exercise to help arm you for any such encounter.

As you associate with friends, family, and colleagues, and the issue of the soul or spiritual dimension comes up, it's likely you'll confront someone who holds opposing views. In some cases, you'll be faced with profound vitriol. You'll be challenged to offer verifiable physical proof of the soul's existence. It's a bit of a misguided request. The faulty logic stems out of the desire for physical proof of something that is non-physical. It's like being asked to provide a Tupperware container filled with your most vivid thoughts, neatly packed in an airtight container to maintain their freshness. Then hearing the argument, you couldn't possibly have any thoughts since you're unable to deliver them in such a container.

Should you find yourself in this situation, here's a crafty way to engage in spiritual conversations using a little word game. Rather than calling it a soul, or spirit, refer to it simply as the subconscious mind. This clinical term will not arouse knee-jerk reactions, as spiritual doubters tend to have admiration for theories on which Freud and Jung built their careers. Once you have mutual agreement on the validity and existence of the subconscious mind, you can turn the table by asking your skeptic to prove the existence of the subconscious mind by quantifying its physicality…where does the subconscious mind resides, how does it function, and what is its cellular composition? Ask for physical proof of the subconscious mind. When that can't be delivered, draw the comparison of the subconscious mind to your soul. Neither of them can be wrapped in a fancy box and delivered by 2-day express mail.

However, that alone is not proof of their non-existence. This should provide a crack of reason and openness to allow for a healthy, respectful spiritual discussion. And if that doesn't work, you can always fall back on Ole Faithful – a rarely-cited quote from one of my favorite thinkers, Albert Einstein, in which he said, *"We are souls dressed up in sacred biochemical garments and our bodies are the instruments through which our souls play their music."* Imagine that, Albert Einstein believes in the existence of a soul, that's a pretty solid ally. Then hit them with, *"So, nanny-nanny-boo-boo!"* Followed by an imaginary mic drop. I'm not sure that line of reasoning will hold up in court or peer-reviewed scientific journals, but it'll give you a temporary feel-good moment.

Alright, back to the case. The body has been shown to be a vehicle for the mind to experience the physical world. All your bodily systems have been designed and built precisely for that experience. From the nervous system, to the body's automatic functioning, all the way down to the individual cells, all aspects of the body are precision-perfect tools to be used by the mind. The marvelous beauty and functionality of the body should never be underestimated nor taken for granted, but rather appreciated as a priceless gift.

Unfortunately, many feel burdened with their bodies. Just observe the people around you, in your community, at the stores, cafes, schools, and businesses. You'll find a preponderance of them whining and complaining about their size, shape, age, looks, and shortcomings. People should honor their bodies as that which it truly is - a gift. Gifts are meant to be cherished, appreciated, and enjoyed to their fullest potential. A gift given with loving intent should always be treasured, regardless how small or unnecessary you may believe it to be. An interesting thing with gifts is like our senses they're also examples of duality. With gifts there's a giver and a receiver, which raises another intriguing question, "If our bodies truly are a gift, who is the giver and who is the receiver?"

We've just touched upon a VERY deep and meaningful question. The giver of this great gift is what we'll build to in future chapters, but a little hint is that it's also the source of Vital Life Energy that permeates the universe and the subatomic energy that constitutes the physical world. So, let's postpone exploring the giver portion of this dualistic example for later chapters, which leaves us with the other half to explore now - the receiver. Who is the receiver of the miraculous gift known as a human body? How does the receiver take possession of this gift? And since a truly meaningful gift fulfills a need, what need does the gift of a human body fulfill?

Me, Myself, and I

The questions raised above tie back to questions asked at the end of Chapter 5. It turns out the one who listens to that voice in your head, who directs the physical body, who interprets the senses, happens to also be the recipient of the gift of a human body. And who exactly is that? It's none other than the true essence of you - your soul.

I'm going to assume that every reader of this book is familiar with the word "Soul." It's part of everyday vernacular. You may have heard certain things are *"good for the soul,"* or *"the eyes are the window to the soul."* You can be the *"soul of the party"* or have *"heart and soul."* You may have been called a *"good soul,"* a *"kindred soul,"* or a *"lost soul."* You can be asked to *"bear your soul,"* put your *"heart and soul"* into something, or even to *"sell your soul."* We have *soul music, soul food, soul brothers,* and *soulmates*. There are many iterations of the soul. Religion refers to the soul as a *spirit* or a *heavenly body*. New age groups call it a *pranic body, etheric body,* or *spiritual body*. Science likes to call it a *bio-plasmic body, dark plasma*, or even a *spiritual quantum field*. I've even heard it called *shadow matter* or *subtle body* - all these ubiquitous terms and expressions for the soul. But, when you refer to the soul, what exactly are you referring to? It's funny how people can have such an affinity with a word that is used virtually every day in conversation yet have little understanding of it. When you stop and think about it, do you really know what a soul is?

Don't feel bad if you don't, the complexities of a soul are something man has pondered for centuries. The entire notion of a non-physical immortal entity that animates the body isn't new. Its mystery predates historical record, but how did the idea of a soul, something that bewilders science and society today, even become a topic of study way back thousands of years ago during these 'simplistic' civilizations? Back in ancient times, people didn't have things like Fortnite, Snap, Instagram, Spotify, YouTube, 24-hour news cycles, tax deadlines, frequent flier miles, Xtreme-Sports, smart phones, broadband, Wi-Fi, video streaming, theme parks and all the other preoccupations in life we are faced with. So, what else did they have to do in their down time than ponder the mysteries of life? This led them down a path of theorizing about the non-physical aspects of humans. They searched to explain the abilities humans possess that other forms of life don't. Our ability to think, to reason, to hold memories, and to have emotions. It forced them to question these abilities and develop a sense of self-reflection and self-awareness that is severely lacking in today's A.D.D. culture.

Ancient philosophers from China, Egypt, and Greece spent centuries deliberating the spiritual body and developing concepts that influence what we think of a soul to this day. Plato got the ball rolling in his neck of the woods with theories of dualism, which were picked up by Socrates and Aristotle who expanded on them, speculating the soul is a separate living body. These beliefs were passed on through the Epicureans, the Stoics, and carried through the Middle East and Europe by Hellenistic philosophers. Over time, the notion of a soul began to seep its way into religion, philosophy, and mythology. A similar process occurred in ancient China with the dualistic notion of *Hun* and *Po*, Chinese names for an ethereal and corporeal soul. This proliferated within Chinese philosophy, medicine, and Taoist practices throughout the East as the underpinnings of much of Eastern spiritual beliefs. Flash forward thousands of years and this conversation continues to this day! So, what have we learned about the soul after all these centuries of study and debate?

If you go to Merriam-Webster® you'll find the word "Soul" is defined as:

1: the immaterial essence, animating principle, or actuating cause of an individual life
2: the spiritual principle embodied in human beings, all rational and spiritual beings, or the universe
3: person's total self
4. a: an active or essential part
   b: a moving spirit: leader
5. a: the moral and emotional nature of human beings
   b: the quality that arouses emotion and sentiment
   c: spiritual or moral force: fervor
6: person (not a soul in sight)
7: personification (she is the soul of integrity)
8: strong positive feeling (as of intense sensitivity and emotional fervor) conveyed especially by black American performers

These formal definitions may provide words and terminology for a soul, but quite honestly, they don't tell us much about how a soul relates to your life experiences. So, let's get intimate with our spiritual sides and learn about the characteristics and functions of a soul.

Simply put, the soul is an intelligent, independent, energy-based, immortal entity that fuses with a physical body. The soul is what provides life, emotion, thought, free-will, and purpose to the atoms, molecules, and cells that make up your physical body. A soul has memory and can record all the events and emotions experienced throughout a lifetime. The soul has extreme wisdom and can be an incredible source of creativity and guidance. It can access the source of universal intelligence we examined in chapters 1 and 2, making the soul a consummate problem solver that can help overcome difficulties and adversities.

A soul has its own attitudes and emotions, which combine with, or conflict with, memories stored at the cellular level known as '*body memories*' or '*cellular memories*.' While the soul is not limited by physical boundaries, its energy center is based in the lower abdomen. This is considered its home within the human body. Have you ever had an incident when you experience an uneasy feeling in your stomach giving you warning things aren't as they should be? Or you really screw up royally and you get this sinking, nauseating feeling in the pit of your belly. It's almost an uncanny paranormal sensation. Well, this 'gut feeling' is your soul talking to you, sending you guidance. As you tune in to these spiritual signals, you'll being to trust and rely on your intuitive gut feelings.

You may find it unusual for the soul to be described as a separate entity, a whole different being living inside you, but that's what it is. Your soul is distinct and independent from your physical body. Strange and confusing…yes, but the universe functions in many strange and magnificently confusing ways. One of the more illuminating examples I've found to describe this phenomenon comes from an unexpected source not normally associated with spirituality…Arnold Schwarzenegger. Yes, the bodybuilder turned action star turned governor. Not Eckhart Tolle, Deepak Chopra, or the Dalai Lama, but Arnold!

We all have different people we find inspirational, Arnold happens to be one whose tenacity, confidence, and accomplishments have always amazed and inspired me. I was watching an interview with Arnold years ago in which he gave advice on how to maintain peak workouts. During the interview he spoke of shocking your muscles by avoiding routine patterns to your workouts. If your workouts become routine, over time your body will learn that routine and adapt to your workout pattern causing your results to plateau and limit growth. By shocking the muscles, your body never knows what to expect putting it in a constant state of improvement. Using this technique, Arnold was able to achieve unprecedented success in body-building history. Which brings us to the million-dollar question, what's all this got to do with the soul?

When Arnold talks about lifting weights, he refers to his body as a separate entity from his mind. He talks about entering the gym and executing a series of exercises and routines designed to fool the muscles, as though his muscles aren't privy to the workout routine in his head, even though it's all part of the same body! He speaks in ways that separate his physical body from his thoughts, as if his muscles anticipate a set of 10 reps of a certain exercise, but he deceives them and does 25 reps of a different exercise. Arnold's mind is thinking and reacting differently than Arnold's body is thinking and reacting, like they are two separate entities. This separation of mind and body is the essence of the soul being in control of the body. I don't know Arnold personally, and I can't say whether he fundamentally understood how to access the soul and the power it unleashes, or if it was merely his unyielding drive that tapped into his soul power. However, what I do believe is Arnold owes much of his success to the power of the soul being in command of his body.

At the end of chapter 5, we raised an introspective question about who are YOU? It's the same YOU Arnold has mastered control over. If you pay attention to your mind, you'll find it's constantly talking and interrupting your pure thoughts with incessant chatter. When you tell yourself, "*Come on, you can do it!*" Who are you talking to and who is doing the encouraging? When you have an internal debates on whether you should do something or not, like ask the person of your dreams on a date, confront your boss with a long overdue raise, or spend money you don't have on a special occasion, who exactly are you debating? Talking to yourself inherently implies a conversation with more than one individual. Well, it turns there is. One of the most fundamental understandings of the soul is to recognize the true YOU. YOU are not the erratic voice in your head. YOU are the immortal being who hears it. And if you're like Arnold and you form the ability to subdue and control that voice, along with controlling your body, you will reach a point where your soul is the one calling the shots.

I recognize how much easier it is to differentiate between your body and your mind. Your body is the physical matter that constitutes your shape, size, and appearance. It's the person who would get described in a police lineup, swiped left or right in an online dating app, or be identified by facial recognition software. However, how do you differentiate between the mind and the soul? Aren't they the same? I mean, we've all heard the expression *"Body, mind, and soul,"* but how does the soul differ from the mind? Distinguishing between the mind and the soul can get confusing since both are non-physical, but here's a simple way to differential between the two. Your mind is associated with your physical body, while your soul is associated with your spiritual body. Got it? The mind is part of the physical realm. It's the source of your internal chatter. When the physical body dies, the mind dies with it. Often you will hear the mind being referred to as the *'ego,'* particularly within the metaphysical community. The soul, on the other hand, is part of the spiritual body. The soul is immortal, when the physical body dies, the immortal soul continues in the spiritual realm. Still confused? Well, there's a little analogy I like to use to help distinguish between the mind and the soul, I call it *"The Casting Call of Life!"*

To play along you must think like an actor. Take any A-list actor or actress. For our example Tom Cruise. When Tom Cruise commits to a new film, it typically involves a character he's never played before, unless of course he's doing a sequel. The new character is defined with its own unique and distinct set of traits, flaws, characteristics, personality, and idiosyncrasies. This new character is also immersed into an entirely new storyline filled with action, adventures, conflicts, emotion, twists and turns, and character development. However, with each new role Tom Cruise portrays, there are elements of his real-life persona, the persona of Tom Cruise, that seep into the character. Regardless if Cruise is playing a vampire, a Top Gun pilot, a Mission Impossible agent, a mummy hunter, or the last samurai, there are attributes of his true self that become part of the character he's portraying.

Each character in each movie has a different personality and goes through different stories and adventures with separate experiences. However, Tom Cruise the person experiences all these stories and adventures from all the movies in which he appears. Now, let's get back to you. Think of your soul as the actor playing a role, in this example Tom Cruise is the soul. Your mind is the character within the movie that experiences all the action, events, and drama of that particular film. Your soul controls the mind of the body living your life experience, just like the actor Tom Cruise controls the mind of the character in his film. The character in the film defines the personality for that movie, much like your mind defines the personality for that physical body.

You can do this with any other actor or actress – Brad Pitt, Natalie Portman, Johnny Depp, Meryl Streep, Christian Bale, or Adam Sandler - they all take on different personas in each new movie they star…Well, I suppose you could make the argument that all Adam Sandler movies pretty much portray the same character, but you get my point. When Johnny Depp emerges from make-up dressed as a pirate, he becomes the character and personality of Captain Jack Sparrow. During filming of the *Pirates of the Caribbean* movies, Depp acts and behaves as Jack Sparrow, not as Jonny Depp. However, Jonny Depp the person influences certain attributes of Jack Sparrow's character and he comes away with all the experiences and knowledge gained from playing that role. Likewise, when your soul incarnates in a body, it takes on the character and personality of that body, which are defined by the environment, era, family, geographic location, and cellular structure. Drawing this analogy between your soul and actors role-playing, your soul becomes the physical actor and your mind becomes the character portrayed in each movie. When your soul enters your body, it's playing the character of you, living and experiencing the adventures and drama of your life. When the movie of your life is over, your soul comes away with all the experiences and knowledge gained from that lifetime. Your soul is the actor inside the body that takes on the role and storyline of that lifetime. Your mind is defined by the specific physical aspects and circumstances of your life's movie. And like an actor who has control over the character they're portraying, your soul also has control over the body you are occupying. Just as the actor gains experience and growth from each film they star in, your soul too gains experience and growth with each body it occupies. Understanding this is a critical component to appreciating your purpose in life and how to control and achieve that which your soul has set out to accomplish.

Let's take a little breather and let all this information about the mind and the soul sink in. Make sure you feel comfortable in understanding this as it's one of the more important concepts in this book. There are many characteristics of the soul, but this one may very well be the most significant. The soul is an extension of God. Let that sink in for a moment, don't simply breeze over this. The soul is an extension of God. That means it is a part of God itself. Your soul, the energetic non-physical component that animates your body is a beautiful and glorious fragment of the Creator. That fragment lives within you, is part of you, IS you. YOU are a fragment of God. You are not merely made in his image - you ARE a living fragment of the creator himself. I recognize how this can be a very powerful concept to digest in a way that you unequivocally believe, but believe you must, for this is what makes each and every human on this planet an amazing gift of the highest order.

Remember I spoke of the ability to remove a cell from your body and keep it alive in a petri dish under proper conditions. Well, apply that concept here. Imagine a microscopic cell from your body maintaining itself in a petri dish. This tiny cell contains DNA with all the genetic codes of your entire body. It is a unique and distinct fragment of you, a tiny part of you living its life independently in a petri dish. This is what a soul fragment is in the scope of the universe. The energy of your soul is a small fraction of the original Source energy, the Universal Intelligence…God. And just as a cell lives independently in the petri dish as a fragment of you, your soul lives independently in your body as a fragment of God. If the cell is replaced back in your body, it reunites with your body and goes on living and functioning just as it did prior to being placed in the petri dish. Similarly, when your body dies, your immortal soul reunites with its spiritual body. Believe in yourself as a fragment of God and you will soon see life as a gift to cherish.

Taking this new perspective of the soul into consideration, let's reflect on a question posed at the beginning of this chapter – *If the human body is thought of as a gift, who is the receiver of this gift?* At this point the answer should be of no surprise – it's your soul. The human body is a glorious gift for the soul, a finely tuned, precision vehicle for the soul to experience all the physical world has to offer. The Creator in its consummate wisdom crafted the human body as a device for the energy-based soul to experience the mass and density of the physical world.

As we learned in Chapter 5, the senses serve as a bridge between the physical and spiritual realms, giving a whole new meaning to the body's function. You've probably imagined hundreds of different possibilities for your body, from athlete to astronaut, but how many have thought of it as a vehicle for the soul. All this leads to the next pertinent question…*If the soul is the recipient of the precious gift of a human body, how does the soul take possession of this gift?*

Bonding with Your Soul

I told you things were about to get unreal, and I hope you're not disappointed in how wildly exciting the exploration of the soul can be. There are plenty of people who believe in a non-physical component of the body, but how many simply accept it unquestioned? From the start I've encouraged you to ask engaging questions that challenge your perceptions of reality, like the ones above. This type of inquisitive outlook leads to questioning such mysteries as how a non-physical soul joins with a physical body. We all know the development of a human being begins at conception, when a tiny sperm cell fertilizes the ova merging the male and female chromosomes. That union bursts into the formation of a zygote, which begins to divide rapidly. Soon the zygote implants itself in the uterine wall and becomes an embryo. In the coming weeks, placental blood begins to circulate, hormone production begins, a new heart starts beating, and the embryo develops into a fetus. Over time, the fetus becomes a newborn child. A human being doesn't just materialize in one flashing swoop, it takes about 40 weeks. During the 40-week development of a human, when does the immortal soul enter and bond with the body?

Evidence to answer questions of this nature requires research and investigation in non-traditional methods. One of the most thorough, leading-edge and groundbreaking researchers of the soul is Dr. Michael Newton, a Ph.D. in Psychology. Dr. Newton has conducted revolutionary studies of the soul and the afterlife that are presented in an excellent series of books he authored titled, *"Journey of Souls," "Destiny of Souls,"* and *"Life Between Lives."* I highly recommend these books as must reads for anyone interesting in life-between-lives. (I'll cover this more in Chapter 7.) As a certified master hypnotherapist, Dr. Newton pioneered life-between-lives (LBL) research by conducting thousands of cases of spiritual regression. His comprehensive work supports many of the spiritual teachings passed on by sages, shaman, clairvoyants, and energy masters through the ages that includes how your soul merges with your physical body.

To begin, your soul is an immortal intelligent energy with a vibrational frequency in the same range as the light spectrum. This is why you'll hear the soul or spirit referred to as a *"light being."* At this frequency the soul vibrates at such a high rate it's not detectable by any of the human senses (remember the hummingbird wings from Chapter 4). The soul can function freely in the spiritual dimension because the ether of that dimension has a similar high frequency. However, the physical realm vibrates at a much lower frequency and has a greater density. When the frequencies and densities of these two worlds overlap, their differences are too great for the soul to interact. In order for the soul to function in the physical world it needs a low frequency, low density body. For this reason, the soul takes on a 'vessel' with the capabilities of functioning in the physical dimension. That vessel comes in the form of a human body.

Think of it like this...let's say you wanted to explore and experience the deepest depths of the ocean. You would have to submerge yourself in vast ocean canyons with depths exceeding 8,000 meters (over 5 miles deep). At these depths, the environment is pitch-black, bone-chilling cold, and has pressures exceeding eight tons per square inch! These pressures would crush a human body like a paper cup, making it impossible to experience this world on your own. However, despite conditions that are extreme to the human body, life does exist at these incredible ocean depths...and their creepiness is just as extreme, like this deep-sea darling (see Figure 19).

Figure 19- Anglerfish

To experience the world miles below sea-level you need to immerse yourself in a specially constructed submarine capable of withstanding immense pressures. In this example, the submarine becomes the vessel for your human body to experience life in a world it wouldn't otherwise be able to experience. Applying this example to your soul, the human body provides a vessel for your soul to experience life in a world it wouldn't otherwise be able to experience. Make sense?

As an independent intelligent being complete with free-will and thought, the soul's first step in the incarnation process is to choose to become flesh and blood and experience all the wonders the physical world has to offer. (I'll address the soul's decision-making process in Chapter 7 when we investigate the little-known period of life-between-lives.) Once the soul makes the decision to incarnate it prepares to take-on its chosen body, much like an actor prepares to embark upon a role in a new film. When an actor takes on a new film, he/she lives sort of a dual life, one as the character in the movie and one as themselves. During the time a film is in production, the actor only takes on the persona of the film's character for a portion of his life. While the actor is at home, off-camera, driving to and from the set, during breaks and on hiatuses, the actor is not in character but becomes his true self. Only part of the actor's life is dedicated to the character in the film, the other times he/she is their true self – a celebrity, parent, businessperson, family member, etc.

Your soul acts in much the same way. The totality of your soul's spiritual energy is not all projected into the human body, only a portion of the total spiritual energy incarnates. And like an actor, your soul leads a dual life. During your waking times you become the character in the film and your life becomes the film's plotline. During sleep or periods of unconsciousness you become your true self. While every soul and lifetime are different, on average only about 50-70% of your total soul energy gets projected into the physical body. The extra soul energy remains in the spiritual dimension and stays connected to the incarnated portion through an umbilical-like cord of energy. The portion of energy that remains in the spiritual dimension is called the '*higher-self*' or '*over-soul*.' The over-soul fundamentally defines your true essence. The amount of soul energy projected into the body is predicated on the type of body and the nature of its life experiences. Typically, a greater percentage of soul energy is required for bodies that are severely disfigured, handicapped, or are overwhelmed with hardships.

The ability to access our over-souls is something we all possess. It can be achieved through practiced prayer, meditation, or yoga. You also have the ability to temporarily draw upon some of your over-soul energy during challenging or traumatic times when the physical body is suffering from energy depletion. The transfer of energy between the physical body and the over-soul usually occurs during sleep, deep meditation, or when the body is in a state of unconsciousness.

Let's follow the soul as it journeys into the physical realm. The formation of a human begins when a woman becomes pregnant. The mother carrying the child becomes instrumental to the incubation and development of the fetus. For this reason, the mother's spiritual energy is also instrumental to the development of the incoming soul. The mother's spiritual energy interacts with the spiritual energy of the incoming soul. This interaction occurs in the spiritual dimension as part of the soul's decision to incarnate. Remember, the mother also has an over-soul that exists in the spiritual dimension. The mother's over-soul works with the incarnating soul to help with the soul's decision on the type of life it wants to experience. Once conception occurs, a connection is formed between the incoming soul and the developing embryo to create an energy 'womb' that protects the soul. This helps isolate the incoming soul, so it only has the spiritual energy of the mother to contend with.

As the fetus develops within the mother's womb, the soul remains connected via the energy link until roughly 3 to 4 months. At that stage, the soul begins the process of binding itself with the developing fetus. The soul enters the fetus through the crown chakra at the top of the head. Throughout the pregnancy, the percentage of soul energy fluctuates between the physical and spiritual realms. The soul's job is to develop the energetic body of the new child, while the mother works on developing the physical body. The soul gets to work building and refining each of the seven chakras. The root chakra is a particularly important chakra which the soul spends special time building out. If you remember from Chapter 4, "*The Magnificent 7*" section, the root chakra ties you to the physical world helping to form your identity. For the incoming soul, establishing roots to the physical world is extremely important, so care is given in the development of the root chakra.

From conception through to birth, the incoming soul works with the mother's over-soul and the mother's incarnated soul. This "soul" connection in both the physical and spiritual dimensions shapes what is known as a paranormal bond between mother and child. You've all heard stories, and perhaps experienced them yourself, of a parent who instinctively knows when something traumatic happens to a son or daughter, regardless of the distance that may separate them. This is due to the spiritual bond that develops during pregnancy in both the spiritual and physical realms.

During the second and third trimester, the soul slowly begins to become fully connected to the developing baby. At this stage, the 'heaviness' of the lower frequency and lower density physical world starts to set in. This frequency adjustment can be traumatic for the soul and the mother's energy helps the soul acclimate to the discomfort of the physical realm. It's important for the soul to have the protective physical and energetic wombs of the mother as it goes through this assimilation process. During the third trimester all the soul energy that will incarnate is sent to the developing child. The soul understands when it incarnates it will experience a memory loss of the spiritual world. This is done to assure maximum benefits for the soul to learn and evolve through experiences in the physical world (more on this in Chapter 7). During this point of development, the process of spiritual amnesia begins. Remember, a good portion of the soul remains in the spiritual realm as the over-soul, only the incarnating energy experiences memory loss of the spiritual dimension.

Finally, after forty long weeks, once the spiritual body has fully developed alongside the physical body, it's time for this miracle of life to enter the world. Mommy gets hit with a series of panicking contractions, her water breaks, and after numerous herculean pushes, the tiny blessing enters the physical world independent for the first time. It's then greeted with a welcoming smack on the backside to prepare it for all the physical punishment it's about to go through. The birthing process can be very traumatic for the soul, oftentimes more so than the death process. This may make more sense if we go back to our deep-sea example. Journeying to the deepest levels of the ocean, your body would experience more traumas coping with the harsh pressures and conditions of the ocean's depths, even within a protective vessel. When it returns to the surface, the normal atmospheric conditions would be met with a welcoming relief. This is similar to the relief a soul experiences when returning to its home in the spiritual realm.

Once the child is born, the soul breaks free from the mother's protective wombs. For the first time, the soul becomes subjected to the influences of the physical environment and begins to acclimate with the energy frequencies of the physical world. At birth, the soul 'forgets' its spiritual identity and starts taking on the personality of the host body. The body's personality is formed from the combination of cellular memory stored in the body's DNA and spiritual energy of the soul. This combination produces a single, temporary soul-body personality that's unique to the individual during that lifetime.

The soul still depends on the spiritual support of its mother as it assimilates to the physical realm. The paranormal-like connection between mother and child exists throughout the life of both. However the bond is at its strongest during the child's infancy. The process of the soul awakening to the physical world continues in both dimensions. During the infant years, the baby sleeps often to allow the soul to seek guidance from its over-soul as it struggles to acclimate to the limitations and heaviness of the physical world. (The whole purpose of sleep gets a closer look in Chapter 11.) Over time, the physical and spiritual bodies grow, develop, and learn in tandem to navigate life on the physical plane.

The first five years are when the soul fully adjusts and adapts to the different frequencies, densities, and limitations of the physical world. It's no coincidence that this is also the period that most child psychologists and behaviorists say are the most crucial to a child's intellectual, social, and emotional development. There's plenty of scientific research to support this, but from a spiritual perspective, this period coincides with the soul settling into its new 'vessel.' Providing the soul with a loving, non-traumatic environment to build out the energy body offers significant benefits to the overall development of the individual. Finally, around ages 6 or 7, the chakra systems reach a stable level and are able to protect the spiritual body from external energy influences and fluctuations. This energetic field of protection gives the child a subconscious boost in confidence which becomes evident on the physical level when children of this age begin showing increased independence.

Now, just as there are limitations and rules governing the physical body, there are also limitations and rules placed on the soul. Since the human body is a melding of the physical and spiritual worlds, we need to recognize the influence the physical body plays on the soul. The cells of the body contain DNA with genomes passed on by the parents. These are the physical traits passed from one generation to another such as eye and hair color, body size, gender, facial features, etc. However, physical traits are not the only attributes stored at the cellular level. Cells also store memories from experiences and emotions that include trauma, fear, pain, suffering, and pleasure. These cellular memories collect over time and build inherent behaviors into the genome, for example the natural fear of fire, survival instincts, fight or flight reactions. It's one of the ways we as a species evolve. There are instincts and knowledge inherent within the genomes of millennials that are absent from the genomes of baby boomers. These stored cellular memories help the soul adapt to its new environment in the physical world.

A little sidebar here on cellular memory as this may be one of those areas that raise eyebrows of skepticism. A real-world symptom of cellular memory is evident in organ donations. Each year thousands receive organs from another person. Everything from livers, hearts, lungs, pancreas, intestines, kidneys, and corneas get donated, and if you're one of those unfortunate urban legends, you'll wake up in a tub of ice in a Vegas hotel room missing a kidney!

Often organ transplant recipients take on traits of the organ donor, such as cravings for certain foods, or changes in their taste of music, art, recreation, and career interests. In some cases, the recipient has memories and dreams associated with the donor. For example, a woman who received a heart and lungs from an 18-year-old male involved in a motorcycle accident began craving chicken nuggets and beer. These cravings were odd since prior to the transplant the recipient didn't like either. She also began having reoccurring dreams of a man named 'Tim L.' The woman later discovered her donor's name was Tim L who had a love for chicken nuggets and beer. In fact, Tim L was returning from a fast food restaurant at the time of the accident that took his life and was carrying a bag of chicken nuggets. In another case, a liver transplant recipient suddenly developed a deep sense of civic duty. Even stranger, she found herself wandering into hardware stores instinctively knowing her way around, with knowledge and skills of home repair. She later discovered her organ donor was a former US Marshal who loved working on home renovation projects. These incidents are quite common and can be verified by a simple Internet search, but the larger question is, *"what causes this phenomenon?"*

The answer brings us back to cellular memory. The recipient is implanted with a donated organ that spent years inside someone else's body. The donor's cellular memories are as unique and distinct as the donor's soul-body combination. When the donor's senses picked up years of physical experiences, which you now know occur within the body's spiritual energy, they become infused as cellular memories within the cells of the donor's organs. When an organ is removed and placed into a recipient's body, the cellular memories are implanted with it. Once in the new body, the donor's cellular memories intermix with the spiritual energies of the recipient. This influence then surfaces as new, unusual, and unexpected traits, cravings, and behaviors, which become inexplicable tales of the paranormal. The reality is, there's nothing weird, mysterious, or paranormal about them, it's all very normal and easily explained as cellular memories. That's all there is to it. It only gets churned into fanciful tales of the paranormal when one ignores the realities of a spiritual dimension.

An interesting side note of organ transplants is research shows heart transplant recipients are the most susceptible to experience traits of their donor. Think about that for a moment. With your knowledge of the energy chakras, would you like to guess why heart recipients are affected more by cellular memory? Going back to Chapter 4, you'll remember that the heart chakra is the energy powerhouse of the body. With such a powerful spiritual energy center surrounding the physical cells of the heart, you can see why the heart would absorb a greater amount of cellular memories.

Going back to rules placed on a soul...When a soul blends with a physical body, the body's cellular memories intermix with the soul's energy. As we've learned, the soul exists on a higher vibrational frequency in the spiritual realm than the physical world. When the lower cell frequencies of the body intermix with the higher frequency of the soul the combination results in the soul's vibration being lowered. It's similar to plopping an ice cube into a bowl of hot soup. The interaction of the cold ice cube with the hot soup results in the soup's temperature being lowered. What this means for you is your soul vibrates at a lower frequency when in a body than it does in the spiritual realm. So, your incarnated soul vibrates slower than your over-soul. This is one of the reasons why the over-soul isn't readily accessible to you. However, through deep practiced meditation, you can learn to change your vibrational frequency and gain access to your over-soul.

Throughout this chapter I've talked about the soul as though it was a separate entity, and it is. And like all independent bodies, the soul comes complete with its own set of attitudes and emotions. Likewise, the cellular memories passed on through genetics have their own attitudes and emotions. When the soul merges with a physical body it needs to contend with the cellular memories of the body. Combining these two distinct sets of attitudes and emotions can work in harmony, or they may result in conflict. Depending on the severity of the conflict it can give rise to instability or even mental illness. To minimize this, when a soul decides to incarnate, it consults with the mother's over-soul to identify if the soul and the genetic cellular memories will harmonize.

Finally, what will seem to be a limiting attribute of an incarnating soul is the complete amnesia of the spiritual realm and all its accumulated memories. While on the surface this can be thought to have adverse and damaging effects, the reality is the absence of these memories allows the soul to benefit, learn, and grow more completely in the physical would. Without this amnesia, growth would be severely restricted. As a result, soul memory is knowingly and willingly concealed from consciousness upon incarnation. However, you as an individual are guided by the soul's accumulated wisdom via subconscious thought patterns that engender certain favorable actions. Throughout life there's a continual sharing of thoughts, attitudes, emotions, and knowledge from the over-soul with the incarnated soul and the physical body.

This leads us to ask what happens to the immortal soul once the life of an individual reaches its end. The concept of death from a spiritual perspective doesn't exist. The soul is an immortal energy being. When the physical body no longer functions, whether due to age or tragedy, the soul returns to its high frequency home in the spiritual realm and rejoins its over-soul. The returning soul brings with it all the experiences, emotions, trauma, lessons, and knowledge gained from the lifetime it just experienced. Returning to the relief of the spiritual realm also offers the returning souls an opportunity to rest, regenerate, and reflect on its physical world experiences.

This section contains a lot of soul information to absorb, particularly if you are hearing all this for the first time. As you analyze the process and limitations for an incarnating soul, it has got to make you to wonder why any 'intelligent being' would submit itself to such a taxing routine. I've been defining souls as intelligent energy beings of immense knowledge and wisdom. If that were the case, why would a being of such wisdom go through the trials and tribulations of incarnating and take on the unpleasant heavy densities of the physical world? What's the point? This seems like another fascinating area to investigate. So, let's get to it.

The 3 R's for the Soul

Have you ever been told the importance of learning the *"3 R's"* - Reading, wRiting, and aRithmetic? I know, it's one of those expressions that's always irked me. The message is supposed to instill the importance of education and the person who came up with it obviously didn't apply those standards to themselves, since there's only one word in this educational trifecta that actually begins with an "R"!

Anyway, we all get the point of the vital importance of education. If you're like me, the learning process never ends. I love to learn and absorb as much as I can about virtually anything. Today, a good education is crucial to the foundation and development of children, adults, and society at large. We've created an entire infrastructure around education. From the time a child is born, parents begin the teaching process, some parents even begin while the child is still in the womb. Eventually we turn education over to professionals for years and years of fundamental and advanced learning. It can start as early as pre-school, then on to kindergarten, grade school, middle school, and finally high school. Many decide to continue their education by attending college or university where they go on to earn associates, bachelors, masters, and/or doctorate degrees in a wide array of disciplines. Across America and around the world, educational institutions are filled with billions of people learning everything from the basics to the most advanced theories and principles. All these lessons and curriculum taught throughout the world are designed to help you navigate and achieve in the physical world. If the body truly is a blending of a physical and a spiritual component, why is there no schooling for your soul? How does it learn? What are the "3-R's" for the soul, and where are the Ivy League campuses for the soul to enroll?

Well, you don't have to search far and wide to find the administration office of Soul University…you're sitting in it right now! That's right, Earth. The planet you are living on now is the soul's educational campus. The physical dimension is precisely where the soul goes for its lessons and advanced degrees. Imagine the planet as one giant classroom for the soul where billions of souls go to learn. It's a place where souls experience all the essential lessons the physical world offers. The "3 R's" for the soul can be studied and acquired right here on the 3rd Rock from the Sun. This is the reason an intelligent energy being of immense knowledge and wisdom would embrace the trials and tribulations of the physical world - to learn.

Now, earth is a big place and there are many, many different soul lessons going on simultaneously. In fact, each and every soul incarnated in this world has a unique and distinct lesson to learn. And just as our educational institutions teach courses with different levels of difficulty – from pre-school to Ph.D. - souls also have varying degrees of education. '*Young souls*' are here learning the rudimentary lessons that are equivalent to preschoolers, kindergarteners, and grade school students, while older more mature souls are immersed in more advanced life lessons. They are the soul equivalence of university or graduate school students. Life lessons are nearly limitless and range from basic survival to lessons dealing with anger, boundaries, responsibility, attachment, ego, fear, infamy, greed, jealousy, power, pride, selfishness, wealth, love, faith, service, altruism, family, and much, much more.

Everything you experience, regardless of how painful or undeserving, carries important spiritual lessons. All things happen to serve as a valuable lesson in your soul's curriculum. It doesn't matter if it appears to be trivial or traumatic, friendly or hostile, life-altering or commonplace, hilarious or heartbreaking, in some way all your experiences go towards your soul's education. It's the reason your immortal and intelligent soul decided to enter the physical world – to learn!

Everyone's life is different, and every soul is different. Each has its own distinct lessons to learn for its own distinct reasons. Lessons and purposes vary greatly from soul to soul. Your life lessons are not the same as your spouse's, family members,' friends,' neighbors,' or work associates.' Resist the temptation to compare your struggles, obstacles, adversities, conflicts, setbacks, and triumphs with those of anyone else. These events are as unique to you as your personality and fingerprints.

The peculiar thing about soul lessons is they must be learned, there is no such thing as failure. It's no different than a required class at a university. The lessons are taught, if you don't learn them, you fail and don't receive credit for the class. If you want to graduate, you'll have to take the class all over again. The soul is no different. Lessons your soul must learn are taught through life experiences. You are given the chance to learn or fail. In the event you fail, the lesson will be presented again in a new set of similar circumstances. The lesson will continue to appear in your life over and over until you pass the test.

Always remember YOU (meaning your soul) chose to incarnate in a physical body because YOU wanted to learn this lesson. You wanted to feel the pleasures and pain of your experiences. You came to this planet with a commitment to learn, and learn you will, for if you don't, the lessons continue to repeat over and over and over. You may have experienced this already. Have you ever felt like certain aspects of your life is a real-world version of '*Groundhog Day*'? Where the same thing seems to repeat itself again and again? Or you make the same mistakes over and over? Perhaps you find yourself in the same caustic relationships one after another. These are all indications of soul lessons repeating themselves. The remarkable and frustrating thing about the physical world being a classroom for the soul is life will continue to send you back to class over and over until you get it right. There's a built-in component to your soul's development that no matter how many times you get it wrong, the universe never gives up on you. You are always permitted to try again. And the great thing is you can take the class as many times as you like and not run up an astronomical tuition bill that keeps you in student loan debt for decades!

When the soul decides to learn a certain lesson, it does so willingly by choice to help it develop and evolve. Once this decision is made, the work to accomplish this lesson must be completed. There's no turning back. It can't be skipped, dropped, or failed. It's no different than setting out to achieve a law, engineering, or medical degree. There are certain classes that are part of the required curriculum to graduate. They must be completed. The same holds true for the soul. The only difference is with the soul, there's no option for dropping out! (Don't worry, we'll get into how to graduate from Soul University in later chapters.) The physical world is the University for the soul, to master it you must love the learning process, not resist or fear it.

Souls are also like students in the physical world in their education levels. Have you ever heard the expression, *"He/She is an Old Soul?"* It implies some souls are older, wiser, more mature, and more experienced than others, which is true. Some souls are very new to the physical world and are referred to as *"Young Souls"* or *"Infant Souls."* Often young souls are still acclimating to the densities and vibrations of the physical dimension, have difficulties adjusting, and often end up leading troubled lives. Some souls are in the equivalent of first grade, some are eighth grade students, some in college, and more mature or old souls are in graduate school. And just as you would never criticize a first-grade student for not understanding complex calculus; you should not criticize a young soul for their lack of understanding of certain life issues either. Everyone is on their own spiritual path. There is nothing better about your path, nor is there anything worse about someone else's path. They are simply in different stages of development. As you make your way through life, look to form an understanding of situations and experiences around you. Every event, relationship, experience, family member, friend, acquaintance, and passing strangers on the physical plane offers a lesson to enhance and expand your soul. All the events in your life offer a window to your true self and your true purpose. When you accept that all your life's experiences serve to elevate your soul, you begin to understand your purpose and life becomes more manageable.

An intelligence of a higher order has created the physical world for the soul to learn and grow. None of us are here by accident, and the events which affect your lives are not accidental either. Knowing this reality will allow you to accept what happens as essential soul lessons that you have chosen. They are not curses, plagues, jinxes, or misfortunes. You elected to have these experiences. Recognizing and acknowledging this as a truth will allow you to become less resistant to adversities. The less resistant you become, the less conflict these events will generate, and life will begin to flow more smoothly. The strife, anger, clashes, discriminations, and bigotry throughout society gradually begin to wash away, and become supplanted with peace, love, tolerance, understanding, and compassion. It begins on an individual level, builds to a community level, then a cultural level, and finally a world level. This may sound a bit lofty, but it's easily achievable through spiritual understanding. Everyone living on earth today has earned the right to be enrolled as a student in Soul University. It's really quite a blessing to be here. This gift of life unfortunately is largely unknown and taken for granted by most of the world's population, but it doesn't have to remain that way.

Try to accept what life presents you, even the tragedies and hardships. Accept them as if you had chosen them to occur, as though you specifically asked for them to happen. Do this because you did ask. You did ask for these tragedies and hardships for the knowledge, experience, and growth they offer your soul. Learn to accept and work with these events, don't resist them. You asked for these experiences through a spiritual agreement called a *"Soul Contract."* I've dedicated an entire section to 'Soul Contracts' in Chapter 11, so I'll only touch upon it here briefly since soul contracts are also relevant to soul lessons.

Earth is a place of great beauty, joy, and wonderful marvels, but it also harbors ignorance, hate, suffering, disease, pain, hunger, and fear. We live in an environment where natural disasters are common, a world filled with earthquakes, hurricanes, volcanoes, floods, tornadoes, droughts, mud slides, wildfires, tsunamis, and other natural disasters over which we have no control. Coping with the brutality of the physical world makes for a very difficult school for incoming souls but learning from these traumatic events on the physical plane is by specific design of the Creator. The greatest lessons for the soul to grow and learn are ones that require the greatest efforts.

I know many are wondering how such human suffering can be allowed to occur if the universe is the creation of a loving higher intelligence. How could such an infinite source of intellect, knowledge, love, and wisdom allow the horrors of this world to befall the innocent? This type of thinking is what drives people away from religion, away from the belief in a Creator, and into the arms of atheism. I've maintained from the beginning I'm not out to convert your beliefs, but I do want to challenge them. I also want to challenge you to apply critical thought and intellectual honesty to your beliefs, and if you don't feel your current belief system holds up, then be open to others.

Why does God allow the horrors of humanity to take place? All the suffering, starvation, abuse, murder, and torture…what kind of evil creator would allow such pain? Well, without trivializing or minimizing the actual pain and trauma felt by the individual, the reason such horrors occur in great abundance is because these are life lessons souls have chosen to experience through soul contracts. The soul has purposely selected a life of pain or hardship to experience what such pain feels like. It's the only way for the soul to fully understand and empathize with those feelings. I recognize that hearing this for the first time will sound a bit crazy, but once you chew on and digest it, it'll start to make sense. Let's put it into more palatable experiences than human torture, again not to trivialize the brutality and suffering, but to allow you to relate to the concept. How about we shift and analyze what it's like to have a great head of hair.

Who wouldn't want to have a thick, flowing, full-bodied head of hair! It's the envy of men and women alike. Now, let's assume it's your desire to know and appreciate what it truly means to live a life with such a wonderful mane. Who would appreciate it more – the person who possessed that thick flowing beautiful hair since birth, or the person who has lived a life with thinning baldness and was suddenly granted Rapunzel-like hair? How about a different scenario…To whom does the meal taste the sweetest, someone who dines on fine cooking every day, or a person on the cusp of starvation? Ask the same question regarding eyesight. Who appreciates the gift of sight more, the person born with 20/20 vision who has maintained perfect eyesight for 50 years, or the person born blind who through a medical miracle is given eyesight for the first time? It is through lack that the soul learns to appreciate. By taking away that which has always been there, or that which one covets, the heart and mind are stretched to recognize their importance. It's a fundamental tenet that gives rise to the expression, "*Absence makes the heart grow fond*."

This is the case in many aspects of life with how the soul learns. Experiencing a life of confinement allows the soul to truly appreciate and understand the gift of independence. To experience great penury the souls truly appreciates the gift of wealth. Without the hardships there is no appreciation of comfort. Without pain, there is no appreciation for pleasure. Without suffering, there is no appreciation for love. Some of the most powerful growth lessons for the soul are ones that cause the greatest hardships. As you go through these adversities, always bear in mind that the universe only gives that which the soul is capable of enduring. Great tests are only given to great souls. When you accept this and release the need to know why things happen as they do, you begin to make enormous strides in spiritual growth. Trust the reason behind your experiences is part of a higher purpose designed to benefit your spiritual growth, and life begins to flow with much less resistance.

There you have it. Earth is the soul's schoolroom. We've learned about the soul's bonding with a developing child, and the lessons it learns over the course of a lifetime. This all leads us to two things they say are certain in life – death and taxes. And since I've been told the taxman is without a soul that leaves us with death to examine. Once a soul's purpose has been fulfilled and lessons have been learned, the soul has accomplished its earthly mission. At this point it is time for the soul to return to the spiritual dimension. The soul is immortal and the spiritual dimension in which the soul returns is most often called the "*Afterlife*" or "*Heaven.*" When the physical body is no longer needed, the soul prepares to reunite with its over-soul. The soul waits for the right moment to transcend the body and the process of death begins. Now, death has come to be known as a harsh term, but what we call death is really a term specific to the physical body. When the physical body dies, YOU don't die nor do YOU cease to exist. Your soul simply passes from one state of reality to another. It just transcends the physical dimension and continues its existence in the spiritual dimension. When the soul disengages from the body and leaves the physical world, the soul energy reunites with the over-soul. The amnesia caused by the physical incarnation is lifted and the soul continues in the spiritual realm with all its accumulated memories.

Cramming for Finals

I've dedicated this chapter to the soul, and what a soulful chapter it's been. Throughout all our exploration of the soul you may have noticed that I've minimized references to physical science. It's a bit of a deviation from other chapters in which I've layered science as a foundation. Now in this chapter I present spiritual and soul concepts as though they are a fait accompli. Well, let's give science its chance since it adds credibility to evidence. What type of scientific research do we have to support the immortal soul?

I've mentioned the work of Dr. Michael Newton, but any reliable research should have more than one source. Recent breakthroughs from well-respected scientists studying human consciousness have begun to assert that consciousness is immortal, and it continues after the death of the physical body. Scientists have begun to define consciousness as packets of information stored at the subatomic level in what are being refer to as '*microtubules*' within human cells. The ground-breaking research claims to have found evidence of consciousness stored in these microtubules which is released into the universe after a person dies. This same consciousness then returns to the body if it is brought back to life. This type of revolutionary research is being conducted at renowned institutions such as Cambridge University, Princeton University, and the Max Planck Institute for Physics. Researchers at the Max Planck Institute contend that the physical universe is just a perception, and once the body dies there is an infinite life beyond.

Other prominent physicists are reporting similar findings. Dr. Hans-Peter Dürr has recently stated, "*What we consider the here and now, this world, is actually just the material level that is comprehensible. The beyond is an infinite reality that is much bigger. The body dies but the spiritual quantum field continues. In this way, I am immortal.*" In this quote, the 'spiritual quantum field' is just scientific speak for the soul.

Dr. Christian Hellwig of the Max Planck Institute for Biophysical Chemistry reported, "*Our thoughts, our will, our consciousness and our feelings show properties that could be referred to as spiritual properties...No direct interaction with the known fundamental forces of natural science, such as gravitation, electromagnetic forces, etc. can be detected in the spiritual. On the other hand, however, these spiritual properties correspond exactly to the characteristics that distinguish the extremely puzzling and wondrous phenomena in the quantum world.*"

And the late quantum physicist David Bohm, a student and friend of Albert Einstein, once stated, "*The results of modern natural sciences only make sense if we assume an inner, uniform, transcendent reality that is based on all external data and facts. The very depth of human consciousness is one of them.*"

Other researchers are going as far as claiming the soul is more than the interaction of neurons in the brain, but it is constructed from the very fabric of the universe and may have existed since the beginning of time. These are all scientific ways of explaining the existence of a soul. But there's also research supporting some of the attributes of a soul, for example the parent-child intuitive connection we spoke of.

Psychotherapy Digby Tantam recently presented a theory that helps to explain this intuitive phenomenon commonly call your 'gut feeling.' He theorizes the human brain is interconnected to others through a type of Wi-Fi that allows people to pick up information from one another. Tantam calls this connection "*the interbrain,*" which gives people the ability to pick up one another's emotions. His work is detailed in a book titled "The Interbrain." And this is just the tip of the iceberg. Some of the most advanced researchers and thinkers are now coming forward with evidence of an immortal interconnected consciousness (or soul). One of the things I find surprising about these recent discoveries is that they took so long! These are concepts taught by spiritualists and philosophers for centuries. It's interesting to see another example of science catching up with ancient spirituality.

This has been a very important chapter that has uncovered a plethora of powerful information on the soul. We've learned the differences between the soul and the mind; that the soul is an intelligent, independent, immortal energy being; the body is a precision vessel designed to house the soul; the process for the soul to enter and bond with a human body; the soul's work to form the energy body concurrent with the development of the physical body; and the reason why a soul incarnates. Whew! That's a lot to learn.

And learn we shall. Over the course of a lifetime, the soul learns through its physical experiences, but there are SO many life lessons to learn, how is one soul supposed to learn them all? Souls are as unique and distinctive as individuals, as a result they also learn at different rates. Some are fast learners, while others require more time. So, how are all souls expected to learn all life lessons equally? Is life supposed to be one endless all-nighter of cramming the day before finals? The harsh realities of life show us that not everyone has the same amount of time on this planet. Some are gifted with an entire century of learning, while others have their lives cut tragically short only after a few brief years. What happens to their souls? Does their education end quickly and they are forced to live in the afterlife missing out on all the lessons they never had a chance to learn? Do their immortal souls return to the spiritual plane with only a preschool education, while other souls return with advanced degrees? Is it just spiritual tough luck for them? That doesn't seem very fair. In fact, there are so many lessons and experiences, how is it possible to learn all of them in just one lifetime even if you do live to be 100? This has got to get your mental wheels turning.

How does a soul learn everything it needs if one lifetime just isn't enough? Well, here we go again. Another profound question leading us into a new chapter…

Ch. 7: Life on the Other Side

"It is the secret of the world that all things subsist and do not die, but only retire a little from sight and afterwards return again." - Ralph Waldo Emerson

Dying to be Born

Our exploration of the soul has really taken us down one very intriguing rabbit's hole. As we look to answer the questions raised at the end of chapter 6, we'll travel further into this spiritual tunnel. There may be some readers who are journeying down the path of spirituality for the first time, while others have plunged in with great depth already. In either case, the excitement with journeying into the unknown lies in the mysteries and questions that arise up along the way. Most people have a good understanding of the physical world, after all it's a world we've live in and learned about all our lives, but the spiritual world continues to remain largely cryptic. Every turn of the way it gives rise to new revelations and enigmas. As you struggle to make sense of it all, undoubtedly questions and skepticism will arise. My goal is to answer and address as much of this as possible. So, let's burrow deeper into our spiritual rabbit hole in search of answers.

We ended Chapter 6 wondering how a soul could possibly acquire all it needs to know in just one lifetime. Since everyone's life is uniquely their own, it makes this task even more challenging. From the geographic location you are born, to the family you're born into, your socio-economic standing, your religious and ideological beliefs, your parental support, your circle of friends and their influence, your career path, and all the multitude of choices you make along the way, your life is distinctly unique. It's virtually impossible to find two people who have led identical lives with identical decisions and identical life lessons. There are an infinite number of events and circumstances that sets your life apart from anyone else's. However, despite all these variations, the one thing we all have in common is if we were born onto this planet, one day we will leave this planet. There's no avoiding it - one day every one of us will face the realities of dying. We've even come up with some colorful euphemisms to express this reality. You can *Take Your Last Breath, Assume Room Temperature, Buy the Farm, Cash in Your Chips, Drop Like a Fly, Go to the Big Place in the Sky, Become Worm Food, Join the Invisible Choir, Kick the Bucket, Meet Your Maker, Push up Daisies, Go Six Feet Under, Take a Dirt Nap, or Bite the Big One*! Despite how you say it, the inevitable truth is we're all going to die.

If this is a touchy subject, don't feel bad. Acknowledging your own physical mortality is discomforting to most people. The fear of dying is nearly universal. It's a natural human survival instinct. Staring death in the eye and accepting its fate can cause quite of bit of anguish. However, is death something that needs to be feared? Or does the fear of death arise from the belief you'll never have another opportunity to see and experience worldly pleasures again? Is losing the joy and companionship of those you love the underpinning of our anxiety?

Death doesn't have to engender negative sentiments. It all depends on the perspective in which you view death. In fact, death from the spiritual perspective takes on a completely different meaning than it has from the physical perspective. From the soul's vantage point, death is a completely different experience altogether. For the soul, death of the physical body is simply a transition from one state of consciousness to another state of greater awareness. In fact, for the soul the birthing process and the dying process are somewhat inverted experiences.

When your soul is born into the physical world it goes through a type of spiritual death. As we've learned, the soul endures the heaviness and limitations of the low frequency, high density physical realm, and loses memory of its spiritual home. The soul transitions from an existence of unconditional pure love and tranquility to one of turmoil, pain, and hardships. It shifts from a state of consummate bliss to one of adversities and suffering. Then, when the physical body dies, the soul is 'reborn' into its spiritual paradise. It's liberated from the physical world.

From a soul's perspective, death of the body is a return to its spiritual home and the state of purity and love. After a long, challenging life in the physical world, often a soul embraces its return home. Isn't it interesting how the same event, death, can have two entirely different implications depending on the perspective? And, since the body has both a physical and spiritual component, does death mean something different for each?

Kicking the Bucket

It's time to set aside any squeamish tendencies you may have about death. Death is something we all must deal with in life as friends, family, and colleagues pass on. Eventually, you too will join everyone else in human history and pass from your physical body. Getting comfortable with the subject of death now, will only help prepare you for when your time does arrive. When you think about the grand scheme of things, you're only one person occupying a small space on a very large planet, and Earth is only a teeny-tiny spec in a massive Universe. However, despite your infinitely small size within the entirety of the universe, have you ever wondered what it takes to keep your body going year after year?

During an average lifetime of nurturing and sustaining your body you'll consume about 50 tons of food! 50 tons! That's the equivalent combined weight of a jet fighter, an armored truck, a school bus, a large granite monument, 10 vending machines, and 25 telephone poles! Line all these items up in a parking lot, grab a knife and fork and start munching. In addition to 50 tons of food, you'll hydrate yourself with over 25,000 gallons of water, grow nearly 600 miles of hair, take about 50,000 showers, shed over 20,000 square feet of skin (enough to cover a football field), drink 70,000 cups of coffee, walk over 215 million steps (enough to circumnavigate the globe 5 times), your heart will beat over 3 billion times, you'll take 675 million breaths, produce 25,000 quarts of spit, and you'll flush the toilet nearly 200,000 times! That's a whole lot of feeding, watering, cleaning, caring, and toilet paper for the mass of cells you call your body. Then, after a lifetime of all this upkeep and maintenance, your ticker stops ticking, your brain waves flat-line, and your body up and dies. Then what? What happens to all those 30 trillion cells that you spent a lifetime nurturing and grooming?

We've seen how the physical body is a precision machine designed to function and sustain itself in remarkable ways. And what's true in life also holds true in death. The changes a body experiences leading up to and after death, are not simply random bio-chemical reactions, but are part of the miracle of a body's intelligent design. There are different stipulations used to declare a person 'deceased,' some include the absence of a pulse, breathing, and/or reflexes; no pupillary constriction when exposed to a bright light; or the lack of brainstem reflexes. Regardless of how you are pronounced dead, once life departs your body, all humans go through the same stages of death, unless of course certain preservation techniques are employed, like embalming or mummification. So, hold onto your lunch, we're about to examine how the entire process plays out in all its ghastly detail.

Shortly after the body 'dies,' there's a brief and momentary surge in brain activity. The muscles relax sending the body into a state called '*primary flaccidity.*' This relaxed muscular state causes the eyelids to lose their tension, the pupils dilate, the jaw falls open, and the extremities become limp. Moments after the heart stops, the body grows pale as blood no longer circulates and drains from the small veins in the skin. The pale tone is known as '*pallor mortis.*' The skin begins to sag making joints and bones appear as though they are protruding. Internal cells begin to die and break down from lack of oxygen. The body's temperature drops about 2 degrees Fahrenheit per hour from its living temperature of 98.6° until it reaches the surrounding temperature. This '*death chill*' is more formally called '*algor mortis.*' Forensic scientists use the difference in the body's temperature with the ambient temperate to help determine the approximate time of death.

After a few hours, calcium builds up in the muscles causing them to stiffen, which is a term you may have heard called '*rigor mortis.*' The muscles first affected by rigor mortis are the eyelids, jaw, and neck. It then spreads downward through the chest, abdomen, and limbs. Rigor mortis lasts about 1 to 2 days before the muscles eventually relax from chemical changes within the cells. During this time, gravity pulls the blood downward where it pools in areas of the body closest to the ground. If the body is undisturbed the pooling of blood creates a reddish-purple bruising-like coloration known as '*livor mortis.*'

After a couple days, the skin begins to shrink as it dries out, making the hair and nails appear to grow and eliminating the need of any further

Botox treatments. After a couple weeks, bacteria combines with enzymes in your organs and the body begins to decay. Finally, in about 4 months, all your soft tissues fully decompose leaving only your skeleton. Ewww! Thanks goodness we're done with that. However, it is remarkable how even in death the body continues to perform like a precision machine.

With the knowledge of what happens to this vehicle you've inhabited all your life, it's time to explore what happens to the energy body once the physical body ceases to function. Does the death of your physical body mean the death of YOU and all you've accomplished, experienced, and achieved? While your body goes through a rather gruesome decay, what happens to your soul? Does it go through a spiritual equivalent of a decomposing body? I'm sure the suspense is just killing you! (Ha! Couldn't resist that one!)

Rebirth of a Soul

I've made the case that humans are comprised of two parts - a physical body and a spiritual body. The physical body is the vessel the spiritual body uses to experience life in the physical world. We've now reached the point in our investigation where we need to gather information and evidence on what happens to the immortal spirit when its vessel stops workings. Where does it go when its '*out of body*' and what does it do?

As we dig into this investigation and analyze findings, it's important to acknowledge that there are many theories, ideas, speculations, and beliefs about what happens to the soul upon death of the body. Some theories complement one another, while others are contradictory. Some are based on credible scientific research, and some are the work of charlatans. I've studied life after death researcher for over 20 years. I've weighed corroborating evidence against speculative theories and distilled information from thousands of cases and volumes of research down to a consolidated synopsis. I believe the information presented in this section isn't simply speculative conjecture based on hunches, but truthful evidence complied from worldwide research that includes hypno-regressions, near death experiencers, clairvoyants, channelers, shamans, yogis, ancient knowledge, native healers, spiritual adepts, Qi Gong and energy Masters, mediums, psychotherapists, and scientists. While you may find some professions in this group lack credibility, the independent corroboration of information, regardless of who gathers it, that transcends religion, culture, demographics, boarders, ideology, language, and time are some strong motives to pay attention to this research.

For instance, you may have heard of the Tibetan monks. There are a lot of people who think of them as an odd group of Buddhists with shaved heads who wear funny cloaks, pray a lot, and make bizarre noises when they meditate. The same people wouldn't consider these monks credible sources of human physiology. However, Tibetan monks have studied the physical and spiritual aspects of humans for centuries and have developed abilities consider superhuman. Through the mastery of their energy bodies, they're able to dry cold, wet sheets wrapped around their bodies by raising their body temperature, or stab an index finger knuckle-deep into a solid tree trunk, or sit unscathed in a pot of boiling oil, or use Chi energy to keep a power drill from drilling a hole into their temple. Their amazing superpowers have been analyzed and documented for all to see. Just run a YouTube search if you want a glimpse of these astonishing feats for yourself. In addition to superhuman powers, the Tibetan monks have developed a clear understanding of death and the afterlife through centuries of deep transcendental meditation. Much of their sacred knowledge kept secret for centuries by monastic vows is now being shared with the world. Nothing they've learned is fanciful imagination. It is spiritual truths.

Other sources factored into our after-life exploration include accounts of people reporting Near Death Experiences (NDE's). Now, I have to concede in the name of full disclosure that I haven't actually died myself…at least not yet! I'm not part of the .5% of the population who have gone through a NDE, which is roughly 35 million people worldwide. That's a lot of first-hand information on the afterlife. Extrapolating common patterns described by near death experiencers provides profound insight on the afterlife. These two examples illustrate some of the information amassed in this section.

Let's step through what happens to the soul once the human body dies. We've learned the soul is a form of fine energy vibrating at a very high frequency that provides life to the body. If you've ever seen a dead body, you recognize how devoid of animating life it is. It's just a giant mass of inert motionless matter. However, just because the vital life energy has departed the body, doesn't mean that energy ceases to exist. Remember from our investigation of energy in Chapter 3 we learned that energy can neither be created nor destroyed. Well if the soul is energy, and energy can't be destroyed, where does it go when it no longer has a body to house it? And, since the soul is intelligent energy, what exactly does it do when it's not in a body? Without a physical brain, does it lose its ability to think?

We learned earlier how the physical body transitions through universal stages of death. And like the body, souls also go through their own universal process when its host body dies. The first of two fundamental stages of a soul's transition back to the spiritual realm depends greatly on a few factors; the type of death the body undergoes (peaceful or tragic), the age and experience of the soul (young soul or old soul), and the mental state at the time of death (influence of the mind). For instance, old souls with lots of experience can transition back and forth between the spiritual and physical realms without incident, while younger less-experienced souls have a more traumatic transition. A tragic unexpected death creates more confusion for the soul than a peaceful passing during one's sleep. We'll explore all of this in much more detail, but let's first begin with the basics.

Each time a soul incarnates in a human body it does so to fulfill a specific lesson that will aide in the soul's evolution. Once that life purpose has been achieved, the soul has accomplished its mission and it no longer needs to be incarnated in a body. The soul recognizes it is time to return to the spiritual realm to analyze its experiences and signals the body on a super-conscious level of its inevitable departure.

The soul's desire to shed its human body causes the body to decay since the body is a programmed vessel operated by the soul. Most people will not have a conscious knowing of this as it occurs very deep in super-conscious mind. In the case of a natural death, the body subsequently begins to break down in preparation for the soul's withdrawal. The soul's yearning to return to its spiritual home is what gives credence to the expression *"losing the will to live."* Ask any doctor, once a person has lost the will to live, it's virtually impossible to keep the body alive. The soul is the source of that will for life. In the case of unforeseen or tragic deaths, arrangements are made in the spiritual realm for the life to end via accident or sudden unexpected illness. We'll explore this further in soul contracts.

Inevitably the time comes when the body kicks the bucket. Fortunately, death in the physical realm is nothing more than the soul's separation from the body in the spiritual realm. The soul disengages from the body and begins its first stage of transitioning back to its spiritual home. We learned in the previous chapter that when a soul enters the body of a developing child in the womb, an energy cord is created linking the over-soul with the incarnating soul. Upon death of the body, this energy cord is severed. The incarnated portion of the soul energy is no longer connected with its over-soul. In this regard, the death of the body truly becomes a rebirthing of the soul. It's a neat little twist on perspectives...the body's death corresponds with the soul's rebirth. The soul's separation from its host body to be left on its own draws a very similar parallel to an infant baby being left to breathe and function on its own after separating from the mother's host body. Even the cutting of the infant's umbilical cord and the severing of the soul's energy cord share parallels. It's why an inverse relationship is said to exists between birth and death depending on the perspective. The birth of the body is the death of the soul's spirituality, while the death of the body is the rebirth of the soul. Interesting, isn't it?

Once the soul leaves the body, it becomes a whirling ball of energy with no physical restrictions. Suddenly, the soul is no longer confined to the 3-dimensional physical world or the limitations of the five senses. However, immediately after death the soul brings all the personality, character traits, and memories held and experienced during its physical life. Often, these temporary influences of the mind will cause the soul to believe it is still alive, yet it no longer has a vessel to interact with the physical world. In the spiritual realm the soul only perceives things energetically, not physically through the body's senses. The soul can feel surrounding energies and their emotions. So, when loved ones suffer deep emotional grief the soul feels those negative energies. In its temporary state of confusion, the soul can become compelled to remain and interact with loved ones. Many people report 'feeling' the presence of their deceased for days afterwards. This is because the living person senses the soul's energy, just as you can 'feel' the presence of someone standing behind you even if you don't see them.

Remember, when a soul incarnates it agrees to do so with amnesia of the spiritual world. The soul literally forgets who it is. We learned in Chapter 6 the differences between the mind and the soul. The mind is affiliated with the personality of the physical body and the soul is affiliated with the energy of the spiritual body. We used the analogy of an actor taking on the role of a character in a movie to differentiate between the mind and the soul. Continuing with that analogy, often when an actor completes a film, some character traits will continue to influence the actor's real personality, perhaps it's an unusual walk, mannerism, or accent. For a short time after the actor has moved on from the role, they find themselves instinctively slipping into that character out of habit.

For those of you who aren't actors and don't fully relate to this analogy, here's another way to look at it. If you've owned a car for a period of time, take note at how you are able to operate it almost instinctively. You know exactly where to reach for the parking break, the wipers, lights, shift, radio, A/C, etc.…you don't even think about it, you control everything on reflex. Then, after years of driving this car, you trade it in for a new car whose interior design is completely different. Suddenly all your driving instincts are off. You find yourself reaching for the emergency break when the new car's emergency break is a foot pedal. You grab for the shift, reach for the radio or A/C where it was positioned on your old car, only to realize it's not in that position on the new car. This goes on for a few weeks until your body finally forgets about the old car and adjusts to the design of the new car. The memory of the old car carries over into the new car and temporarily influences your body on a subconscious level. Well, this is very similar to the temporary influence the mind has on the soul shortly after the death of the body.

During the period of temporary disorientation, the soul needs to be reminded of its true identity. This becomes particularly apparent for younger souls. There are groups of highly evolved spiritual entities called *'Spirit Guides,'* whose job is to assist souls transiting from the physical realm back to the spiritual realm. You may also have heard spirit guides being referred to as *'Angels.'* Spirit guides hover around the individual in the days leading up to the soul's scheduled departure to balance energies and help stabilize the soul's confusion during its transition. Ironically, it's these benevolent spirits that give rise to tales of dark spiritual apparitions like the '*Grimm Reaper*' or '*Angel of Death*' who arrive to seize your soul prematurely.

Older souls with experience transitioning from many former lives are able to escape the influences of the mind and don't fall into a state of confusion. They immediately become aware of their departure from the body and are able to return to their spiritual home with very little guidance. On the other hand, young souls become easily disoriented and can remain attached to the physical world after the death of its body. For these souls, spirit guides work closely to assure their return home. Some of you may have heard stories of people claiming a deceased loved one physically appeared before them after their death…not in mind or feelings, but in the physical! I personally know two people who swear this phenomenon occurred. In both cases it was a parent who made a brief appearance shortly after their death. Apparitions of this sort are somewhat common. It occurs when a soul manifests its etheric body to appear physical by slowing down its energy vibrations through concentrated thought. Only mature, advanced souls are capable of doing this. If you ever encounter someone who swears this has happened to them, don't write it off as their crazy imagination so quickly.

For the surviving family and friends, the passing soul benefits the most if you celebrate its life rather than mourn it. This is an important aspect of life, since everyone at some point is faced with the loss of a loved one. Why is it important to celebrate and not mourn a soul returning to their spiritual home? Remember you are an immortal soul having a human experience. While you are within your human vessel, you experience the physical world through the body's 5 senses. However, the body has 6 major functions – the 5 senses and feelings.

In addition to seeing, smelling, tasting, touching, and hearing, you also feel. And just as the eyes can see multiple colors, the nose smells multiple scents, the tongue tastes multiple flavors, the skin detects multiple objects and surfaces, and the ears hears multiple frequencies, you feel multiple emotions. When someone asks, *"How you feel?"* You almost always have an immediate response. I'm tired. I'm happy. I'm excited. I'm sad, afraid, angry, disgusted, surprised, worried, eager, disappointed, delighted…there are just so many. Now, ask yourself, *"If my body has 6 basic functions, the 5 senses and feelings, and then my physical body up and dies, what function is left?"* Feelings!

When your body dies and your soul returns to its spiritual home, all it can do is feel. And it does so by picking up on the emotional frequencies of those in its immediate surroundings, which are your loved ones. Shortly after the passing of a loved one, extreme despair and anguish is felt by the departing soul which can disrupt its acclimation back to the spiritual realm. The soul is much better off transitioning when loved ones' express gratitude for shared experiences and celebrate the soul's passing to a place of universal love. Grieving for months only creates distress for the soul. Spirit guides remain after the soul departs to help rebalance energies of living individuals traumatized by the loss of their loved one.

Once the soul moves on from the physical environment of its recent life, it will find itself in a locality that complements the belief systems it had in the physical world. In the energy state the soul is able to manifest instantaneously. Since it hasn't yet fully accepted its non-physical existence, the soul creates an environment projected from convictions it carried over. This could be a home, a church or temple, a frequently visited park, or other meaningful location from its prior life. Nothing in this stage reflects the soul's true spiritual home, but rather it's like a dream state created by beliefs from the soul's physical experience. The greater the convictions a person carries over from their physical life determines how strongly a soul will be impacted in the afterlife. This is one of the ways the mind plays an influence in the soul's reemergence. While in one of these mental locations, the soul is joined by enlightened spirit guides who help to reorient and guide it back to its spiritual home. The soul's home in the spiritual realm is sometimes called its *'soul family'* or *'soul group.'* In addition to spirit guides, the spirit of deceased family and friends often appear to the soul while in its calming location.

The manner in which the body dies also plays a powerful role on the soul's transition. Was the person's death quick, violent, peaceful, drawn-out, painful, traumatic, etc. All these factors determine the type of spirit guides needed to aid in readjusting to the lighter, higher-vibrational energy. Those who are blessed with a peaceful natural death simply say goodbye to their physical incarnation and smoothly transition to a calm state of spiritual consciousness. However, when a person dies a sudden, tragic, or unexpected death, as with an accident, the soul often doesn't realize it has passed over. The consciousness remains as clear as when the soul was in a physical body, but the soul is no longer physical. This abrupt shift can cause a temporary state of confusion. The soul believes it's still alive and becomes puzzled why it cannot do the things it used to do, or why people are not responding to it.

While less common, another situation that creates discourse for the soul is the individual's mental state just prior to death. If the soul believes it has unfinished business in the physical world, or if there is resistance to death, or if it carries a sense of rage in the manner it died, these convictions will remain temporarily with the soul. All these circumstances can cause the soul to fixate on the physical world and prevent it from crossing over.

In these cases, the soul ends up staying behind and remains attached to families and loved ones becoming what we call 'ghosts,' 'apparitions,' 'evil spirits,' or 'demons.' This is most common when a parent leaves a young child, or when a soul experiences a lifetime with an addictive personality. The strong personality weighs so heavily on the soul energy it results in an unusually powerful attachment to the physical. These souls become so focused on a house or location that it becomes the afterlife for them, they simply don't want to leave it. They try to communicate with the living, remain in homes, and manifest as apparitions.

Some souls will attach to a living person to cling to an earthly pleasure that fueled their addiction, like the taste of alcohol, cigarettes, food, etc. This is always to the detriment and harm of the living person, as the soul interferes with the energy body of that living person. Typically, this situation only occurs with young souls who don't realize the harm they are causing. In these cases, spirit guides intervene and assist in the adjustment process. While a soul may occupy a location for years, or decades, in earth time, in nonphysical spirit time it amounts to only a few passing moments. These souls are not stuck in purgatory so much as they simply reject returning to the spiritual world. The soul is never forced to act in any way. If the soul desires to remain on the physical plane or stay in a self-imposed exile, it is given the leeway to do so. The soul is always in control of its energy and destiny. It is always a self-imposed situation.

Once your soul accepts it is no longer 'alive' in the physical world it shifts to its next transiting stage where it reunites with its over-soul, joins its soul family, and returns to its immortal existence. When this occurs, the soul has fully assimilated back to its true essence and begins its *'life-between-lives'* work. We'll explore what happens with the soul during this period in a section all to itself, but before we move on to that topic, I'd like to take a little detour to explore a prevailing belief that has become instituted in the psyche of many. So, grab a leather jacket and a bottle of Jack Daniels, we're about to hop on our Harleys and take a rebellious ride on the highway to hell…

Hell on Earth

There's a popular belief held with strong conviction of a purgatory filled with fire and brimstone, supervised by a sinister dark angel where the wicked are doomed to suffer for eternity should they lead a life of sin. The notion of Satan's underworld for the truly evil is somewhat of a distortion from the realities of the afterlife. If you're wondering whether there is a place filled with pain and suffering where an imperfect soul is confined, the simple answer is, "*Yes! There is.*" But, as we step through the cycles of reincarnation, and you gain an understanding of how it functions, you'll see hell isn't quite the place it's been depicted over the centuries. You see, if you're sitting in a quiet place right now reading this book, you are actually sitting squarely in the infernos of hell! That's right, you're in hell right now as you read this book. I don't mean for this to be a shocking statement, but I'm drawing attention to how the reincarnation process has become distorted over time. I'd like to clarify how these fear-inducing tales of Satan's torturous purgatory got their origins.

There are two principal circumstances associated with the birth of 'hell' and how it has become distorted throughout time. One embodies stories of people who have had NDE's or vivid dreams in which they visited and suffered the horrors of hell. These accounts have been reported for centuries and some have become timeless, like the 14th century epic poem '*Dante's Inferno*.' The other more ubiquitous way involves an inaccurate interpretation of the reincarnation process. Through no fault of their own, the process of the soul's incarnation cycles has been misinterpreted and altered, much like the game of "Telephone," where a story morphs as it's told from person to person until the final tale no longer resembles the original. Let's first look at people who claim to have taken a horrifying elevator ride down to the Devil's catacombs only to return with disturbing Dante-like tales.

If in your physical life, you develop rigid beliefs of a hell, or of God's wrathful judgment, or if you cling to patterns of hatred or anger, you carry those powerful beliefs and emotions into the nonphysical realm when you die. Remember how the pesky mind can influence the soul in the immediate stages of the afterlife. In the nonphysical the soul produces instantaneous manifestations of thought. When these strict beliefs are carried over by the subconscious mind, your soul ends up creating this reality as your initial place of arrival in the afterlife. The expectations that your physical mind carries over will create your initial experience - a heavenly paradise or a hellish hollow - it's up to you. If you believe firmly in your physical life that hell is a torturous place of pain and suffering where sinners of all kind are destined to spend eternity, then upon passing you will experience this hell as it has been etched into your subconscious mind. The intensity of your beliefs will determine the vividness of your initial afterlife experience. In a strange way, you are the one who creates the hell you experience. The soul remains in this torturous place of pain and suffering until it realizes that hell, as imagined, is nothing more than a temporary construct of the physical mind. After which, the soul moves on to the true loving nature of the nonphysical realm. Those returning from a NDE before coming to this realization, return to the physical world with strong convictions of a legitimate hell in the afterlife. They don't understand that they simply experienced a manifestation of their own mind. However, their terrifying tales of life on the 'other side,' go on to influence and frighten others who are equally unknowledgeable of this self-manifestation.

This is one way the parable of 'hell' has worked itself into our psyche. The other more prevalent means stems from the misunderstanding of reincarnation. In the traditional telling of heaven and hell, when a person dies, if you've lived a benevolent life you ride the escalator 'UP' to heaven to be greeted at the pearly gates by Saint Peter. On the other hand, if you've lived the life of sin, you take the escalator 'DOWN' where you're met by the dark angel Lucifer for an eternity of suffering. Up or down, you determine the direction of your elevator ride based on the life you choose to live. Here's how the distortion comes into play.

When your soul transitions to the spiritual realm, there is no judgment of your physical experience by a wrathful God armed with a clipboard of your sins, who enforces which elevator button gets pushed - Up or

Down. The judgment comes through your own deliberations of lessons learned and values gained. Not only of your most recent life, but the collective entirety of all your lifetimes. There is no condemnation, punishment or hell issued to you by a higher authority. Your soul is in a constant state of evolution. It learns, grows, and evolves through experiences in the physical until it has learned all it can from the physical world. Until it reaches that level, it must continue to return for more lessons. As a soul, you know this, and you agree to it because it is what you want. When you go from the perfect loving home of the spiritual world and incarnate into the not-so-perfect physical world, the soul grows and evolves from the contrast. It is YOU who willingly and eagerly makes the decision to push the 'Down' button and return to the physical realm to continue your spiritual growth.

When you do, you return to a world of pain and suffering. Life on earth is messy and filled with all kinds of unjust hurt and misery. We've all witnessed and experienced a world overflowing with temptations, war, greed, poverty, conflicts, disease, famine, natural disasters, indecency, contempt, road rage, and people who chew with their mouth open. Earth is the learning grounds for the soul, a giant classroom where the soul experiences the delights and pleasures and learns the differences between good and evil. But to learn the good, it needs to experience the evil. It's in the physical world where physical and emotional pain are felt, not in the loving realm of the nonphysical. Going "Down" to incarnate in the pain-filled physical realm, instead of remaining "Up" in the unconditional loving spiritual realm is how the entire concept of heaven and hell, above and below, has become distorted. So, when I say you are sitting in the fiery chambers of hell as you read this book, you now understand my reference. You see, hell does exist, and you are here in it right now with all the rest of us incarnated souls. It's a place of great pain and great suffering, but also a place of great beauty, pleasure and reward. Most importantly, it's a place you willingly and enthusiastically chose to come.

Anyone fearing an afterlife filled with agonizing punishments doled out by a wrathful God, can be comforted in knowing you will be treated with love even if you've lived a life of sin. There is no hell where you'll suffer for eternity, but don't start planning your next bank heist just yet! You will be held accountable for your actions in the physical world. There is great compassion for human weakness, but inhumane, selfishness, and intentional evil, hurt, and pain you impose on other incarnated souls generates great negative karma for you. All the negative karma you generate through pure and willful acts of evil must be repaid in future life(s) on Earth. Negative karma is only worked off through future lives of extreme difficulties and challenges where you will feel and experience physical and emotional pain equivalent to that which you've caused. We'll learn more about this in Chapter 9, for now let's continue with the soul's journey to return to its immortal home and see what life is like for a soul when it is no longer incarnated in a human body. This period is often called '*Life-between-lives*,' which is the topic of our next section…

Life Between Lives

In Chapter 6 we raised an intriguing question, "*If the body is a blend of the physical and the spiritual, how does the spiritual component learn and grow?*" We then went on to investigate and learn that the physical plane, the brick and mortar, meat and potatoes world in which we live IS the soul's classroom. Each time a soul incarnates into a new body it attends Soul University, has new earthly experiences and adds to its growth, development and evolution. A soul making its way through Earthly lessons draws parallels to students making their way through our educational institutions. Every time a student enrolls in a new class, he/she learns something new that applies towards their educational growth and development. If a student fails, they'll have to take that class over again. The same holds true for a soul as it attends Earth's classroom. Each time the soul 'enrolls' in a new life, it learns something new that applies towards its growth and development. If the soul fails the lesson, it is destined to relive that life lessons again and again until it gets it right.

This brings us to another questions. If the physical world is the soul's classroom, then what does the spiritual world correspond to? It's really an interesting comparison to consider. Think about all a person goes through from the time they are young until the time they find their path in life. Through all the trials and tribulations of trying to figure out *"what I want to do when I grow up,"* a person seeks and is given a wide mixture of advice from family, friends, teachers, guidance counselors, recruiters, career counselors, clergy, mentors and everyone else from the barista to the barber! This collective of people doling out their two cents of wisdom helps lead you down the path of success and fulfillment. The spiritual world is very similar, and advice and guidance are also given to the soul in the spiritual realm. Like life on Earth, guidance is sought and given from a wide array of souls who have been there and done that, all in an effort to lead you down a path of growth and fulfillment. The spiritual realm is a time and place where the soul seeks advice and guidance on its growth, development, and evolution. You can look at the spiritual realm as one great big session with your guidance counselor.

After the death of the physical body, the immortal soul reacclimates to the spiritual realm and finds itself in its true spiritual home. Through the help of spirit guides it reunites with its over-soul, rendezvouses with familiar souls of deceased friends and family, and resides in an unconditional loving environment of the nonphysical. Upon its return, your soul is celebrated for its journey into the physical. It's like a big family reunion. But what happens once the accolades are over? If one life in the physical realm doesn't allow enough time for the soul to learn everything it needs to know, how can it learn more? What process does the soul go through to determine new lessons it needs to learn? Where does it go to learn those lessons? All this evaluation comprises the work a soul is faced with in the afterlife, or its "*Life-between-lives*" (LBL). So, let's spend a little time with a soul to get a feel for what goes on in its life-between-lives.

In earlier chapters we learned that the spiritual realm and the physical realm are two worlds existing on top of one another. The spiritual realm is not all that different from the physical world, the energies of each simply oscillate at different frequencies. The physical world is an extraordinarily diverse place. There are many different ways a person can live on this planet depending on your geographic and socioeconomic conditions. There are countless sets of laws, cultures, norms, and challenges scattered across the globe. Life for a Yanomami Indian living in the remote depths of the Amazon rainforest is much different than life of an affluent socialite living in cosmopolitan Paris. From the primitive to the technologically advanced, and everything in-between, there are many levels of existence on Earth. Such is the case for the afterlife. There are various planes of existence in the afterlife that represent different levels of spiritual progress, development, and evolution. Lower levels are occupied with younger, less experiences souls, while more highly evolved souls exist on higher levels.

The afterlife is a time of introspection for returning souls. It's a time for them to reflect on their experiences in the physical world and recharge their spiritual energies. The work a soul does during its life-between-lives differs depending on the soul's stage of evolution. You can think of it like the many different levels of education in the physical world. The work that students in elementary school must do to advance to grade school is at a different level than the work high school students have to complete to advance to college, which is entirely different than the work post-graduate students have to complete to earn their degree. Likewise, young souls have a different level of work to do than mature souls for each to continue their growth and evolution. One is not considered 'superior' to the other, they are simply at different stages of development. Because of the varying degrees of work, there are also different levels of existence for each to perform their work.

The lower levels are destinations for souls who have accumulated a great deal of negative karma through willful acts of evil during an incarnation. It is rare for advanced souls to engage in this level of immoral physical activity, so the lower planes are predominantly filled with infant and young souls who are still inexperienced with handling the negative influences of the physical world. The overwhelming majority of returning souls go to a higher plane of existence to assess their growth and determine future development. However, if you happen to find your immortal butt in one of the lower planes it probably means you haven't been a very good camper in your physical life. Perhaps you exercised your free-will to end your life unnaturally, or you committed murder, or engaged in acts of terrorism, or participated in other acts of pre-meditated and intentional evil. All these negative activities in the physical world cause blockages to the energy network that needs repair. In the physical world, energy blockages can be restored or revived by energy masters such as acupuncturists, Tai Chi specialists, Qi Gong masters, Reiki masters, etc. Likewise, the spiritual world has its energy masters who help to fix disrupted energy. Like I said, the afterlife really is quite similar to life on Earth. Spirit guides direct these imbalanced souls to the lower planes so as not to affect other souls. In a sense, the corrupted souls are quarantined until they are purified of their negative earthly contaminants. Souls in this state are not allowed to reincarnate until the negative energies have been balanced.

Now, don't get these lower spiritual levels confused with hell. There is no hell in the afterlife for souls. It exists only on the physical plane as explained in the prior section. All souls go to the same spiritual realm and are all treated with patience, love, understanding and compassion. No human is born evil, but souls can become contaminated by mental, emotional, or biological damage to their physical bodies. This is especially true for less-advanced souls. Souls who cause great harm to others in the physical world will discover there are consequences for their actions. The negative karma generated by the harmful actions will have to be repaid in future lives. The soul itself will choose the work required to stabilize the negative karma. Through deep reflection and consideration, the soul selects a life of pain similar to the pain they inflicted. This allows the soul to learn specific life lessons and empathize with the hurt they caused. This is not considered a punishment but rather an opportunity for karmic growth which the soul eagerly accepts. Souls that inhabit the lower planes are supported by loving spirit guides who counsel and help them work through the contaminating energy until the soul is ready to return to its rightful home on a higher plane of existence.

Assuming you're not a mass-murderer, terrorist, or some other profound perpetrator of evil, then you will simply arrive back to your spiritual home on a higher plane along with the vast majority of returning souls. Now, here's a fascinating thought to consider…I've mentioned more than once that every human being born on this planet has an immortal soul. That means everyone! From the furthest remote corners of the globe, all 7.6 billion people are immortal souls having a human experience. Over time, what happens to all these humans? They die! Each year 55,300,000 people on this planet will die. That's 151,506 every day, 6,312 every hour, or 105 per minute. That's an awful lot of souls heading back to their home country in the sky. I mean, I get impatient waiting in a check-out line with more than 3 people, how am I supposed to deal with this kind of logjam of souls returning to the afterlife!

The Universe is a very big place, and the Creator designed it in an amazingly efficient manner. Just consider the marvels of how efficiently the 30 trillion cells work together in the bodies of all 7.6 billion people. The miracles of the physical also extend into the nonphysical. The soul's journey home does not resemble a New York subway car during rush hour. Instead, the soul is automatically guided to its afterlife destination based on the frequency of the soul's energy. And while billions and billions of souls populate the afterlife, your soul will return to its specific spiritual home inhabited with souls of similar frequency.

Here you'll reunite with a collection of souls known as your *'soul group.'* Your soul group is simply a group of souls that consist of family members, close friends, extended family, and other close associates who have been part of your life on Earth. We've all had classmates that come in-and-out of our lives year-after-year, some more influential than others, and continue to be part of our lives. Soul groups are the spiritual equivalent. The souls in your soul group will come in-and-out of your physical lives lifetime-after-lifetime, in some lives more influential than others. For example, you may have lived a lifetime in the 15th century in which your parent is an incarnated soul from your soul group. Then in another lifetime, say one set in the 21st century, that same soul may be incarnated as your spouse.

While different lives, in different eras, many of the souls from your soul group occupy your inner circle of close friends and relatives. If you pay attention to your intuition, you'll be able to detect people from your soul group. For example, have you ever run into a total stranger and been struck with the uncanny sensation that you've known this person for years? When this happens, it's very likely that person is an incarnated soul from your soul group. Embrace those moments when they happen, it very well could be a dear old friend! If I've piqued your curiosity about soul groups, hang on tight, we've got lots more on soul groups when we explore the topics of soulmates and soul contracts.

Getting back to life-between-lives and the soul's task at hand during this period. Once the soul has made it back to its spiritual home, it needs to do something. The one thing it won't be doing anytime soon is reincarnating into another life. It is extremely rare for a soul to jump into a new body immediately upon the death of its former body. Life-between-lives is a time for the soul to rest and rejuvenate its spiritual energy. On average a soul will spend about 5-10 Earth years before reincarnating. During this period, you review and evaluate all you have accumulated during your incarnations. You'll analyze your recent life acknowledging the highs and lows. You are your only true critic, there is no one else to judge you than yourself.

This is both the good and the bad, since you are the ultimate judge, you must confront your shortcomings with honesty. You cannot deceive and exonerate yourself of your failures. If the soul does try to deny itself of its own realities it will continue to repeat its failures until it learns to become truthful...there's no getting around it. As you recognize your lessons learns, areas of improvement, and karmic obligations, you begin to resolve your need to return to the physical for further growth. To do so, you must determine the type of lessons and life you want to experience to compliment your growth. The soul relies on advice and guidance of other more advanced souls and masters to help make these determinations.

You, as a soul, examine the activities of your recent lifetime by doing a *'life review.'* Your entire life will pass by with clarity, almost like a movie or vivid dream. All the choices you made and lessons you learned are reviewed. The pains and challenges of your time in the physical world are explored to fully understand their purpose, cause, reason and their contribution to your spiritual evolution. In addition, your evaluation encompasses not only your recent life, but the soul's entire existence. Your successes, mistakes, and sins of all your lives are recounted. All the many lives you have lived contribute to your process of self-discovery. All these experiences become integrated into the fabric of your soul. If all this judging and self-evaluation seems a bit overwhelming, don't worry, there are loving and wise spiritual guides to support and help during these reviews. Your guides evaluate, critique and suggest what you could have done differently in your physical experience. You freely express and discuss your desires and regrets on the choices you made. Your guides help you gain an understanding of your growth and lessons that remain.

After reviewing and evaluating all the lessons learned and failures made, it's time to plan your next incarnation. Just as students return to campus in the fall for a whole new set of learning experiences, souls return to the physical world for their new learning experiences. You work closely with your guides to help determine your new curriculum in Soul University. Together you assess the life lessons that are needed to advance your growth, what karma needs to be dealt with, and any negative belief systems that need to be cleared. It's important to note that you are never forced to reincarnate. The opportunity to incarnate and experience the physical to further spiritual growth is considered an honor that souls pursue with enthusiasm. It is always entirely up to you.

Whenever a soul incarnates, it weighs two kinds of objectives it hopes to accomplish – a personal achievement and a world achievement. On a personal level, you look for a lifetime that will provide important life lessons your soul needs to further its development. In addition, you also look to contribute in some way to the world at large, this gift becomes your world achievement. Often your two purposes overlap. For instance, a scientist brings the important work of discovery, a doctor offers the gift of healing, an author contributes inspirational writings, a mother her nurturing and love, etc. As you can see, you've got a lot to consider before jumping back into the physical world. Once all your work is done - you've evaluated all the criteria, determined what lessons are instrumental to your growth, and what personal and world goals you'd like to achieve - all you have left to do is figure out the time, place, and person who will provide these experiences. Sounds simple enough, but exactly how are you supposed to do that?

Let's all take a deep breath, because I'm about to test your faith in me. I'm well aware that all this information about life-between-lives can strike some as being a bit fanciful. After all, I'm the one trumpeting science as the foundation of spiritual concepts. Now, it appears I've completely jumped off the deep end into a vast pool of fantasy. However, the information I've presented has been corroborated by thousands of independent cases, as is the case for the information I'm about to present. The next stage in your life-between-lives is to determine who, when, and where you will incarnate. How that is done may test your skepticism, but at this point, if you're in for a penny, you're in for a pound!

You've completed all your self-evaluations, and through the help of spirit guides, you gain a strong understanding of the type of life that will be the most beneficial to your spiritual growth. As an immortal, intelligent soul, you are given the opportunity to review all the events, people, and circumstances the desired host body will encounter in its lifetime. You actually have the ability to peer into the future of the life you've selected and see scenes of people and incidents you will face in the chosen life. You explore your childhood, adolescence, and adulthood that shows potential paths you may take in this body. You choose your parents, your physically inherited characteristics, your set of probable realities, and the life work you will do in that specific body. In essence, you select beforehand all of these complex mixtures of people, places, and events for the specific purpose of achieving your soul's desired goals.

It sounds crazy, I know, but that's how it done. It's like a giant spiritual Red Box where instead of selecting a new movie DVD you select a new lifetime. It's very important to understand that your immortal soul knows in advance the hardships and challenges it will face in the physical world. The soul willingly and enthusiastically chooses these hardships for its own growth. There will even be lifetimes of physically handicapped bodies and extreme difficulties you voluntarily select to address karmic debts or to work on aspects of a lesson you've had trouble with in a previous life. YOU are in control, and it is YOU making these decisions. In fact, it is more common for mature, advanced, and old souls to take on extremely challenging or traumatic lives. As you confront difficulties in the physical world, bear in mind that you likely knew of these troubling incidents and purposefully choose them for your own personal gain. Also, bear in mind the Universe only presents challenges to the degree a soul can handle them - extreme hardships are signs of a powerful soul!

Although you have a full understanding of the life you've selected for your next human experience, you still live this life under the auspices of free will. The events, incidents, and lifestyles shown to you are potential realities, none are fully predestined. Your fee-will allows you to alter the lifetime, making your lessons occur sooner, later, or perhaps in another life. Nothing is predestined. Life unfolds based upon decisions and choices your soul makes using its free-will in the physical world. Knowing this provides options you don't have in the absence of this knowledge. You now have the option to take steps in your current life to form an awareness of your soul. To study and learn ways of strengthening the alliance with your soul and take control of your life.

In the physical world, when you are preparing to engage in a physical or mental challenge, like running a marathon, taking the SAT's, or passing the bar, you typically try to get some rest before the event. Once again, the spiritual world mirrors the physical world. Prior to the soul taking on a new incarnation, it also gets a little R&R before taking on the grueling challenges of physical life on Earth. After that rest period, when the soul feels it is time to return to the physical plane, you say a temporary goodbye to your soul group and begin the incarnation process. The reincarnation cycle begins at conception when an energy cord is formed between the over-soul and the developing child. The energy body begins to develop along with the physical body inside the mother's womb, the incarnating soul gradually experiences memory loss of the spirit world, and the human experience process repeats itself. Your guides continue to watch over your soul throughout your time on Earth. As you become more aware of this, you are able to call on them for affirmation and support. There you have it. All the fascinating things your soul does when it's not down here on Earth worrying about bills, traffic, retirement, or how many 'likes' you can chalk-up on social media! It's another aspect of the marvels of creation.

This has been a rather full chapter of discovery. We began by stepping through the ghastly decomposition process of the human body after it dies. Then, we saw how the energy body goes through its own process after death of the physical body. Death even tossed us a curveball when we saw how death in the physical world corresponds to a rebirth in the spiritual world. Once the soul leaves the body, it goes through two fundamental stages of transitioning to the spiritual realm. The first involves the assimilation of the soul energy back to the spiritual realm while under the temporary influence of the physical mind. This stage causes short-term confusion as the immortal soul adjusts to life without the limitations of a physical body. Stage two occurs once the soul has fully reintegrated to the spiritual realm and made its way back to its spiritual home, reuniting with its soul group. This period is known as life-between-lives.

During the life-between-lives period, you as an immortal soul, review all the life experiences from your most recent incarnation, along with other previous lifetimes. You evaluate all the lessons learned, mistakes made, karmic obligations, and areas of future growth. Finally, you select the new human experience to provide the new life lessons needed to compliment your spiritual growth.

I realize the world of the afterlife I've depicted can read like it came straight from the imagination of J.K. Rowling. With spirit guides, life reviews, screenings of your future life…I mean, how are we really supposed to believe this 'afterlife' isn't just conceived from the creative minds of wishful thinkers and wannabe believers? If all this evaluation and preparation in the afterlife is to prepare yourself for a new incarnation, what evidence is there for a soul, any soul, returning to the physical world? How are we supposed to believe in reincarnation without some sort of proof…even a tiny bit? These questions and apprehensions are all valid. And by now, you should know whenever faced with valid questions needing further corroboration it's time to shift our investigative minds into overdrive. So, let's roll up our sleeves and get to work!

Ch. 8: Come Here Often?

"It is not more surprising to be born twice than once; everything in nature is resurrection." — Voltaire

Reincarnation

Welcome back to the real world. Having spent an entire chapter in the spiritual realm it's nice to journey back to a reality we are more intimate with, the physical world we awake to every morning. We all have our familiar touchstones that reassure us we're firmly planted in a place called home. There's the morning alarm, the repetitive banging of the snooze button, then a caffeine jump-start launching us into a day filled with screaming kids, rush hour traffic, work deadlines, 24-hour news cycles, mortgage payments, interminable bills, juggling calories and calendars, all the while trying to stay current on the latest pop culture before it becomes passé office conversation! Ahhh, life in the physical world. In this chapter we'll be staying right here in the hustle and bustle of the physical world while investigating the past. But this isn't a past that harkens back to your childhood memories, rather a past of a different kind. It's a past you may not even be aware of, but one that continues to influence you to this very day.

I'm about to step through some common events and coincidences which I'd like you to see if any have occurred to you. Often, they go by without much thought or fanfare, but they deserve much more attention. For instance, have you ever experienced a haunting sense of déjà vu that stops you in your tracks? The kind that feels like someone threw a bucket of vertigo at you. When this happens, how do you react? Do you try to determine the source of the sensation or simply shrug your shoulders with a "*Hmm*?"

What about a paralyzing phobia that has no real-world connection – fear of snakes, heights, water, spiders, dark rooms, etc. Do you wonder how the phobia originated, or do you just accept it as part of your personality? Perhaps you have a certain talent you've mastered with little to no formal training – musical, artistic, engineering, etc. Why are you proficient at this talent and not some other skill? Have you ever visited at a new location and inherently knew the way around, or met a total stranger you were convinced you knew? Where did these familiarities come from? Have you met this person before or travel to this location as a child? Are you drawn to certain time periods or geographic locations? Why these specific eras and places? What makes them special? Maybe you or a someone you know are involved in a group that recreates historic battles - Civil War, Medieval, or Ancient Roman? What is the attraction with those battles? How did such an obsession form? Do you have an unusual birthmark and wondered about its origins? These seemingly innocuous events are experienced by people all the time, but they're rarely given much thought or explanation. We're about to change that.

I want you to consider all these common events and think about why they occur. Probe these seemingly ordinary circumstances of life and question their origins. What would you attribute them to? How would you explain them? Go ahead, give it a try, it'll be interesting to see what you come up with. The answer to these questions is precisely what we'll be investigating in this chapter. I'll give you a hint…they may all be symptoms of your past. That's right, your past. It's a phenomenon known as '*past lives*' and I assure you our exploration into this topic will be one remarkable trip. Because you know what they say, *"You only live once!"*...or do you?

To give past lives their fair shake, we really should take a big step back to its origins – reincarnation. Reincarnation is the belief that the soul is immortal, and it goes through a cycle of being born into a physical body, dying, and being reborn again in a new body. This cycle continues with each life contributing to the soul's evolution until it reaches a level of understanding where it frees itself from the reincarnation cycle. I made implications about this in chapter 6 and spent all of Chapter 7 discussing what happens when a soul departs the body, so it's safe to assume my belief in reincarnation is rock solid. But I recognize yours may not be, so let's fill in the backstory of reincarnation, and then get onto examining evidence of its existence.

The concept of reincarnation has been around for a long, long time...it goes so far back that we're not quite sure where its origins were established. We do know that ancient civilizations on all 7 continents – American Indians; Eskimos; African Tribes of Yoruba, Ibo, and Bassongo; Koreans; Siberians; the monks of Nepal; Brazilian shaman; Australian bushmen; and Chinese and Greece philosophers – all believed in some form of reincarnation. Its name even stems from ancient Latin roots that literally means *"to enter the flesh again."* Throughout time and across the globe, there's scarcely a religion that doesn't accept the continuance of life beyond death in one form or another. However, it's primarily the Asian religions, Hinduism, Jainism, Buddhism, Sikhism, and early forms of Christianity and Judaism that hold the belief in the soul returning. While being able to come back and enjoy life again and again may sound hip and cool, in the ancient Eastern religions, reincarnation was not considered a good thing. They believed that for a soul to achieve the ultimate state of nirvana it had to escape the cycle of reincarnation. Being born into a human body was rather clear evidence that your soul hadn't yet achieved nirvana. Maybe that's where the tradition of getting a good smack on the backside as your welcome into the world got started.

Most of these religions hold similar beliefs in reincarnation with just some minor nuances that separate them. For instance, Hinduism believes your soul accumulates karma during a physical lifetime which determines the quality of life you'll experience in your next incarnation. Accumulate positive karma and experience a pleasant life, or a life of hardship to pay off negative karma. While Jainism, a popular religion in India, holds the belief that karma is a fine particulate substance that settles on the soul. New karma gets added to the existing karma depending on your deeds in life. In this regard Jainism is quite similar to Hinduism. Another religion grounded in reincarnation is one that most people have never heard of – Sikhism – but it's actually the 5th most popular religion in the world. Sikhism believes that human beings spend their time in a cycle of birth, life, and rebirth, with the quality of each life being dependent on how well or badly a person behaved in their previous life. The only way out of this cycle is to achieve a total knowledge of and union with God. See, we're just talking about small nuances that separates these different religious beliefs in reincarnation.

You may have noticed that early Christianity and Judaism made the list of religions that subscribe to reincarnation, and some may take issue with that. However, the key word in my statement is "early." Judaism held the belief in reincarnation, or *gilgul*, right up until the early 1800s, so not very ancient at all. It wasn't until the Jewish people migrated from Eastern Europe to the West, and entered the Age of Enlightenment and science, that the belief in reincarnation went underground. However, the Chassidic (Ultra-Orthodox) populations still hold the believe in reincarnation. In Christianity, reincarnation found itself going underground much earlier. Back during the 6th century, the Second Council of Constantinople officially declared reincarnation to be a heresy to the church. As Christianity became a state religion, the Romans excised the notion of reincarnation, replacing it with the belief of a Judgment Day in an effort to engender more rigid control of their followers.

Where does all this bring us to today. Well, about 2/3 of the world's population believes in some form of reincarnation. That's about 4.75 billion people who think they've been here before in another body. However, the numbers in the US don't stack up quite as high. Only about 40% of Americans aged 25 - 29 believe in reincarnation, and for those above retirement age it drops to only 14%. So, you stand a greater chance of having a conversation about reincarnation with millennials than with baby boomers…although you may have to carry that conversation over social media!

Just for the fun of it, I did a Google search and an Amazon book search on "reincarnation." Google churned out 22,800,000 results and Amazon showed over 10,000 books (Amazon stops counting after 10,000). And I'm certain I've read just about every one of them. So, you can see there's no shortage of information supporting reincarnation. It's out there, lots of it! Each book and website providing a nugget of truth and real-world examples of past life cases. This raises another interesting question to consider. With all this information on reincarnation at everyone's disposal, why is it that so few know about and believe in the realities of reincarnation? Interesting thing to think about isn't it? What are the forces in society, culture, and your life that keep reincarnation from being openly discussed and taught? Think about the people and institutions who stand to lose should reincarnation become more widely accepted. I have my theories and suspicions; however, my role is not to preach, but rather raise eye-opening realities for you to explore and come to your own conclusions. Whatever you determine the societal forces acting on you, wouldn't it be nice to see them erode and the cultural stigmas dissolve so the effects of reincarnation can become an open aspect of life? Now that we have the background covered, let's grab those passports and start our journey into the past...past lives that is.

A Passport Through Time

Have you been here before? Living in a strange body on the other side of the globe, speaking a foreign tongue during a bygone era. Perhaps you were a man? A woman? A King? A Peasant? A Savior? A Murderer? A Knight? A Slave? A Monk? Maybe you helped build the Great Pyramids? Lived off the land in Native America? Drowned on the Titanic? Fought alongside Alexander the Great? Died in Pompei? Became a made-man under Al Capone? What about all the above?

One of the biggest misconceptions I hear when people first begin to explore past lives is they think they've only had ONE previous lifetime. That's it, just one. It's almost a universal reaction. I remember having the same thought when I first began to study past lives. At the time I assumed that if past lives were true, who was I before? Not, what were my many previous lives, but which one life did I live before this one. It's funny how the mind works.

Back when I began my pilgrimage into past lives, I met a very powerful 'seer.' He was a young guy with incredible abilities to read energy – both physical and spiritual. His abilities allowed him to access astonishing spiritual knowledge. He told me things about my soul that were truly life-altering. One of the things he mentioned, which at the time I thought was total nonsense, is that I'm currently living my 863'rd life! I couldn't help but laugh out loud…remember, I was a bit arrogant in my younger days. Eight hundred and sixty-three lives! I couldn't help but ask, *"Why so many?"* He told me I was an *'Old Soul.'* I responded, *"Yeah, and obviously not a very quick learner!"* He was rather patient with me and went on to explain that it was normal to have more than 1,000 lives before reaching the point in which the soul no longer needs to incarnate in the physical plane and continues its evolution in the spiritual realm. To be honest, I don't know what the magic number is for how many lifetimes it takes to break free from the reincarnation cycle, or if I really am on life 863. However, I do know that I've had far more than a handful of past lives. What about you? How many lifetimes do you think you've had? One? Two? A dozen? A Hundred? Well, it's a pretty good bet that this isn't your first or second incarnation.

Truth be told, you have been here before, in many, many different bodies of both sexes, ethnicity, culture, location, ideology, religion, and time period. Each lifetime has contributed to who you are today. All the experiences, the good, the bad, and the traumatic, collectively form and shape your inner soul, which in turn shapes and forms characteristics of your personality. Isn't that an amazing concept to think about? It just blows me away to contemplate the life-altering enormousness of this. You may be wondering how this is possible. How do all these previous lifetimes influence you today? How can a trauma that occurred thousands of years ago in ancient Greece still affect you today? After all, in today's pervasive 24/7 news cycle catastrophic events seem to fritter away in a matter of days!

All humans experience a wealth of emotion. It doesn't matter who you are, where you live, your profession, or socioeconomic standing. We all have a built-in system of emotions. Whether you're a celebrity, a doctor, a welder, a parent, a teacher, a farmer, a religious leader, an angst-driven teen, or a corrupt politician, we all have feelings. Over the course of a lifetime you experience a wealth of emotion, trauma, loss, pain, joy, heartache, and pride, all of which collects deep within your subconscious mind, leaving an imprint on your spiritual body. When the physical body dies, those emotional imprints remain with the spiritual body and become a permanent part of your soul.

As your soul reincarnates in subsequent lives, these deep emotional memories manifest as personality traits in the form of idiosyncrasies, phobias, disorders, fascinations, obsessions, addictions, innate skills, and internal wisdom, from the benign to the extreme. Emotions that have the greatest influence on the soul are grief, anger, fear, anxiety, and joy. So, except for being joyful, you may want to give your soul a break and do your best to consciously avoid the others. Earlier in this chapter I alluded to some psychological behaviors and physical attributes that can be linked to past lives, Table 3 gives a more comprehensive list.

Attributes Connected to Past Lives

- Unfounded Fears or Phobias
- Birth Defects
- Unusual Birthmarks
- Child Prodigies
- Idiot Savants
- Fibromyalgia-Chronic Fatigue
- Obsessive Compulsive Disorder (OCD)
- Extreme Eating Disorders – Obesity, Anorexia, Bulimia, etc.
- Schizophrenia and Multiple Personality Disorders
- Love at First Sight
- Fear or Hatred at First Sight
- Gender Uncertainty or Confusion
- Fascination with Historical Periods, Figures, and/or Places

- Recurring Nightmares
- Unexplained Pains and Injuries
- Xenoglossy (the ability to speak or write in a language that has not been learned, sometimes occurs during sleep)
- Déjà vu
- Mastery of Skill or Natural Talent with No Formal Training (art, music, engineering, etc.)
- Inherently knowing a Location You've Never Been

Table 3 - Attributes Connected to Past Lives

How's that for a new way of looking at life? All these disorders, physical anomalies, and behaviors can be linked to previous lifetimes. What a novel way to re-evaluate yourself. Think about the ways it can provide an entirely new paradigm for how you view yourself. Even if you're not fully onboard the reincarnation train, this can be a fun exercise and may lower any cynicism you may have about reincarnation.

Ask yourself if any of the traits in Table 3 affect you or someone close to you? Do you have a birthmark and wondered about its origins? How about a reoccurring dream that unnerved you as a child? Perhaps you obsessively collect items from a certain time period? Or feel naturally at home when visiting a foreign destination? Do you have a tattoo of an object you are inexplicably drawn to? These and many other traits have successfully been associated with pivotal events that occurred in a previous life. In fact, there is now a burgeoning branch of psychology called *"Past Life Therapy"* that deals specifically with these symptoms.

Past life therapy was almost unheard of until the mid-1980s when Dr. Brian Weiss published a non-fiction book about one of his patients titled *"Many Live, Many Masters."* Dr. Weiss is a graduate of Yale Medical

School, so he's no lightweight. While treating a patient who wasn't responding to traditional therapy, Dr. Weiss noticed his patient began to recall past-life incidents that seemed to alleviate anxieties and phobias in her present-day life. Dr. Weiss was initially skeptical of the results, so he began studying the phenomenon in greater depth. This led him to mastering past life hypno-regression and influencing a whole new form of psychotherapy. Past life therapy uses hypnosis and other relaxation techniques to regress patients to lifetimes that contributed to their present-day disorder. As patients identify with and build an awareness and understanding of the trauma and its origins, the effects are mitigated freeing the patient from the trauma's paralyzing impact. Today, thousands of past life regression therapists practice in the United States, and tens of thousands practice throughout the world.

But having prior lifetimes doesn't always mean you'll be faced with psychological disorders. Far more benefits come from the inherent wisdom past lives provide your soul, guiding you to navigate the physical world in ways most people write off as 'instincts.' Those instincts are actually learned lessons you mastered in previous lifetimes. Stop for a minute and take an introspective look at yourself through a past life looking glass. Ask what drives and motivates you? What are your fears? Are there certain situations you avoid at all costs? Do you possess certain inherent talents? Is your bookshelf lined with books of specific genres or periods? Are you confrontational, or conciliatory? Adventurous or cautious? All the characteristics that make you unique from anyone else, didn't just blossom from the day you were born. They've been developing for centuries! They also reveal important clues about your many past lives.

Here's a fun little experiment you can do to help identify lifetimes in your distant past that may still be influencing you today. Often, they're hiding right in plain sight. As you go about your normal day-to-day activities, pay attention to instances when you feel a strong attraction towards something. Perhaps it's a movie set in a certain time period, or an exhibit opening at a local museum, or a television program about a historical event, or an affinity for a certain genre of music, or an advertisement for a travel destination. I'm not talking about a generic liking for something, like a flavor of ice cream, a song at the top of the charts, or a picture of beautiful sandy beach. It's when you get a strong attraction pulling you towards a particular item – a film, show, music, location, or event. It's almost as though it was produced specifically for YOU. This type of magnetic attraction is usually a good indicator that the item is a reminder of a powerful experience that occurred in a past life. Being aware of these moments will help you recognize them when they occur. The more you train your mind, the more you'll notice. And you'll see them popping up all the time. Viewing your world through past life goggles provides a whole new perspective on behaviors and idiosyncrasies you previously attributed to environmental, cultural, or learned.

I'm sure all this talk about past lives can make you a bit curious about your own past lives, and what kind of role they play on you today. It's a fun to uncover some of the many previous lifetimes you've lived. They can lead to life-altering revelations. Some will trickle into your dreams, some will find their way into your meditations, others are best uncovered through the guidance of a past life hypno-regression specialist. Whatever technique you use to discover them, you will find each one provides insight to your life today and alters your perspective on humanity. The more people identify with past lives and who they were in those lives, the more the walls of prejudice, bigotry, and hatred will come down. Imagine a misogynist learns he was a woman in a prior life. Or, even more powerful, that he will reincarnate as a woman in a misogynistic world he helped to define. You can substitute any combination to understand how an awareness of reincarnation can transform the world – a homophobe reincarnates as a gay man, an Islamic radical reincarnates as an 'infidel,' a racist reincarnates as an African-American, a self-centered person of wealth becomes homeless in their next life. Knowing that your actions today will directly impact your future lives, truly knowing this, not having a flimsy belief, but a true knowing, will alter how you treat others.

As you explore your past lives, it's also important to understand the purpose of each life. Many people get excited to uncover the who, what, and where of a past life, which is fine. There is a lot of excitement in learning the cities and centuries in which you've lived, but don't stop there. It's equally important, perhaps even more so, to reflect on the 'why.' The why of a previous life reveals the purpose and lesson of that lifetime, which provides growth to your soul. It may sound like a subtle nuance of words, but the difference is profound. The who, what and where tie into aspects of your physical life, but the why gives a much deeper psychological insightful on the true you…your soul.

For example, you may learn that you were an explorer who helped settle the New World in a previous life, but you did so to discover the marvels of the physical world. Or, you were a sculptor in ancient Rome, but took on this life to learn to art of discipline. Perhaps you lived an ordinary life as a parent of ten, but through this life you learned the value of patience and virtue. You see, the 'why' far outweighs the who, what, and where. This also holds true for the life you are currently living. This is a very powerful introspective question *"Why did I take on the life I am currently living?"*

What we've been talking about in this chapter is truly transformational. How we view and treat ourselves, others, humanity, and the future of the planet, becomes completely transformed when we understand that the future we create is OUR future. Not simply a future for our offspring and distant descendants, but a future in which YOU and I will be living...all of us! You will face the hardships and prejudices of tomorrow that you foster and create today. Imagine the impact this can have on humanity if it was understood by all seven billion people on the planet. I recognize for this to truly have any lasting impact, it need not simply be talked about, but rather believed at a consummate level. Believed not as an interesting theory to ponder, but a core value that guides your thoughts and decisions.

One of the best ways for a concept to become a belief is proof of its existence. Given that challenge, we'll soon look at some actual cases of past lives that provide some solid evidence of reincarnation. I want to challenge you when reading the next section to truly weigh the contents of every case, evaluate the facts, analyze how lives separated by time and distance could intersect with such profound personal information, and then form a conclusion. Don't simply read the next section and come away from it saying, *"huh, cool."* It's indispensable to draw your own conclusion on reincarnation. Even if it disrupts your personal belief system, take the time to think this through and make a choice. This is truly one of those issues in life worthy of contemplating, researching and forming a well-informed conclusive belief. Alright, enough said on this topic, time to get into past life cases that may test your skepticism, but I assure you, all of them are true.

Past Life Cases

Since I've tasked myself with the arduous tasks of providing some genuine and irrefutable evidence supporting reincarnation, I thought I'd start off with a person most people are familiar with, Jetsun Jamphel Ngawang Lobsang Yeshe Tenzin Gyatso. But you may know him as the 14th spiritual leader of the Tibetan people, His Holiness himself the Dalai Lama. The people of Tibet go through an absolutely fascinating ritual when the spiritual leader dies. Unlike the Catholic church where a new Pope is decided by a conclave of senior ordained bishops who gather in secrecy to choose a new Pope, the Dalai Lama is not chosen, but rather he is found.

It's predicated on the belief the Dalai Lama has the spiritual power to choose the body in which he will be reincarnated, returning to fulfill his destiny as the high spiritual leader. If you paid attention in Chapter 7 during the 'Life-between-lives' section, this special power won't come as much of a surprise. In fact, it won't seem all that special either. You don't need to be an extremely enlightened spiritual leader of millions to have this power, we ALL have the ability to choose the body we'll be reincarnated into. The real magic lies in the hand of the High Lamas. The High Lamas are spiritual masters who receive signs that point them in the direction of the reincarnated soul of His Holiness. It's really a remarkable and accurate process. But for it to begin, there first needs to be an end. Back in December of 1933, the 13th Dalai Lama's reign came to its end when he passed away, leaving the physical world for reflective time in the spiritual realm. The death of the 13th Dalai Lama then set in motion the process to find his successor.

To do this, the High Lamas come together and meditate for signs or a vision containing information on the whereabouts of their spiritual leader. It typically takes a few years for His Holiness to be found, the recent Dalai Lama took four years to locate. When the High Lamas feel strongly about a vision, they set off in search of the child using the premonition as a guide. When the child is located, a series of tests are conducted to ensure they have found their true spiritual leader. The most notable test involves placing several articles in front of the child, only some of which were owned by the previous Dalai Lama, to see if the child is able to select those specific items. Additionally, former servants of the Dalai Lama meet with the child to further confirm his identity. Finally, the High Lamas step through various tests known only to them for the final confirmation. Once the child is determined to be the reincarnation of the Dalai Lama, he is taken with his family to the Drepung Monastery to begin his studies as the new Tibetan spiritual leader. Let's see how this ritual turned out with His Holiness number 14.

This little guy is Lhamo Thondup. He was born on July 6, 1935 to a loving family of farmers in a small provincial hillside village in Tibet. He has two sisters and four brothers. He's a cute little fellow, who even as a toddler carries a wisdom and stature beyond his tender age. When Lhamo was a young boy, he would often pack a bag and tell his mother that he'll be going on a long journey to Lhasa, the area where the Drepung Monastery is located. He also insisted on being seated at the head of the table during mealtime.

When Lhamo was two years old, the High Lamas began their search to find the new incarnation of the Dalai Lama. One of the High Lamas received a vision during a meditation in which he clearly saw the Tibetan letters Ah and Ka, followed by an image of a three-storied monastery with a jade-green and gold roof. The monastery had a path leading toward a hill upon which a small house with turquoise roof tiles and strangely shaped gutters stood. With this vision in hand, the High Lama's sought guidance on where to search for this monastery and house, so where else would they turn? How about the 13th Dalai Lama!

Now this part is rather interesting. When the 13th Dalai Lama was embalmed, during the mummification process, his head turned to face toward the northeast. The High Lamas saw that as a sign. And what do you know, looking northeast they found a small village in the province of Amdo, which happened to have a three-story, jade-green and gold roofed monastery named Kumbum. The High Lama was certain the letters from his vision - Ah referred to Amdo and Ka referred to Kumbum - so it was here they searched.

The path near the Kumbum monastery seen in the High Lama's vision really did exist and it led right to a small house on a hillside with turquoise roof tiles and strangely shaped gutters. They were now confident the new Dalai Lama would not be far. Within this tiny home lived a small child named Lhamo Thondup. Keeping their purpose secret, the leader of the search party disguised himself as a servant and made his way into the home where he could spend time observing the children. Lhamo immediately recognized him and called out "*Sera lama, Sera lama.*" They had found their man…or child, His Holiness.

To assure themselves of their intuition, they presented several possessions belonging to the 13th Dalai Lama, together with several similar items that did not. In every case, Lhamo correctly identified those belonging to his predecessor saying, "*It's mine. It's mine.*" This confirmed to the High Lamas they had found the new incarnation. Lhamo was taken to the Potala Palace, where he was officially installed as the spiritual leader of Tibet, assuming the new name, Jetsun Jamphel Ngawang Lobsang Yeshe Tenzin Gyatso, aka the Dalai Lama.

That's quite an impressive search and discovery. As I mentioned earlier, some of this will test your skepticism, but stop and think how is it possible that a group of people meditating hundreds of miles away, are able to get signs specific enough to lead them to a house that has a child exhibiting usual behavior of a leader, who subsequently identifies the search party by name, and personal belonging with 100% accuracy. How is that possible?

This is the type of questioning I was driving towards in the start of this section. Don't simply read this story and think, "Hmmm, that's interesting!", then go about life as if nothing earth-shattering has just been revealed. Look at this as an example of a spiritual phenomenon smacking you in the face. Then react with dumbfounded curiosity that demands an explanation. An explanation that only YOU can come up with. You see, this type of self-determining Q&A will shape your belief systems into ones that reflect the realities of the physical and spiritual worlds as you determine them to be. Not the distorted interpretation someone else has defined for you. You'll discover the more you use your own innate critical analysis, the more clearly the truth of the world becomes. OK, are you still not convinced about reincarnation? That's fine, I did say we'd look at cases…with an 's.' So, let's move on to our next case.

With this one, we'll be bringing it home to right here in good ole U-S-of-A, Lafayette, Louisiana to be more specific. This remarkable case of reincarnation involves a young boy by the name of James Leininger.

From a very early age, James was always fascinated with airplanes and the South Pacific. He possessed an unusually extensive knowledge of WWII fighter planes, so much so his parents called it an obsession. I don't mean to give a spoiler alert, but I think you know where this past life story is heading. It's the exact path that the astonished parents of James were led down. Let's follow the journey that brought these two parents into the life of a deceased Navy pilot.

James Leininger was born to loving parents, Andrea and Bruce, and raised in a traditional American household, nothing odd about that. However, as James grew older, some highly unusual things began to occur. His parents noticed James only played with his toy airplanes, in fact he had a particular fascination with crashing them, so much so their furniture became covered with gouges and scratches. The toddler would conduct preflight inspections of his toy planes with unusually advanced knowledge of jet fighters. At first his mother found it adorable, but one day when she commented on a "bomb" on the underside of a toy plane, the tiny child quickly corrected her, calling it by its proper name - a "drop tank." His mom began to recognize his knowledge of planes wasn't merely a child's imagination at work and wondered how a boy so young could know such specifics.

With their curiosities piqued, James' parents begin to pay more attention to their son and logged what they thought was unexplained behavior. In one instance, James named his G.I. Joe dolls Leon, Walter, and Billie. When his father asked about the names James told him, *"because they greeted me when I went to heaven."* The first time Andrea cooked meatloaf for James, he told her that *"he hadn't had meatloaf since he was on the Natoma Bay,"* which struck her as an odd thing for a child to say. His father took James to the Cavanaugh Flight Museum in Addison, Texas where he was mesmerized by the planes. James kept wandering back to the World War II section and wouldn't leave for hours. When Bruce finally tried to take James from the exhibit, the boy started to cry. To calm him, Bruce bought James a Blue Angels Navy flight demonstration videotape, which James played so much he practically wore it out.

The strange behavior took a turn for the worst when James began having regular nightmares in which he'd scream out, "*Airplane crash on fire, little man can't get out.*" The nightmares grew out of control with the young child violently kicking and screaming almost nightly. Concerned for their son's wellbeing, Bruce and Andrea began talking with James about his dream to try to repress them. James told them astonishing details about "his" plane and events that led up to its crash. He described the plane he flew as a "*Corsair that flew off of the Natoma,*" and that they had problems with the Corsair getting flat tires. He spoke of getting shot down by the Japanese after taking off from a ship on the water. When Andrea asked the name of the pilot her son simply replied, "*James.*" Later, James told his stunned parents the name of a fellow pilot, '*Jack Larsen.*' Then one day James was sitting on his father's lap who was thumbing through a book on the South Pacific. As Bruce turned a page, James suddenly burst out pointing to a map and yelled, "*Daddy, that is where my plane was shot down.*" The map the child pointed to was of Iwo Jima.

The astonishing details recounted by their son sent Bruce on an investigation of his own, mostly to prove to himself it was all just a series of bizarre coincidences. What he uncovered instead altered his perception of the world. During his exhaustive research, Bruce discovered in U.S. military records a World War II fighter pilot named James who was part of an elite special squadron. His full name was Lt.

James McCready Huston Jr. Bruce found a photo of Lt. Huston standing beside his plane and sure enough the plane was a Corsair fighter jet.

Bruce also learned from a retired pilot who also flew the Corsair that the tires were in fact prone to blowouts on landing. Digging deeper Bruce confirmed that Lt. Huston was stationed in the Pacific Ocean during World War II for five months during which time he flew off an aircraft carrier named U.S.S. Natoma Bay. Interviews with Navy vets stationed on the Natoma Bay verified they were served meatloaf regularly and that Lt. Huston did fly with a fighter pilot named Jack Larson.

In official military Aircraft Action Reports, Bruce found that James Huston was shot down on March 3, 1945 at the age of 21 during a special strike mission in Futami Ko Harbor near the island of Iwo Jima. According to U.S. Pacific Fleet records, 21 men were lost from the Natoma Bay. Among the fatalities were three pilots who flew with Huston's squadron - Lt. **Leon** Stevens Conner, Ensign **Walter** John Devlin and Ensign **Billie** Rufus Peeler...the angels who greeted James Leininger on his way to heaven and names of his G.I. Joe dolls. For Bruce, his research corroborated all that his son recounted, but it gave no clue as to how this young child could possibly know the life details of a man who lived over 50 years prior. Everything his son spoke of - the Natoma aircraft carrier, Jack Larson, the Corsair fighter plane, his fellow pilots, being shot over Iwo Jima, even the meatloaf - were all real!

Bruce couldn't overlook the stunning accuracies and write them off as simply coincidental. He pushed further and discovered James Huston's sister, Anne, was still alive. Bruce contacted Anne and explained his son's experiences. Over time they formed a friendly relationship and Anne sent James photos of her brother, along with several of his personal artifacts which became treasured keepsakes for James. Anne went on to declare, "*This child couldn't know the things he does – he just couldn't – so I believe he is somehow a part of my brother.*" She also wondered, "*There must be a reason for it, but I have no hint of what it could be. It's some phenomenon that I don't understand.*" This unknown phenomenon that Anne simply couldn't understand is not all that mystical. In fact, nearly 67% of the world's population and 100% of the readers of this book know precisely what this phenomenon is…reincarnation.

You have to admit whatever your stance on reincarnation, this really is quite a fascinating case. As with the Dalai Lama example, let's analyze this one. It's important to get into the habit of thinking through the underpinning of 'paranormal' incidents. In this case, the two intersecting lives are James Leininger and James Huston, one a 5-year-old child living in Louisiana, the other a WWII fighter pilot who died in 1945. It's incumbent to ask yourself how it's possible that this young child could know such specific details of James Huston's life.

It's not as though the boy provided details of a famous historical figure, say George Washington, which could have many different explanations. One might speculate the child somehow learned details of Washington subliminally and later recalled them from his subconscious mind. You could argue that perhaps the boy heard a documentary as an infant. However, this argument doesn't hold up for the Leininger's case. James Huston was not a public figure. There were no documentaries made about him, public or private, that the boy could have inadvertently overheard. The life details specific to WWII fighter pilot James Huston were known only to him, his immediate family, and fellow pilots, none of whom were known to the Leiningers.

Following another argument, you could claim that James's memories were imbued in him through cellular memories, or etched into his DNA, as we have seen previously with organ recipients. However, neither Bruce nor Andrea were related to the Huston family in any manner, which pretty much dispels this argument. Maybe you're not willing to make the leap to reincarnation but are open to lend credence to an immortal soul. And from that belief argue that it is the soul of James Huston who is communicating with the young boy from the spiritual realm. The child being so young isn't capable of understanding the spiritual communications and believes the messages from the other side are of his life. OK, that's a credible argument. However, to accept as an explanation for this case you also have to accept the reality of a spiritual realm in which souls exist and are able to communicate with the physical realm. If the soul of James Huston knows details of James Huston's physical life, you must accept that souls can incarnate at least once, which makes the step to believing souls can incarnate more than once isn't much of a leap.

Whatever your approach to analyzing this fascinating case, please be sure that you draw a conclusion on how you believe a 5-year-old child could know what he did about a deceased WWII fighter pilot. As I've repeated over and over, YOU are the one who should determine your belief system using your own critical thoughts and reasoning. I've told you that there are millions of examples of reincarnation from every walk of life. Reincarnation is not bound by age, race, gender, ethnicity, religion, geography, nor any other barrier. So, let's look at a case that transcends cultural and continental boundaries. For our next incident we'll be jetting off to India to meet a child named Titu Singh.

As with the previous case, this one also involves a young boy. When we learned about a soul taking possession of a body in Chapter 6, we also learned about the 'overlay' effect, in which fresh traumas can be carried over by the soul and influence the new body. If you recall, I drew the analogy of reflexes you form when driving a certain car for an extended period. Everything about the vehicle becomes a reflective instinct – where you grab for the emergency break, the instrument panel, wipers, radio, etc. Your body becomes programmed. Then when you drive a different car whose interior has a different configuration; those old reflexes carry into the new vehicle. Suddenly you find yourself grabbing for an emergency brake that isn't there or reaching to turn on the radio that happens to be the A/C fan. This continues until your body adjusts to the new car's configuration. The same thing happens when a soul enters a new vehicle after 'driving' one for an extended period. This soul overlay takes time to adjust to the new body and is most prominent in the first 5 years of life. As a result, past life influences are more pronounced with young children.

Back to India where I'll introduce you to a little boy named Titu. Now, Titu was not like other children his age. When he was only 2 ½-years-old, and just learning to talk, he began speaking of some rather extraordinary things. The defiant child insisted his mother was not in fact his real mother, and that Titu wasn't his real name. The boy maintained his real name was Suresh Verma, that he owns a video store in the town of Agra with his wife, Uma, and two children. Initially his mother placated to the little boy's wild imagination, but as the child revealed more details and grew stronger in his conviction, the mom came to recognize there was more than childhood imagination at play.

His mother listened more intently to her son who went on to reveal that in his life as Suresh, he was shot and killed while sitting in his car, his body was cremated, and the ashes thrown in the river. Unable to contain the child's demands to visit his 'real' family, the mother acquiesced and brought her son to the small town of Agra.

As she drove into town, she came upon a video shop named "Suresh Radio." She entered the shop in a state of astonishment, where she was greeted by the shop owner, a widow named Uma. After a brief conversation, Uma confirmed that her husband had been shot, cremated, and his ashes thrown in the river. The mother explained to Uma the stories her son had told, and Uma agreed to meet the boy. When Titu entered the shop, he correctly identified changes Uma had made to the shop since the death of her husband. Looking out the shop window Titu saw a group of kids playing in the street, and properly identified 'his' two children among them. But what really stunned Uma was when Titu told her the details of their first date, where it occurred and the specific honey sweets he had given her. Uma knew instantly this child could not have known this information and became convinced she was being visited by the reincarnated soul of her former husband.

As Titu and Uma stayed in touch and talked about his life as Suresh, the issue of the unsolved murder came up. Titu went on to describe how he was sitting in his car after arriving home from work one night, when a man approached and shot him in the head. Not only did Suresh's autopsy report confirm the boy's story, but it also provided evidence from the spiritual realm. The autopsy detailed the exact size and location of the bullet's entry and exit wounds on Suresh's head, which matched precisely where Titu had indicated. Even more astonishing the entry wound coincided exactly with a round, indented birthmark on Titu's head, and the exit wound coincided with a second protruding birthmark on the opposite side of Titu's head. The child's two birthmarks aligned exactly with the entry and exit wounds from Suresh's autopsy report. Titu then revealed the name of his murderer, a businessman named Sedick Johaadien, which was provided to the police. When they presented the man with the details of the crime, Johaadien confessed to the murder. Talk about karma coming back to get you!

If this story doesn't make you leap from your chair and say, *"Holy crap!,"* you need to check for a pulse! This is truly an incredible case that is very challenging to explain as anything but reincarnation. The specific details this child knew about his former life, verified and corroborated by numerous people, police, and autopsy reports, should make even the most hardened skeptic open to the realities of reincarnation.

So far, you've seen some pretty convincing evidence and we've only scratched the surface. There are thousands and thousands of past life cases to scrutinize, each with their own astounding details. Obviously, we're not going to look at thousands of cases, but we're not done yet. In the previous section I presented a list of attributes that can be related to past life trauma, if you recall, unusual birthmarks made the list. Titu's case exemplifies this phenomenon, as will the next case. And if you thought Titu's story was astonishing, this next one is just as amazing.

This case centers on an adult, a hero of sorts, named Jeffrey Keene. It's one of the more convincing cases of reincarnation I've seen, since it includes physical evidence and remembered memories that were not brought about through hypnotic regression. Jeffery's amazing journey is documented in his book, *"Someone Else's Yesterday,"* which I recommend if you're interested in learning more of this highly unusual story.

Jeffrey is a retired Assistant Fire Chief from Westport, Connecticut, and his story goes back to a series of uncanny events that opened his eyes to the realities of reincarnation. In the

Jeffrey Keene

Spring of 1991, Jeffery took a vacation with his wife in Maryland where they visited the site of a Civil War battle known as the Battle of Sunken Road. Jeffrey had an overwhelming desire to visit this site. Walking through the battlefield Jeffrey suddenly became wracked with an intense and inexplicable wave of anxiety, grief, sadness, and anger. He was consumed by emotion and for no reason collapsed and began crying uncontrollably. He gasped for air finding it difficult to breathe. After the wave of anxiety lifted, it left him confused and disoriented. Jeffrey regained his composure and kept the incident to himself. However, before leaving he purchased a Civil War book from the battlefield's gift shop.

John B. Gordon
Confederate General
Army of N. Virginia

Returning home, he tried to forget the incident and tucked the Civil War book out of sight in a dresser drawer but try as he might the experience kept weighing on his mind. For reasons he didn't understand at the time, it caused him to reflect on another incident that happened a few years prior. He would later discover the alarming connection. On Jeffrey's 30th birthday he was hit with an intense burning pain. It began in his jaw, ran down through his neck and into his shoulder. With his EMT training Jeffrey feared he was having a heart attack and rushed himself to the emergency room. Doctors examined the firefighter and ran an EKG, but it showed no signs of heart problems. Jeffery was released with nothing physically wrong despite the burning sensations he felt in his neck and jaw. Unable to find answers to the pain, Jeffery again put the incident behind him. Then a year and a half after his experience at Sunken Road, the answer surfaced. Jeffery decided to finally look at the Civil War book he filed away in a drawer. As he thumbed through the book, he turned to a page that featured a picture of General John Gordon, who fought at the battle of Sunken Road. Jeffrey found himself in stunned silence. In his own words, Jeffrey states, *"I knew the face of General John Gordon quite well…I shave it every morning."*

General John Gordon Jeffrey Keene

The above photo is not a picture of Jeffrey Keens at a costume party, but rather it's an actual photo of General John Gordon. The same photo that left Jeffrey breathless. Imagine flipping through a book about a war that took place over a century ago and finding a picture of yourself in it. That's how Jeffrey felt when he made this discovery. Their likeness is truly astonishing. In side-by-side comparisons you can see how closely they match. The shape of the head, the hair line, the eye sockets, jaw line, the bridge of the nose, even the personal choice of facial hair. If you didn't know better, you'd say these two were separated at birth…or in this case, reconnected at birth!

But the physical likeness isn't the only extraordinary events in this case. What Jeffrey was about to learn helped answer many mysteries that had disrupted his life. He learned that General Gordon did in fact fight in the Civil War battle at Sunken Road. During that battle he incurred multiple gunshot wounds and nearly died in the very spot Keene was stricken with uncontrolled anxiety.

He also discovered when General Gordon was 30, he was shot in the face and the bullet traveled through his neck and out his shoulder. Precisely the same path of the burning pain Jeffrey experienced on his 30th birthday. As Keene dug deeper into the life of General Gordon, he noticed a zigzag scar on General Gordon's face that matched a similar zigzag scar on his own face. Additionally, Keene has three other markings on his face in the same locations where General Gordon was wounded: under the left eye, on the forehead, and across the right cheek.

Being convinced that he once fought in the Civil War as Confederate General Gordon wasn't the end for Jeffrey Keene. The further he dug into his life as General Gordon, the more supernatural the story became. Keene found other Confederate soldiers who served with General Gordon. The first was Confederate General Cadmus Wilcox, who Keene noticed resembled someone very close to him, fellow Westport firefighter Wayne Zaleta.

But, don't take Jeffrey's his word for Wayne's resemblance to General Wilcox, decide for yourself. The photo on the left is of General Wilcox, the photo on the right is firefighter Wayne Zaleta.

General Cadmus Wilcox Firefighter Wayne Zaleta

It still doesn't end there. Keene also found a photo of Union General Wesley Merrit who served along with General Gordon, who Keene recognized as another contemporary serving with him, firefighter Rob Yost. After comparing their photos, you can begin to understand how the lines between Jeffrey Keene's past and present became blurred.

Union General Wesley Merritt Firefighter Rob Yost

Jeffrey Keene's story is a remarkable telling of a man, who through no prompting of his own, was led to discover a past life in which he fought in the Civil War as a Confederate General. It's also a story that introduces the phenomenon we touched upon in Chapter 7 of *'soul groups'* or *'soul families,'* where souls reincarnate as friends and family members in different lifetimes. In Jeffrey's life as a Confederate General, the men who put their lives at risk serving alongside him on the battlefield, were doing it again only in this lifetime they're at a fire station in Westport, Connecticut.

While there are thousands and thousands of incredible past life cases to explore, and I encourage you to research as many as you can, we'll only examine one more in this chapter. This one happens to fall close to home as it's a past life story involving yours truly. I've mentioned my fascination with the paranormal, spirituality, and consciousness since childhood, and that fascination has inspired many projects I developed and produced as a professional in the television business. One project I conceived was a reality show that would solve mysteries and enigmas in people's lives by looking into their past…not their childhood past, but their past lives. I called it "P. L. I.," for Past Life Investigators.

In the entertainment business, you used to be able to sit with a network executive, pitch them a concept, and they would be able to visualize it and order the show in the room. Well, those days are gone. In today's program development cycle, producers are forced to create elaborate presentations called '*sizzle reels*' that provide a visual representation of the show. To produce a quality sizzle reel, you must cast it with talent who will appear in the series, along with sample stories that help depict the show's core concept. It's like a movie trailer but only for television shows.

For my "P. L. I." sizzle reel, finding a past life regression therapist who was 'camera friendly' with an engaging personality and accurate past life hypno-regression experience took me over a year. Finally, after a long and arduous search I had found my host. Next step was to bring in some willing participants who were curious about their previous incarnations. I was looking specifically for individuals who had an unusual and unexplained phobia or obsession in their current life that we could resolve with past life therapy. So, we put out a casting call and the flood gates opened.

We sifted through many candidates with interesting tales of previous lifetimes, but none were wrought with a present-day mystery disrupting their life…until Karine showed up (not her real name by-the-way). Karine was different. Most people were coming in with common fears of snakes, heights, or water, or stories of love at first sight, but not

Karine. Her issue was one that we not only didn't ask for, it was a condition we had not even considered. Karine told us she suffered from severe migraines, that would strike without warning with such intensity she often found herself racing to the emergency room.

The first time it happened was a real scare, but after numerous occasions the ER doctors got to know her on a first name basis. Specialist after specialist were unable to find anything wrong. Drug after drug had no effect, and treatment after treatment did nothing to relieve her head-pounding pain. She explained in detail how the pain would start at the base of her neck and flow up engulfing her entire head, with a suffocating pressure that felt as though she was being crushed. It would cause waves of nausea, anxiety, and panic. Then, as quickly as it would develop, the pain would dissipate. Now, I had no idea how we could ever bring relief to what seemed to be a medical condition by digging into her past lives, but there was something about this woman I was drawn to. So, Karine became our first test case.

Having knowledge of Karine's condition, our host hypno-regressed her in an effort to bring her back to the lifetime that contributed to her migraines. Her entire regression was recorded with multiple high-def cameras and a full audio crew. Here's where the story really becomes wild. Karine immediately regressed to a life that she described in vivid detail. She was a 19-year-old girl living in 16th Century Belgium. Karine was able to describe the specifics of her home, her family, her clothing, her village in the north, the Dutch language she spoke, and the horrifying death she suffered during that lifetime. What was amazing to me was how Karine not only spoke and acted like a 19-year-old teen from northern Belgium, but she relived the emotional trauma of the events that took her life in a very real and dramatic way.

Karine told us that she was part of a small middle-class family, not poor but not wealthy either, and she was very close with her mother. She said what made her 'different' within this community was that she was very spiritual, not psychic, but she had a connection and understanding of consciousness that she spoke of freely. In that era and location, this type of talk was perceived as witchery and heretics against the church. When she refused to denounce her beliefs, she was formally accused of heresy. Her case was decided by a group of five men within the town, who among themselves determined her guilty of the crime and sentenced her to the mandated punishment – to be buried alive.

Karine then took us through the harrowing event, moment by moment, of the night her sentence was carried out. She talked about the velvet lined white dress she wore while at home with her family, and her scuffed black leather shoes. While enjoying the tranquility of the evening, the door to her home suddenly burst open and in walked five men dressed in black robes looking for Karine. She made herself known, and without explanation, the men forcefully grabbed her and dragged her from the house. Her last memories before being ripped from the house was looking into her mother's eyes and wondering with a deep sense of betrayal why she was not doing anything to protect her.

The five men dragged her to a nearby shallow grave, where a small wooden coffin barely her size sat. She was then hit on the back of her head with a solid blow from a metal object causing her to collapse. The men believed she was unconscious, but Karine claims she was well aware of events going on around her. They placed her inside the crudely made wooden coffin which she scarcely fit into and lowered it into the grave. Then without any lid on the coffin, the men began filling the grave one shovelful of dirt at a time.

While lying on the couch of our studio with cameras running, Karine began to relive this incident. With each pile of dirt tossed down on her, she felt a suffocating pressure. Her hands began to shake, and her heartbeat quickened. Her panic intensified as she cried out, *"They're burying me."* Her entire body began to tremble. I was getting nervous that we didn't have an EMT on site. Finally, in a quick and sudden flash, the trembling stopped, and Karine simply stated, *"I'm dead."* The entire regression session was quite surreal to me. I wasn't sure if what I just witnessed was an actual incident her soul experienced back in 16th Century Belgium, or the entire thing was a figment of her imagination. Regardless, I was certain what we captured was great television!

With a successful past life regression 'in the can,' we proceeded to the next phase of the show – bringing in a historical expert to verify facts presented during the regression. We brought in a history professor from a prominent local university who had a Ph. D in history, specializing in medieval European religion. When we first presented him with our findings, he felt we had gotten our facts messed up. He explained that Belgium at this time spoke French, not Dutch, velvet was an expensive fabric for the time and not available in this region, and burial by death was not a punishment for heretics. He was aware of instances where people were burned at the stake, hung, imprisoned, or executed in other ways, but not buried alive. When we finally revealed how we obtained these facts, he couldn't contain his laughter. However, we were paying him for his research, so off he went to prove his case and us the fools.

About 2 weeks went by and the history professor returned to our office with his research report. Gone from his face was the smirk he left with. One by one he stepped through the facts revealed during Karine's regression. He began by showing us photos retrieved from a museum in Europe of black leather shoes from 16th Century Belgium fitting the description Karine gave. Next, he showed us paintings from the era depicting women wearing the same white dress Karine described. He explained that he initially thought the expensive velvet fabric was unavailable in northern Belgium, but he proved himself wrong when he discovered the fabric was indeed being produced locally in that region. He told us it would have been highly unlikely for a family of her means to obtain enough velvet to piece together an entire dress, but it was common for middle-class women during that time to instead line portions of their garments with velvet, just as Karine has described. He also confirmed that while French was the language spoken in the southern parts of Belgium, Dutch was spoken widely in the North. Now, all of this can be determined on your own, it doesn't provide concrete evidence of this past life. It becomes a bit more intriguing when the woman who provided the information had never been to northern Belgium, and certainly was not a scholar of 16th Century Europe. But the professor's next discovery really added credibility to our case.

After extensive research, he was able to find a very specific edict issued by Charles V of Netherlands that ordered men who committed heretics against the Church to be *"killed by the sword,"* and women who committed the same crime to be *"buried alive."* This discovery even surprised the professor, who then expanded his search and found a documented case of a woman who was buried alive for heresy against the church - Anneken Vanden Hove. She was buried alive in southern Netherlands (now Belgium) on 19 July 1597! While we don't believe Karine was the reincarnation of Anneken Vanden Hove, the details of Hove's persecution and burial for identical crimes corroborate Karine's story, down to the black robes of the men conducting the burial described during the regression (see Figure 20). We were also informed that women were placed in crudely made wooden boxes as it was believed this would contain the evil presence within them. Finally, regarding the men dressed in black, the professor initially believed that clergy didn't conduct this type of trial and execution. However, a religious diary was found that provided firsthand accounts of various executions committed by clergymen serving under Charles V.

Figure 20 - Burial alive of Anneke van den Hove, Brussels, 1597
Engraving by Jan Luiken. Source: Rijksmuseum.

Needless to say, we were all blown away by the professor's findings. He left thanking us for including him in what he now called a truly fascinating case. All we had left to do was present Karine with the findings and capture her reaction. Now, if there weren't enough twists and turns in this story for you, hold on to your stomachs, we're about to go through an inverted double-corkscrew!

We sat Karine down and revealed all the historical facts that corroborated her story. We also spoke about the physical evidence of the incident, for example how the blow on the back of her head just prior to her burial correlated with the trigger point of her migrates. The suffocating pressure, anxiety and nausea matched symptoms she experienced during the burial. We even showed her the video of her regression reliving this experience, all with the hopes of somehow mitigating the intensity of her migraines. She stared at us in what we thought was stunned disbelief, but what she was about to tell us spoke of a different emotion.

As she wiped tears from her eyes, she revealed what none of us expected, not even herself. You see, this lifetime wasn't being revealed to Karine to address the physical aspects of her migraines, but rather the emotional implications, which as it turned out were even more damaging. Karine proceeded to tell us about her daughter, a beautiful and caring young woman full of energy and compassion. She volunteered with the Peace Corp and was doing philanthropic work with impoverished communities in Columbia. She went out for a hike near a powerful river, slipped and fell in. Her body was never found.

Since losing her daughter, Karine carried the weight of a thousand lifetimes of guilt for not being able to save her daughter. Learning of her past life in Belgium, reminded her of the betrayal she felt as her mother watched helplessly while she was being dragged to her shallow grave. This deep sense of betrayal remained with her soul to this lifetime. Experiencing the same helplessness as a mother and connecting these two incidents on a spiritual level caused a powerful release of guilt, which Karine later discovered was the trigger of her migraines. She soon began to cope with the repressed guilt and found the migraines not only reduced in intensity, but also in frequency.

Well, we're not quite done with this story. Once Karine had composed herself after going through a myriad of emotions, I asked her a question from out of the blue. I wanted to know if there was anyone who she recognized from her life in northern Belgium, who is a figure in her life today. Her jaw fell to the floor and the blood drained from her face. I thought, *"Oh no, what did I step into now!"* She stuttered and stammered through a couple of incoherent sentences until finally admitting that,

"Yes, there was someone...You!" "Me! What!" All I could think was, *"I'm just trying to create great television, why do you have to pull me into all this. I'm supposed to remain behind the camera!"*

She went on to explain that I was one of the five men dressed in black robes who stormed into her house and participated in the burial. Wow! I didn't see that one coming! I tried to deny everything, *"But, I don't even own a black robe!"* It was no use, I was being outed some 4 ½ centuries later! It really floored me and now I was the one carrying the guilt. What she then explained struck me as a message coming from a source beyond Karine, perhaps wisdom from the spiritual dimension. Karine looked me in the eyes and calmly said that I was meant to find and help her in this lifetime to correct the injustice I did in a previous life. Boy, karma sure is a bitch, and I discovered there's no statues of limitations on it! But in the end, I had my show, Karine had her life back, and we both had cleansed some serious karma. Don't worry, we'll be learning all about karma in the next chapter.

That about wraps it up for our scrutiny of past life cases. We've only examined a few, in fact you can count on one hand the number of cases we looked at, unless of course you joined an organized crime syndicate and lost a pinkie in the process. There are thousands and thousands of intriguing, dramatic, and equally inexplicable cases of past lives if you feel the need for further evidence.

Now, the challenge I presented at the beginning of this section was to draw a conclusion based on evidence presented. Remember, you're a detective. This is life-altering evidence you've been given, don't simply read it and think *"Hmmm, interesting,"* and then go about life as usual. This is one of those earth-shattering moments that I'm pushing you to seize. It's the detective equivalent of investigating a crime scene and being told the victim died of suicide. Then you arrive on the scene to discover a shotgun blast to the back of the victim's head that's impossible to be self-inflicted. As the lead detective you look at the shotgun evidence and say, "*Hmm, interesting. Oh well, I guess it was a suicide after all.*" These cases are the shotgun blast to the back of the head of cultural norms ridiculing and mocking reincarnation. You've just seen evidence indicating that things aren't as you've been told. So, take the challenge and develop a conclusive answer to where you fall on the realities of reincarnation…it truly is a subject that can change your entire outlook on life.

Connected Souls

Before we conclude our research on reincarnation and past lives, I'd like to touch upon a subject that is relevant to both – soulmates. You hear the term '*soulmate*' typically being used as a romantic expression of true love. In social media it's common to find cute postings of kittens with the message "*Friends yesterday. Lovers today. Soulmates forever,*" or expressions indicating your soulmate is "*Not one you can see yourself with, it's the one you can't see yourself without.*" While these deeply sentimental expressions may appeal to the pursuers of romance, the spiritual meaning of a soulmate is something completely different. Soulmates on a spiritual level are not simply a saccharine coated relationship that develops between two people with similar interests. Spiritually speaking, we have many different soulmates, each of whom serve a different purpose. Soulmates are not just romantic partners, but rather any soul originating from your soul family. In any one lifetime, you will meet multiple soulmates.

In the physical world we associate with certain groups, souls also belong to and associate with a specific group of souls in the spiritual realm. Your soulmates have been associated with your soul family since their creation. Every soul family contains souls at higher levels of knowledge and evolution who serve as teachers or spiritual guides. Soulmates from these families incarnate with one another and assume meaningful roles in each other's lives on Earth. We saw an example of this in the past life case of Jeffrey Keene, and with my incident with Karine.

Soulmates are souls with similar vibrational frequency, originating from the same soul family, who enter your life in many different capacities – siblings, parents, cousins, close friends, colleagues, and yes, sometimes as lovers. We learned in Chapter 7 that when you incarnate there are specific life lessons you set out to achieve. Soulmates are souls who have incarnated alongside you to help you learn those lessons and achieve your evolutionary objectives. They can come into your life for a brief period or be a lifelong companion. Sometimes it can be as innocuous as bumping into a stranger on the street. However, unlike the amorous connotations, a spiritual soulmate doesn't always enter your life under romantic auspices. Sometimes a soulmate is an individual who forces you to question things, pushes your buttons, disrupts your reality. Regardless of how a soulmate enters your life, their participation is always done out of spiritual love and there's always something for your soul to learn from them. Soulmates are a necessary part of your purpose in this physical lifetime.

A soulmate from your soul family who forms a deep, long-lasting partnership, such as a spouse, sibling, or parent, is known as a *'Primary Soulmate.'* These are people who become your best friends, confidants, and loyal supporters. They're very important relationships who you connect with on a deep level. Another type of soulmate is called a *'Companion Soulmate'* or *'Kindred Spirit.'* They are also from your soul family, but in your physical life they don't serve as deep and long-lasting a relationship. They are still influential people who teach certain life lessons. Typically, a companion soulmate will be a family member who you don't communicate with on a regular basis, friends who served an important role at one point in your life who you've since lost contact with, or teachers and advisors who helped you overcome a specific hardship. Whether a primary or companion soulmate, they all bring exactly what is needed to experience a karmic lesson in your life.

What does this mean for the vast number of people who come in and out of your life on a regular basis? How do you know if the person you just met is simply another soul in the physical school of life, or if it's a soulmate sent for a specific purpose that you just blew off! Well, unfortunately, nobody is going to walk up to you and say, *"Hey, guess what? I'm one of your soulmates and this is our karmic lesson for the day!."* However, you can train yourself to tune-in to the intuitive connection your body feels when in the presence of a soulmate. During your life-between-lives, your soul spends a lot of time analyzing its next incarnation. Part of this process includes seeing people your soul will encounter including those from your soul family. When you do meet a soulmate in the physical realm, you connect with their energy frequency on the super-conscious level. There's an intuitive 'knowing' that comes with meeting a soulmate, which you can train your body to pick up on. Being in touch with your energy body through meditation and an awareness of your chakras will help heighten this sense.

The people with whom we share our lives have something to teach us, just as we have for them. The lessons are countless, involving issues such as jealousy, greed, arrogance, intolerance, compassion, allegiance, power, trust, honesty, commitment, failure, etc. For these lessons, our soulmates assume many different roles of a 'teacher' and bestow lesson upon us. Bear in mind, you're not always the students in Earth's classroom. You also act as an instructor providing your own lessons to souls from your soul family. It's a two-way street of knowledge interchange. Each interaction serves a purpose to your experience. Life is not just an accidental hodge-podge of unrelated events. All the chaos and craziness does serve a purpose. You may not understand that purpose as you are thrust in the center of life's whirlwind, feeling like all the universe is working against you, but there is a beautiful and meaningful purpose to your life.

Each person is a soul having a different experience, and each soul has a different level of soul consciousness. Young souls who are relatively new to the physical realm arrive with a certain innocence and naivete of the physical dimension. For their own protection, young souls incarnate into simpler lives with limited risk and human challenges. Perhaps a life in a remote area that is rudimentary and basic as the soul becomes familiar with the densities and experiences of Earth. Over time and through various lives and lessons, the soul becomes more adept and aware of the connection between the spiritual body and the physical body. It begins to take on lives with more responsibilities and hardships knowing the soul can handle them. In many circumstances the soul's evolutionary benefit is directly proportional to the hardships experienced in the physical world. A soul needs to be more advanced to handle these hardships.

So, the next time you stare into the eyes of someone leading a life of challenge, regardless of their social standing, keep in mind you may be peering into the window of an extremely wise soul. A homeless person begging in the street may very well be a spiritual master who took on this life of destitute to experience the virtues of humility, lack, or generosity. When you do look into those eyes, will you see the beauty of a wise soul?

Every morning, when you wake up to a new day, be grateful for the opportunity to experience the magnificent school of the physical world and all the rich lessons it provides that feed your soul the nutrients it needs to grow and evolve. Embrace joyfully the knowledge you are learning and show gratitude for this opportunity.

We've spent the past few chapters learning quite a bit about the spiritual realm and how it interacts with the physical world. In fact, I've discussed the spiritual realm as though it were a fait accompli. But is it? If the spiritual realm were a genuine dimension, like the physical dimension we are so certain of, would there also be rules and laws that govern it? After all, there are many physical laws that govern our world. Try standing under a grand piano dropped from a 5-story window, and the law of gravity will play a very sour note on your head! Which brings us to ask, are there similar Universal laws that apply to the spiritual realm? That's an interesting thought. What are the laws of the spiritual realm and how are they applied? Hmmm, looks as though we just stumbled upon a new subject to explore.

Ch. 9: Bound by Laws

"The entire Universe is conspiring to give you everything you want." - Abraham-Hicks

Throw the Book At 'Em!

I hope you had fun journeying into a past dating back long before the day you were born. Now that we've examined past lives, let's take a deeper look at the life you are leading today and all the rules and laws you are bound by. Like every great rebel, the first thing we'll do before digging into rules and laws is to break one! Now that we're swimming in the deep end of the spiritual pool, I'll spare you the traditional recap and dive straight into this chapter's subject – rules! I know, we're really living life in the fast lane.

Like it or not we live in a world defined by rules. Rules of many different distinctions. There are benign rules like don't eat before swimming, don't serve red wine with fish, never wear vertical and horizontal stripes together, and of course the big rule of social etiquette never stir your tea clockwise (it should be in a back and forth motion)!

All kidding aside, we really do live in a world that is governed by rules and laws. When you stop and think about it, there is virtually nothing in the physical world that isn't in some way governed or regulated by a law. It may sound crazy but stop and think about it and you'll see exactly how many rules and regulations dictate your life. Take walking for instance, you'd think something as natural as putting one foot in front of the other would be free from laws, but there are plenty of pedestrian laws dictating how, when and where you can walk, run, skip, and hop. And of course, we all know the cardinal rule about running with scissors.

What about eating? FDA has that covered with thousands of laws and regulations defining what you can and can't eat, what goes into your food, and nutritional information that must be displayed on the packaging. We have housing laws dictating where and how you can build your house. Traffic laws governing how to operate your vehicle. FAA that defines how to travel. Social services that specify how to raise a family. SBA for how to conduct your business. SEC to regulate publicly traded companies, and of course the IRS to enforce how much of your hard-earned money goes to the government.

The federal government alone has over 430 departments, agencies, and sub-agencies that pump out regulations and laws each and every year. Add to that state, county, and local agencies and you begin to understand just how voluminous these governing rules and laws truly are. Most are common-sense laws to protect the safety and well-being of society, but when it's all said and done, there are hundreds of thousands of laws defining every tiny aspect of life. In fact, the average person in America breaks 3 laws a day without even knowing it. Yikes, that's over a thousand a year! I suppose next time I get a parking ticket I should be grateful for the 999 tickets I got away with...

With all these laws, some outrageous ones somehow got passed along the way and oddly enough remain on the books. Did you know that in North Carolina it's against the law to have a Bingo Game lasting more than 5 hours? In Connecticut its forbidden to walk across the street on your hands. Women in Vermont must obtain written permission from their husbands to wear false teeth. In Florida, you must pay the parking meter if you tie an elephant to it, and don't drive in Massachusetts with a gorilla in the backseat of your car or you'll be violating state law! These goofy laws didn't just magically appear as legal statues and codes; groups of well-intending public servants came together, discussed and analyzed them at length, then memorialized them in convoluted legalese to be enforced. It really makes you wonder who are these brain trusts that oversee our wellbeing.

Despite the absurdity of some laws, what they have in common is they are all man-made. We can change them, amend them, abolish them, violate them, and create new ones. However, there are some laws which we don't have quite as many options called *Universal Laws.* For instance, there's the *Law of Growth and Abundance* that states in nature everything innately grows in size and number. A seed grows to a tree, a tadpole grows to a frog, one sunflower can produce an abundance of seeds, a sea turtle can produce an abundance of offspring, etc. There's also the *Universal Law of Circulation* that says nature is in a constant state of circulation. Plants grow with the aid of minerals, animals eat plants, animals die and decompose in the soil leaving behind minerals that plants use to grow. Water in a lake evaporates, becomes vapor particles in the air, accumulates as storm clouds, falls as rain, runs into a lake to evaporate again...it's the whole circle of life theory. And of course, we can't overlook the Universal Law that probably impacts us the most...*Murphy's Law* stating that if something can go wrong it will!

Now, we can't forget about the matriarch who has her own set of laws that preside our world...Mother Nature. Her laws go beyond "clean your room!" to define the constitution of the physical world. Some of the greatest thinkers and scientists over the centuries have discovered these laws and developed mathematical formulas to express them. Sir

Isaac Newton's groundbreaking work defined laws of motion that explain gravity and the forces that act on bodies in motion. You may have even heard some of Newton's theories, like *"a body in motion (or at rest) will remain in motion (or at rest) unless acted on by an external force,"* or perhaps, *"for every action there's an equal and opposite reaction."* Newton isn't alone in defining Natural Laws, there are many, many others.

For instance, Blaise Pascal came up with a discovery back in the mid-1600s that lead to his very own law of fluid mechanics called *Pascal's Law*. This mathematical equation is used to calculate a change in pressure of an enclosed fluid and has become the basis for hydraulic machines today. Later an English physicist named Robert Hooke joined the ranks by discovering a law that applies to the tension strength of springs. *Hooke's Law* is still used widely today from wind effects on tall buildings to the vibrations of guitar strings. Working with gases in fluctuating volumes, chemist Robert Boyle got his law when he devised an equation to calculate how gas pressure changes in proportion to the volume of its container. And, we can't leave out astronomer Johannes Kepler, who expressed the planet's orbital patterns around the sun in what came to be known as *Kepler's Laws of Planetary Motion*.

There's the *Law of Conservation of Energy* stating energy can neither be created nor destroyed, which you should be familiar with by now. Even Graham has a Law that states when acted upon by toasted marshmallows and melted chocolate, a Graham cracker reconstitutes into a Smore! Ha! Just making sure you're paying attention. Actually, *Graham's Law* applies to the effusion rates of gas. With Nature being as grand as it is, you can imagine the sheer volume of natural laws. There are Laws of Thermodynamics, Electro-Magnetics, Mechanics, Fluid Dynamics, Chemistry, and all sorts of wonderfully complicated laws of physics and quantum mechanics. They've all been devised, tested, and proven by minds far superior to mine, but the one thing they all have in common is they are descriptive and mathematical equations that define how the physical world operates.

So, you see, we DO operate under many, many different rules and laws. Some have been created by humanity, others by Mother Nature. Which raises an interesting question, if the physical world is governed by so many laws, what about the spiritual dimension? If the spiritual dimension is just as real as the physical, does it get a free pass on rules and regulations? Is the soul absolved from abiding by laws?

Unfortunately, there is no "Get Out of Jail Free" card once you enter the spiritual realm. There are rules and regulations governing the spiritual dimension you'll have to follow just like everyone else. But the good news is spiritual laws are much less convoluted and FAR fewer. Spiritual laws are natural in concept but abiding by them is an entirely different story. It's important to understand that despite living in the physical world governed by thousands of man-made and natural laws, we also have a spiritual component. Whether we consciously know it or not, that spiritual component is bound by spiritual laws, even when incarnated in a physical body…like yours. Your physical life is inseparable from your spiritual life and vice versa. Like it or not, there's another set of laws governing your life that most people don't know about. These laws are much more powerful than any law written by man, or even Mother Nature, so it's probably a good policy to get to know them.

Spiritual Laws have been recorded and debated throughout time and in certain instances have been documented in texts like Hermetic and Cabalic writings. Early scholars and philosophers considered spiritual laws the foundation of life, yet popular culture has drifted to where most people are not only unfamiliar with these laws, they don't even know they exist! Of all the various spiritual laws, there are two that are so important I've dedicated an entire section to each. I call them the *Supreme Laws of the Soul*. They are the *Law of Attraction* and the *Law of Karma.* But, before we get into the meat and potatoes of those spiritual laws, I'll give a brief overview of other laws presiding over the spiritual dimension.

Let's begin with a Spiritual Law known as the *Law of Balance and Polarity.* This law essentially states that everything contains an opposite, nothing is one-sided. If there is light, there must also be dark. A positive charge has a negative charge. The polarity for happiness is sadness, prosperity is poverty, health is illness, etc. On a spiritual level, your soul's objective is to recognize, understand, and accept the Law of Polarity for it to achieve balance. This law gets enforced by assuring your soul experiences polarity in its many lives, so eventually it achieves balance and understanding. When you experience a lifetime of wealth and riches, you will also experience a life of poverty. If you are an oppressor in one life, you will need to experience a lifetime as a victim. It's important to note that polarity is not a punishment. As a spiritual being, you desire these experiences to compensate for your prior behavior and to balance your understanding, all in the name of spiritual evolution.

Another important spiritual law is the *Law of Vibration.* It states that anything existing in the Universe consists of pure energy resonating at a certain frequency. We've examined this law back in Chapter 3 when we investigated energy and learned that all matter, thoughts, and feelings have a unique vibrational frequency. This law comes into play with the Law of Attraction and its importance will become clear when we examine that law.

There's also a law known as the *Law of Rhythm,* which states the energy in the universe is like a pendulum. Whenever something swings to the right, it must then swing to the left. Everything flows, pulses, and moves. Tides flow in and out, the seasons come and go, everything is either growing or dying. The *Law of Gender* states that all things possess a masculine and feminine trait. Every person contains psychological characterizes of both male and female; likewise all things in the Universe, from matter, to plants, to animals also contain masculine and feminine characteristics. There's a spiritual law stating we live in a Universe of abundance. Most believe we live in a finite world of scarcity, but the *Law of Abundance* maintains it's one where abundance dominates. You will soon learn that every one of us has within ourselves everything needed to manifest the life of abundance we desire. The law that helps guide this principle is called the *Law of Chaos and Order.* This law is profound both in its simplicity and power. Simply stated, when you fight the flow of the Universe chaos results. However, when you embrace that which the Universe delivers, order ensues. This can be observed in the natural world where when left to its own devices operates in a state of ordered balance. Humanity operates from a belief that it must control all aspects of life, resulting in chaos to both the balance of nature and the balance of your happiness and wellbeing.

There's a law called the *Law of Universal Life* that states all forms contain life. It's not just the plant and animal kingdoms that contain life, according to the Law of Universal Life everything, from the sidewalks you trample across to the water in your toilet, everything contains life. OK, the toilet analogy is probably creating some disturbing imagery…how about we change that one! Let's go with…Everything, from the sidewalks you trample across to the Siachen Glacier on the Himalayan mountaintop…everything contains life. Animals, oceans, mountains, trees, flowers, buildings, Earth, the planets, the sun, the moon, stars, and galaxies – all contain life. In eastern cultures and Native American tribes, many pray and speak to the life, or souls, of all these material forms.

Rounding off the spiritual laws are the two powerhouses I refer to as the *Supreme Laws* - the *Law of Attraction* and the *Law of Karma.* Both are so powerful they effectively control your life, and all your future lives! It's a shame these life-altering laws are not openly taught side-by-side with Newton, Einstein, Faraday, and Kepler. This knowledge gives everyone the choice and ability to refine and master their life. When you are unaware of these laws and how they govern your life, inevitably you'll end up violating them just like the three municipal laws you violate every day without knowing. However, unlike man-made laws where violations are paid in the form of a fine or jail time, violation of these spiritual laws are paid with toil, heartache, and adversities. However, the beauty is when you become aware of them, you can use their power to your advantage. How's that for a great secret of the Universe! Wouldn't it be far more desirable to be in control of your life instead of reacting to it? The improper management of these spiritual powerhouses' result in your lives - past, present, and future – becoming equally mismanaged. Many life lessons get repeated over and over, throughout one lifetime and into another, simply because these fundamental spiritual laws are unknown and ignored. But today is different, because today is the day you will learn about these laws and how to gain control over them…well, assuming you continue reading that is! Let's take the first steps of shifting your life from autopilot into the captain's seat and charting a course with intent and purpose.

Law of Attraction

The first of the two Supreme Laws will strike you as very rudimentary in concept; however you'll soon see how very few have mastered it. The basis of this powerful spiritual law simply states, *"That which is likened to itself is drawn."* Another way of stating this is similar energies are inherently attracted to one another. It applies to energies of matter, spirit, and thought. Whatever you put out into the Universe will be reflected back to you. Whether you realize it or not, you attract into your life things you focus on most often, think about most intently, hold the strongest beliefs in, expect to occur on the deepest levels, and imagine most vividly. It's that simple. That which you are preoccupied with becomes your reality. Quite rudimentary, right? However, mastery of this law…not as simple. You could liken the Law of Attraction to playing chess. Understanding the basic movement of each piece is not that difficult, just some basic rules. However, learning the skills to master the movements of these 16 pieces around 64 squares to become a world class chess champion is a horse of a different color. But, don't let all this discourage you; with practice, patience, and a little diligence, you'll be one of those rare few who actively uses the Law of Attraction to invite all you desire into your life.

Let's start with the basics. I'm not much of a gambling man, but I'd bet the farm there are quite a few things taking place in your life right now that can be attributed to the Law of Attraction. Why am I so sure? The reason something occurs in your life is because you called it into action. You did so by believing in your heart and mind that it's what you deserve. It doesn't matter if you believe it consciously or subconsciously, the fact is, it occurred because of YOU and the powerful and irrevocable forces of the Law of Attraction.

One of the first steps in seizing control over this spiritual law is simply to understand its principle and accept fully that YOU are the one creating and manifesting your life. If you truly want to be in control of what enters your life – prosperity, peace, and happiness, or struggle, strife, and conflict – then accepting the Law of Attraction is an essential beginning. One of the most powerful factors with the Law of Attraction is the Universe doesn't know nor care if the thoughts you are thinking and beliefs you are believing are from your subconscious mind, your imagination, your observation, or your deliberate intention…it acts on all thoughts and beliefs equally without discretion. But beware…this beneficial aspect can also become a great adversary. Whether you deliberately focus and control your thoughts and beliefs, or they unintentionally preoccupy your mind, the Law of Attraction will respond to them and bring into existence that which your mind thinks and expects. It doesn't matter if your thoughts are positive or negative.

We learned in Chapter 4 that your thoughts are energy of different vibrational frequencies. We also learned of technologies that detect your thought energy and use them to control physical devices from video games to fighter jets. It's simply a scientific principle that as you think, you produce brain waves of different vibrational frequencies depending on what is racing through your mind. It's these vibrational thoughts that become the magnetic force of attraction that sets this spiritual law into action. If you believe the Universe has cursed you because nothing ever goes your way, every turn in life is plagued with trouble, drama, and conflict, then that's what will be attracted into your life. And if this describes you, it's very likely your mind has been preoccupied with negative thoughts and emotions for quite some time creating a self-perpetuating cycle.

Gaining understanding of this, acknowledging what comes into your life is of your doing, and taking proactive measures to change your thoughts and behaviors will bring about fundamental changes in what you attract. Simply by focusing on things that make you feel good, that fill you with loving feelings, will raise your vibrational thought frequency and alter your attractive forces. Whatever you think and feel, you bring into your life. Whatever you meditate upon, focus on, and believe in, you become. Contemplate and show love and appreciation for health, peace, harmony, and success, and you'll find these things manifesting in your life. However, if you dwell on thoughts of hate, envy, criticism, resent, ageing, illness, and struggle, and allow these thoughts to propagate and fester, then you will find these things manifesting in your life. It's that simple! What you are thinking and what enters your life are always a vibrational match. It's a powerful spiritual law and the basis of how the Law of Attraction works. I told you, it's a rather basic concept, right? Doesn't seem all that challenging to conquer does it? Of course not. That's the spirit. Now let's take that positive energy and jump into how you can proactively apply the Law of Attraction to your life.

You may not realize it, but the Law of Attraction cleverly sneaks its way into your life all the time. You even refer to it without knowing. For instance, when you use the expression *"Birds of a feather flock together,"* you are essentially paraphrasing the Law of Attraction. Or, when you make comments like, *"They're two peas in a pod," "We're on the same wavelength," "They're cut from the same cloth," "You reap what you sow,"* or *"Think Positive!"* These are all ways of expressing the belief that you attract what you think. And you do!

There are cute little rituals that set the principles of the Law of Attraction into motion. For example, have you ever made a wish before blowing out your birthday candles? How about wishing on a falling star? Or believing green M&M's bring prosperity? What about finding a four-leaf clover and think you're about to have a string of good luck? When I was young it was popular to carry a rabbit's foot for good luck. I remember as a kid I had a key chain with a real rabbit's foot attached, the furry little thing was even dyed red. I'd carry that rabbit's foot everywhere thinking as long as it was in my pocket luck was on my side. Imagine that. It sounds a bit ghastly to me now, but I carried it for years and I didn't even have any keys! Have you ever had a Thanksgiving tug-of-war with only a dried wishbone between you and your opponent? When it snaps the person with the larger piece is supposed to be granted a wish come true. Go figure. The dried bone from a turkey carcass now competes with the power of a magical genie in an oil lamp! Or, if you're an old schooler like me, you may still toss pennies into fountains making a wish as it flips through the air. All these rituals have one powerful thing in common, they can all work! But the magical power doesn't derive from a rabbit's foot, nor dried turkey bone, nor shiny penny, shooting star, birthday candles, nor four leave clovers. The real magic of all these rituals comes from YOU! And the powerful force of your mind. Because the strength of your belief in any of these rituals is equivalent to the strength of the force you activate with the Law of Attraction.

I'd like to share a little story that happened to me to help illustrate the power of the Law of Attraction and how it operates in the most unusual ways. At the time this event occurred, I wasn't even aware of this spiritual law, but when I reflect on this experience it shows itself as an illuminating example of the Universe flexing its muscles for me. Several years ago, I went through a divorce that left me in a state of emotional and financial collapse. My two children were 9 and 11 at the time and I did all I could to insulate them from the emotional trauma a divorce can inflict. I had moved out and gotten a nearby apartment, so the kids wouldn't feel as though they were living out of suitcases when they traveled between homes. It wore on me mentally since I had always seen my life playing out into its golden years with a family who had spent a lifetime together. All that came unwound and forced me to reconceive the second half of my life.

The confusion took its toll and had a profound effect on my work. Within a short period of time, my finances were running on fumes. Months ticked by, my debt accumulated, I had less than $100 in the bank, rent was due, and I needed to take care of my children. I had no idea how I was going to pay for anything. Eviction loomed over me. How would I feed my kids? Cloth them? House them? Even buy small comfort items to keep them free from the stings of divorce. I was at the end of the line and the end of my wits. I really didn't know what to do. At the time I was reading a book on Eastern Medicine, self-healing, and other meditative practices. There was a chapter in the book about a simple spiritual cleansing prayer in which you ask for forgiveness then follow it with a heartfelt request for a blessing. When I first read the prayer, it seemed a bit goofy to me and quite honestly, silly for a grown person to recite and believe anything could actually come from it. But, in the desperate situation I found myself, I thought, *"What the hell have I got to lose!"*

So, I sat alone in my dark apartment as the hours approached midnight, cast aside my pride and humility, and began reciting this silly little prayer. At first, I felt awkward, but soon it became natural. After about 10 minutes I began to believe it had a chance of working, I mean if it didn't work, I literally had nothing else to fall back on! So, with conviction and gratitude I recited the prayer over and over. I went to sleep that night and didn't give it another thought.

The following day I awoke and set about my normal morning routine having virtually forgotten about the previous night's prayer. However, I couldn't escape the stack of bills and pending rent despite how hard I tried to wash it away with my morning coffee. Then, around 11:00 AM, my phone rang and on the other end was an individual I hadn't spoken with in about 6 months. We had worked together on a project in the past and it was great to hear from an old colleague, even more so from a person who had become family-like to me. I was looking for an ear to vent my situation, but it turned out to be a very brief call with no shoulder to cry on. Soon after our cursory greetings, this individual cut right to the chase and out of the blue blurted, *"Hey Dan, you know that project you and I worked on in the past, it struck me how much work you did on it. I'd like to send you a check for $10,000."* I was floored, not only by the generosity of this man, but by the powerful message the Universe was sending me. While I had all but forgotten about my previous night's prayer, as soon as this blessing was offered it hit me like a ton of bricks. It was as if the Universe was telling me, *"See you knucklehead, it does work this way!"*

I'm forever grateful to this individual for helping me when I needed it the most, and so appreciative to the Universe for giving me an eye-opening experience that pushed me in the direction of spiritual understanding. Now, I know with a teaser story like this, you're all wondering what the heck is this prayer, I want my shot at 10 grand! Well, I can't guarantee a check in the mail for everyone, but if you're interested in reading a life-changing book, I highly recommend *"Soul Mind Body Medicine: A Complete Soul Healing System for Optimum Health and Vitality"* by Dr. Zhi Gang Sha.

Alright, back to the Law of Attraction and how you can make it work to your advantage. You can see from my rousing story that the focused strength of my thoughts and emotions triggered the blessing into my life. These are the essential dynamics behind the Law of Attraction. As you begin choosing your thoughts with deliberate intent, your body provides an inner tool of guidance - they're called your emotions. Pay attention to your emotions, how you feel, your gut instinct, and they'll let you know if your thoughts and beliefs are on target. It's easy to do, you simply need to train yourself to have an awareness of what is going on inside. For instance, have you ever noticed when you entertain a negative or hurtful thought how it makes you feel? Try it now. Take a moment to clear your mind, then fill it with some cringe-worthy thought. (But don't make a habit out of this, it's JUST for illustration purposes here.) As you do this, pay close attention to how this thought makes you feel. Notice that feeling in the pit of your stomach. Be aware of the negative energy, the discord, and anxiety that settles within you. Have a recognition of this sensation. Identify and remember that feeling. This is your emotional guide letting you know that the thoughts you are thinking are not a vibrational match to that which you desire.

Now, let's do the opposite. Fill your mind and spirit with positive, loving thoughts. Remember a moment that brought you great joy and love. Hold that memory in your mind and pay close attention to how it makes you feel. Can you notice the difference? Do the positive loving thoughts make you feel warm, alive and energized? Can you sense the warmth radiating from your heart? Isn't that interesting? The only thing you've done in this simple experiment is alter the thoughts that fill your mind. This was only one brief moment in your life. Imagine the shift if you were to have this level of deliberate control over your thoughts on a permanent basis.

It's so incredibly important to recognize and understand that whatever you project into the world will be reflected back to you. It doesn't matter if it's conscious or subconscious, YOU are the one in control of what enters your life based on the vibrational energies you emit. Now, I recognize many readers are thinking, *"Give me a break! You can't expect me to believe that if I merely think positive thoughts, they'll come true. Please, real life doesn't work like a Disney fairy tale."* Alright, I can identify with your thoughts, I held those beliefs at one point too. So, let's examine this spiritual law through the lens of science. That way we'll have a nice credible foundation to mitigate the 'Tinkerbell' perceptions some may experience. But, as we head down this path keep in mind that throughout his life Walt Disney was criticized by many, many people of being an impractical, naive dreamer. However, through the power of mind and his positive thoughts, look at all the magnificent ways Walt Disney's dreams have manifested. Not so fairy tale are they! So, let's get into some science and see what kind of light it sheds on the Law of Attraction, perhaps you'll discover that pixy dust isn't just for cute animated characters.

There's a scientific principle in physics known as the *"Law of Harmonic Resonance."* What makes this scientific principle relevant is a characteristic it shares with the Law of Attraction…either one can be your best friend or if used improperly, your worst enemy. We've talked a lot about all things in the Universe having a natural vibrational frequency. If left alone with no external force, everything breezes along in their natural vibratory state. However, should an external force be applied, the object's natural frequency can be altered. This is where it gets interesting. When you apply an external force that has a frequency equal to the object's natural frequency, a phenomenon called *"Harmonic Resonance"* occurs. It's an amazing condition where the object's natural frequency gets amplified by the external force causing it to build upon itself, sometimes at extreme rates. I know this all sounds a bit esoteric at the moment but keep your attention on the part about frequencies becoming amplified. It's this power of amplification that ties into the Law of Attraction.

Physicists have long-established that energy and matter interact through dynamic fields called *EMF's* (Electro-Magnetic Field). EMF's are measured by frequency (the number of times it occurs in any given timeframe), wavelength (the distance between each wave peak), and amplitude (the height of the wave). To put this in familiar terms, imagine you're at your favorite beach enjoying a blissful day in the sun. You look out into the blue water and see a surfer sitting on his board waiting for the mother of all waves. As he sits and waits, he'll experience the frequency, wavelength, and amplitude of the ocean waves passing beneath his board. Roughly every 15 seconds a new wave comes by, which is the wave's frequency – once every 15 seconds. The waves are separated by approximately 250 feet, so as the surfer lets a wave pass and looks into the distance at the next wave it will be about 250 feet away. This is the wavelength, the distance between waves. And the amplitude is the height or peak the wave reaches. Our surfing dude sits and waits for the maximum amplitude to 'hang 10'! That gives a basic understanding of frequency, wavelength, and amplitude. Keep this surf scenario in mind to help conceptualize these terms when they arise in other examples.

Let's now step through some real-world examples of harmonic resonance and all this science mumbo-jumbo will fall into place. Remember, everything has a natural frequency, there's no escaping it. In fact, one of the most advanced thinkers in human history, Nikola Tesla, stated, "*If you want to understand the universe, think of energy, frequency, and vibration.*" The three things we're talking about now. So, stick with it as we gain a better understanding of harmonic resonance, since it's a key underlying principle of the power behind the spiritual Law of Attraction.

Everything has a natural frequency or resonance. Everything. Resonance appears in diverse and countless forms even in everyday life. When a parent pushes a child on a swing, they use the principles of mechanical resonance to maximize the swing's arc and the child's happiness. The parent times each push with the child's swing to build upon the swing's arcing momentum. If the pushes are not synchronized with the swing's back-and-forth frequency, then the swing gets disrupted. This is very easy to test, just try pushing someone when the swing is in the middle of its arc instead of at the top of its arc. You'll quickly find yourself on your fanny. However, time your pushes at the end of the swing's arc and you'll find each push makes the swing go higher because you are timing your 'external force' of pushing with the swing's frequency. This building of the swing's energy is due to the harmonic resonance between the swing and the person pushing it.

Where else can you find harmonic resonance? Every time you tune your radio to a favorite station you are using the principles of electrical resonance. Dialing in your station changes the frequency of the radio's electrical circuit making it equal to the frequency of your desired station's radio signal. When the two frequencies match, harmonic resonance causes the energies to build and your station becomes the only one you hear. When you pop something in the microwave you use resonance to heat it. The microwaves from the oven form a resonant frequency with the water molecules in the food, causing them to vibrate at an extreme rate creating friction that heats your food from the inside! Pretty neat huh?

Now, do you recall what I asked you to remember? Resonant frequencies get amplified and build upon themselves. These amplified frequencies can either be good or bad, depending on the system involved. Resonant frequencies can grow strong enough to have disastrous consequences when the power builds stronger than the system can handle. A small-scale example of this is when an opera singer hits the right pitch to shatter a wine glass. When the sound waves emitted from the opera singer's vocal chords hit the resonant frequency of the wine glass, the sound waves begin to amplify. As they build upon themselves, the sound waves grow stronger and stronger until they exceed the tensile strength of the glass. Once this happens the glass shatters. This is due to harmonic resonance. This phenomenon can sometimes occur in nature. In extreme cases bridges have begun to oscillate from an external force, like the wind or a military troupe marching in perfect synchronization. When the external force reaches a resonant frequency of the bridge, they build upon themselves until the harmonic resonance exceeds the structural strength of the bridge causing it to collapse.

Let me share a funny and disastrous story about how resonance frequencies brought down a summer delight for me as a kid. Keep in mind the surfer example for understanding the concepts of wave frequency, amplitude, and wavelength. We had a cheaply made above ground 16-foot circular pool in our backyard. The water in that darn pool was always some shade of murky green, but it served up hours of relief from the summer's sweltering heat. One day we discovered if you stood in the middle and jumped up and down with a float, a wave would radiate out, much like the circular waves radiating outwards when your toss a stone into a still pond. In a circular pool, when the wave hits the side it reflects back toward the center. Then, if you timed your jumps precisely when the reflected wave meets in the middle, you could quickly create a giant oscillating wave that would go out and come back to meet in the center. Out and back, out and back, each time building and building on itself until we had an enormous tsunami-like wave right there in our back yard…at least it seemed like a tsunami. When the wave went outwards the water level at the center of the pool sank just about to the bottom, then as the wave returned all that water would converge in the middle creating a waterspout that would shoot up about 6 feet. Pretty cool since the pool itself was only 4-feet deep! It was a fun home-made wave machine…until one day, the center wave went out, but never came back. By timing our jumps, we created a wave of such power that the sides of our cheap pool couldn't handle it. Our summertime relief flooded out across the backyard leaving us sitting on floats in the center of a drained pool. Thanks to wave frequency, we were able to create a gnarly wave-machine, and thanks to the law of harmonic resonance that wave built enough force to burst through the sides of our pool. In this case, resonance truly was our best friend, until it turned on us and became our worst enemy.

But harmonic resonance isn't all negative. Medical professions use resonance in MRI's and ultrasounds. Engineers use resonance in the design of bridges and high-rises. Resonance also exists throughout the universe, from the tiniest wave-like vibrations of sub-atomic particles, all the way up to massive orbital resonances of spinning galaxies. There's no getting away from it. If you live in this Universe, resonance and vibrational frequencies will find their way into your life. And the power of resonant frequencies building upon themselves simply can't be understated or overlooked.

Alright, I know you're chomping at the bit to find out how all this talk about resonant frequency relates to you and the Law of Attraction…after all, that is what this section is about! Well, we know that everything in the Universe is composed of energy vibrating at a specific natural frequency. This includes the very substance of your body and the energies of your thoughts. Your physical and mental energy fields are unique and distinct, each vibrating at a rate determined by the frequency of the thoughts you put out. Your thoughts drive your physical and spiritual frequencies. Have you ever noticed how you feel a sense of comfort and ease when you are around people with similar outlooks? We'll even say things like "*we're in sync*" or "*we're on the same wavelength.*" Notice the subliminal use of energy terms to express this alignment!

So, how do you use the Law of Attraction and the power of harmonic resonance to turn your life into all that you desire? I'll go back to the simple answer: control what you think. Everything has a natural frequency, and that frequency becomes amplified when acted on by another force of the same frequency. Together, the two frequencies have the power to influence and build upon each other, like when an opera singer shatters a wine glasses or rambunctious kids create a tsunami in a backyard swimming pool. The frequency that you resonate is going to match the thoughts that you think. It's that easy. Just noodle that for a minute. Your thoughts are energy of a certain frequency, and like all other energies in the universe, are bound by the law of harmonic resonance.

Let me give you a little test to see how well you've been paying attention. I'd like you to apply what you've learned about harmonic resonance to determine the outcome of this scenario. What happens when the thoughts you are thinking and the energies they create, encounter other thought energy vibrating at the same frequency? Remember what the law of harmonic resonance does to energies of the same frequency…alright, what's your answer? If you said the frequencies will amplify and build upon each another, you've hit the nail on the head. The thought energies do build upon and amplify one another. Have you ever worked on a project with someone and everything you did just seemed to fall into place with ease and perfection? Your work and progress become seamless and you built a sense of being unstoppable. You say things like, *"We're in the flow now!"* Well, this is an example of harmonic resonance acting on thought energies, building and amplifying common frequencies.

Now, let's put that into context. Positive thought energies build upon themselves to create and attract more positive energies. However, the flip side is also true. Negative thought energies also build upon themselves to create and attract more negative energies! See how that works. Whatever you think of your life, your life becomes. So, birds of a feather really do flock together. And phrases like "*when it rains it pours*" and "*bad news comes in threes*" also ring true, thanks to the Law of Attraction and harmonic resonance. Given the choice, which frequency would you rather have building, amplifying, and resonating in your life - positive or negative? Now I'm going to let you in on one of the greatest secrets in the Universe…you do have a choice!

You and you alone determine what your mind focuses on. And this mind of yours is no trivial thing. Your thoughts, your beliefs, your emotions, they are all powerful determining factors of your life. It's a common belief among many spiritual masters, adepts, yogis, and shaman that thoughts are not just brain wave energy but are actual living forms. When you generate a thought, it lives on beyond the momentary flash of it racing through your mind. The energy of that thought remains until it becomes absorbed either by the originator or the person it was directed towards. Thoughts are just as much an action as any other physical act. When you generate a thought filled with hate, it actually causes great damage to the energy body of the person to whom it was directed. This is the reason spiritual masters are profoundly in control of their negative emotions. It would be a rare occasion to see the Dalai Lama, Gandhi, a Tibetan monk, or Shaolin master burst into road rage, or berate someone for getting their take-out order wrong. They know the hidden powers of thoughts. Now, don't misinterpret this into believing you must suppress ALL emotions and live in a zombie-like trance. The key here is to suppress the negative thoughts and emotions and replace them with positive thoughts and emotions. Take our friend the Dalai Lama, you'd be equally hard-pressed to find the Dalai Lama go more than a few minutes without a smile!

Different thoughts engender different frequencies. Negative emotions – hatred, envy, disdain, fear, vengeance, violence, greed, etc. – are all low frequency thoughts. While positive emotions – love, affection, joy, caring, compassion, etc. – are high frequency thoughts. If your mind is dominated with low frequency thoughts, then low frequency energy will be drawn to you and your physical and emotional attitudes will deteriorate. However, a mind filled with positive thoughts will draw high frequency energies promoting physical and emotional health. Have you ever noticed people who do the most complaining are also the ones constantly battling some type of illness?

The choice truly is yours to make. Strive to make positive thoughts and beliefs dominate your mind. Use all your will and energy to fill your life with joyful, loving, peaceful, prosperous, and happy thoughts. Force them upon yourself. As you proactively engage in positive thoughts, the Law of Attraction and harmonic resonance will step in and help you along bringing you more and more positive energies. Then, day by day you'll begin to see your life being consumed with joy, love, prosperity, and happiness. This is reflected in the wisdom of ancient philosophy that states, *"A great person is one who controls their thoughts and actions, so that all their energy and expenditure are constructive."*

When you make the conscientious effort to replace a negative thought with a positive thought, you raise the frequency of that which is attracted to you. Having positive thoughts running through your mind will in turn increase the spiritual and physical energies of your body. In the end, it's the control and filters you impose on your mind that become the reality of the physical world you experience. The world is a mirror that reflects what you choose to see. If you convince yourself the world is filled with racism, you'll see it and experience it in every action and occurrence you observe. Innocent and innocuous events will take the form of racism to you. If you believe the world is filled with crime and corruption, you'll find it abound on every street, business, and elected office in the country. If you believe society is fundamentally hateful, guess what your life will be overpowered with? But remember, the Universe and the Law of Attraction act exactly like a mirror and reflect whatever you put in front of it. So, by altering your perceptions and look instead for the beauty in the world, you'll find and experience that too. If you believe in the kindness and compassion of humanity, your life will soon be filled with that. View the world as a place of magnificent marvels and life will become a majestic wonder. The mirror is what you define it to be. The outside world you experience is created inside your mind. Create a world of love and beauty and all you are left with doing is to live your creation.

There are over 7 billion people on this planet. Trying to get each and every person to live THEIR life to YOUR standard is a task as silly and impossible as it sounds. Yet, most people do exactly that. You can't control the outside world, but you can control the world within. You alone determine how you will reaction to outside events. The more you tune your inner mirror to reflect positive, loving, and inspirational beauty, the more you'll avoid dark, negative, and hateful events entering your life. Love yourself for who you are as you are, and love others for who they are as they are without judgment or criticism and you'll be on your way to peaceful positive mental energies.

Back in Chapter 6 we learned the difference between the mind and the soul. The mind is a function of the physical body while the soul is a function of the spiritual body. We used the example of an actor taking on a new role in a movie to distinguish between the physical mind and the soul. The character in the film is the physical mind, the actor playing this character is the soul. This parallel also applies here. Use the power of your soul to control the physical mind and you'll gain control of your reality. Whatever you hold within your soul's mind will manifest in your life. It is spiritual law.

You have the power to manifest anything you desire. You create your reality with every thought you think through the powerful Law of Attraction. Anything you can imagine can be yours. When you ask yourself what you want and why you want it, you begin the process of activating the forces of the spiritual law that brings it to you. Your brain becomes magnetized with the dominant thoughts you hold in your mind. These magnetic thoughts attract the energies, the people, and the circumstances that will dominate your reality. The more intense your thoughts and feelings, the faster it is brought to you. But remember, this works with both positive and negative thoughts. Now that you've been given this information, and you know how attractive forces work, don't you think it would be prudent to force yourself to hold positive dominant thoughts all the time?

Begin today. Start making conscientious efforts to control how you think. Look for the beauty in life instead of focusing on the doom and gloom. Strive to be grateful for what you have and not envious of what you don't. Look around the world and recognize the conditions of abject poverty the vast population is living and be grateful for the blessed life you have. Be thankful for your health and the health of your loved ones. Show gratitude that your refrigerator and cupboards are filled with food, heck be grateful you have a home with a refrigerator and cupboards! Quit bitching about everything that's wrong with your life and replace those thoughts with ones of love, compassion, and appreciation. That's really all there is to it. Stop dwelling on what is wrong in the world with hateful negative thoughts and focus instead on bringing forth those things in life you love. Make the conscious determination to magnetize your mind with intense thoughts and desires for the positive things you want – health, happiness, loving relationships, prosperity, adventure, friendship, etc. Your soul is the master of your reality, not its servant. Take control of your soulful thoughts and you take control of your life. It's all just a matter of making a concerted and conscientious effort to refocus your thoughts, perceptions, and beliefs. Whenever you notice a negative, hurtful, or judgmental thought entering your mind, don't entertain it. Immediately eradicate it and replace it with a positive one. That's all there is to it! No magic, just knowledge and practice. I've given you the knowledge, it's now up to you to engage in the practice.

Unlocking the ability to create with your mental willpower kind of sounds like you've been given superhuman powers. The truth is you have! But everyone has these powers, unfortunately most will never discover this gift and learn how to unleash it. But you are different. You've now been given the key to unlock your spiritual superpowers. It's like Stan Lee has just rewritten the script of your future. And you probably know from all the Spiderman films, "*with great power comes great responsibility!*" Well, it's no different with this power. If you ignore the inherent responsibility life will constantly prod you with misery.

When you train your mind to harbor all that is good, automatically good begins to flow to you. However, you must also learn to accept all that occurs in your life with gratitude, even those events that on the surface appear to be setbacks. The outside world marches to a beat of its own drum and things will occur that you have no control over. Life can be confusing at times, particularly when trying to find reasons why bad things happen to good people, and vice-versa. You can't change that and will drive yourself senseless trying. However, you can change how you react to these events. The inner world of your mind and how you react to outside events is completely and totally under your control. Trust that the Universe is bringing exactly what you need, fully accept the perfection of why it is there and be grateful for the experience! This is the awesome responsibility you have as a spiritual superhero.

It's story time again. Let me tell you about an incident that happened to me to help illustrate this concept. Now, I recognize this incident in the scope of all the horrors and tragedies occurring in the world is trivial. However, it's a good example of how to shift your mind with ordinary life events. I mentioned earlier about a divorce I went through years ago. Once I had recovered emotionally and got my life back in order, I decided I didn't want to spend the rest of my life alone. So, I put myself back in the game and began dating. Although I met many women, I hadn't really connected with any. I began to wonder if I wasn't meant to remarry. Then I met a very attractive woman who I related to on many levels. I was excited to get to know her better and we scheduled a date for a dinner and a movie.

I had recently purchased my dream car, an Atlantic blue convertible 6-Series BMW, and was heading out to meet my dream date on an evening that couldn't have been more perfect. Well, perfection didn't last very long…on my way to pick her up my pricey new car decided to die. Right there in the middle of the street, for no reason this very expensive vehicle that was supposed to set the standard of excellence in engineering just went ka-putt! I literally had to push the darn thing through a busy intersection to the side of the road and wait for a flatbed tow truck to arrive. It ruined my night and a date I was excited to go on. On top of that, it set me back a couple grand for towing and repairs.

Now, I could have cussed out the car and the Universe for ruining my night. I could have sat there seething while I waited hours for the tow truck. I could have raged in anger at how the world was out to get me. But, doing that wouldn't change the situation at all. My car would still be stalled, my date would still be ruined, and my wallet would still be a couple grand lighter. Getting angry and upset would only wear on my nerves and call undo stress into my life. Instead, I simply thanked the Universe for its decision. A decision whose purpose I didn't know or understand, but I accepted the Universe in its infinite wisdom had orchestrated this for my benefit. Perhaps if my car hadn't conked out, I would have gotten into a serious accident on the next block. Perhaps I wasn't meant to meet this woman. Perhaps had we gone on our date and sat together at the movies it would have prevented two other people from meeting who were supposed to meet that night. The thing is, I'd never really know. But accepting this situation as that which was best for me, made it all ok.

Now, it took me a while to reach this level of calm understanding. I certainly had plenty of incidents where I'd scream at the Universe for unjust misfortunes. Remember, I'm the guy who has spent a lifetime asking questions, and *"Why me?"* was a big one I repeated often. But, through my studies and pilgrimage in spirituality I came to understand that my position is not to try to figure out WHY such events happen, but to recognize that everything in my life serves a purpose for the evolution of my soul and the betterment of me and the world at large. I could never truly know why certain things happen, and what purpose they serve. I could speculate until the end of time, but ultimately all that is simply speculation. However, by shifting perspectives towards accepting what life doles out and being grateful for it, not only makes adversities and setbacks easier to accept, but it changes your personal frequency and opens the door for positive things to enter.

And that's exactly what happened with me after my disastrous car-stalling date. Life went on. My mind and emotions were not clogged with negativity and positive things flowed into my life. Shortly after a woman of both inner and outer beauty entered my life in an unusual way -- which is another story in and of itself -- who is now my wife and the true love of my life. And most of all, a silly little thing like a stalled car didn't keep me from laughing and enjoying life. So, the moral of that little tale of adversity is stay positive and be grateful for all you have, especially during times when it seems you don't have much to be thankful for.

As you begin to shift your negative thoughts to positive ones, you will notice more positive events, people, and situations 'resonate' in your life. Harmonic resonance and the Law of Attraction will work their magic without you even knowing or trying. Then, things start to build upon themselves and life just sings in harmony. You can think of this as your personal harmonic resonance. But never lose sight of the fact that both the Law of Attraction and the law of harmonic resonance are non-discriminatory. It makes no difference if you are thinking destructive thoughts or constructive thoughts, thoughts of prosperity or thoughts of poverty, thoughts of envy or thoughts of compassion. Your thoughts act as a magnet attracting the things, objects, circumstances, environments, and people that match what you think and believe. During this process learn to relax, enjoy life, and just allow these positive things to flow into your life. Maintain the temperament of accepting all the Universe delivers, even if it seems undesirable at the time. Recognize that the wisdom of the Universe and the higher intelligence that created it is infinitely wiser than you. Believe in your heart that everything you experience in life is done so as a gift…a special gift delivered to you. A gift of spiritual growth. Even things that appear harmful and cruel serve a beneficial purpose to you and your soul.

Alright, I think 25+ pages on the Law of Attraction should give you a pretty good understanding of how your thoughts influence what manifests in your life, which raises some intriguing questions. With the world being a mirror reflecting your thoughts and beliefs, what happens when you act on all these events resonating in your life? After all, we are here to live and experience the physical world, not just think about it. Are there spiritual consequences to your actions in the same way there are for your thoughts? Is there some type of spiritual rap sheet that tracks your hurtful behavior and a Nobel Prize given for acts of benevolence? Do we have an account that logs positive credit for good virtue and negative debt for objectionable behavior? If so, how does it work? How do we spend our good credit and pay off our bad debts?

These are all wonderful questions that will get answered as we gain further understanding of the second supreme spiritual law known as the *Law of Karma*.

Law of Karma

Now that I've got you questioning every thought that races through your mind, let's look at what happens when you act upon circumstances and events in your life. You've heard the expressions, *'what goes around comes around,' 'an eye for an eye,' 'reap what you sow,' 'honor the Golden Rule.'* These are reflected in popular stories of how karma can really be a bitch. Like the big game hunter who gets trampled by an elephant; or the man on his way to a job interview who rudely cusses out a subway passenger only to discover the employer he's interviewing with is that same subway passenger. There's the age-old story of a man who tried to cheat the system by paying for one paper in a newspaper box but taking two, only to get his shirt stuck when the box slammed shut and having to pay again to free his shirt. One of the richest karma tales is an employee who stole a co-worker's ice cream bar from the company refrigerator to later learn it wasn't ice cream but dog laxative for his colleague's pet! Ha! I'm sure he had a fun weekend alone in the bathroom. This is truly a case of karma kicking you in the butt!

But karma isn't all negative. There are just as many stories illustrating the positive aspects of karma. For instance, a homeless man found a diamond ring worth $4,000 and went through great efforts to return it to its rightful owner. For his act of honesty thousands donated money to the homeless man, so much so that he was able to buy a new house, ending his homelessness. And karma isn't always instantaneous. There's a wonderful story of a baby born premature in critical condition whose life was saved by a caring pediatrician who didn't leave the infant's side for days. Thirty years later, the baby now a paramedic, arrived at a terrible car accident where he risked his life to save a man trapped within a burning vehicle…you can probably guess who the injured man in the burning car turned out to be…that's right, the doctor who saved the paramedic's life 30 years earlier.

These stories never get old, but are they just that…stories? Have we created a term we call *'karma'* as a way of referring to these arbitrary events, which are nothing more than coincidences of profound irony? Or, is there really a powerful force in the Universe directing the tides of karma? If there is, are we helplessly at its mercy, or are there things that can be done to minimize the bad karma and maximize the good?

Let's begin with a little history lesson on karma and build on this supreme spiritual law from there. The word karma is derived from the Sanskrit word *"karman,"* which means action, effect, or fate. Sometimes it's referred to as the Law of Cause and Effect, which basically means every action has a reaction, which in turn causes another action. We'll soon see how these series of actions are interdependent.

The core principles of karma first became identified thousands of years ago in India through the practices of Hinduism. In the ancient scripture, the Rigveda (1,500 BCE), there are references to the philosophical belief that your actions come with spiritual consequences. This belief was echoed and expanded upon in later texts that include the Upanishads (800 – 300 BCE) and the Bhagavad Gita (200 BCE). The notion of karmic influence soon emerged in Buddhism and Jainism around 500 BCE. Then for centuries the knowledge and understanding of karma quietly remained secluded within the inner teachings of monasteries and temples in the East, rarely being shared with the West. The concept of karma as a spiritual teaching didn't make its way into the zeitgeist of American society until being introduced by pop culture icons, such as the Beatles back in the 1970's. As Eastern practices like yoga, meditation, reiki, and certain disciplines of martial arts grew in popularity and influence, karma began to take its foothold in Western culture. Today only about one third of the population has an understanding and belief in karma although many do place faith in the general concept of 'reaping what you sow.'

We've seen how the Law of Attraction is much simpler in concept than it is in practice, and this may very well be a prerequisite for becoming a supreme spiritual law because the Law of Karma is no different. While *"What goes around comes around"* may be an obvious descriptor of this law, there are much deeper and significant forces at play that need to be understood. In the most simplistic of terms, your actions and behavior falls into two categories – good or bad. Now, I fully understand there are many shades of gray and degrees of good and bad, but for conceptual purposes let's stick with good and bad for the time being. Under this premise, acts that benefit humanity and the universe in a positive way fall into the category of good karma and acts that harm humanity and the universe in a negative way are categorized as bad karma. I don't think I've lost anyone yet.

With this understanding, the powerful spiritual Law of Karma states, *"a person who engages in good behavior will generate good karma and receive positive blessings from the Universe. A person who engages in bad behavior will generate bad karma which must be repaid through an equally negative hardship."* Positive blessing can include things such as good health, relationships, finances, family, and every aspect of life, while bad karma can result in hardships in all the same areas. That's all there is to it. As I said, like the Law of Attraction it's simple to understand but not so easy to master. You may not believe in karma, but as with all spiritual laws regardless of your beliefs you are still subject to their governance. Non-belief or ignorance doesn't absolve you from its effect. It's up to you to work on your level of conviction, but my objective is to provide you with karma's rules of engagement, so you can no longer make the claims of ignorance.

I've classified the Law of Karma as one of only two supreme spiritual laws, why? One of the fundamental reasons we incarnate in a human body is to accumulate and resolve karma. With this being a primary force of our physical incarnation, it makes sense to elevate it to supreme status. It's like the Supreme Court being the final say with physical laws binding society, karma provides the final say with the blessings and hardships we face in the physical realm. Let's slow down for a moment to reflect on some of what I just said. I'm curious if anyone has picked up on the statement about a fundamental reason for incarnating is to resolve karma? What's does that imply? How could you possibly have karma that needs to be resolved when you're born? What kind of bad behavior can you engage in as an infant? Urinate on the pediatrician on the way out? Where does negative karma originate for a newborn? This is a terrific line of questioning. Those of you who had these thoughts have become rather profound thinkers!

We've seen real stories where the effects of karma appear instantly (the man who took 2 newspapers and got his shirt caught in the newspaper box) and others that occur years later (the paramedic who saved the doctor who cared for him as a baby). However, the big hitch many don't understand is karma can be carried over into different lifetimes.

I can hear the screams now, *"What! You're telling me that not only do I have to worry about my behavior in THIS lifetime, but previous ones as well!"* While this may sound nutty, it's a fundamental tenet of karma. Your actions in the physical world set energies in motion, forming your experiences and providing lessons your soul needs to learn. You know if you're generating good or bad karma just by paying attention to your emotions. Just as your emotions provide indicators of your thoughts with the Law of Attraction, they can also be used to as a guide to your karmic activities. When your actions create discord in another person, you will feel that discord. If you form an awareness of your emotions, you'll be able to detect this discord. Likewise, if your actions create harmony and empowerment in others, you will also feel that harmony and empowerment. Forming an awareness of your emotions will allow you to pick up on these feelings. Using your inherent system of emotions provides a gauge to identify the effects of the karmic energies you create. No matter how you slice it, responsibility gets brought back to you and you alone. You are the one who must learn to create karma responsibly.

When you choose behavior through your own free-will that causes pain or suffering in another, you build negative karma. This is your choice, as a result you are the owner of the subsequent karmic energy. The greater the pain you cause, the greater the negative karma you create. Certainly, this must be an understandable concept to everyone. However, what may not be understood is negative karma does not dissipate nor terminate with the death of the physical body. It stays with your soul until it is repaid in full, and it must be repaid. Repayment can come in the form of personal hardships equal to the suffering you caused. Your hardship will teach a life lesson necessary for your soul to truly understand and empathize with the pain you caused. The debt may also be settled through service, aide, protection, help or other support given to the soul you harmed. Remember back in Chapter 8 I shared a story of a woman buried alive in 16th century Belgium, and how my participation in that event stayed with my soul until being repaid in this lifetime. Your actions and behavior carry consequences that stay with you. You are held responsible for your actions, thoughts, and intentions. This is such a powerful spiritual understanding. Now that you know this would you not agree it is wise to be aware of all your actions, thoughts, and intentions? Choose them in accordance with the life and experiences you desire to produce.

Getting back to behavior in previous lifetimes that tarnish the purity of your soul, what are we supposed to do about karma from a lifetime we may not be aware of? In today's society you're barely held accountable for your own actions. How can you be held accountable for actions of a person from a time and place of which you have no knowledge? The thing about spiritual laws is they apply first and foremost to the spiritual realm, which in this case means your soul - that immortal energy inhabiting your physical body. It's that immortal energy we need to be concerned with when applying the Law of Karma.

Let's go back to our actor analogy where an actor portrays different characters in different films. Each film is analogous to a different lifetime. Let's say our actor has a fantastic performance in one role winning him an Oscar. His performance in that film will impact future roles. He'll be offered better parts and higher pay. While the movies and characters portrayed are unrelated, the actor behind those roles is the one receiving the blessings. Conversely, should the actor bomb and instead win a Rotten Tomato Award, it'll impact future roles in a different way. He'll be less desired, and his acting fee will take a hit. Good performance in one film impacts future films, as does poor performance. Now, use this analogy and replace the actor with your soul, and each new film with a new lifetime. Your soul is like the actor. If your soul performs well in one lifetime it'll be rewarded with positive blessings in future lifetimes. However, if you live a lifetime of behavior comparable to rotten tomatoes, you'll pay the consequences in future lives. Make sense? Live a good life today and you won't have to worry about hardships in future lifetimes. But live a hurtful destructive life and you can look forward to lifetimes of adversities and suffering. It's that easy. Your soul must experience the effects that it has caused to become whole.

As I said, it's a pretty basic and simple concept. But, as you know, most people don't have the will and desire to plan and manage 6 months out, how are they expected to live today for an unknown future lifetime! Part of that lies in the belief of reincarnation - that one day you will return in a future life. The other part involves the belief in karma, whether that karma is delivered today or far in the distant future. Combine the two with unwavering conviction and you'll live a life today that offers a blissful future. Doubt in these two items can cause confusion and the repetition of certain life lessons. For example, it's common for a person to experience the ramifications of negative debt created by their soul in another lifetime that is being repaid in this lifetime. Without the knowledge of your soul, your past lives, and the law of karma, these situations can become challenging and confusing. However, your gift of understanding places you in a different position, one where you can accept these hardships with clarity, offer appreciation for the experience, and recognize the value of its meaning.

I make comparisons of the physical body with the energy body throughout this book. Back in Chapter 4 we learned about the 7 'magnificent' chakras that control and regulate the flow of energy. Sometimes these energies can become blocked which can lead to physical illness. Specialists in the field of human energy - acupuncture, Reiki, Qui-Gong, Tai-chi, etc. - help in clearing blocked energy. Well, your spirit energy can also form blockages. Spiritual blockages result from negative karma. Any harmful act, negative behavior, or even negative thoughts, from the most heinous to the benign, create spiritual energy blockages that stay with your soul until cleansed. And just as you can strengthen the physical body with healthy and nourishing foods, you can also strengthen your soul with healthy, nourishing sustenance. What is the nutritional food for the soul? Well, it isn't chicken soup, as a successful series of books metaphorically implies, but it is virtue. That's right - virtue or positive karma feeds the soul and helps release blocked energy. Good virtue nourishes the soul while bad intent damages it. So, you see, the power and understanding of karma truly does run much deeper than the simple expression *"what goes around comes around."*

Never lose sight of the fact that the karma you generate is YOUR karma. It can't be traded, swapped, nor dissolved. Even spiritual masters cannot remove karma, nor can they assume responsibility for your life and the choices you make. Your life is totally and completely under your control. Others can only help you understand your choices and the consequences resulting from your thoughts, actions, intentions, and behavior. It's you who experience the benefits or hardships of your actions. Knowing this, wouldn't you much prefer generating positive nourishing karma than negative corrosive karma? Of course! So how do you do that? Good karma is created by acts of love, caring, compassion, sincerity, honesty, integrity, generosity, purity, charity and unconditional service. Good karma can absolutely bless your life, bringing you happiness, health, peace and harmony. It can transform your life, help you reach soul enlightenment, and foster a purer, more loving, more peaceful, and happier life experience.

Conversely, bad karma is created by hurtful acts, such as murder, abuse, deceit, lies, jealousy, greed, selfishness, indecency, and theft. Bad karma is the root of most hardships in life. If you caused terrible pain, or were involved in a horrible act, in this or another lifetime, you will have to repay the debt. It is karmic law. Suffering, unhappiness, conflict, heartbreak, illness, bankruptcy, and other hardships are the currency used to repay karmic dept. The inability to achieve success in relationships, accidents, and business failures are events that can all be karma related. Struggles, pain, and difficulties are all part of the cleansing process. They cannot be avoided. If not in this lifetime, then in the next, you must return virtue to the souls you owe. For your soul to become whole, it must experience the effects it has caused. Whether you believe in karma or not, this is spiritual law.

So, what should you do when you're hit with a string of bad luck or unjust misfortune? Even when you play by the rules, you don't cheat on your taxes, you live with principle and integrity. Despite all this, the Universe still spits in your face with a cruel and unjust hardship. There's no explanation and you're left shaking your head asking *"Why me?"*

Everyone goes through spiritual testing in some form. The teacher of growth in the physical realm is adversity. It is how we gain spiritual knowledge. With challenge comes growth. The more evolved a soul, the greater the challenge. This is because old souls innately understand and are better suited to cope with hardship having experienced it more. The Universe only doles out what your soul is capable of handling. In a strange way, you can view enormous adversity as a compliment. It's a testament to your spiritual wisdom. But to overcome these obstacles, it's important to keep a clear understanding of the Law of Karma and the Law of Attraction.

Avoid focusing on the temporary pain, setback, or hardship the circumstance brings. Look beyond the present conditions and be grateful for the opportunity to repay your karmic debit and gain spiritual growth. Trust the Universe is delivering everything that is essential for your soul development and be appreciative for it. Offer gratitude and unconditional love with faith and trust, and your hardship will end much sooner. On the other hand, clutter your mind with anger and victimhood, and guess what the Law of Attraction will bring to your hardship…more of the same!

Now that you know about karma and how it is generated, you can use this knowledge to mitigate negative karma. The means for doing this is pretty simple - generate positive karma. If you become disciplined and committed to serving humanity, you can cleanse bad karma. Positive virtue softens and mitigates potential adversities. The more you serve unconditionally, the more blessings you will receive. Combine the Law of Karma with the Law of Attraction you can begin to understand just how powerful your thoughts and actions are in manifesting your life experiences. Your thoughts do matter. Your behavior does matter. Feed your soul good virtue and positive thoughts then just watch the blessings it'll have on your life.

Some of you may be wondering about that person in life who seems to get away with everything. You know the type who never gets caught for any indiscretion. They're as slippery as Teflon, nothing sticks! Why do they get away with everything? How come karma doesn't set up camp in their lives? If there are similarities between the physical and spiritual realms, is this one of them? Do some people simply get away with bad behavior? How can we be so sure there is a price to pay for bad behavior? Is behavior somehow being tracked? Is it possible a little slip up here and there could fall through the cracks?

Well, it's a nice try to proceed with this line of thought, but you can't fool the Universe. It's like lying to yourself, the only person you're fooling is you. As far as tracking your karma, there is a means in which all activities, behaviors, and thoughts of your life are recorded. It's called the *'Akashic Records,'* or *'The Book of Life.'* It's like a spiritual Library of Congress that contains the history of every soul in the Universe since its creation. Think of it as an energy based super-computer of the Universe. I know this sounds like something from the imagination of J.K. Rowling, but it does exist. You can even train yourself to access it and draw upon Universal Intelligence.

The Akashic Records act as a central storage of all information for every individual who has ever lived. Each record contains every deed, word, feeling, thought, and intent that has ever occurred since the beginning of creation. While most understand the Akashic Records to contain records of human experiences, they also contain information on all phenomenon and knowledge of the entirety of the Universe. The concept of an all-encompassing database dates back centuries. Cultures throughout the world speak of sages from ancient times to the present who access this knowledge, cultures that include Indians, Moors, Tibetans, Himalayans, Egyptians, Persians, Greeks, Chinese, Hebrews, Christians, Druids and Mayans. In ancient Egypt, the Pharaohs were advised by those with the ability to read the Akashic Records. The French physician and clairvoyant, Nostradamus, known for his prophesies claimed to access the Akashic Records utilizing methods of ancient Greek oracles. Still today many spiritualists and energy masters provide Akashic Record readings and teach individuals how to train themselves to access them on their own. The Akashic Records impacts our everyday life, relationships, feelings and beliefs. While you may think you or someone you know has gotten away with something in this lifetime, just know that act has been recorded and its debt will be repaid.

Taking in all we've learned about the Law of Karma we see how, like the Law of Attraction, it's indiscriminate in its application. It doesn't matter who you are, how well-connected or ordinary, celebrity, a man of the cloth, politician, criminal, or philanthropist, if you act in positive virtue the Law of Karma brings positive blessings to you. However, should you decide to engage in abhorrent behavior, the Law of Karma will generate negative debt that must be repaid through hardship or service. The Law of Karma is unbreakable.

If you prefer prosperity over penury, then give and practice charity. If you prefer cordiality and peace, then be courteous and respectful. If you don't want to be cheated or swindled, then treat others with honesty, integrity, and fairness. Use the Law of Karma to your advantage to avoid undesirable things by generating more positive karma than negative debt through purposeful and deliberation actions and behavior. Treat all living beings with respect, not just humans but all life – humans, animals, even plant life.

The senseless torture or slaying of animals without respect, appreciation, and gratitude will also incur negative karmic debts to your soul. This is why cultures who are in-tune with the spiritual dimension show respect and gratitude for their kill when they hunt. They offer a prayer beforehand and show reverence for the soul of the creature that has sacrificed for their sustenance. Gandhi believed that the evolution of a culture can be gauged by the respect it pays to animals, not by its technological achievements. Everyone must take personal responsibility to act in kind, decent, civil, and respectful manners to every other soul. It's just simply that basic and straightforward!

That about wraps up our study of the Supremes, and not the ones who backed up Dianna Ross, but the ones who back up you and your soul.

We've come to explore and understand the mechanics behind the two supreme spiritual laws, which can neatly be summed up by the Chinese proverb, *"Life is an echo, what you send out comes back."* You've learned enough to now recognize that the world is a reflection of your thoughts and beliefs. What you have, what you experience, and what you are, all depend upon what you think, what you believe, and how you behave. You are responsible for every action, thought, feeling and intention. There's no one else to pin it on, it's all you.

So, be aware of the thoughts and intentions that fill your mind. Are you radiating love and compassion, or judgment and criticism? Do you choose anger and resent over understanding and forgiveness? Do you look for ways to find laughter or scour for things to complain about? Are you showing gratitude for the beauty and abundance that surrounds you, or do you whine with envy over what you don't have? Are you thinking powerful thoughts of success and prosperity, or bemoaning that which you can't afford?

Ask how you can adjust your thoughts and actions to attract and manifest all you desire from life. Look for ways to be grateful even if there's nothing to be thankful for. Find something, one small item, then focus all your positive thoughts and beliefs on it, and soon you'll discover more and more to appreciate. Little by little your blessings will grow and build upon themselves until your life is filled with such beauty and abundance you won't have any problem finding gratitude. Choose your beliefs, intentions, and actions in accordance with the life you want to produce. The alternative is to abdicate it to the control of the two extremely powerful supreme spiritual laws that will manifest your random and arbitrary thoughts whether good or bad. The choice is yours to make. Your thoughts and actions really do matter. Gain control over them and you'll discover you gain control over your life and the events that enter it. You are a creator, so create with deliberate intent to control your destiny and obtain all you desire!

Now, all the while I've been lecturing about controlling your thoughts and actions, I've also been indicating that mastery of them isn't easy. So, you're probably wondering if there are routines and practices you can do to help you achieve mastery over your mind. Well, wonder no more. To find useful everyday tools you can use to sharpen your mental skills all you have to do is turn the page and begin to learn.

Ch. 10: Fine Tuning the Mind

"The most powerful energy in the universe is a thought, which becomes the quantum intelligence within every atom and molecule." – Unknown Source

The Rock in Your Head

After exploring laws that govern our world, lives, and souls, we've come to recognize the long arm of the law is much longer and multi-limbed than we thought. It makes you want to run out and pass the bar. All kidding aside, while a fancy law degree may give you a legal edge when battling the IRS or a parking ticket, it's not going to tip the scales of justice with any of the natural or spiritual laws. As I always say, you don't have to believe in gravity to get conked in the head by an apple. We have Isaac Newton to thank for discovering and defining that natural law. But Newton wasn't just a one-hit-wonder, he made many other discoveries in the fields of optics, motion, and mathematics. In fact, Newton was first recognized for his scientific achievements in the design and construction of a reflecting telescope, and it was Newton who theorized that white light is composed of all the colors of the spectrum. His work was so influential he was knighted by Queen Anne of England in 1705, making him 'Sir' Isaac Newton. But with all his contributions to science, few know that Newton also had an obsessive pursuit that eluded even him - the *Philosopher's Stone*. Newton, along with a long list of brilliant minds, searched and experimented for years to find this mysterious substance rumored to have magical properties.

Newton's quest is supported by a recently discovered manuscript that reveals Newton's handwritten notes of his infatuation with the Philosopher's Stone. Now, you're probably wondering what the Philosopher's Stone is, which oddly enough isn't a stone at all. You may also be curious why so many brilliant minds were racing to uncover this magical secret? Well, glad you asked...

Dating back to the Middle Ages, a magical substance which came to be known as the Philosopher's Stone, was tenaciously sought-after in the world of alchemy. According to legend, the Philosopher's Stone could transform any base metal into a precious metal - gold or silver. On top of the riches it could bring, it also offered something you couldn't put a price-tag on – immortality. It was believed to cure illness, restore youth, and grant immortality. For those reasons, alchemists in 17th-century England engaged in a tireless quest for its discovery...and our ole friend Sir Isaac Newton eagerly jumped on the bandwagon. But their efforts weren't entirely futile, their exploration of countless elements and experimentation built a base of knowledge that spawned the fields of chemistry, pharmacology, and metallurgy.

However, long before Newton many others had hunted for the powerful substance that could transform lead into gold. Their quests were ignited by extraordinary legends, religious texts, and myths that gave accounts of such a magical substance. There are references throughout these ancient texts of an *'Elixir of Life'* that could impart immortality on whomever ingested it. In Greek mythology ambrosia and nectar were the food and drink reported to make gods immortal. It's said that ambrosia was used to cure diseases, restore physical injuries, and perfectly preserve the bodies of the dead. Vedic mythologies refer to a special drink prepared by extracting the juice from plants that gave gods immortality. Ancient Egyptian legends refer to gods drinking a substance which produced immortality. In Sumerian texts there's mention of the gods and kings drinking a magical milk to extend life and grant immortality. The Epic of Gilgamesh gives account of a thorny plant found at the ocean's floor that induces immortality. And the Taoists of ancient China took the search one step further by developing techniques to achieve immortality through internal alchemy - meditation, breathing exercises, diet, and energy flow.

You can appreciate with so many tales circulating about a magical substance offering great riches and immortality, that all the exceptional minds and powers of the time would relentlessly pursuit it. During this era, those pursuing the Philosopher's Stone kept the knowledge of its existence secret. This was a period of high illiteracy and a poorly educated populous, and rumor of this powerful substance was kept only among a very few 'in-the-know' individuals. Additionally, it was commonly accepted that the Philosopher's Stone was a substance found in abundance yet despite this it continued to remain unrecognized and unappreciated. Interesting characteristics, aren't they? Think about the prospects of discovering a powerful substance granting wealth and immortality to anyone who possess it, that can be found everywhere yet remains hidden! Can you imagine the frustration these great minds faced in their struggles to solve this enigma?

After centuries of tireless searching and experimentation, the idea of a Philosopher's Stone-like substance that grants wealth and immortality, which can be found everywhere, and yet goes unrecognized and unappreciated, is one that still baffles many today. Now, after 9 chockfull chapters of examining and questioning the world, I'm certain you've become quite a crack gumshoe capable of solving such mysteries of life. So, let's give this centuries-old enigma a shot. What can you think of in the human experience that is found everywhere and is widely unrecognized and under-appreciated?

Think back to earlier chapters and see if you can come up with something you've learned that previously went unrecognized and under-appreciated in your life. If you need a little clue, peek at Chapter 6…Have you got it? The soul? That's right, it is the soul! The very thing that makes you who you are and your reality what it is. The Philosopher's Stone sought by so many for so long can be thought of as nothing more than the spiritual body. All those failed lab experiments and formulas over the centuries searching for an Elixir of Life concoction when all along it was within them. The soul IS the Elixir of Life. When understood and mastered, it can grant you all the riches of the physical world while offering the spiritual gift of immortality. That's a pretty neat twist on an old tale wouldn't you say.

When we examine it from the perspective of spiritual consciousness, you can see how it all falls into place. Back in Chapter 5 we learned about the differences between the soul, the mind, and the body, and how your soul is the true manager of the mind and the body. It directs the body how to walk, what to say, how to function, how to heal, how to sustain itself, when to laugh, what to create, how to interact, and how to love. All these glorious things result from your soul's mastery of the physical matter making up your body. The soul is the director of the body's chemistry. From the conscious, to the subconscious, to the super-conscious, it is your soul that dictates the actions of every limb, organ, muscle, and cell within your body. Each of these limbs, organs, muscles, and cells are made of molecules, which are made of atoms, which are made of subatomic particles which are nothing more than energy. So, if the soul controls the limbs, organs, muscles, and cells of the body, it stands to reason the soul also controls the energy that makes up the cells of the body.

If you acknowledge your soul has control over the atoms of your body and the manifestation of your reality, then you should have fun with this extrapolation. We know from the study of physical matter that the atoms making up your body come from external sources through the foods you eat. Most people today are ingesting physical matter that originate from all over the world. For those who don't think of themselves as an international jetsetter, here's a perspective that may change that. The atoms making up the bones, muscles, skin, blood, and organs of your body come from the foods you eat. If you shop in a normal supermarket in the United States, your food supplies come from the farthest reaches of the planet. The foods on your plate have originated from countries all over the world. As your body digests this food, their atoms and molecules go into building the foundations of your body. Isn't it cool to think that in one meal you can ingest atoms from spices grown in Morocco, atoms from wine produced in France, atoms from vegetables grown in China, and atoms from beef raised in Texas? Matter from all corners of the globe are sitting right there on the same plate about to be digested and converted to cells that make up your body. You are an international player built from atoms of food from around the world!

Do you remember another important characteristic of physical matter? It's all made from energy, and energy can neither be created nor destroyed. Every subatomic particle of the atoms making up your body and the atoms making up all the physical matter on earth are energy from the same Universal source, which is the same energy that constitutes your spiritual consciousness. As a result, the atoms of external matter can also respond to the desires of your soul in the very same way the atoms of your body respond to your soul's desires. Did you get that? It's important enough to repeat. Your soul controls the energy of your physical body, which comes from the same source as the physical world surrounding you. Meaning your soul also has the potential to control the energy of the physical world. The soul incarnated in your body has the very same ability to influence all energy from Universal source. The limitations placed on this are self-imposed and stem from a lack of awareness and understanding of the soul's abilities. Mastery of the spiritual mind unlocks unimaginable powers over the physical world. Your ability to affect the reality around you through your connection with your soul is one of the biggest secrets in humanity. And now, you are in on it. You are one of the 'in-the-know' individuals who has obtained the secrets of the soul and solved the ancient mystery of the Philosopher's Stone.

With all the talk of magical superpowers we need to come back to earthly reality to acknowledge it takes years and years of practice, study, and concentrated effort before having Yoda-like powers over external matter. Skills of this level have been achieved by masters throughout time. A simple Google search can provide an abundance of supporting evidence, but the important thing to note is that these spiritual masters are no different in their physical and energy composition than you. The powers and capabilities they've achieved can be mastered by anyone with the desire and will. With that in mind, let's focus our attention on using your spiritual consciousness to gain control over your life, and we'll leave the Tibetan monks to master their Jedi powers. It's time for us to look at some of the practices and techniques which can help turn that lump of granite in your head into a true Philosopher's Stone!

By All Stretches of the Imagination

You've learned a great deal about yourself since beginning this book. You now recognize that in a broader perspective you are much more than a massive clump of cells and organs. You've seen evidence the real YOU is an immortal energy being occupying a physical body for the experience to learn and evolve. You've also learned a portion of your soul energy incarnates in your physical body while the remainder exists in a higher spiritual dimension. Since your true self is this higher spiritual consciousness, wouldn't it be great if you could use it to help navigate the physical world? Well, guess what…you can. Everyone has the ability to tap into their higher soul consciousness. It's actually quite easy and can be fun with proper instruction and practice. So, why aren't more people utilizing this ability to guide their thoughts and beliefs to attract their desired reality? The issue goes back to being informed. Most people are not even aware they have a higher consciousness, let alone how to access it. But here's the good news…you're not one of them! So, let's breakdown the process of tapping into your soul consciousness to gain a firmer control over your physical experience. First, I'll fill in some of the backstory.

Your thoughts are energy, and the contents of your thoughts become the basis of your reality. This has been hammered into you in the previous chapter. Your reality is molded by your thoughts. But your abilities to control your own reality goes beyond what we've learned about the Law of Attraction and Harmonic Resonance. The physical world that surrounds us is not dead empty matter, it's composed of energy. And the energy that makes up the physical matter of our world stems from the very same energy of your higher-self. It's all part of the original

Source energy. How's that for a profound concept to chew on. Take a moment to really contemplate this because it's one of those weighty concepts that has the power to alter your perception of reality. The energy of physical matter and the energy of soul consciousness originate from the same source. What does that tell you about the very solid physical world you wake up to every morning? Everything you can see, feel, touch, taste, and smell, all the worldly possessions were all at some point uniform energy, nothing more than soul consciousness. Everything that exists in the physical world has first been thought energy of the spiritual dimension.

I fully recognize how this may strike you as quite a radical concept. It's such a stretch of the imagination to think every physical form is energy brought into existence through spiritual consciousness. That the physical world is merely spiritual energy lowered in its density. That no form of matter exists without it first being spiritual consciousness. I know it defies all you have come to understand about the physical world. It's an unconventional belief to wrap your head around so take your time. It's not every day that someone walks up and tells you the entire structure of the physical world with all its solidity - the buildings, the streets, the infrastructure, all the products and merchandise, even earth itself - all began as pure soul consciousness lowered in frequency until it achieved the density of physical matter. However, it's one of those sublime topics to wrestle with since your ability to grasp this concept is an important aspect in your ability to manifest your desired reality.

If you reflect to our first topic of investigation - how life on this planet began – you'll remember our analysis revealed the theory of intelligent design. During our investigation we uncovered many great scientific minds who believed the structure of the Universe, from the design of an atom to the coding of genomes, had a helping hand from a higher intelligence. The evidence of intelligent design is so great that even the most brilliant quantum physicists agree it couldn't happen by random chance. Now, if that were true, it forces us to inquire further about how this higher intelligence would be able to create physical matter? How could an ethereal consciousness form the atoms of amino acids and assemble them into genetic codes that sparked life on earth? The spiritualist belief falls right in line with the radical concept I've just outlined, by lowering the vibrational frequency of thought consciousness to the density of the physical plane. The physical world you experience and all the physical matter that occupies it are the end results of spiritual energy. The very same spiritual energy of your higher consciousness.

The reason I'm spending so much time drilling this into you is because having this awareness is a core component in the manifesting process. You'll need to develop the belief and conviction that you do possess the ability to create the life you want, without any doubt or skepticism. Knowing how the system behind your amazing ability to create operates will reinforce your belief in your own abilities. Health, prosperity, happiness, loving relationships do not occur by happenstance, they manifest through the thoughts and beliefs you accept as true. You are a magnificent fragment of the Creator. You share in all its divine powers. In the exact proportion you believe this of yourself is the same proportion you are able to master your physical experience. Your life is determined by your beliefs. You are either a slave to them or you become their master. Mastering your thoughts and beliefs is the key to unlocking the control room to your future. Enough of the pep-talk, I'm sure what you really want to know is how it's done? How do you alter your thought frequencies to create the life of your dreams?

It turns out the actions involved are quite basic. In fact, the process can be summed up in two easy steps:

> **Step 1**: Determine with clarity and specificity what you want.
> **Step 2**: Convince yourself you already have it.

That's all there is to it. If you're able to master these two steps, you'll soon begin attracting and resonating the life experiences you desire. It's that simple. Just state what you want, then make your future dream a present fact. Sounds rather easy doesn't it? Well, as we've experienced with mastering other spiritual tasks, this is yet another one that appears simple on the surface but is unusually challenging to master. So, let's break the process down in such a way that anyone can become a master creator.

In the last chapter we investigated the Law of Attraction and learned how this spiritual law can be used to manifest your desires by controlling your beliefs with deliberate intent. Once set in motion the Universe will provide the means and circumstances for your wishes to be fulfilled. It's up to you to recognize, acknowledge and accept them when they appear. Let's bridge this spiritual law with the deliberate creation process beginning with Step 1: *Determine What You Want.*

The first essential step in manifesting what you want is to first know what it is that you want. As ridiculously obvious as this sounds, it's probably one of the biggest mistakes made. Often people have a vague generality of what they desire from life. I'm sure you've heard friends and family make statements like, *"I just want to be happy,"* or *"All I want is someone to love,"* or *"I wish I was wealthy,"* and of course, the one shared by 70% of Americans, *"I want a job I don't hate!"* Sound familiar? Perhaps you've uttered one or two of these statements. While all these wishes are fine and universal, they don't define what it is that will make you happy, or who you can love, or what constitutes wealth – money, health, ability to love, etc....?

Understand that vague desires yield vague results. Here's a painfully obvious example to underscore the point. If I send you to the grocery store with the vague request to pick up some '*food*,' the sky's the limit as to what you bring back. Anything from breakfast cereal to potato salad to Puppy Chow would fit the bill since they all adhere to the request. And guess what, I'd have to accept what I got since it's exactly what I asked for - food. However, if I ask you to get '*93% lean ground turkey with Italian seasoning*,' then I shouldn't expect you to return with a container of blueberry yogurt. Specific requests yield specific results. You need to be just as specific when determining what you want from life. To bring forth something into your physical experience you must learn to develop an intense, burning desire with specificity and clarity. Think of it as the grocery list of your future. I'm not talking about ambiguous wants or halfhearted wishes along the lines of "*yeah, it'd be nice to have such and such...*' You need to develop the ability to form a fierce, burning hunger with all your heart. You must want a reality different from what you are currently attracting. Your energy flows where your attention goes. A clear desire starts with your attention focused like a laser on exactly what you want. The intensity of your desire regulates the speed it occurs.

It's equally important that you focus your desires on that which you want, and NOT on that which you are trying to AVOID. There's often confusion with this so here's an example to add clarity. If you are longing for a loving relationship, your desire should focus on all the characteristics and qualities you WANT in a relationship. For instance, "*I want to be with someone who shares my interest, has an outgoing sense of adventure, looks for laughter in every moment of life, wants a loving family, has a close relationship with his/her parents, etc…"* List all the specific things you are looking for in a relationship. Avoid focusing on the things you DON'T want. For instance, don't state your desire as, *"I no longer want to be lonely, my life match can't be boring, I don't want someone who lives with their parents, a poor sense of humor is a turn-off, he/she can't have a drinking problem…"* Do you recognize the difference? These statements all focus your attention on the negative – lonely, boring, drinking problem... By doing this, your energy inadvertently focuses on these negative attributes. And since Law of Attraction is indiscriminate in its actions, guess what resonates in your relationships? A boring person with a drinking problem who lives with their parents and can't hit a punchline. Got it! Statements of this type feed into your fears, not into your loving desires. Trying to bring forth your wishes through avoidance of the negative emotions, worry, doubt, greed, etc., will only resonant experiences with those negative attributes. So, focus your attention and desires on the positive attributes and you'll attract positive results.

It's also important to strive for blessings that are honorable, constructive, and worthy of your energy. You are a divine spiritual being given a precious opportunity to be in this physical realm, use it lovingly and responsibly. Examine the integrity of your wishes, don't focus on things whose sole purpose is to gratify the physical senses. Make sure there are no lurking feelings that you'll benefit from your desire at the expense of another. Remember that little thing called 'karma' hangs in the background! Be honest to yourself and society at large. Think through your desires in every possible way. Be certain no part of you feels you are undeserving of it. These subliminal doubts will only neutralize the process, or worst, attract the opposite. To be clear, I'm not advocating that you should not yearn for and enjoy many of the pleasurable things the physical world offers. The note here is that you are not driven solely by capital vices and cardinal sins. Your life wishes should not be defined by the 7 deadly sins. As a refresher, they are – pride, greed, lust, envy, gluttony, wrath, and sloth. Avoid falling into any of these 'sins' and you'll stay on a positive and productive life experience.

Once you've successfully determined what you want with clarity, detail, and worthiness, and all parts of you are in alignment with it, you're ready to move on to Step 2: *Convincing Yourself You Already Have It*. I need to warn you that the single biggest breakdown in the creation process occurs during Step 2. What makes this so challenging is you must unwind all you've been taught about the physical world to bring forth the feelings of your wish being fulfilled when everything and everyone in the real world is telling you just the opposite. To effectuate this belief, your wishes, your desires, and your wants need to take a journey from your conscious mind, travel through your subconscious mind, and impress themselves upon your super-conscious mind. You must persist in and concentrate on your desire with such feeling and conviction that your super-conscious mind becomes filled with such certainty it pushes out all other doubts.

You may have noticed I like to anticipate your thoughts, and right about now I'm anticipating that you're thinking, *"Alright Captain Know-it-All, it's easy enough to put these obscure statements on a page in a book, but how am I supposed to apply them in the real world? Last time I checked, my 'super-conscious self' hasn't friended me!"* I understand the concern. Up until now I've been providing you an overview to delineate what occurs internally during the creation process. The method we'll use to impress the belief of your wish being fulfilled on your super-conscious mind before it has manifested is a technique called *'visualization.'*

I'm sure you've heard this term before, but don't confuse visualization with something that pertains solely to sight or mental images. As we'll see, proper visualization technique requires you to summon your emotions and all your senses. It really should be called *"Feel-ization,"* since you must master the feeling of your wish being fulfilled with all the sensory and emotional radiance of reality. Visualization in the creation process means you must believe you already are what you want to be or have what you want to have and live that reality with conviction and confidence. Your desire can only manifest through your absolute faithfulness to the belief you already have it. If you can pull this off, you will never have to pursuit it. It will find its way into your life experience. It is spiritual law. However, if you cannot believe yourself as something other than what you are, then you will remain as you are. You must completely abandon the beliefs that differ from those of your desire. So, how are you supposed to accomplish this feeling of belief with natural conviction? Well, that secret lies in a little gift we've been given that no other organism in nature has – an imagination.

The amazing thing about humans is we have a powerful tool to imagine and create with our minds that all things are possible. Believe yourself as something other than what you are, or have what you don't, are realities that can be achieved by using your imagination. Use your creative gift to imagine yourself being what you want to be or having what you desire. The intensity and brilliance of your imagination governs the strength in which your desires will be etched in your super-conscious mind. But what about those who are new to this, whose imaginations are tepid at best? There are some who can create incredible worlds of augmented reality in their heads, while others are lucky to dream up a stick figure. Does this mean they won't be able to manifest their destinies? Is it limited to only an artistic mind? Of course not. Some people just need a little work. Your imagination can be strengthened just like any other aspect of your being. It's no different than building your muscles or strengthening your cardio-vascular systems. It just takes some diligent exercise. You can do the same with your imagination. It just takes practice, patience, and determination. So, let's work on building our imaginations.

Once you begin to flex your imagination, it'll expand and develop just like any other part of your body. One method for building a robust imagination requires a slight change of your perception. Don't see yourself as a curious onlooker of your desires but rather as an active participant living your desires now. For instance, think about what you experience in real life when something you've been wishing for, yearning, and wanting finally arrives. It could be a loving relationship, a job, a dream vacation, a home, whatever. When something like this happens, how do you react? What are your feelings? What emotions do you express? Try recalling an incident where this did happen and relive the emotional experience. Remember in detail what it felt like. Did you scream with excitement? Was there a big, broad smile plastered across your face for hours? Did your body feel light and airy, like you could walk among the clouds? Were you unable to contain your enthusiasm? Did the entire world suddenly become hopeful and optimistic? Did everything in life radiated joy? It's not just a superficial feeling, but one that runs deep to your inner core. You become filled with a great sense of completion and fulfillment. Positive energy swirls through your body. Your senses come alive. Think of the sights, the sounds, the smells. All the things to relive that moment again with all its vividness and clarity. Remember these feelings. Hold onto them as these are the emotions, feelings, and sensations you'll need to recreate with your imagination.

Now, try the same visualization technique calling upon your imagination to invoke all your emotions and senses, but this time let's do it using something that has not yet occurred. Our objective is to imagine your wish being fulfilled using just your mind. Close your eyes and relax in a deep, quite meditative state of mind. Start from your toes and relax each muscle working up to the top of your head, letting all tension flow out of your body. Breath deep and slow from your belly. When you've reached a deep relaxed state, imagine the thing you want exactly as you'd like it. It can be anything, a new home, a new partner, a new job, a thinner body, a respectful relationship with a child…anything that you currently desire. Once you have it in mind, create a vivid and clear picture or movie in your head of your desire playing out in your life now as you sit and relax. Form a mental image of the person you want to be, and experience that person now, as you are. Fill in all the details to make it as real as possible. Imagine yourself in the physical setting you would like, doing what you enjoy, receiving appreciation and financial compensation. Add more details that are important to you. Bring forth the emotions and feeling that you are that person or are experiencing that situation now. Whatever it may be, see yourself living in the house of your dreams, succeeding in the career of your dreams, surrounded by everything that makes your dream a reality. Invoke all your senses. Remember our investigation in Chapter 5 where we learned all our senses occur in the mind, well use that knowledge here to make the senses of your desire play out in your mind. See the sights, hear the sounds, smell the fragrances and aromas, taste the deliciousness, feel the emotions as though it actually exists. Envision yourself doing all the things you would be doing while living this desire. See all this in your mind, feel it with your emotions, sense it with your senses. Believe it to be true. Get from it all the pleasure and enjoyment you would if it was yours now, belonging to you, already in your possession. Have fun with it, enjoy the experience. Achieve the feeling that this IS possible. Be grateful for having your desire. Take that emotional energy and flood the desire with more and more feeling. Imagine it becoming more real. Load positive emotions into your creation - confidence, acceptance, excitement, joy, and pleasure all create a powerful visualization. Surrender yourself completely and totally to these feelings until your whole being is possessed by them. This is the full scope of the visualization technique that uses the power of your imagination combined with your senses and emotions to energize your desire. Practice and master this and the dreams of your imagination will soon become the realities of your future.

I recognize all this can sound a bit counterintuitive. How are you supposed to believe you have something with total conviction when the physical world is showing you the complete opposite. If your wish is to be thin, how can you convince yourself of it when the reflection in the mirror says otherwise? Well, you must learn to see reality different than it is if you want it to change. It may sound crazy, but it's done all the time. Look at virtually any champion for inspiration and example. Most people who have risen to the top of their field, whether an athlete, politician, entrepreneur, spelling champion, chess master, musician, or salesman, will tell you that long before they were crowned champion of their domain, they saw themselves at the top. They knew years before they achieved the top spot that one day, they would be a champion. They knew it, they saw it, they believed it with all conviction. Champions see themselves as a champion, know they are a champion, they talk as though they ARE a champion long before winning the title. And nothing anyone says can change their belief. They know it's their destiny to become a champion, and so those thoughts resonate, and it becomes their reality.

Now, don't expect to visualize with imagination and emotion once and suddenly "poof," your desire materializes as though a magic genie just granted you a wish. It's done through repetition. Every creation takes energy to come into existence. Once you have a clear desire that is focused with a positive attitude, you will need to continue giving energy for your desired to manifest. The energy must build and coagulate. It is not enough to feel yourself into the state of the wish being fulfilled, you must persist in that state. Make a routine of giving thanks for having what you desire, despite not having it. You must persist in drawing upon the feelings of your wish already being fulfilled. If you are shameless in this assumption, it shall be given to you.

There are some useful things you can do to maintain focused energy on your desire. Find pictures that represent your desire and match them as closely as possible with the images in your head. Place these pictures in locations you frequent throughout the day - bathroom, kitchen, office, car, etc. Along with pictures you can also write a short, powerful, and positive statement of intent. Keep it in the present tense, as if it is already happening. Instead of statements that begin with *"I Will...," "One Day...," "I Want...,"* use statements that begin with *"I AM...," "I Have...," "I'm grateful for...."* Place your written statement in similar locations as your pictures. Turn your statement of intent into a mantra. Repeat it to yourself throughout the day as you visualize your focused intention and feel the sensation of it already being realized.

Now that I've filled you with all the positive aspects of creating your reality, I do need to touch upon another aspect of manifesting your destiny. Visualizing with intensity and consistency doesn't always guarantee it is going to materialize. Wanting something and visualizing intently with positive emotions doesn't mean you'll get it. There are some obstacles that may block your desires from entering your life. For instance, you can run the risk of using too much willpower to force something to materialize, which unintentionally focuses your mind on NOT having it. As we now know, the Law of Attraction acts on your intent, which is what the non-discriminating Universe delivers – you NOT having it.

You can also inherently see your desire as being separate from you, which will keep it separate from you. You may harbor deep feelings that you are not entitled to or deserving of what you want, or perhaps you truly don't want the changes it would bring. If you subconsciously believe a prosperous life will become overwhelming, you'll subconsciously block it. If your desire is saturated with fears or doubts of failure, it will neutralize your efforts. All these blockages will put you on an imaginative treadmill of wish fulfillment where nothing materializes. Therefore, it is extremely important to take the time defining and examining your desire in Step 1.

To increase success practice positive affirmations and expressing gratitude for your wish being fulfilled. Adapt these into your daily routine. Don't get trapped into thinking you're an innocent bystander in life. You are the one creating your life, it's not just a bunch of coincidences. You must believe in yourself. You must believe that you can make your perfect life — even if you can't see the whole picture just yet. Developing a confident attitude and belief in yourself is a choice. You must choose to believe that you can create any dream you set your mind on. Telling yourself this daily will retrain your brain to believe that you can accomplish it because your thoughts are what drive your success.

Once you call upon the forces of the Law of Attraction and energize it with powerful visualization techniques, you then must learn how to allow things into your life. Relax with the confidence that your wish will be fulfilled. Don't agonize over the means for how your desire will be accomplished, turn the outcome entirely over to the Universe. Allow the universal forces to take control of your wishes. If you can visualize the thing you want, if you can impress upon your subconscious mind the belief that you already have it, you can safely leave to your higher consciousness the means of it being fulfilled. Trust the Universe will show you the way. Don't end up discussing or debating your desires with your friends and family. It'll only reinforce doubt and feelings of not having. You want to reinforce your desire with regular visualizations, but you don't want to hijack your mind 24/7. During your day try to forget about your wish, knowing it's in the good hands of your higher-self. Don't' continue to analyze it, evaluate it, or anticipate it's arrival. All these will also highlight the not having.

Signs and circumstances relating to your desire will begin to show themselves. It is incumbent to train yourself to recognize these opportunities when they happen. Manifesting your dreams is a process, a series of events and circumstances that all lead toward your wishes being fulfilled. It doesn't all happen in one swoop. For instances, if you invoke the 2-Step process to attract the love of your life on Monday, don't expect on Tuesday while walking through the mall to get a tap on the shoulder by a stranger saying, *"Excuse me, I'm the perfect love you've asked for,"* and on Wednesday you're on a honeymoon flight to a romantic island get-away. The manifestation process typically develops through a series of events that seem to defy coincidence as the Universe delivers more and more energy of matching frequency into your life experience. These incidents are called *'synchronicities,'* more on them later in the chapter. Over time you'll begin to recognize these moments.

When they occur, you must seize them, for they have come into your life as part of your request. Follow Steps 1 and 2 diligently and day-by-day you will begin to see changes. Your mental and emotional states, along with your actions, will begin to shift towards your desired wish. You'll begin to notice coincidences and synchronicities that support your desire popping up all around you. They are signs you are on the right track. Make the most of them for they are opportunities to fulfill your desires in ways you might not imagine.

Now that you've been given the details of this two-step creation technique, let's look at some of the helpful ways you can maximize your success. Visualizing with the full intensity of your imagination can be done just prior to falling asleep when your mind is in a relaxed alpha state. It's also good to do in the morning just after you wake, or as part of your meditation routine. Don't struggle or force yourself, learn to let go, relax, don't try so hard that it becomes a manipulation. If you place too much negative emotion on whether you will attain your goal, it'll work against you. You implant in your subconscious mind the fear of NOT getting what you want. Make your visualization process a regular part of your life. Train yourself to have a routine of visualization meditations for 15 minutes every day, either in the evening before you go to sleep, in the morning, or during a relaxed point of the day.

To illustrate all I've discussed, it's story time again. This one is a 450-horsepower yarn of how I used visualization to drive off in the car of my dreams. Now, before I get started, I fully recognize that I'm using a story about obtaining a material possession after lecturing the importance of honorable and virtuous desires. Keep in mind that ALL desires don't have to be noble, just as long as their intent is not hurtful. This is one such desire. To give you a little backstory, I've worked hard all my life. This story occurred at a point in time where, after many struggles, things were going well for me. I had sacrificed for others for years and felt it was finally time to do something for myself. OK, in hindsight it does seem a bit selfish, but none-the-less that's how I was feeling. I set my sights on the car of my dreams – a BMW 6-Series convertible. It's just a beautiful vehicle top to bottom. Every car I've ever purchased has pretty much been a one-day process. I would decide it's time for a new car, head to a car lot and by the end of the day I'd drive home in a new vehicle. I figured my dream car would be no different. So off I went with the full determination of driving home in luxury…until the reality of the sticker price hit me with the full force of a wrecking ball! But I was dead set on getting this car, so I'd have to go about it a different way. If my checking account couldn't materialize this vehicle, my only other option was to visualize it into existence.

Off I went and began the 2-Step process. Each day I'd meditate, visualize, and add positive energy, thoughts, and beliefs to my dream. I'd create very vivid mental images of driving this gorgeous car with the top down and the sun radiating its warmth on me. I'd feel the wind in my hair, enjoy the rush of the power under the hood, even breath in the new car smells. I actually got to where I'd beam with pride during my visualizations sitting behind the wheel of my imaginary car. During this time, I'd routinely check various car listings for the perfect vehicle. To my delight, many BMW 6-Series convertibles were available, but to my disappointment, none were in my price range. I began to think I set my sights too high. Then the Universe delivered its first synchronicity. About 2 weeks into the process, I spotted an ad for an Atlantic Blue BMW 450ic convertible that seemed to leap out of the ad and grab my attention. When I saw the price, I thought it was a misprint. So, I called the dealership and sure enough the price tag was correct. I jumped with glee. Here's a dream car I could actually afford! Now, I had to bring myself down from the clouds understanding that the devil is in the details – where is the dealership? Has the car been damaged? Will insurance make it unaffordable? All these dream-busting questions needed answering. So, the legwork began.

One by one a series of 'coincidences' occurred that began to defy belief. I was struck by synchronicity #2 when the dealership turned out to be only a few blocks from my office, so I could check out the car in person during my lunch break. I ran a title report which generated synchronicity 3#, the vehicle came up clean. I couldn't believe my luck. The pieces of the puzzle were falling in place. Last came the dreaded insurance call. I thought for sure the rates on a car like this would put a fast and firm end to my dream. So, I reluctantly called the insurance company only to be left speechless with synchronicity #4 – the rate was only $25 a month more than what I was paying on my Toyota! Holy smokes, this thing was really happening.

The next day I went down to the dealership and there it was, sitting on the lot like an Atlantic-blue chariot of the Gods was MY convertible BMW. I approached the car studying it intently, fully expecting to be swarmed by salesmen, but none arrive. I was able to spend a good 15 minutes inspecting and enjoying the car all to myself. It was just as I had imagined – synchronicity #5. After being fully satisfied this was my dream car I was determined to come back to see if I could negotiate a deal.

I arrived back at work and couldn't contain my enthusiasm. My boss at the time was a bit of a car aficionado, so I told him all about my discovery. It was a Thursday afternoon and he asked if I was going to buy it. I told him my plan was to go down on Saturday and see if I could negotiate a deal. Then, synchronicity #6 occurred. My boss, the man paying me to produce work for him, told me not to wait until Saturday, to go tomorrow (Friday) and make a deal. I told him that it'll take too long, I'd miss too much work. He insisted I go tomorrow despite me insisting I wait until Saturday. Finally, he ordered me to go tomorrow to buy the car. Now, can you imagine your boss ordering you to take half a day off work to do a personal errand. Well, that's exactly what happened…and who was I to argue!

Friday came and off I went to the dealership that was holding my affordable dream car. Now, I know how car dealerships can sense when they have a customer hooked and I was in hook-line-and sinker on this car. So, I pretended to be 'just looking' for a convertible. There were 3 other BMW convertibles on the lot and sure enough the salesman showed me all three, but never even mentioned the Atlantic blue dream car. Finally, after entertaining his salesmanship I pointed to my chariot and said, *"What about that one?"* His answer gave a sinking feeling in the pit of my stomach, *"Oh that…that one's sold."* I was stunned and wanted to scream *"Noooooooooooo!"* as I turned towards the heavens like a melodramatic scene from a B-movie. But instead, the words that came out seemed to be coming from someone other than me, *"How can it be sold if it's sitting right there?." "Oh, well it was an out of state purchase, we're shipping it out tomorrow."* Synchronicity #7 - my boss was right! Had I waited until Saturday the damn thing would have been on a car-carrier heading toward the opposite coast. The foreign voice inside took over and said, *"Well, since it's not shipped yet, can I talk to the sales manager?"*

A few minutes later I'm in the sales manager's office who is showing me a copy of the check the purchaser has written for the car and the shipping documents, both were arriving the next day. However, the strange thing is I had convinced myself that this was MY car, and it didn't matter what he showed me, I was leaving with MY car. So, I said, *"Sir, you know very well that a deal isn't closed until the check clears, and you haven't even received the check yet. You sell that car to me today, and you can be assured the deal is done."* He didn't want to budge, he had already committed the vehicle to an out of state buyer. He couldn't take the risk. He told me if he did this deal, he'd get his ass chewed out. I had come this close. All the hopes and visualizations brought me to this point and now it was slipping through my grasp. In a final desperate attempt, that unbeknownst voice emerged and asked the sales manager how often he got his ass chewed out. He said, "*Well, about once a year.*" So, I explained that it'd be in his best interest to get his ass chewed out today, you won't have to worry about it for another year and at least you'll have a nice deal to show for it! The guy then made this ear-to-ear grin, looked me dead in the eye, and hit me with synchronicity #8. He put his hand out and said, "*OK, you have a deal.*" I was shocked! I was leaving with MY car.

Finally, to top everything off synchronicity #9 arrived during the negotiation process. The sales manager out of the blue told me that he's looking for a Toyota Camry for his son. Well, guess what car I was trading in? Yes, a Toyota Camry! I got maximum dollar for my trade-in and left the lot sitting behind the wheel of my dream car that cost me less than $100 a month more than what I was paying for my Camry. As I looked back at the series of events that lined up to make this possible, they seemed to defy statistical mathematics. And all those emotions and sensations I imagined while visualizing my dream car, were now mine to experience for real.

Despite all my blabbing about manifesting your fate being a simple two-step process, I sure have complicated it with pages and pages of details. So, here's a bullet-point recap of the process:

1. **Determine Your Desire**
   - Use clarity and specificity when forming your desire
   - Determine why you want it, be sure no part of you feels undeserving of it
   - Assure your desire is not at another's expense
   - Focus on the positive feelings of the want, not on the negative attributes you are trying to avoid
   - Develop an intense, burning desire through visualization

2. **Convince Yourself You Already Have It**
   - Use visualization to create a mental imprint on your super-conscious mind of your wish already being fulfilled
   - Master the feelings, emotions, and senses of your wish completed with all the radiance of reality using your imagination
   - Make your visualization a daily routine
   - Show gratitude for possessing your wish despite not having it
   - Use pictures and statements of intent to maintain your focus
   - Relax and allow your desire into your life
   - Learn to recognize synchronicities and seize them when they occur

Earlier in this section I made reference to incorporating your visualization technique into your meditation routine. You may be wondering when I was planning on providing some insight on how to meditate. After all, it's quite an important aspect of manifesting your desires. Well, the wait is over!

A Clean Slate

For thousands of years, people have received great benefits from the practice of meditation. Millions worldwide turn to meditation for health, balance, and well-being. You may hear friends and colleagues talking about meditation and various disciplines they've tried. Perhaps you've given it a shot yourself. You might think with all the talk about meditation and its inherent benefits that the ancient practice is making a big revival. Well, don't worry, you haven't missed out on a pop-culture comeback. Only about 8% of the US population practices meditation. 8%...that's it! 92 out of 100 people don't meditation. 8% is such a paltry number when compared to the staggering amount of stress and anxiety-related conditions that plague the United States.

About 77% of the U.S. adult population report experiencing physical symptoms caused by stress. Nearly half say their stress levels have increased in the past 5 years, and over 50% have gotten into fights with people close to them because of stress. Can you imagine, half the people you know have picked a fight with you merely due to stress. It becomes even more disheartening when you learn what Americans claim are causing them stress…well…it's virtually everything! Work, money, relationships, media, divorce, moving, illness, pregnancy, death of a loved one, pressure to conform, personal appearance, competition, loss of job, weddings, retirement, child leaving home, in-laws, school, recreation and social activities, vacation, Christmas, and traffic violations. What's left? Getting a pampered massage? I'm sure even that is stressful to some!

How is anyone supposed to go through life avoiding all these things? No wonder road rage is on the rise. No wonder prescription drugs are at epidemic levels. No wonder inappropriate behavior and vulgarities across social media platforms are not only commonplace, they're EXPECTED! No wonder people are arguing and brawling at events that are intended to promote companionship, camaraderie, or debate. Society is reaching a stress event horizon. Individuals need to reevaluate the true source of their stress, I assure you the above list isn't it. They are merely symptoms, not the root cause.

We need to consider the inability of ordinary people to calm and control their temperament as the REAL root of our stressed-out society. All the events being blamed as stress-inducing are simply triggers. Well, guess what? We're not going to be one of the 77% with stress related ailments, or the 50% who fight with their loved ones due to stress. Life is a gift meant to be cherished with a loving, peaceful, and fun disposition, and that includes every 'stress-inducing' event listed above. Make it a personal objective to experience the glory of life with enthusiasm and joy. You may be wondering how you're supposed to do all that while walking through the pressure-cooker of life. Well, an effective means of reaching a calm controlled state is to incorporate meditation into your daily routine.

We've learned about the visualization process and how it can be used to manifest the life experiences of your desires. One of the primary drivers to your success is the ability to guide and control your mental powers through deep relaxation and focused thought, or what is commonly known as *'meditation.'* It's a wonderful practice to incorporate into your daily routine. In addition to lowering stress levels, there are many other uses and benefits of meditation. You can use meditation to boost your body's energy intake and direct the flow of Chi. It can be used to manifest your desires (as we explored in the previous section), or as a form of self-healing. People use a type of meditation as prayers to send blessings to loved ones, while others meditate on perplexing problems to derive solutions. Artists and performers gain creative inspiration through meditation, and people of all walks meditate on important life issues to seek inner guidance. But perhaps one of its most valuable functions is as a vital tool to advance your spiritual journey.

e, there are numerous studies and research that show reduces tension and stress, alleviates anxiety and hronic pain, improves heart health, boosts the enhances metabolism, lowers blood pressure, g, improves learning and memory, accelerates cognition, sharpens concentration and multitasking, enhances self-awareness, and enriches sleep. Imagine that, all those benefits with no prescriptions, no addictive drugs, no bills from the shrink, no fighting with your health care provider over coverage. The positive benefits to meditation are so numerous it's a wonder why everyone doesn't make it a part of their daily routine. Meditation is a marvelous gift from the Universe, and to think only 8% make use of this gift. Hopefully you'll begin gaining all these wonderful, life-affirming benefits of meditation…that is, if you're not already doing so.

There are many styles and forms of meditation that have developed around the world. Some techniques use visualization, others strive to achieve a perfectly empty mind, while others combine meditation with chanting and/or specific body positions. However, they all share a common objective to develop a sharper, more focused mind. This mental clarity not only benefits all the conditions referenced earlier but is an essential component in the efficacy of manifesting your life desires. And getting started is so much easier in today's connected world. You don't need to journey into the Himalayan mountains in search of a Shangri-La utopian monastery or turn over your way of life to join the monks of Tibet. Today, there are many apps you can download that get you on your way and help monitor your progress. Some of the more popular ones include; *Buddhify, Headspace, Calm, 10% Happier, Mindful, Insight Timer,* and *Smiling Mind.*

Now that you've heard my sales pitch on meditation, I'm sure you're wondering when I'm going to drop the bad news…I mean, it can't all be rainbows and gumdrops with no downside. What will it take to work meditation into a hectic lifestyle? How much time will it eat up? How many years before the benefits kick in? What are the costs…do I have to give up coffee, sugar, red meat, and sleeping in on rainy days? The pressures and responsibilities of life already erode every waking minute of the day, how is the average person supposed to find time to sit around chanting *"Ohmmmm*?" Isn't that for the privileged with a team of servants and assistants to handle their thankless grunt work? There's got to be some sort of letdown! Well, don't worry there is no bad news. Meditation is easy to learn, takes very little time, and the benefits begin kicking in right away. A good meditation routine only takes 15 – 20 minutes each day, and this small commitment will yield an amazing return on your investment. With a clear focused mind, you'll be able to accomplish far more in less time. Your meditation abilities will advance just as natural as any other activity you practice with earnest intent. Once you realize the ease and simplicity of meditation, and how little time it takes, you'll question why you haven't tapped into this powerful tool sooner.

But before you begin, let's step through a few basic pointers that will greatly improve your effectiveness. You'll want to first figure out the Where's, When's, and How's. Where to meditate? When to meditate? and How to prepare? Each one is important to the success of your session. Let's start with the 'Where.' The environment and location in which you meditate play a significant role in reaching a deep state, particularly during the preliminary stages. Until you've gained masterful control of your mind, you'll be easily distracted by external noises preventing you from reaching a deep state. Find a quiet, peaceful location that's free from clutter. Don't try to learn while the kids are screaming, the TV is blasting, the phone is ringing, and you're rushing to be somewhere. Even the slightest of sounds, the ticking of a clock or dripping of a faucet, can become distracting and offset your concentration. You really want to separate yourself from the hustle and bustle of your life. Establish a quiet place in the beginning allows your mind and body to learn how to reach a deep theta state uninterrupted. As you become more experienced, you'll be able to achieve a deep focused state just about anywhere, from a crowded subway car to the middle of a Door-Buster Black Friday Sale! But for beginners, start in a serene isolated spot that you can turn into your personal meditation sanctuary.

Boosting your energy level is a terrific byproduct of meditation. Since nature is teaming with life and energy, you will discover heightened energy benefits when you introduce nature into your meditations. Surrounding yourself with nature is a terrific way of achieving a peaceful relaxed mind. Simply sit in an outdoor garden or beneath a large tree to pull in tremendous energy flows of nature. However, if weather or circumstances do not allow for outdoor meditating, just place a few house plants nearby as an alternative. As you advance and gain the ability to reach a deep state quickly, you'll be able to have mini-meditation sessions throughout the day just about anywhere. I've had wonderful meditations during lunch breaks, on commuter trains, in the airport, waiting for meetings to begin, even while on the phone with my mother. Don't laugh, I'm sure you've tuned out during one of your mom's interminable stories. The point is, it becomes easier in practice and you'll begin to look forward to your escape from the busyness of the day and search for those moments in the most unusual of places.

Once you've established your meditation sanctuary, you'll only need to set aside 15-20 minutes a day to conduct your session. I enjoy meditating in the morning, before starting the day, but I'll often get in a quick session while lying in bed just before falling asleep. During the early stages you'll want to use a non-jarring timer to prevents yourself from going longer than planned. I use the harp alarm on my iPhone. While there is no harm to extending your meditation beyond the 15-20 minutes, it's actually a good thing, you might become discouraged if your sessions end up eating more of the day than you bargained for. After a while, you'll find yourself emerging from your mediations within seconds of your alarm and can gradually do away with the timer.

With the Where and When are covered, let's finish off with the How. To prepare yourself, avoid caffeinated drinks and large meals for 1 hour before your session. Wear loose fitting clothes so you're comfortable and relaxed. Avoid clothes that tug, pull, or act like a tunicate on your legs. Restricted blood flow causes discomfort and inhibits energy flow. Remove your shoes and socks to allow for unobstructed energy flow into and out of your feet. Sit with your spine straight and maintain lucid control of your mind. You can also meditate laying down, but you risk falling asleep in the lying position. If you have the flexibility, sit in the full or half lotus position (crisscross applesauce) with your hands resting comfortably on your lap or on your thighs. If you're unable to sit comfortably in a lotus or half-lotus position, stretch your muscles and ligaments a little each day so that you can achieve this position. Until then, sit in a comfortable straight back chair. Don't slouch, sit upright.

A big challenge many beginners face is concentration. A still, pure, unobstructed mind is the secret passage to the soul and all its inherent powers. The more emptiness you experience, the more benefits you will receive and the faster your creative abilities will develop. For many beginners, the simple instruction to 'stop thinking' is almost inconceivable particularly to someone who has lived their entire life with vigorous unrestrained thoughts racing through their head. Getting control over these wild uninhibited thoughts can become frustrating. Don't struggle to still your mind, don't force it, or suppress your thoughts. Let your mind think. Let your thoughts flow naturally.

When unwanted thoughts do pop into your mind, place yourself in a superior position and 'observe' the thoughts. Think of your mind as separate and apart from you, an entity that is creating these thoughts independent of you. Treat these errant thoughts as a neither good nor bad but just as the mind's byproduct. Simply observe the thought from your superior position, and lovingly discard the thought and move on. Do that for every unwanted thought that comes to mind. Treat each one with loving appreciation, then set it aside. Don't get frustrated. It may take some time to gain control over your busy mind, but practice and be patient. Gradually this unrestrained chatter will diminish, and a still mind is easily achieved.

As meditating becomes a natural part of your daily routine, you'll find yourself getting more and more proficient. You'll be able to reach a deeper state quicker and accomplish your mediation goals in less time. During these still moments, when your mind and body are relaxed is when the physical and spiritual components of your body merge. A lucid union forms between the ethereal dimension and the incarnated portion of your soul to establish a powerful means of transforming thoughts into action. Your higher spiritual consciousness flashes knowledge and inspiration to you through this connective bridge. Original ideas spring into your consciousness, answers to complex questions materialize, and guidance to challenging situations emerge. You'll learn to cultivate and harvest these flashes of wisdom into actionable endeavors. When your meditation sessions are over, you return to your waking world armed with vigor, confidence, and solutions to many of your challenges. Spending a few moments each day with your higher-self expands your mind and in a short time you'll recognize your infinite capabilities. You gain self-control, confidence, compassion, understanding, and an enthusiasm for life.

The more you practice, the greater access you gain to your spiritual reservoir. Soon, you'll find yourself diving into this pool of knowledge during brief moments throughout your day – in the car stopped at a red light, out for a walk, brushing your teeth, standing in line, waiting to cross the street, or watching a sunset. Suddenly, a thought or creative idea will flash through your mind with vivid detail that relates to issues or desires you're working on. In practice, you'll recognize these flashes as communication from your spiritual self and you'll welcome them like an old friend. This simple daily routine that doesn't cost a single penny, will return priceless benefits.

Alright, it's time to read your mind again. Right about now you're thinking, "*Wait one stinking minute! I thought we're supposed to be imagining all these vivid and brilliant images to manifest our desires. How are we supposed to do that if we need to empty and still our minds?*" Good question. Think of your mind as a complex blackboard crammed into your skull. The blackboard gets written on throughout the day with all sorts of random thoughts and ideas. By the end of day, it's a chaotic mess of chalk scribblings. Day after day goes by with more chalk scribblings being added to the blackboard. Soon every teeny-tiny spot is filled with scribbles. Then, you're approached with a problem to solve and the blackboard is so full and in such disarray there's no room to work out your problem. Instead, you procrastinate because there's simply too much clutter in your way. The only way of working through the problem is to wipe the blackboard clean. When you do, it's like an enormous relief. Ahhhh! A fresh clean and empty blackboard. Now, you can focus with intent on working through that problem with no chalk-filled clutter. Well, that's what meditation does with your mind, it wipes the slate clean! Clearing your mind's blackboard gives you a clean slate to create uncluttered vivid visualizations with no distracting aberrant thoughts. Meditation will train your mind to master the visualization process.

The Mind-Body Refresher

So, you've established your quiet meditation sanctuary, you've blocked out 20 minutes of your day to calm your mind, you're dressed comfortably and are ready to start meditating. Now what? What do you think about? Are you supposed to breath in a certain way? What do you do with your hands? Do you play meditation music? Burn incense? Ring a Tibetan gong? Geez-Louise. Who would have thought meditation would be so stressful! Well stay calm and don't let the unknown abyss of what to do and how to do it trigger those stress levels we're trying to get away from. There are plenty of styles, methods, and techniques for meditating. I advise you to do some independent research to find the technique that is the most enjoyable and effective for you.

I've studied many different methodologies and created my own meditation routine that I like to call the *"The Mind-Body Refresher."* I've taken some of the best techniques that have resonated with me, improved upon some, adjusted others, and tossed in a few of my own creations. In the process I've developed a very effective meditation designed to relax the body, clear the mind, improve energy absorption and flow, supercharge your subconscious mind, and make you feel refreshed and bubbly. The Mind-Body Refresher steps through a few stages to bring the body and mind to a state of complete relaxation. I'll guide you through each stage in beat-by-beat detail, but first I want to call your attention to the importance of breathing.

There are three sources of energy your body needs to survive – food, water, and air. Which of these three sources do you think is the most important? We certainly spend the most time on food. Just watch a few episodes of any cooking competition series and you'll see the lengths people go to in their food preparation. But, would it surprise you to know that of the three, breathing is by far the most important…the other two don't even come close!

Think about it. How long can the average person go without eating? Two Days? Ten days? Two weeks? In fact, most people can survive between 30 – 40 days without food. That's pretty shocking huh. Especially since I have a tough time getting through a 2-hour movie without reaching for a snack! What about water, how long can you go without water? The answer to this one is a little different; on average you can only survive for 3 -4 days without water. Making water about 10 times more important to your survival than food. Do you spend 10 times longer preparing, planning, and understanding the water you drink than the food you eat? Very doubtful.

Now ask, how long can you go without breathing? On average most people become unconscious in only 3 - 4 minutes. We'll eat about 3 meals a day, drink approximately 64 ounces of water a day, and take over 23,000 breaths a day. How's that for putting things into perspective. Of the 3 ways to provide energy to your body, the one we know the least about and give the least amount of attention to, is the one that has the most significance. Now that you recognize the importance of breathing, I encourage you to take some time to learn about proper breathing techniques, at least give it the time you would to prepare just one gourmet meal.

You've discovered how the physical body is a vehicle for the soul in Chapter 6. You've been given this gift of a physical body and you are responsible for maintaining it. It's up to you, and you alone, to control all the energy you take into your body – the food, the water, and the air. The sustenance needed to nourish and maintain your body are also gifts from the Universe. Cherish and show gratitude for them. Give thanks to Nature whenever you consume food or water for its sacrifice, so your vehicle may continue. And as for breathing, when you inhale you are not just taking in oxygen, Vital Life Energy also enters your body with every breath. It's something most people don't recognize. This vital energy is the 'oxygen' that nourishes your energy body. Your breathing is not only extremely important to your survival, but it plays an important role in the relaxation and mediation process.

When you meditate using The Mind-Body Refresher, you'll use a form of breathing called *'Diaphragmatic Breathing.'* This is a breathing technique that employs the diaphragm to help regulate the inflow and outflow of air to the lungs. The diaphragm sits at the base of the lungs, during diaphragmatic breathing when you inhale, your diaphragm moves downward creating more space for your lungs to expand. When you exhale, the opposite happens, and the diaphragm moves upward pushing air out of the lungs.

Diaphragmatic breathing is performed by inhaling through your nose and exhaling through your mouth. Begin with a slow, deep inhalation through your nose for about 2-3 seconds. As you inhale, simultaneously push your stomach out. Imagine there's a string attached to your bellybutton that gently pulls your stomach out as you inhale. Focus your attention on the air entering through your nostrils and flowing down into your abdomen as your stomach expands. Your chest and lungs should not expand, only your stomach. At the completion of your inhalation, hold the breath for a full second before slowly exhaling. On the exhale, crack your lips slightly and gently begin pulling your stomach back in towards your spine. Use the same imaginary string attached to your bellybutton to pull your stomach back. Your exhale should also last about 2-3 seconds. Practice this a few times until it becomes natural. You'll use this form of breathing to help relax your body during the stage 1 of The Mind-Body Refresher.

With the breathing lesson out of the way, let's begin the process for The Mind-Body Refresher. The first phase of this mediation works on relaxing the body. Tension and stress in your muscles will stand in the way of your mind entering a deep theta state, so it's important to bring your body to a state of complete relaxation. Some people will be able to reach a relaxed state in very little time, others will have to work a little harder. However, as this becomes a daily routine, you'll be able to become extremely relaxed in very little time. In the beginning, it may take 5 to 10 minutes of your session before your body fully relaxes, which is normal. When I first began, I'd sometimes sit for my entire 20-minute session and never reach a state of full physical relaxation. Now, I can relax my body in a matter of a few deep breaths.

I've provided estimated times for each stage of this meditation, but don't get discouraged if you're unable to complete the stage in the allotted time. These are timeframes you can work up to. As you begin, keep your focus on remembering and completing the process. The more you practice the more the meditation becomes instinctual and soon you'll be completing all the stages in under the suggested time.

Stage 1: Physical Relaxation (Approx. 2 ½ minutes)

- POSITION: Sit comfortably with your spine straight. No slouching or slumping. If you have the flexibility, sit in the full lotus or half-lotus position. This is where you cross your legs and place each foot on the opposite thigh. If you're not able to twist yourself into a pretzel like this, not a problem, just sit upright in a firm comfortable chair with your feet flat on the floor.

- HANDS: Place your hands in either of these positions;

    a. Turn both hands so your palms are facing up and set the back of your right hand in the palm of your left hand. The fingers of each hand should be pointing in opposite directions. Then slide your hands so the thumbs are gently touching. With the hands in this position, rest them on your lap, palms up, with the base of your hands touching your lower abdomen just below the belly button.

    - OR –

    b. Place your hands on your thighs with the palms facing up and fingers pointing towards the knees. Left hand on the left thigh, right hand on the right thigh. Don't force your hand position, they should be resting naturally on your thighs. Bring together the right thumb and right index finger so they are lightly touching making a circle like the 'OK' sign. Do the same with the left thumb and index finger. The remaining fingers should be extended outward in a relaxed position.

- PREPARE THE MIND: In order to relax your body, you'll need your mind to be open and not preoccupied. Gain control of your thoughts by dismissing all worries and problems of the day. Eliminate any negative thought you may have dealing with vengeance, hate, jealousy, etc. as well as any busy-body concerns about deadlines, meetings, housework, chores, schedules, or obligations. Simply tell yourself now is not the time for these thoughts and set them aside. Allow yourself to sink into a mental state of calm by pushing away these thoughts and filling your mind with a sense of peace.

- BREATHING: Close your eyes and take a deep breath. Your breathing is extremely important in the relaxation and mediation process. Begin the meditation with Diaphragmatic Breathing as instructed earlier. Gently close your lips with the tip of your tongue lightly touching the bridge of your mouth where it meets the back of your two front teeth. Slowly inhale deeply through your nose for 2-3 seconds. Focus your attention on the air entering through your nostrils and flowing down into your abdomen as your stomach expands. Your chest and lungs should not expand, only your stomach. At the completion of your inhalation, hold the breath for a full second before slowly exhaling. Crack your lips slightly and gently begin exhaling for about 2-3 seconds. Continue to use diaphragmatic breathing for the duration of Stage 1.

- RELAX THE BODY: Many people have difficulty reaching a relaxed state. This little method I've developed works wonders at driving out muscle tension. Starting at your feet, focus your full awareness on the muscles in your toes. When your eyes are closed it's natural to perceive that your mental awareness is in located in your head. However, you can shift this mental awareness anywhere in your body. Imagine you are inside your body and bring your awareness down to your toes. Focus all your attention on the muscles in your toes. Concentrate on relaxing your toe muscles completely and entirely for a couple deep diaphragmatic breaths. As you inhale focus your awareness on your toes, on the exhale shift your focus on relaxing the muscle. When your toes are fully relaxed, move to the muscles in the arches of your feet. With your awareness now fully in the arches of your feet, focus on relaxing the muscles there for a full deep breath or two. Once your arches are fully and completely relaxed move on to the ankle muscles. Continue this process as you move your awareness internally up the body taking 1 – 2 diaphragmatic breaths as you relax each muscle group. Don't move on to another muscle if you sense any tension. It's OK to go back to a muscle to relax it again should you sense tension returning. Including all your muscles as you travel your awareness up from the ankles to the calves, then to the thighs, stomach, lower back, chest, upper back, hands, arms, shoulders, and neck.

- RELAX THE FACE: When you reach your head, do a quick scan of the body to make sure no muscle tension has returned. If it has, go back to that muscle and relax it. With the body in a completely relaxed state, it's time to focus on the head where much of your tension gets stored. You'll want to focus on each individual muscle of the face. First bring your awareness to the muscles of your jaw relaxing them during a couple diaphragmatic breaths. Include all the facial muscles as you work toward the top of your head. Move on to the muscles at the front of your chin, then to your lips, upwards to your lower cheeks, then to your upper cheeks, next the muscles beneath your eyes, your eye lids, your eyebrows, and your forehead. By the time you've reached the top of your head, your entire face and body should be completely relaxed. Do another quick body scan and re-relax any muscles in which you sense any tension. Now that the body is in a completely relaxed state, it's time to work on the mind.

Stage 2: Clear the Mind (Approx. 2 ½ minutes)

- FOCUS ON BREATHING: It's time to let go of the external world and enter the universe of your internal mind. Your breathing will now shift from the deep diaphragmatic breaths to a normal gentle breath. Inhale and exhale through the nose. Keep your lips gently closed with the tip of your tongue lightly touching the bridge of your mouth where it meets the back of your two front teeth. Shift the focus of your mind to your breathing. With each breath, imagine the air flowing in through your nose, flowing throughout your lungs and body, and exhaling out through the nose again. Breath in positive rejuvenating energy and exhale all the stress and toxins of the day. Energy in, stress out. Breath in thoughts of unlimited health, happiness, and love. Breath out all thoughts of sickness, failure, and fear. In and out. Continue this for a few moments.

- CURB ERRANT THOUGHTS: In the beginning, it's inevitable your focus will drift as errant and random thoughts enter your mind. This is perfectly normal, don't get frustrated. Don't try to battle these thoughts or struggle to suppress them. Just allow them into your mind and gently move them along. The key to doing this is to take on the perspective of an observer who sits and watches these thoughts. Notice them in a detached way, as though they belong to someone else. It's like you are the parent of your mind and these thoughts are hyper-active children getting into mischief. Simply shoo them along like a loving parent as you calmly refocus your attention back to your breathing. It may be awkward at first, but with a little practice it'll begin to feel natural.

- OPEN ENERGY CENTERS: In the same way that you've learned to bring your awareness to various muscle groups throughout the body, you can also bring your awareness to various locations in your head, an area it's most familiar. You'll use this technique to open energy vortexes in the head, which aid in the flow of energy throughout the body. Begin by focusing your awareness at the very top of the head, or your crown vortex. Your awareness should be about 1 inch beneath the surface of your skull, not on the outside. With your awareness at the crown, think to yourself, "*Open this energy center.*" This simple command instructs the energy body what to do, all you need to do is keep your awareness focused at the crown and concentrate on "*opening the energy center*." Do this for a few complete breaths repeating the statement in your mind as you exhale. Your consciousness will do the rest.

- After a few breaths you'll move your awareness to open other energy centers inside the head. From the crown proceed to the center of your forehead about an inch above the eyebrows (the 3rd Eye) and repeat the process you did at the crown. Then move your awareness to the center of the temples (you can do them individually or split your awareness and do them both at once). Then proceed to a point just behind your eyes, and lastly, you'll finish with the pineal gland (a point where the spinal nerves connect with the brain). To bring your awareness to the pineal gland, imagine a point that is centered over your spine which sits at a height level with your eyes. After opening all these energy centers, your mind should be lucid and revitalized. It should feel clear, light, and refreshed. This exercise of opening energy centers within the head can also be performed by itself as a stand-alone technique whenever you need to clear your mind. It's especially effective when your head is feeling 'cloudy' and you can't seem to concentrate.

Stage 3: Recharge the Energy Body (Approx. 5 minutes)

- SPIRITUAL ENERGY FLOW: Your body is now completely relaxed, and your mind is thoroughly clear and vitalized, the final thing to complete is bolstering the flow of Chi energy throughout the body. This will recharge your spiritual body, which you know takes the lead in maintaining physical health. We learned about the 7 chakras in Chapter 4, this part of the meditation gives them all an energy boost. If you remember, there are 2 chakras that extend up and down vertically (the crown chakra and the root chakra), while the others extend horizontally outward from the body. In this portion of the meditation we'll be focusing on the root and crown chakras, at the base of the tailbone and top of the head respectively. Visualize a tube that encircles your spine which runs up through the top of your head, and downward through the tip of your tailbone. The diameter of the tube should be about the size of the circle you create by touching your thumb to your index finger. Chi energy flows into this tube from both its top and bottom and meets at your navel (which is the 3rd Chakra) where it radiates throughout the body.

- Continue your normal breathing through the nose with the tip of your tongue lightly touching the bridge of your mouth. As you inhale, visualize brilliant white energy coming in and filling the tube from its top and the bottom. These two flows of energy then meet at your navel and form a sphere of light about the size of a grapefruit. Imagine the energy pouring in on each inhale, and the sphere charging up on each exhale. Continue this for 5 – 6 breaths imagining the sphere growing brighter and more energized with each breath. Once you've gotten 6 or so full breaths completed and your energy sphere is nicely charged, on your next breath inhale normally but on the exhale imagine the energy sphere expands from the size of a grapefruit to a sphere of charged energy that surrounds your body. As you inhale envision the flow of energy in through the top and bottom of the tube, meeting at your navel, and radiating outwards into the energy sphere surrounding your body. Feel the flow of energy and your connection with the spiritual dimension. Your awareness will begin to tune into your spiritual consciousness. The more you practice this, the more you strengthen your ability to manifest reality.

Stage 4: Visualize (Approx. 10 minutes)

- VISUALIZATION: The first three stages of this meditation are designed to enhance your mind and body's connection to your higher consciousness. This preparation will amplify your visualization session. Once you've completed stage 3 you can use all the remaining time of your meditation session to visualize your wants and desires. Follow the visualization instructions provided earlier in this chapter. I also want to give a friendly reminder to keep the Law of Attraction rules in mind during your visualization. Remember, to maintain your focus and concentration on already having that which you desire. If your visualization focuses on the NOT having the want or desire, your mind will emit the mental frequency of NOT having it, and the Law of Attraction will bring forth that reality…the reality of NOT having it.

- While I've presented the Mind Refresher as the foundation for visualization, it can be used as an activator for many other mental actions, some of which we'll discuss later in this chapter. For instance, upon completing stage 3, instead of visualizing a want or desire you can focus on a blessing for a friend or loved one, or commence a self-healing session, a problem solving session, ask for creative inspiration, or retrieval of memories, or simply take the time to continue concentrating on your breathing, energy flow, and stilling the mind to help maintain a sense of calm and focus in your waking life.

Stage 5: Returning

- BACK TO LIFE: Once the allotted time you've set aside for your meditation session has come to an end, it's time to return to the real world. Either your non-jarring alarm has sounded, or as you become more proficient you instinctively know your session has concluded. Take a few deep breaths, open your eyes, and bring your awareness back to your physical environment. Slowly stretch out your arms and legs. If you meditate in the lotus position, you may need to shake out the stiffness. Breath in the realities of your physical world and leave behind the spiritual requests made during your meditation. Remember, you don't want to dwell on your wants and desires to avoid emitting the frequency of 'not' having them, in which case the Law of Attraction draws the 'not' to you. Slowly stand and go forth with a rejuvenated mind and invigorated energy body. You should be refreshed and vitalized, ready to leap eagerly and enthusiastically into the challenges of the day.

There you have it, the Mind-Body Refresher in all its glory! I've gone through many trials and errors refining this meditation to one that works wonders for me. I hope and wish it delivers similar benefits to you as well. The wonderful thing about The Mind-Body Refresher is the first three stages can be used as the basis for other meditative objectives. Since we'll be looking at other ways in which the first 3 stages can be used, I'll refer to them as *"The Mind-Body Primer."* It's amazing what the subconscious mind is capable of when you call in help from the spiritual dimension. You may be wondering how you can apply meditation in other areas of your life. We'll, let's find out...

Instruments of the Mind

Once meditation becomes part of your daily routine, you'll want to utilize it to guide and accelerate other areas of your life. It's not just for visualization. The Mind-Body Refresher is a great foundation for many other life experiences. The first 3 stages of the Mind-Body Refresher, which I'll now call "*The Mind-Body Primer,*" prepares you for other actions, such as to send a blessing to a friend or loved one, for self-healing, problem solving, creative inspiration, retrieval of memories, or stilling the mind in a traditional meditation. To use the Mind-Body Primer for problem solving, the first thing you'll need is a problem to solve. Is there something that's been troubling you that you just can't seem to crack? Whether it's a difficult issue at work, a complex scientific problem, concerns over a relationship, uncertainty with a business venture, developing a new product or service, or any other problem in life you're struggling with, you can offer your problem to your higher-self for guidance.

It's important to have a clear and concise mental impression of the problem you'd like answered before you begin. Prior to starting the Mind-Body Primer, fill your mind with every bit of information you can about the problem. State the problem consciously and flesh out a defined question to cover the answer you're searching for. After rolling it around in your mind and giving it meaningful attention, you're ready to pass it on to your spiritual consciousness.

Sit comfortably in your meditation sanctuary and step through the 3 stages of the Mind-Body Primer to prepare the body and mind to be receptive of the spiritual dimension. Once you've completed the Mind-

Body Primer and you are at stage 4, begin laying out the specifics of the problem. Mentally work through all the issues and concerns you have with the problem and stipulate how you'd like the problem to be resolved. After you've fully created a mental image of the problem, politely command your spiritual self to do your work with the following statement, "*You have access to infinite knowledge. You know the answer to this. It is now YOUR problem. Please work out the answer for me.*" Express appreciation for the work your higher-self will do on your behalf and end your meditation. When you emerge from your deep meditative state, forget all about the problem and the request you've made to your higher-self. In due time, your answer will come. Remain open to recognize and identify the answer when it is delivered as it can arrive in the most unusual of ways.

Here's a short story of how The Mind-Body Primer worked for me in a dealing with a problem I faced, complete with a very usual delivery of the answer. I used this technique to ask my higher-self for advice in a business venture that was presented to me. I had thought long and hard about all the various possibilities and outcomes and whether I should move forward or pass up the opportunity. I was indecisive and couldn't quite make a firm commitment in either direction. Finally, I resolved to turn the decision over to my higher-self by using the Mind-Body Primer meditation.

The following day on my drive into the office I came to a red-light and was unexpectedly struck by a very strange experience. As I sat in my car at the traffic light, the world around me suddenly became irrelevant and my attention was inexplicably drawn to the car immediately in front of me. It was as though there was some external force focusing my awareness on this car. I experienced a sort of a tunnel vision where things in my peripheral vision became blurred. Only the vehicle in the center of my eyesight remained focused. Nothing else mattered but the vehicle directly in front of me.

Then bizarrely, my attention overwhelmingly became drawn to the car's license plate, which read "NOT NOW." At the time my mind was far removed from the business venture I had meditated on the previous day. I was either immersed in listening to morning talk radio or belting out my version of carpool karaoke. However, the moment my eyes connected with that license plate I inherently knew it was the answer I had asked for. There it was, stamped in raised blue letters on a California license plate, the answer to my question - "NOT NOW!" I thanked the Universe for the clear message and politely turned down the business venture. Months later I learned the business partnership had been sued for fraud. As I said, the answers can arrive in unusual ways so stay open and alert.

Now, some may wonder why *'prayer'* was included in my list of meditation activities. Often prayer gets associated with a religious ceremony done fully conscious, in a non-meditative state. Prayer is linked with things like rosary beads, 'Hail Mary' and 'Our Father,' kneeling at the foot of the bed before going to sleep, bowing in prayer multiple times a day, or holding hands around a dinner table. Yes, these are all forms of prayer, but they're different from the style of prayer I've referenced. Prayer from a spiritual perspective takes the form of deep, relaxed, and focused thought utilizing visualization with the full engagement of feelings, emotion, and the senses. Sounds a lot like the visualization process...well it is. Spiritual prayer differs from the visualization process of manifesting your desires only in who the intended recipient is of the want or desire. All the positive thought energy you use to attract wishes and desires into your own life experience can also be used to project wishes and desires for the benefit of others. When you do this, it's considered a '*prayer*' in a spiritual sense.

You can offer a prayer of health, prosperity, good fortune, or any other positive benefit to anyone. To do so, you must first suspend all negative thoughts and be in a neutral mental state. You want your prayer offering to come from a state of strength and positivity. You can use the Mind-Body Primer to begin your prayer session up until stage 4. At this point, simply begin offering your prayer blessing instead of a self-directed visualization. Remember that prayer is just like your own personal visualization, so be sure to engage all the senses – smell, sight, taste, touch, hearing – and 'feel' the results of your wish, as if it's already happened. If you are praying for a loved one to recover from an illness, visualize that person fully recovered, as though they were already healed. Believe it! See their healing as an accomplished fact. Use your power of thought, feeling, and emotion to wish your blessing upon your loved one. Conclude your prayer by showing and feelings appreciation and gratitude for the opportunity to radiate positive energy upon your loved one and the Universe's power to grant your prayer. It's such an awesome feeling to be able to help people you care about on a spiritual level. Even if they don't believe in the concept of spiritual blessings, your work will still provide benefits. Be assured that prayer is effective and can work miracles.

We've seen how the Mind-Body Refresher can be used to solve problems and send blessing to others, so what other type of mind miracles are you capable of? Well, plenty! This next one is a real humdinger, but I may need you to sign a legal waiver before continuing as this one involves self-healing. Have you ever had a cramp, sickness, injury, flu, aches, pains or other illness and just didn't have the time to head to Urgent Care or the desire to wolf down a bunch of pills? Well, there is another way to find relief…yourself. That's right, through the power of your mind. Now, I do have to make a very firm and clear caveat. Self-healing is a very advanced practice that should not be attempted by beginners without the supervision of a doctor or in conjunction with seeing a doctor. This discussion on self-healing is for informational purposes to illustrate the power of the mind and how self-healing under proper training and supervision has shown to be very real, to the astonishment of many doctors.

With the legal disclaimer addressed, I'm sure you're itching to know if we really do have the ability to heal ourselves. Some say *"Absolutely!,"* while other emphatically insist *"It's impossible!,"* but I assure you it is very real. I always find science to be a terrific way of supporting positions that some find farfetched, and self-healing certainly falls into that category. So, what type of scientific evidence is there to support self-healing? Lots!

When doctors, medical researchers, and pharmaceutical companies develop a new or experimental drug, they'll often conduct detailed clinical trials that monitor all variables and conditions. In these studies, a means of determining the efficacy of the new medicine is to employ the use of a placebo. Researchers take two groups of patients suffering from the same condition and give one group the experimental drug while the other group is given a treatment with no medical effectiveness, essentially a sugar pill or saline solution called a *'placebo.'*

Repeatedly these studies have generated miraculous healing results researchers call *'The Placebo Effect.'* In these cases, patients given the fake placebo treatment end up completely cured, eradicating all signs of their illness. Since these patents have not received any medical treatment their cure has been effectuated by themselves. Simply their belief the sugar pill will cure them is powerful enough to rid their body of the disease. The remedy to their illness comes from their mind.

A common case of the Placebo Effect plays out much like this; A patient is found to have incurable cancer and has been given only months to live with a tumor the size of a grapefruit. The patient has been told a miracle drug has been discovered shown to dissolve their specific type of cancer with a 100% cure rate. The patient is then given a placebo. Shortly thereafter, the patient is reexamined, and doctors are astonished to discover the grapefruit sized tumor has dissolved and the patient is now cancer free.

There's are thousands and thousands of cases in which the placebo effect has occurred. This mountain of clinical research gives incontrovertible evidence of the body's awesome ability to self-heal. You can easily do this research to prove this phenomenon to yourself. In fact, on the day I wrote this section, an article appeared in the news about an 11-year-old girl who was diagnosed with a rare, inoperable brain tumor with no cure. The little girl was given months to live. Her parents told her she'd be fine and prayed for a miracle. The little girl believed her parents wholeheartedly. A couple months later their wish was granted. The tumor had completely disappeared leaving doctors to scratch their heads in disbelief. This is just one story in thousands that show how the mind has commanding influence over the body, as we have learned throughout this book.

Every cell is controlled by your energy body, even the ones causing pain or illness. Every person on the planet has the innate ability to direct their energy body to self-heal. These cases merely provide the scientific evidence of this ability. But I want to reiterate that self-healing is a very advanced practice that should not be attempted without the proper training, and supervision or consultation of a doctor, particularly when dealing with a disease or illness that is life threatening.

With all these cases of self-healing occurring all over the world, it's got to make you curious about how the self-healing process works. What are the mechanics within the body that regulates self-healing? If self-healing is so effective, why doesn't my doctor write me a prescription to just sit and think about curing myself? Well, one of the issues with self-healing is if done in the masses, it'll put a whole lot of physicians, drug manufacturers, and medical specialists out of work. To get a better understanding we'll need to take a step back and analyze the macro picture.

There are different perspectives on the cause and treatment of disease and illness. Western medicine holds the belief that illness is caused by nasty microscopic creatures like bacteria, germs, or viruses, or it stems from emotional stress or psychological disorders. There's nothing inaccurate with this belief. Disease and illness are caused this way. However, since western doctors believe the illness is initially caused by a foreign organism or external condition, the approach to curing the illness requires the removal of the invading organism or eliminating the stress-inducing situation. I'm sure this is how many of you have learned to treat and recover from illness. It's the American way.

There's another perspective that involves the energy body, which takes on more ancient roots and is unfortunately neglected by most Western medical professionals. This perspective subscribes to the belief that the energy body serves as a protective shield against germs and disease and plays a crucial role in the causation and treatment of illness. We've learned that all matter at its core is energy, including the cells of your body and the cells of infectious organisms. Each of these in addition to having physical matter also have an energy component.

According to a spiritualist, disease and illness initially develop when there's an energy imbalance in the energy body before it manifests in the physical body. This means disease can be detected in the energy body before the illness develops in the physical body. For example, should the energy body associated with the throat become depleted and remains unrepaired, disease will inevitably manifest in the physical body as a cough or throat infection. The practice of self-healing utilizes the mind to repair the energy body, or to maintain its protective balance. In turn, the physical body is healed, or remains healthy. The beauty of this belief system is it's a whole lot easier, faster, less expensive, and less painful to treat an illness in the energy body before it manifests in the physical body.

Bringing all this back to our nifty little friend the Mind-Body Refresher, reminds us the importance of working meditation into your daily schedule. You don't need to become an advanced self-healing guru. You can simply use the Mind-Body Refresher to bolster the flow of energy through your 7 chakras and energy centers as preventative maintenance. Remember that you are responsible for the creation of your own health. So, it stands to reason that you also participate at some level in the creation of your own illness. As the creator of your illness, you can also become the healer of it. Inner peace and a strong energy body are keys to building a strong, impervious immune system. Imagine, all these benefit from a brief daily meditation that only lasts about as long as it takes to cook a pizza!

The benefits of keeping a calm inner peace in every aspect of your life can't be overstated. But we are human, and you can't be expected to maintain a perfectly calm demeanor all the time. So, when you do find yourself becoming frustrated or agitated, stop it in its tracks. Recognize your anger or irritation and focus on calming yourself right away. Don't be afraid to treat yourself like two separate individuals – the physical you and the spiritual you. Have your spiritual-self talk your physical-self off the ledge. Speak from your higher-self and remind your impetuous physical human to remain calm and loving. Talk to yourself out loud if necessary, again and again until to your inner peace returns. Your body, mind, and soul will thank you for it!

Speaking of thanks, is there someone in your life who you've done a disservice and have not asked for forgiveness? How about switching the roles…is there someone who has caused you pain that you are still harboring resent over? I'm sure we can all find someone if we give it a little thought, perhaps many with a lot of thought. Well, forgiveness is another action you can add to the Mind-Body Refresher list.

When it comes to the cleansing and purifying the body, we have a plethora of choices at our disposal. There are all sorts of crazy diets, exercise regimens, herbal supplements, and exotic treatments. Some are extremely beneficial while many are simply marketing ploys. In this chapter, we've discussed the many important benefits that come with cleansing and stilling the mind. With all these cleansing remedies logic dictates that cleansing and purifying the various components of the body are a good thing. And they are. But have you ever thought about cleansing the soul? In fact, how many are even aware that you can clean the soul? Doesn't your soul deserve a good ammonia-based scrub-down every now and then? Sure, but how?

You won't find soul purification products on a late-night infomercial, you won't find them advertised on your favorite social media site, nor will you see them plastered across a billboard as you sit in traffic. Despite all the attention given to purifying the body, very little importance is given to cleansing the soul. When in fact, purifying the soul is just as vital to your energy body as a healthy diet and exercise is to your physical body. When you purify the soul, you are cleansing the mistakes you've made in this life and in previous lives. Here's the dirty little secret for scouring the muck from your soul - forgiveness. Sounds crazy doesn't it? But not when you understand the true nature of forgiveness, which is often misconstrued.

This single word is the brawny solvent you can use to wipe free some of the physical, emotional, mental, and spiritual buildup clogging your soul. Forgiveness is a powerful spiritual tool to heal the damage caused by anyone who has brought you pain. If you can offer unconditional forgiveness to those who hurt you, without asking or expecting anything in return, you will receive incredible relief and positive blessings. *"How it this possible?"* you may wonder, *"After all, the people who cause the pain should be the ones offering comfort and love for their actions, not me!."* Yes, that is true. However it all comes back to the concept of being in control of yourself and NOT trying to control others. Let me explain how this relates to forgiveness.

When someone causes you pain, that pain leaves an impression on the various components of you - your soul, your subconscious mind, and your physical body. These impressions go on to create an imbalance between your physical body and your energy body. If left unchecked the energy imbalance can develop into a physical illness on the body. It's a natural instinct to become angry and resentful when you are hurt or betrayed by someone. That's just human behavior. However, emotions such as resent, anger, hatred, jealousy, and other negative feelings are toxic poisons to your soul. As you harbor these emotions and allow them to fester, over time their toxicity invades the cellular structure causing damage to your physical body.

Ask yourself whose body is suffering from the physical damage caused by these emotions, yours or the offenders? It's YOUR body that is being poisoned, not the body of the person who caused the pain. But if you offer complete and unconditional forgiveness to the offender, the impressions of pain get washed away. The act of forgiveness doesn't just heal your emotional and mental pain, but also prevents physical illness from developing.

It's important to point out that when you offer spiritual forgiveness it does not imply you are releasing the person who caused your pain from blame, responsibility, or applicable ramifications. Forgiveness means releasing the control that person has over your psyche. It's a spiritual and emotional act for you, not the offender. You should care enough about your own wellbeing to offer forgiveness to those who have harmed you to prevent that pain from inflicting further damage. You see, by not offering forgiveness, the offending person hurts you twice. Once from the initial incident, and again from the long-term toxicity it imposes on your emotional and physical being. When you forgive, you liberate yourself from the influence the harming individual has over you. Does that make a little more sense? You offer forgiveness for yourself. That may sound a bit self-serving but serving yourself is an obligation.

Here's something that's really unique about the forgiveness process. Since forgiveness is an internal action, you don't have to physically confront the person who offended you to offer them forgiveness. While that may be something you want to do, it's not a requirement. Forgiveness can be done on a spiritual level. This is where the Mind-

Body Primer can be employed as a handy tool. Employ it as you would with any other spiritual task. First step through the 3 stages of the Mind-Body Primer to prepare yourself for spiritual blessings. As you enter the 4th stage, shift your mind to concentrate on the person who has caused your pain. Visualize this person and the pain he/she has produced. Establish a connection with the soul of the offender, then release the hurt and acknowledge you no longer hold the person responsible for the damage they caused. Recognize they are also a spiritual being having a human experience and are learning through their mistakes. Appreciate that you have been part of their spiritual education and forgive their actions. Don't just think the words, you must truly mean and feel forgiveness. Spend a little time with these feelings, nurturing them, accepting them, and becoming comfortable with moving on from them. When done, emerge from your meditation as you would in any other meditative session.

An important aspect of forgiveness you must avoid is when you unconditionally forgive others for the hurt they have caused, don't feel you are the one who has been taken advantage of. In addition to freeing yourself from the emotional pain and preventing physical illness from manifesting, you also receive spiritual blessings. Your spiritual blessing may not come in the form of like a large chuck of money falling in your lap, but you will receive incredible blessings. For example, positive opportunities will present themselves more quickly, your relationships will become more loving and meaningful, your business will run more smoothly, your health will be less prone to illness, disasters will be averted, and other such blessings will come your way.

It's also important to recognize that forgiveness is a 2-way street. You can also ask for forgiveness from those whom you have hurt both in this life and in previous lives. The asking of forgiveness with humility and sincerity is just as vital as the offering of forgiveness for the cleansing of your soul. And just like giving forgiveness you can ask for it in the same spiritual way during meditation. Again, you may find emotional relief by asking for forgiveness in person, but on the soul level it's not necessary. Use the Mind-Body Primer as your foundation and at stage 4 concentrate on the person you have hurt to connect with their soul. Visualize this person and the pain you have caused and ask with loving sincerity for forgiveness. Be genuine in your request, show remorse. Apologize to the soul of the person for your actions and offer gratitude for their compassion, love, and forgiveness. You must truly mean and feel the remorse and sorrow for what you have caused. The more forgiveness you offer and ask, the sooner you will experience the muck and sludge dissolving from your spiritual body. Forgiveness is the Lemon Scented All-Purpose Clorox of the soul!

I recognize it's much easier to put words on paper than it is to enact these words in the real world. Unconditional forgiveness for those who don't deserve it may be easy to say but it can also be difficult to do, particularly when the pain is great. However, keep at it since the more you can offer unconditional forgiveness, the more physical and emotional benefits you will experience. Bear in mind the ancient Chinese proverb, *"If you devote your life to revenge, first dig two graves."*

With all the visualizations, meditations, and prays you'll be doing, your life will begin to move and reshape in extraordinary ways. Strange and unexpected coincidences will begin to occur that will give you a moment of pause. The more you participate in manifesting your reality, the more you will connect with the spiritual dimension, and the more these coincidences will occur. Since these strange coincidences will become a new and frequent part of your life, it's important to understand what they are, how to recognize them, and how to invite them in. So, let's get to know a little more about your new life companion - synchronicities.

I Can't Believe That Just Happened!

Get used to this expression. If you maintain a consistent meditation schedule, then you'll begin to experience events that'll trigger expressions like this on a regular basis. Eventually you'll grow tired of saying, *"You'll never believe this one...," "I was just thinking about you!," "Oh come on! How is that possible!,"* and *"What are the chances of that happening!."* You'll come to the conclusion that all these experiences triggering these expressions are not just coincidences but are in fact normal. You'll stop being amazed by them and begin to recognize them for what they are, *"synchronicities."*

The term 'synchronicity' refers to random and unrelated events that are unlikely to occur by chance yet are experienced together in a way that defies rational explanation. While that may be the formal definition, on a spiritual level a synchronicity is merely a way in which the connectivity of the Universe reveals itself. You think of a friend you haven't seen in years and suddenly that friend calls, or a recent argument is weighing on your mind when out of the blue a stranger tells you, *"Go ahead and apologize."* They are little messages acknowledging our spiritual nature and reminders to stop and recognize there's more to life than your physical surroundings. If you ask a physicist to explain the phenomenon, he/she will tell you synchronicities are examples of nonlocal quantum entanglement occurring outside the space-time continuum, which is simply a fancy way of saying we're all connected on a spiritual level. Regardless of the vernacular, synchronicities will become a very real part of your life.

Your initial instincts will be to treat them as cool experiences. Then as you grow in your spirituality, you'll accept them as evidence of your heightened connection to the spiritual dimension. But there's more to synchronicities than what you experience on the surface. When you analyze synchronicities closely, you'll find at their core is spiritual guidance. There is often deep spiritual meaning behind them relating to your life's journey. Learn to use your intuition to understand the message from your soul when synchronicities occur. Intuition is the voice that speaks to you from the spiritual dimension. Trust your intuition as much as you rely on your physical senses. When you base your life experiences using only your 5 senses the understanding you take away is solely that of the physical world. Which is fine, there is much to learn from your physical experiences, but 5 sensory learning is a longer, slower process. When you divorce yourself from your physical senses and enact your intuition, you'll better understand the meaning of your experiences, how they came to be, what they represent, and your role in creating them. The lessons are learned quicker and on a much deeper level allowing your decisions to be made more wisely and with more compassion.

If you'd like to develop and strengthen your intuition, then it's important to clear yourself of the emotional impacts of daily life. Just as you bathe your physical body daily, you should also cleanse the emotions that can clog your intuition. A wonderful way to do this is to free your mind at the end of the day, never go to sleep angry. If there is something upsetting you from the day, identify the source and dissolve the emotional anger before falling asleep.

Another thing is to learn to trust your intuition and honor the guidance it gives. This helps strengthen your belief in and sensitivity to intuitive messages. Remain open to life and trust there is a reason for all that happens. While you may not understand the reason, be confident it's always compassionate and good, even in the face of hardships and pain.

There's a terrific stage of mind called *'pronoia'* that you should strive to achieve. What is pronoia? Well, it's a recently coined term that means the opposite of paranoia. With paranoia, you develop a fear that there's always a conspiracy out to harm you in all aspects of life. Pronoia flips this around and takes on the belief that the Universe is conspiring to help you in every way. It's a mental state of going through life with the firm conviction that you have a golden cloud over your head, because you do. Everything that happens to you is exactly what you need, delivered at the precise time you need it.

You know by now that I'm a big proponent of asking questions. Your intuition benefits in a major way when you get into the habit of asking 'why' events take place. Each time you ask introspective questions behind the meaning of life experiences you invoke spiritual guidance. The answers to your questions will come but they won't be handwritten on a note in your mailbox. You'll need to develop an awareness for recognizing them as often they'll arrive in the form of a feeling, a synchronicity, a memory, or a random thought. It's your intuition that will help you discern them. So, learn to remain open and alert. Just as you can develop and discipline your mind to cogitative thought, you can also develop your intuition. Lastly, when you do recognize and acknowledge an intuitive message, give thanks for it. Showing appreciation to your higher-self and the Universe at large. It's a sure way to keep the communications flowing!

We've done quite a bit of fine tuning of the mind in this chapter. You certainly have lots to think about and work on, from filling your mind with vivid images to manifest your reality, to wiping clean your mental slate for a pure, still mind. I've made the point that this life is yours and it's up to you to determine how you want to live it. The Law of Attraction will bring you a reality that matches the vibrational frequencies of what you choose to focus your attention on.

You choose each moment of your life. It's your choice how you want to perceive and react to the physical world. You can choose to grumble about aches and pain in your body, or you can choose to celebrate life. You can choose to whine about a rainy day spoiling your plans, or you can choose to be grateful for nature nourishing itself. You can choose to complain about all that's wrong with your work, or you can choose to show appreciation for having a job. You can choose to become envious of others who have more than you, or you can choose to be thankful for that which you have. You can choose to wallow in self-pity over everyone who hasn't 'friended' you, or you can choose to honor the loving relationships that you do have. You see, the choices are all yours. The reality you create is one that you and you alone choose. It's as easy as choosing the thoughts and feelings which align with the reality you desire. Choosing your thoughts and feelings is one of your greatest responsibilities. Why…

Whether you consider the billions who came before us, or the billions who shall come, or the billions who are here today, the most amazing, life affirming fact in all of creation is we are all God. That's right, YOU, me, all of us are God. You are a fragment of Universal consciousness. You are a portion of the divine creator, that Universal Intelligence we explored in Chapter 2. You are not made in God's likeness, you are not subservient to an almighty being, you ARE a part of God. This is the great secret known by the sages, shamans, and prophets throughout the ages. Robert Cumming Neville put it succinctly when he wrote, "*In all creation, in all eternity, in all the realms of your infinite being the most wonderful fact is – You are God."*

Becoming aware of this isn't enough. You must convince yourself of it with all the conviction you can muster. Viewing the world through the perspective that you are a fragment of the creator, gives you the conviction of being a creator yourself. It reinforces your abilities to manifest your own reality. The world takes on a profound awe and meaning. Everything becomes the miracle it truly is. Your reverence for life in all forms intensifies. Your life grows richer with wonderment, and you become closer to fulfilling your purpose. And just what is that purpose? Well, stick around for another chapter and you may just find out.

Ch. 11: Singularity

"You are the quantum singularity interacting with itself."
– Unknown Source

Worlds United

We've investigated an awful lot in the past 10 chapters, and soon we'll have to gather up all our research and evidence to form a decision. There's one last chapter of exploration before we draw our conclusions. In this chapter we'll look into the spiritual body and its role and participation in the physical world. To do this, let's first reflect on a concept we broached back in Chapter 5, dualism.

If you recall, we studied how our five senses pick up energies generated in the physical world which are interpreted in the mind. This was demonstrated using the philosophical enigma of a tree falling in the forest. If nobody is present to hear it, does the tree make a sound? We learned that the falling tree generates an energy pulse which is interpreted in the mind as sound. The 'noise' actually occurs in the mind. Such is the case with all the senses. The interpretation of energy vibrations in the mind allows us to navigate the physical world through vision, hearing, taste, touch, and smell. We defined this as a dualistic system. For every sender there needs to be a receiver. The falling tree is the sender, the mind is the receiver. It's a dualistic relation, hence referred to as dualism. In this sense of dualism, we treat the mind and the physical world as separate, one is internal the other external.

There's another form of dualism that separates the physical and spiritual dimensions. This separation of realms has occurred since the time humans have shown cognitive thought. The perception of two universes, a spirit world and a physical world, continues to be held even today. The Creator (or God) and other spirit-based elements (our soul, ghosts, heaven, etc.) are presumed to be of the spiritual world, while all material things are thought to be of the physical world. This awareness of two worlds that are separate and apart is evidence of our evolution from simple consciousness to self-consciousness. The dualistic nature of the physical and spiritual realms is the commonly accepted relationship in society today. However, there is another way to perceive this relationship that is viewed by many as the next stage of conscious evolution. What if, instead of the physical and spiritual realms being separate and apart, they are actually one and the same? Now, that's a truly alternative perspective on reality, and one that's powerful enough to explore further.

By now you've come to understand that your physical body is an energy-based entity, as is the solid brick and mortar world of everyday life. Going back to Chapter 3, we saw that electrons, neutrons, and protons, which are the building blocks of all matter, are simply tiny bits of swirling energy. If you spent the day on the subatomic level, you wouldn't be able to tell the difference between the atoms that make up you and the atoms that make up inert materials. They are all the same type of subatomic particles - electrons, neutrons, and protons. There is not a different type of electron that appears only in humans. All electrons are the same. The electrons orbiting the nucleus of the atoms in your body are the same as the electrons orbiting the nucleus of a plutonium atom. It's the same with protons, neutrons, and other subatomic particles. They're all the same. You, I, and everyone else on the planet are all built from the same swirling bits of energy as physical matter. Having this in common raises the question of what other attributes we may share with physical matter? How else are we alike? Perhaps there's something we have in common on a spirit level. After all, our physical make up is built from the same swirling energy particles as inert matter and we have a spiritual component, does that imply inert matter also has a spiritual component? Could it be that everything existing in the Universe contains a spiritual underpinning?

This is clearly a question that's taken 10 grueling chapters of investigation and learning to be given sincere consideration. Imagine if I raised this question in Chapter 1, prior to knowing about the makeup of matter and the existence of a soul. *"Hey, do you think a rock contains a spirit? What about your toaster, or a lawn mower?"* I can see you tossing the book in the shredder. However, with your advanced understanding of the Universe, we can now explore this question in a serious and credible way. What if the Universe isn't broken into two separate worlds? What if there's not a spirit side that's separate and apart from the physical side...What if it's all one Universe in which the physical world exists interspersed with the spiritual realm? That all things are as much spiritual as they are physical. That's certainly an interesting concept, isn't it? Is it possible that's exactly how it does exist...the physical and spiritual are both one and the same? They are not separate and apart from each other. They do not represent a dualistic relationship, but rather a *'singularity.'* A Universe where all is one, where all is interconnected.

Well, how's that for a lofty concept to wrestle with? Do we live in a dualistic world with a separate physical and a spiritual realm, or do we live in a world defined as a singularity? (NOTE: singularity in a spiritual sense is different from the singularity of physics or mathematics.) Now, in a singularity the physical world exists interspersed with the spiritual world, each operating together simultaneously as one multidimensional reality. The physical and spiritual interact and influence each other. Everything is interacting energy. All things are energy in various forms of consciousness. Everything. The sun, the moon, Earth, the planets, the oceans, every animal, every tree, every bird, flower, grass, rock, river, mountain, building, every grain of sand, every book, every computer chip, cloud, drop of water, even your toaster and lawn mower. . .everything is alive! Fully alive. Nothing is inert. Universal consciousness is infused in absolutely everything. There's even a term used to describe such a Universe in which everything is imbued with a form of consciousness known as *'Panpsychism.'*

The belief that we are multidimensional beings living in a multidimensional world stems back to ancient Greece with Plato, and is the philosophical underpinnings of Taoism, Buddhism, shamanism, and many of today's quantum physicists. It's also a belief I have personally come to understand and trust. Now, before you think I've fallen off the deep end, it's important to note that everything contains a form of Universal consciousness, but all things do not contain a soul. Universal consciousness energy exists in or around everything, but it is different from the soul that incarnates the human body. A soul exists only in beings capable of emotion, which surprisingly includes species in addition to humans. Animals have intelligence, are capable of emotion, and do have a soul. This isn't merely anthropomorphism, but rather a spiritual truth. Animals may not be able to articulate their emotions or have deductive reasoning at the level of man, but they are living breathing souls who experience emotion and pain. They are not purely biological entities here for the pleasure and sustenance of humans.

As you begin to view the world as one grand singularity, whether it be a person, animal, plant, or elemental matter, you begin recognizing how everything is connected. Everyone on earth emits a certain vibration that radiates outward and touches everyone else, even people you've never met. You are connected to far more than you would ever expect. Physicist refer to this as a form of quantum entanglement. The birth and death of other souls throughout the planet are felt by many. Those who are sensitive can feel the vibrations of other souls. The impression is felt in accordance with the strength of your relationship with other souls. You may be able to sense the energies of souls close to you, for instance your children or parents. This connection becomes more apparent during large-scale disasters when many souls depart suddenly. It's common for this spiritual disruption to be felt around the globe. This connective energy is called '*Chi*.' Not only is Chi the life-force energy that keeps each of us alive, but it also connects us.

Altering your perception of reality from a dualistic view to a singularity may sound nice on the surface, but how do you get beyond the stumbling point of believing in it fully? And why is this perspective even important? Not only is it a good practice to yearn for the truth, but conviction in the world as a singularity is a necessary component of your spiritual evolution and your abilities as a creator. As part of the singularity, you become both the observer and the creator of that which is being observed. This is one of those moments where it's worth spending the time and thought power to grasp this paradox. It's a cerebral enigma that can be awkward to wrap your head around, but there is something you are very familiar with that may help clarify this weighty concept - dreams!

Have you ever awoken from a nightmare with your heart racing as though whatever occurred in your dream actually happened? Think back to a time when you've experienced this. Maybe you were chased by a giant spider, or fell from a high building, or were physically threated, or drowned, or involved in some other traumatic event. Whatever it was, you were startled from your sleep with all the physiological symptoms of the trauma actually occurring. Now, of course you know it was only a dream. After all, you awoke in the comfort and security of your bed, the very place you peacefully settled into prior to falling asleep. Yet, the life-threatening event felt real, as though you really were in that precarious circumstance. Let's examine this for a moment. The dream invoked real emotion, real trauma, real fear, real physiological responses. It caused your heart to race, your mouth to go dry, your stomach to turn in knots, real anxiety set in, adrenaline pumped through your veins as your body prepared for a fight or flight situation. This is all very real. You awoke in a state of panic believing the circumstances of your dream really happened. But who created this dream? Where did it originate?

In your mind. The very mind that also experienced the trauma of this creation. In this nightmarish example, you are both the creator of the dream and the person experiencing the dream. You conceived the situation and were traumatized by it at the same time. How can that be? How can the mind that creates a scenario also be traumatized by it? Should not the creator also know the circumstances are only a figment of the mind? If so, why are the emotions experienced as though the circumstances are real?

Well, this is a nice little example that illustrates a singularity at work. In this singularity you are both the creator and the person experiencing your creation. And you do it all the time…every night in fact. Now, take this dreamtime illustration and apply it to your waking world. Just as you experience the world you create in your dreams, you also experience the world you create in your waking life. That's another reality altering concept to contemplate.

Let's do a quick review to put everything into perspective. A spiritualist's belief is the entirety of the Universe is one vast sea of energy vibrating at different frequencies creating both the physical and spiritual realms. All this energy exists simultaneously, interspersed with itself, and connects everything. The physical dimension and the spiritual dimension are united in one singularity. This union of dimensions results in all physical things also having a component of energy consciousness. You are part of the singularity making you both a creator and experiencer. Forming an awareness of this is part of your spiritual journey. Forming a conviction of it is a steppingstone in your spiritual evolution. And with a steppingstone of this importance, it's incumbent that we take time to investigate the evolution of things.

Inner Evolution

To evolve or not to evolve…that is the questions. There's a funny little concept known as evolution that's commonly associated with Darwin's theory, the presumption in which all the wonderous and diverse life of today arose from a single common ancestor through a process of biological mutation and natural selection. The Darwinian philosophy tells us a cactus, an octopus, and a human all evolved naturally from the same single celled organism. We touched upon some of this in Chapter 1 when we investigated how life on the planet first began. While it's not my intent to do an in-depth analysis of Darwin's theory, I would like to expand on this topic to underscore a pivotal evolutionary problem it faces, and to introduce another theory of evolution.

We live on a planet that offers a spectacular diversity of life, the scope of which is simply miraculous. But to have such vast diversity, according to Darwinists, natural mutations must also be present. For a bird to evolve from a reptile it would require a slow gradual process of thousands of mutations that give rise to dominant traits which offer survival or reproductive advantages. Over time, these gradual mutations spawn an entirely new species. However, most are not aware of the gaping problem with Darwin's theory.

Way back in Chapter 1 when we studied cells and DNA, we learned about the complex structure of genetic codes and the precise combinations of thousands of amino acids that form a functioning gene. If a mutation in a genetic code were to create a new characteristic, then it would require the specific alignment of thousands of amino acids. Darwin's theory ignores this complexity. To demonstrate let's use a simple word game where you 'mutate' the letters of one word to create a new word. For example, by simply changing one letter per generation, a WORM can evolve into a BIRD in just 5 generations, watch:

WORM → WORN → BORN → BARN → BARD→ BIRD

From a Darwinist perspective, the changing of one letter corresponds to a mutation in the genetic code that results in a new trait. On the surface this seems like a reasonable explanation for how things evolve over time. However, when applying this simple word game process to genetic codes as Darwinian theory does, you hit a big fat problem. A genetic code sequence consists of thousands of amino acids, millions in more advanced species. The formation of a new functioning gene requires the precise substitution of thousands of amino acids, not just one as the word game suggests.

More importantly, the word play requires intelligence to know which letter to remove and which new letter to replace it with. If left entirely to natural chance, it's more likely the first mutation generates a 'dead' word, like WXRM, and ends the mutated sequence. In fact, there are 456,976 random combinations of 4 letters. Only about 4,200 form a word leaving 452,776 dead letter combinations. Random mutations are overwhelmingly more likely to degrade the genetic structure than produce a new functioning trait. The odds of a natural mutation of thousands of amino acids to survive and be passed on to the next generation is staggering! Thousands of mutations are required to create just one new trait, let alone form a thumb, a limb, or an exoskeleton. At these rates it makes Darwin's theory a virtual impossibility for the evolution of an entirely new species. Thus, it simply cannot explain how the diversity of life 'evolved' on this planet.

So, if changes in lifeforms have not occurred through a random mutation of genetic codes, how did species change? After all, there are many evolutionary traits that are easily identifiable. The elongated neck and legs of a giraffe seems likely to have occurred through natural selection of horse-like animals who were able to feed at higher levels surviving and reproducing, passing on their height gene until eventually evolving into the NBA of the animal kingdom. In the U.S. the average height has gone from 5′7″ to 5′9″ in just 2 generations.

This is found in many species, like the peppered moth that changes its color from light to dark in a few generations to survive environmental changes. And of course, us humans now walk upright, unless you want to include a handful from my family tree! So, if Darwinian theory hits an impassable blockage, how does life on earth evolve? How did all the marvelously diverse forms of life come to be? How will they continue to evolve? Now that's an interesting dilemma.

Perhaps altering of genetic codes didn't happen through random chance as many anthropologists believe, but through the guiding hand of an intelligent source. What if altered genetic codes responsible for evolutionary change occur at the spiritual level? But, how could that be?

We've learned physical matter is composed of tiny bits of swirling energy called atoms. The cells that make up the human body, animals, plants, and other lifeforms are all composed of these swirling bits of energy. In the previous section we explored the idea of the physical co-existing with Universal consciousness as a singularity, creating a matrix in which everything contains spiritual energy. If all things physical are imbued with spiritual consciousness, this would include the atoms that make up your DNA.

Now, this is important to understand so I'll repeat it. The atoms that form your DNA are nothing more than swirling bits of energy coalesced from universal consciousness. This intelligent consciousness is infused in all atomic particles. It IS the underlying intelligence that makes the complex alteration of genetic codes possible. It's not random but done with the helping hand of a Universal Intelligence. So, you see, there is a source of intelligence involved with evolution…it isn't left to random chance. The physical world and all its growth, change, and evolution are the physical manifestations of spiritual consciousness. A consciousness that YOU are part of. Wow! Take a moment to absorb this before moving on. I encourage you to stop reading and let this concept sink into your mind and soul. It really is a powerful one worthy of your attention.

Let's advance this new theory of evolutionary to the next stage…If humans have a physical and spiritual body, and we recognize our physical bodies have evolved, do our spiritual bodies also evolve? Is there an evolution of the soul? If so, how does the soul evolve? We've learned that the spiritual world contributes to physical evolution, does that imply the physical world also contributes to the soul's evolutions? Well, we seemed to have opened another can of intriguing questions to investigate, so let's get to it.

As an immortal soul, we step into a physical human body and use it as a vessel to experience the physical dimension. Through these physical experiences the soul learns lessons through the lower density of the physical plane where pain can be felt. This is why I refer to Earth as a Soul School. The process of incarnating on the physical plane gets repeated again and again as your soul learns new lessons based on unique challenges each life presents. Through these experiences in the physical realm the soul grows in maturity and wisdom, much like a student grows as they pass through the various levels of school – preschool, kindergarten, grade school, middle school, high school, University, Graduate School, etc. But why is the soul trying to learn lessons and grow in experiences? What's the point? What's it trying to learn? What is the Soul curriculum? Not everyone needs a Ph.D. to lead a productive life in the physical world, why does a soul need continued education?

This is a bit of a complex issue that needs to be answered in sections. Let's begin with how consciousness factors into the physical world. We now recognize that matter is composed of tiny bits of swirling energy vibrating at different frequencies. The frequency that the energy vibrates determines its density. The higher the frequency the lower the density. Think of solids, liquids and gases to help clarify this. Solids have a high density and as the material heats the atoms vibrate faster and the density decreases turning to a liquid, then a gas. As density decreases matter becomes more ethereal. So, as the energy vibration goes up you move closer to the spiritual dimension. Now, how does this apply to consciousness in the physical world?

All the solid elements in the periodic table exist at the highest density. This level makes up the minerals of the planet and is considered high density material. Its firmness and solidity make it extremely difficult for the high-frequency energy of a soul to occupy. For instance, a fish can live and function in water but not in ice, which is the same substance at a different density. Similarly, soul energy has difficulty existing in high density materials. As a result, soul energy doesn't incarnate in minerals. Despite minerals not containing soul energy, they do contain Universal consciousness which forms the atoms of the element. Make sense? Iron, zinc, and magnesium aren't typically known for their free will and emotional sensitivity.

As the frequency of the vibrating energy increases, you enter a lighter density range consisting of simple living organisms. This level includes the plant and insect kingdoms. At this level the density begins to become light enough to sustain life but limited in its degree of consciousness. This density level contains life with *Basic-Consciousness,* which means it is merely capable of sustaining itself. Increase energy vibrations further and you elevate into the density range consisting of lower life forms such as rodents, birds, reptiles, and fish. This density level contains life with *Simple-Consciousness,* which are lifeforms that are instinctual and reactionary to their environment but lack an awareness of their ability to have influence over their surroundings.

Continuing to increase the energy frequency brings us to the density range of life with *Self-Consciousness.* These are lifeforms who recognize themselves as distinct entities apart from their physical surroundings with the awareness of their ability to consciously alter their environment. This is the level of consciousness humans have reached…at least most of us. While many believe humans are the only lifeforms on the planet to reach this state, others feel a significant portion of higher forms of mammals have also reached this state of consciousness. Animals from dolphins to primates to elephants have demonstrated the ability to reason and exhibit emotions for life outside of their own. Critics note that these attributes can be explained away as anthropomorphism or projecting human characteristics onto something that is non-human, like saying your car is acting temperamental. I happen to share the belief that many lifeforms on the planet exist as self-conscious species, but this is a belief you'll have to determine for yourself.

As energy frequencies grow higher you step into the very fine density of the spiritual dimension. This level of energy is vibrating at such a high frequency it is not visible to the human eye. Lifeforms that exist in these higher energy densities, such as your soul, have a body and a world that is as physical and real to them as earth is to you. Many paranormal activities are just high frequency beings operating in this density level. Now, I suppose you are wondering what level of consciousness is associated with this density range?

Lifeforms operating at this level of consciousness are said to have *Universal Consciousness.* This stage also goes by many colorful names, some of which include *Cosmic Consciousness, God Consciousness, Enlightenment, Illumination,* and Gautama Buddha referred to it as *Nirvana.* Universal consciousness is a state that brings intellectual enlightenment with a full awareness of the life and order of the Universe. When you achieve Universal consciousness, you operate from a position of love with a conviction that all things are energy, life is eternal, and the soul is immortal. There's an understanding of the singularity, an elevation of morality, and an absence of the fear of death. Universal consciousness is what many in the metaphysical fields believe we are progressing towards. At advanced stages, individuals can operate in both the physical world and spiritual dimension simultaneously, with full conscious awareness of each. There have been a handful of spiritual leaders, yogis, and philosophers who are said to have reached universal consciousness. Two of the most notable individuals are Gautama Buddha and Jesus. So, humans have achieved Universal consciousness. I bet that makes you wonder just how close you are to achieving Universal consciousness?

Here's the interesting thing. You may not feel like you are on the path of becoming the next Buddha or Jesus figure, but the realization of Universal consciousness is the objective of every soul and the reason why we continue to reincarnate. Once a soul reaches Universal consciousness, its need to incarnate on the physical plane ends. All further evolution of the soul occurs in the spiritual dimension.

If Universal consciousness is the golden ring all incarnated souls are in pursuit of, how do we do achieve it? What's the secret to reaching the next level of conscious evolution and end the cycle of reincarnation? I suppose you're expecting me to tell you that you'll have to shave you head and meditate on an isolated mountain top for a couple years. Fortunately, spiritual growth doesn't mean you have to deprive yourself of material possessions and take the monastic vow. In fact, it's essential to utilize all the physical world has to offer and learn how your physical experiences contribute to your spiritual growth. The essential process in achieving Universal consciousness is to incarnate in the physical world. The more you experience in the physical world the more you grow spiritually. The encouraging news is Universal consciousness is being achieved at a greater rate today than ever before.

You may have noticed a pattern emerge as we stepped through the different levels of energy frequencies. As the energy frequency increases, there's a corresponding elevation in consciousness. Higher frequency correlates with a higher consciousness. Have you ever noticed when you are in a state of consummate love, or are completely overjoyed, your entire presence feels lighter? You describe this sensation with expressions like *"I'm walking on air"* or *"I'm on cloud nine."* This sense of lightness corresponds to the high frequency feelings of love and joy. Conversely, negative feelings give the sense of heaviness. When you're depressed or stressed, you'll use expressive terms like, *"I've got the weight of the world on my shoulders," "I feel sluggish,"* and *"I've got a heavy heart."* This heaviness corresponds to the low frequency feelings. It isn't just coincidence that elated feelings are expressed with terms of lightness and negative feelings with terms of heaviness.

During each lifetime you are faced with a plethora of decisions that contribute to the evolution of your soul. The more you experience, the more you participate in spiritual growth. The rate in which your soul evolves is determined by the choices you make and actions you take. All experiences count. A soul doesn't sort them into good or bad, right or wrong, there is spiritual context within every experience. It all comes down to your choices and actions.

Remember, you are a creator who creates your reality based on the thoughts and feelings you radiate. By raising the frequency of your thoughts and actions you in turn raise the frequency of your energy density and elevate your spiritual consciousness. This is how the soul's evolution works. *"Fair enough!"* you say. *"Now how about telling me what I'm supposed to do to raise the frequency of my thoughts and actions! Nobody has informed me about some 'frequency' dial I can turn to adjust my energy frequency!"*

OK, I certainly don't want to back you into a corner and not give you the tools for getting out! So, you want to know how to raise your frequency? What choices can you make to accelerate your soul's evolution? How can you produce that sense of lightness, joy, and love on a regular basis? Well, it's as elementary as this…If you want to elevate your spiritual frequency, then elevate the frequency of your choices. Simple enough, right? Then, let's get into the details of what constitutes high frequency choices.

A good starting point is a remarkably relevant set of commandments you can adopt to raise your frequency. These commandments are not the ones Moses brought down from Mount Sinai, although adherence to them is a darn good policy as well, but these are the 10 Native American Commandments.

Here's the list:

1. Treat the Earth and all that dwell thereon with respect.
2. Remain close with the Great Spirit (Universal Consciousness).
3. Show great respect for your fellow beings.
4. Work together for the benefit of all Mankind.
5. Give assistance and kindness wherever needed.
6. Do what you know to be right.
7. Look after the well-being of mind and body.
8. Dedicate a share of your efforts to the greater good.
9. Be truthful and honest at all times.
10. Take full responsibility for your actions.

How's that for a concise set of high frequency rules to live by?! Wouldn't it be refreshing if these were reinforced in our children, preached by politicians and CEO's, and were the go-to rules of society? Can you imagine a world in which everyone subscribed to these tenets? Just think how much more loving and respectful society would become. Well, that world CAN exist. It just takes a slight shift in perspective, and it's a shift you can begin with today.

As a society, we place focus on the physical body at the expense of the spiritual body. The importance of the soul's growth is not promoted. But you are different. You are now aware of the importance of the soul and can invert this focus. Begin to shift your perception and make the physical world subordinate to the spiritual. Start viewing the physical world as a learning environment for the soul, where everything that occurs serves the soul's growth. When you align your thoughts, emotions and actions with your spiritual body, you become filled with enthusiasm, purpose and meaning, and adhering to this set of commandments becomes natural.

But the 10 Native American Commandments aren't the only ways to bring higher frequency decisions into your life. Others include work on the mind and work on the body. For the mind, incorporate meditation into your daily routine, look for ways to express gratitude more often, take time to help others, watch less TV and reduce the time you spend on social media, spend more time in nature, and look for ways to laugh through life.

For the body, maintain a good exercise regimen, stretch, eat more fresh fruits and raw vegetables while reducing your intake of processed foods and meats, improve your breathing, maintain a calm and relaxed demeanor, get enough sleep, and walk barefoot, which is known as "Earthing."

As you gradually embrace these lifestyle adjustments and alter your perception to a more spiritual view, you'll begin to recognize and appreciate the beauty in the world. You'll see a precious soul within everyone. You'll discover the power of love and gratitude. You'll learn to appreciate everything as a gift, your life, your experiences, and all you have are cherished gifts. Appreciate and show gratitude for them.

Life's experiences are all beautiful blessings for your soul's growth. Be thankful for everything you experience, even if you don't understand its purpose. Over time and through numerous incarnations, your soul will eventually reach Universal consciousness and evolve beyond the physical realm. The human experience and school of Earthly lessons will no longer be necessary. Your evolutionary journey may take many lifetimes, but you will complete it. All souls graduate. It's not a matter of if, but when.

Those are some of the things you can do to raise your energy frequency and promote spiritual growth, but what are the things to avoid? Are there behaviors, thoughts, and actions that lower your spiritual vibration? Of course. Most are obvious, but let's review them anyway. Avoid making judgments. Socrates has a great quote that speaks perfectly to this, "*Be kind, for everyone you meet is fighting a hard battle*."

It's so true. You have no idea nor understanding of the harsh life others are facing, and until you do, you shouldn't pass judgment on them. You may have made the very same decision you are judging if placed in their circumstance. Release the need to know why things happen and trust that unwanted or spontaneous events are part of your spiritual path. Accept them with the love and belief they happened with your best interest in mind. Recognize there are things you simply cannot change and stop trying to force the world to adjust to your temperament.

And the granddaddy of all, eliminate all hate from your life. This one can be the most challenging especially when dealing with acts of evil. It's important not to show a hatred for those who engage in evil. I know it defies reason and all you've been taught, but by hating you contribute to the absence of love energy and inadvertently end up increasing the evil you hate. When you hate, you bring suffering upon yourself. Hatred affects only those doing the hating. Now, please don't misinterpret this to mean you must become passive and disregard evil actions and behavior. It's totally appropriate to stop evil when you see it, but you also need to show compassion for those doing the abuse. The offering of compassion for those who engage in evil, even as you denounce their actions, protects you from cultivating toxic energy within yourself.

With all the horrors occurring in the world today, it's inevitable that you will feel rage and anger against horrendous acts of evil at some point. When this happens, stop, acknowledge it and dismiss it. Remind yourself that you are a spiritual being living a human experience, and the person who engaged in the act of evil is also a spiritual being living the human experience. The incident is something of profound spiritual significance that extends beyond your understanding. Release the event and offer compassion. This keeps you from fostering negative thoughts that can swell to cause internal decay. Understand the evil doer is also a spiritual being and their actions have spiritual consequences and karmic debt.

For many, much of this will sound esoteric and unrelatable to the real world of physical and emotional pain. There are horrors and abuses that defy mercy. How is one to show compassion for those who torture children, abuse the innocent, or butcher and massacre? How can you ask not to show hatred for these perpetrators of horrific acts of evil?

This is an understandable impulse when all you consider is the physical realm. As a spiritual being, you must first consider the spiritual realm. Like humans, souls are in different stages of development. When you see an infant or young child act out in inappropriate ways, you don't judge them as evil, but rather you see a loving being that you respond to with corrective compassion. This is also the approach you need to bring on a spiritual level.

While you are here in the physical realm you will interact with souls of all developmental levels, from young to old. In fact, there is a famous incident dating back about 2,000 years that illustrates this...the crucifixion of Jesus. Are you familiar with what Jesus said to the men who were about to crucify him? Remember, Jesus had achieved Universal consciousness. Prior to being crucified he said, *"Forgive them, for they do not know what they do."* Can you imagine? Let's transpose this situation to today and put you in the place of Jesus. Imagine that soldiers from Rome had just pounded nails through your hands and feet to secure you to a wooden cross, after repeatedly whipping and beating you. Then, they hoist you up and stab you with a sword, so you'll die a slow death. I think we can agree these are some rather horrific acts of evil. Now, given this situation, think about what words would come from your mouth about these men. Do you think you'd ask for their forgiveness? Very unlikely, isn't it. Why did Jesus do this?

He made this statement because Jesus was a spiritual being who understood the spiritual nature of the Roman soldiers, and their ignorance of their own spiritual bodies. It adds some context to avoiding hatred and showing compassion. Now, if we take the position that Jesus was more spiritually evolved than the Roman soldiers, it suggests there are different stages to a soul's growth. Let's look at the various developmental stages a soul passes through during its cycle of incarnations in the physical world.

The best way to present the soul's development is to put it in terms of our own physical growth. The first stage a soul goes through when incarnating in the physical world is called the *Infant Soul*. The Infant Soul lasts for approximately the first 20% of your lifetimes. During this stage the soul's primary focus is adapting to the heavy density of the physical world. Infant souls experience lessons in survival and environmental awareness. They incarnate into lives of simplicity as new experiences often terrify them rather than motivate. Infant Souls being so new to the Earthly experience truly don't know the difference between right and wrong and often act with violence and cruelty. They typically don't seek higher education, need to be forced to better themselves, act out of lust instead of love, and treat animals poorly. Most of our prisons are filled with Infant Souls. Roughly 15% of the world's population are Infant Souls.

Once a soul has assimilated to the density of the physical world it grows into what is called the *Baby Soul*. This stage takes the soul roughly through the next 10% of its incarnations. The primary focus of Baby Souls is belonging. For this they experience lessons involving rules, law and order, and social behavior. Baby Souls often become pillars of the community, but don't handle opposing views well. They become easily bewildered and angry, expressing hostility, belligerence and negative emotional energy. They tend to seek higher education predominantly in the liberal arts. Baby Souls make up approximately 25% of the population.

Advancing beyond the baby stage a soul reaches the *Young Soul*, which carries it through the next 30% of the soul's incarnations. A Young Soul finds itself focused on independence. It will experience life lessons that deal with self-advancement, personal achievement, and free will. Many Young Souls are in a state of unrest and tend to live in urban locations. They are socially polished and become the movers and shakers of society, driven to achieve. A Young Soul is the type that pushes to get you to change your point of view to theirs. The most valuable spiritual lessons are learned during this stage, but it's also the stage where most mistakes are made. Young Souls account for about half of the population.

By the time you've been back and forth to the physical plane through all your Young lifetimes, it's time to progress to the *Mature Soul.* A soul is considered mature during lives that takes the soul through about 85% of its lifetimes. At this stage the primary focus becomes co-existing with others. Life lessons includes experiences that relate to interdependence, empathy, intimacy, and self-awareness. For many souls the mature stage can be the most difficult as it requires a lot of introspection. There are hard lessons to be learned at this stage causing Mature Souls to question life's motives. During this stage the soul realizes it's pursuing internal questions but is unclear what it seeks causing confusion and frustration. As a result, Mature Souls tend to live in tranquil or isolated environments. Only about 7% of the population today are mature souls.

Finally, at the end of the cycle you reach the *Old Soul* stage. Calling someone an Old Soul is a common expression but is typically misused. Only about 3% of the population are in the Old Soul Stage. This is the final stage of lessons in the physical world and carries the souls through is final 15% of lifetimes. You could probably guess the primary focus for Old Souls is learning to becoming part of the singularity. They are faced with life events that teach lessons about autonomy, non-attachment, and spiritual awareness. People who are Old Souls have an overall casual sense about life and look you directly in the eye with a penetrating stare when talking. They share wisdom and love to explore the world. Old Souls work hard and are profound creators. They recognize the temporary nature of their material achievements so they bounce from one project to another. Old Souls long for spiritual evolution and are very sensual and affectionate.

As your soul develops and matures, it's able to perceive a higher range of energy frequencies. With soul maturity comes a heightened sensitivity to the spiritual realm. When you learn to accept that you are a spiritual being you understand how physical events become tools for the soul. You recognize that positive thoughts and actions raise your spiritual frequency while negative thoughts and actions lower it. When you cling to negative thoughts of hatred, jealousy, bitterness, revenge, greed, contempt, or violence it has a toxic effect on your body, mind, and spirit. While it's normal to become frustrated and angry at times, avoid harboring negativity for the long periods. When you find yourself exhibiting negative thoughts or actions, stop the behavior right away. Don't admonish yourself but recognize it is only your human (human animal) personality. Control it with your higher-self and analyze the event or circumstance that triggered your anger. These events and circumstances are indicators of the lessons you are here to learn. When you become upset, it's as though your oversoul is firing a flare to identify lessons you need to work on. The physical world will bring forth and create situations that serve your growth – good or bad. You can use this to mitigate your negative reactions to events by thinking of them as an opportunity to grow and evolve spiritually. This transforms a negative thought into a positive one.

Let's assume you take all these tips on how to live a high frequency lifestyle to accelerate your spiritual growth, how do you know if you're making progress? It turns out to be quite easy. You can track your soul's progress by monitoring your reactions to those events that trigger your temper. When they occur and you find yourself free from emotional discord and instead calmly addressing the situation with wisdom, compassion, and understanding, it's a sure sign of progress. The more you can step away from the human personality reacting negatively to events in the physical world, the greater your spiritual growth.

As you gain in your spirituality you will open yourself more to understanding the reason behind events and adversities in your life. This is pure soul growth. Often the greatest spiritual leaps come during moments when your life seems the most out of control. When you question what you are meant to do with your life, or why you came to this physical plane? These are the times when you need to be receptive to spiritual guidance. Open yourself to spiritual guidance with faith and trust and the spiritual dimension will reshape your struggles into successes, and your pain into strength. Then your life may move in directions you had never anticipated. Trust that behind all events, no matter how painful, there is a reason from which good can come.

An Old Soul sees the beautiful immortal soul in everyone. An advanced spirit does not ask for more than it needs as it knows whatever it needs the Universe will provide. Advanced souls see the perfection of each situation and each experience. They find perfection in everything. Wherever they look they see the miracles of life. And just like a superhero, advanced spiritual growth brings a higher level of responsibility. The more you understand, the greater the accountability to your soul, and the greater the rewards. It's sort of like knowledge of the law. The more you know, the less you can claim ignorance. If you break the law with the full knowledge and understanding of it, the accountability is greater than if you broke the law out of ignorance.

Let's wrap up this section on spiritual evolution with a brief summary of the key take-away points. Begin to shift your perspective from living in a world entirely of the physical, to one that places the soul first.

Interpret all situations and relationships as having spiritual significance, even if you don't immediately understand them. End your need to know why certain things happen and trust that all occurs for the betterment of your soul. Work on releasing thoughts based in hate, anger, or violence, and refrain from judgment, regardless how evil the act.

Spiritual growth is achieved through self-control and the capacity to work through challenges life presents. Make high frequency choices that serve the evolution of your soul. If you choose anger, conflict, or resentment, the Universe will repeat the lesson until eventually you learn it. Ultimately, you will learn, but only after experiencing a lot of pain, trauma, and loss.

There you have it. A whole bunch of information about the soul's evolution and proactive things you can do to accelerate it. Now, isn't it interesting that you live in a physical world surrounded by friends, family, co-workers, and thousands of people who come in and out of your life every day. Each one is a soul who incarnated to learn and gain spiritual growth. It makes you wonder if any of these souls are here to help you. We're all here to learn, but do we share in the learning responsibilities? Do other souls help you learn and evolve? Are you helping other souls? That is what friends do in the physical world why wouldn't spiritual friends do the same?

What about events that involve multiple people; does the event have spiritual significance for each person involved? Well, we may be onto something here. Do we as spiritual beings help other souls while incarnated in a human body? I think we've just stumbled onto a new topic to explore.

Soul Contracts

Let's spend a moment to take an inventory of the people and relationships in your life. Think about all the people who enter in and out of your life daily - friends, family, co-workers, familiar faces in places you frequent, strangers you pass on the street, in stores, cafés, restaurants, hallways, the park, and every place you journey. How many Facebook friends do you have? What about Instagram and Twitter followers? LinkedIn connections? Think about the depth of your relationships? Are they minor acquaintances or deep seeded friends? With all the vast number of people and types of relationships, do you ever wonder if there's a reason your world contains the people it does?

Some relationships bring great joy, while others bring heartache. There are people who teach you important lessons in life, while others become the beneficiary of your wisdom. There are family and friends you know for a lifetime whose relationship never advances beyond superficial, while a passing stranger can make deep penetrating eye contact that touches your soul with lasting effect. With all these people and relationships coming and going over your life's journey, have you ever stopped and wondered what is the nature and purpose of the souls populating your world? And why are some so heartwarming, loving, and joyful, while other filled with betrayal, anguish, and hurt. What's the purpose of negative relationships…and why is pain such a common byproduct?

When you see, hear about, and experience all the suffering that occurs in the world, it makes you wonder how it could be permitted by a loving Creator of infinite wisdom and knowledge. How could such a boundless source of love allow the horrors of this world to occur? All the starvation, abuse, murder, and torture…what type of Creator would allow such pain?

Back in Chapter 7 we explored the notion of hell being a place of great misery. A place where pain and suffering are experienced. A place where an imperfect soul takes the elevator down to *'atone for its sins,'* or as a spiritualist would say, *'continue its education.'* I made the case that hell plays out right here on the physical plane of Earth. Do you remember who presses the down button and agrees to return to that place? Is it the almighty Creator or You?

When your soul transitions to the spiritual dimension, you are not judged by a wrathful God who seals your eternal fate. You embark upon a process of self-judgment where YOU analyze lessons learned and new experiences desired. Much like selecting your college curriculum, you choose your spiritual lessons. Your soul is in a constant state of growth and it determines when to return, along with the type of knowledge it wishes to gain. You are aware of the life of pleasure and pain you're involved in because you are the one who selects it. It's what you want. You willingly and eagerly decide to return to the physical world to continue your spiritual growth.

The physical dimension can be a place of great pain, suffering and unjust anguish, but it can also be a place of great beauty, pleasure and love. Your life may be rife with abuse, or bountiful in love and wealth. Filled with crippling disease and pain or blessed with health and athletic superiority. Whatever the case, it's a life YOU selected to advance your spiritual growth.

Some of the ironies of life are it takes sadness to truly appreciate happiness, noise to know silence, and absence to value presence. Through lack the soul learns to appreciate abundance. Through suffering the soul learns joy. Through betrayal the soul values loyalty. Through confinement the soul grasps independence. Through poverty the soul respects wealth. Through hardships the soul cherishes comfort. Without pain, there is no regard for pleasure. Without loss, there is no meaning to love. Some of the most powerful growth lessons for the soul are ones that cause the greatest hardships. This is how the soul learns. As you experience adversities analyze their spiritual purpose. Trust the reason behind your experience is to benefit your spiritual growth. Do this and life will flow with much less resistance.

Now, let's toss a complicated wrench into this scenario of self-selected suffering. When you choose to experience the hardships of abuse or torment, you need an accomplice in the physical world to cooperate in your abuse, someone to take on the role of your abuser. How do you find such a soul? Is there a spiritual Craigslist where you place an ad for *"Abuser in the Physical Dimension Wanted! Must be Proficient in Causing Pain and Suffering!"* And, if the spirit world is a place of universal love, how do you find a soul capable of such personified evil? It all seems like some great oxymoron of the heavens.

The souls involved in these challenging lives of hardship or abuse have purposely chosen to participate in the experience to fully understand and empathize with the feelings and sentiments they engender. This goes for both the recipient of the abuse and the abuser. It may seem bizarre to you that a soul who agrees to inflict the pain or abuse is doing so out of love, but that's because you are only considering the physical aspects of the life, not the spiritual or karmic consequences. With lifetimes of this nature, loving souls make an agreement in the spiritual dimension to create the physical experience of hardship or abuse. They agree to go through the trauma in the physical world for the spiritual growth the soul will gain. It's done out of love for one another.

From the spiritual perspective there is very little that happens in the physical world that isn't first established in the spiritual realm. We don't meet people by accident. Lovers, friends, and colleagues don't come into our lives by happenstance. They are meant to cross our path for a reason. All relationships, even the most difficult ones, are meetings that were agreed upon in the spiritual dimension. They become gifts from one soul to another to help with lessons that can't be learned alone. These relationships are called *Soul Contracts.*

A soul contract occurs when souls from the same soul group (also known as a *karmic group*) participate in an agreement in the spiritual dimension for specific events to occur in the physical world to provide one or both souls with spiritual growth. Despite the tragic or horrific events that may occur in the physical world, soul contracts are always executed with loving intent. It's for these reasons you must learn to accept what life presents you, even the tragedies and hardships, as they all occur because you chose them. Accept them despite the pain or unjust nature, because you asked for these experiences in order to gain the corresponding spiritual growth. The greatest lessons for the soul to grow and learn are ones that require the greatest efforts, and oftentimes the greatest pain.

With earthly contracts, we've all heard the expression that "*contracts are made to be broken*" and "*the devil's in the detail.*" So, is it the same with a soul contract…once agreed upon can they be broken? Making an agreement in the spiritual dimension and setting the energies in motion in the physical plane is not something that can be unwound. However, there is some wiggle room due to a little thing known as '*free will.*'

When a soul contract is made, you agree upon certain life experiences in the physical world, but once incarnated you have free will with how to carry out those experiences. You can think of a soul contract like committing to travel to a certain location, let's say you decide to drive to Miami. The choice is made, and you will drive to Miami. No matter what else you do, you're going to make the drive to Miami. How you make the drive is entirely up to you. You can drive slowly, you can speed, you can drive backward, you can drive a scooter, a go-cart, an 18-wheeler, or a Ferrari. You can make the drive in one shot or stop and sightsee along the way. There are choices to be made, but you will go to Miami. In this example, the decision to go to Miami is the Soul Contract, the manner in which you get there is your free will.

So, how does this apply to your life experiences? Let's say you've chosen to experience a lifetime of obesity, which you agree upon through a soul contract with a loving soul from within your soul family. There are various reasons why you may want to experience such a life. Perhaps you lived a life in which all you knew was hunger and you died of starvation, and now you want to experience its opposite. Maybe you recently completed a life as a stunning beauty coveted by all, and you now want to experience the prejudice of being overweight. Whatever the reason, you make the choice to learn important lessons which another soul agrees to incarnate with you as the enabler of your food obsession.

In the physical world, the soul contract may be carried out by a parent or spouse, who is your spiritual accomplice. As you suffer your food addiction, recognize and own that you are in this body having this experience because of a spiritual agreement you made. It's important to understand why you made that decision and consider the lesson you were trying to teach yourself. Why did you choose a life of obesity? Finally, discover ways you can receive the same lesson with less pain. Going through this introspective process brings great resolution to life's dilemmas and struggles. I highly recommend an in-depth book on this subject titled *"Courageous Souls"* by Robert Schwartz that explores souls who choose lives of addictions, deformity, and terminal illness. It's a terrific book that helps to bring meaning to what seems to be purposeless human suffering.

If you as spiritual beings choose and plan your human experience, why don't you remember what you selected? What's the point with having to go through all that pain and suffering, can't we just acknowledge the lesson? Well, the simple answer to this is *"No!."*

Like anything else, there's no substitution for experience. As a man, I could read and study everything there is to know about conceiving and delivering a baby, I could even become a world-renowned obstetrician. However, unless and until I experience the pleasure and pain of childbirth as a woman, I could never truly understand it. This is the same with souls.

To gain experience and growth souls accept willful amnesia of past lives and the spiritual realm as part of the incarnation process. It's a necessity to growth. If you were able to remember the love and pleasures of the spiritual realm you would not want to live out your life on Earth, a place where pain and suffering is felt. Many humans would also seek out retribution against other incarnating souls for wrongs they did in another lifetime. Your mission is to experience and accomplish that which you set out to experience, willful amnesia is essential to doing so. But without memory of our spiritual home or a direct line of communication with our soul family, is there a way to stay connected with our spiritual base? Is there something other than a tarot card reading or fortune cookie for reaching out to our spiritual sides? Well, let's sleep on this one and see where it leads…

Dreamtime

Did you have a nice nap? I hope so because this section is all about dreams, and you'll want to stay wide-awake for it. Sleep is quite an enigma that most people spend very little time evaluating. We're told we need eight hours of sleep a day. There are even theories suggesting the human body can't survive without sleep. But have you ever wondered what purpose sleeping serves? After all, the average person spends about 1/3 of their life getting forty-winks. By the time you hit the rip age of 75 you would have slept about 220,000 hours, which equals 9,167 days, 25 years, or watching *"It's a Wonderful Life"* 97,335 times! That's a whole lot of your life spent lying around on a mattress doing nothing. Talk about being an underachiever.

But, are you really doing nothing when you hit the hay? It turns out some of the most revolutionary breakthroughs and creative artistry have come during sleep. Russian chemist Dmitri Mendeleev got the inspiration for the structure of the Periodic Table while getting a little shut eye. It just so happens that Einstein stumbled onto the theory of relativity, one of the most important scientific principles in history, after having a vivid dream. The father of quantum mechanics, Niels Bohr, was awarded a Nobel Prize in Physics for the discovery of the structure of the atom which came to him while catching some ZZZ's.

On the creative front, Director James Cameron had a fever dream one night that would later become one of the most successful movie franchises in Hollywood history – *"The Terminator."* And he's not the first, Robert Louis Stevenson got the inspiration for the literary classic *"The Strange Case of Dr. Jekyll and Mr. Hyde"* from a terrifying nightmare. I'm sure everyone knows the timeless songs "*Yesterday*" and "*Let It Be*," both came to Paul McCartney in his dreams. Paul McCartney isn't alone with dream-inspired hits, The Rolling Stones' classic "*Satisfaction*" was conceived during a deep sleep, as were "*Just the Way You Are*" by Billy Joel, Jimi Hendrix's "*Purple Haze,*" "*The Man Comes Around*" by Johnny Cash, even the today's pop sensation Taylor Swift has a few dream-inspired hits.

All that amounts to something, right? Sleep isn't a total waste. At least we have dreams inspiring some amazing accomplishments… even if they're only figments of your mind. But, are they really? Are dreams nothing more than mental hallucinations, your imagination running off the rails, the mind left untethered by your conscious thoughts to scuttle amuck? Or, is there something more to dreams? When you rest your head on your pillow and slip into a deep sleep, you enter a world of crazy fanciful imagery where anything can happen. While your physical body is snoring like a chainsaw, there's a part of you off slaying dragons, soaring like a bird to strange lands, encountering friends and family in weird places, getting chased by monsters, and experiencing all sorts of bizarre and fascinating scenarios. What is really happening when you journey to Never-Never Land? Where are you really going, and who's making the trip?

While scientists and researchers have made great progress in understanding mental and biological effects of sleep, they still don't have a conclusive unified answer as to why we dream, what purpose it serves. We do know the body goes through different stages during the sleep cycle. Just prior to falling asleep, your heart rate reduces, your muscles relax, and your brain waves slow to the beta range. As you relax further your brain waves reduce to the alpha range putting you in a state between sleep and consciousness. The first stage of light sleep occurs when your brain waves lower to the theta range, your body temperature drops, your breathing and heart rate slow, and you lose awareness of your surroundings. As you go deeper, your brain waves slow further, and you enter the delta range. This is the deepest stage of sleep prior to the REM stage (Rapid Eye Movement). Once you reach the REM stage, your brain waves remain in the delta range, but brain activity begins to spike, your eyes shift rapidly (hence the astute acronym), and you begin to experience dreams. I refer to this stage of the sleep cycle as the *'dream state.'*

That's a brief oversight of what happens physically during the sleep cycle, but what's going on mentally? If you ask a psychologist why humans dream, they'll tell you, *"Well, uhm...to be honest, we really don't know."* Carl Jung, Sigmund Freud, and thousands of psychologists, neurologists, psychiatrists, and psychoanalysts have batted around this conundrum for centuries and still there's no explanation. Some theories suggest dreams are the brain's response to biochemical impulses during sleep and serve no real purpose, while others theorize dreams are a function to help store meaningful memories; dreams are hallucinated thoughts that help the mind process experiences and emotions from the waking life; dreams are the brain's way of preparing for a fight or flight situation; or that dreams help facilitate the creative process since there's no logic filter during sleep. While there's lots of speculation abound, the one thing we don't have is a definitive conclusion for why we dream. This part of life remains a mystery. How could that be? How can something as significant as dreaming, that occupies such a large chunk of our physical existence, remain unsolved? With all the brilliant minds confronting this issue, why hasn't the mystery been unraveled? Science has been able to decode the complexities of the human genome, yet we still have no explanation for what happens when you enter the dream state. Perhaps the issue that is causing all these great minds to hit a roadblock is they're not considering the spiritual body in their efforts to explain dreams.

When researchers approach dream analysis using the Freudian psychoanalytic method, they look for ways to interpret dreams as the unconscious mind's attempt to make sense of reality. By doing so, they consider only the physical component of the body and fail to acknowledge the spiritual body's contributions. So, does the spiritual body play any role in dreams? According to ancient cultures it does.

There is deep history stemming back to ancient Egypt, Greece, India, and Tibet, along with shamanic teachings of indigenous cultures throughout the world, that believed dreams are messages from the spirits and gods. Still today, many of these cultures and shaman use dreams to diagnose health, as prophetic messages, and as a portal to higher consciousness. Throughout this book we've seen where ancient knowledge has trumped contemporary science, and this may be another case to add to the list.

Earlier in this chapter I posed the paradox of you being both the creator and the one experiencing your dreams. When you have a dream that invokes real emotion, trauma, or fear, the physiological responses to that dream are also real. You are both the creator of the dream and the person experiencing it. You conceive the situation and are traumatized by it at the same time. How can that be? Well, one explanation is that perhaps you are not the sole creator of your dreams. Is it possible that the dream state is simply another dimension of existence you experience with your spiritual body? Are dreams merely events that play out in an ethereal plane that are as real to the spiritual body as Earthly events are to the physical body? While you blissfully sleep on your Posturepedic beauty-rest bed, is your soul off galivanting with other spiritual beings in the spiritual realm? Interesting thoughts, aren't they?

Shamanic and spiritualist beliefs of the dream state tell a different story than Freudian interpretations. Souls are vibrational energy beings, and as energy beings they are never in a state of rest. This state of perpetual energy activity has a draining effect on the soul while incarnated in the heavy densities of the physical world. The free, limitless, enlightened soul is essentially imprisoned by the limitations of its human body. It's similar to sending an electrical current through a resistor: the resistor causes a loss of energy. When a soul is incarnated in a human body, it resides in a vessel that has stark limitations, or 'resistance,' to the freedom it experiences in the spiritual dimension. In Chapter 6 we explored how the soul is confined by the heavy density of the physical world. It needs relief from this confinement, a time to be free from the physical encumbrances to re-energize in its ethereal home. Dreaming becomes an opportunity for the soul to reenergize and seek guidance in order to recharge its batteries due to the loss of energy from the resistance of the physical world. This is the purpose of sleep and dreams from the spiritual perspective. Think of it like the 1-hour of recreation time given to prisoners in solitary confinement to minimize psychiatric issues. The soul's incarnation in a human body is its solitary confinement and the dream state becomes the soul's rec time.

How does all this playtime relief for the soul work? When you enter the REM stage of sleep your brain waves slow to the delta state and your physical body disconnects from its physical surroundings in a state of deep relaxation. Your soul is no longer encumbered by the mind and personality of the physical body. This allows the soul to disengage from the body giving it the freedom to associate with spiritual entities in the spiritual dimension. While in the dream state, only a portion of your soul energy temporarily leaves your body and returns to the spiritual dimension. During this state your soul is able to contact and interact with its over-soul and other souls in the spiritual dimension. These connections and interactions get interpreted by the physical mind as "dreams." However, they are not imaginary or hallucinations. The interactions the soul has during the dream state in the spiritual dimension are just as real to the soul as interactions in the physical dimension are to the human body. It's part of the reason why your dreams 'feel' real when you are startled awake.

Dreams may seem to exist in a magical imaginary world, but that world is real. Shamans, sages, mystics, and yogis have known this for ages. They also know the soul doesn't communicate through the limitations of language. Instead, to express the full range of profound knowledge souls speak to us through alternative means. We've explored soul messages that get delivered via synchronicities and intuition, now we can add soul messages sent by way of dreams. Your dreams are direct symbolic reflection of your soul's communication with its over-soul and spiritual beings and can offer you insights about your life. Every dream has a secret meaning encrypted in it and serve as a portal to the spiritual dimension.

When you intentionally deprive yourself of sleep, you are depriving your soul from connecting with its home. In Chapter 5 we discovered how the soul is the true command center of the body. When the soul becomes deprived of this freedom and drained from extended periods of being 'trapped' in the human vessel, it reacts. It needs time to re-energize and commands the body to sleep so it can seek relief in the lighter density of the spiritual realm. This is why the complete deprivation of sleep causes psychological impairment to the physical body. The soul needs its relief time.

However, sleep isn't the only means of providing relief. The soul can also be rejuvenated through meditation. You can achieve a dream state like condition through advanced forms of meditation. Masters capable of reaching a deep meditative state in which their souls become engaged in the spiritual dimension are said to experience *'Astral Travel'* or *"Astral Projection."* Rejuvenating the soul through meditation explains why people who meditate on a regular basis require less sleep. Now, if dreams do carry insight and messages from the spiritual dimension, wouldn't it be great to remember them? Just think of all those dream time messages you've missed out on! Well, there are techniques you can do to help you remember your dream state adventures.

Just like any other skill you'd like to refine, remembering your dreams only takes a little practice. And like other skills, keeping track of your progress is a great way to monitor your success. I suggest placing a pad and pen beside your bed so that you can write down your dreams as they occur. This will become your dream log. Leave the pad open to a blank page with the pen on top prior to going to bed. There's going to be times when you'll pop up in the middle of the night to scribble down a dream. When that happens, you don't want to search for your dream log and pen, so make sure it's ready to go before falling asleep.

With that in place, you'll want to develop a desire to remember your dreams. Having a genuine belief that your dreams offer communications and insight from the spiritual dimension can provide sufficient motivation to trigger this desire. So, open your mind to the possibilities. With your desire firmly rooted in your conscious mind, follow this simple process before going to sleep. As you lie in bed, take a few deep diaphragmatic breaths to relax your mind and body. Erase all the busy-body activities of the day from your mind. When your mind is cleared and still, program your subconscious mind with the following statement of intent, *"You will remember any significant dream tonight. You will awake immediately after the dream with full memory of all its important details*." This will plant the command into your subconscious mind. You can say it out loud, or mentally. However, if you choose to say it mentally be sure to be direct and firm. As you fall asleep, repeat the command a few additional times.

With practice, you will find yourself waking up after your dreams. Initially you may only remember bits and pieces of your dream but write down whatever you recall. It's important to jot down all the details just after you awake from the dream. I know you'll fight the temptation to fall back to sleep with the certainty that you'll remember a dream with such vivid clarity in the morning. But when morning comes, you'll be kicking yourself for not writing it down as those vivid details escape you. So, write everything down before going back to sleep. Finally, when you wake up in the morning, stay in bed for a few extra minutes and try to recall anything you can from your dreams. Whatever it is, even if it is a vague recollection, write them in your dream log. Don't try to analyze them, just jot down whatever comes to mind. Over time, you will remember more. Soon you'll automatically wake with full memory of your dreams. Afterwards, you can review your dream log for patterns and messages. Strange and bizarre dreams will begin making sense as you tune in to your higher-self.

Tracking and analyzing your dreams provide great insight to your life and can be lots of entertaining fun. As you develop your skills further and become more accustomed to your dreams, you'll be able to perform some dream magic. You can present perplexing questions from your waking life to your over-soul prior to sleep and search for their answers in your dreams. You can advance further to a very powerful technique called *'lucid dreaming.'* This is a magical skill where your body is sleeping, but you are consciously aware and actively able to participate in and manipulate your dreams. Lucid dreaming can be used to make life-altering changes. Have fun, practice, enjoy your spiritual adventures, and get plenty of sleep. Who knows, maybe our paths will cross in the dream state!

On the surface this chapter may seem a bit on the scattered side, but let's review what we uncovered and see how it all fits together. We've considered a Universe where both the physical and spiritual dimensions coexist in one interconnected singularity. A Universe where physical energies and spiritual energies are joined by a Universal consciousness, leading to a world where everything physical is infused with spiritual energy. This led to a revolutionary theory of evolution that implies genetic mutations are not left to random chance, but rather occur through the higher intelligence of Universal consciousness.

By examining energy densities, we were able to recognize a correlation with consciousness. The heavier the density the lower the consciousness, conversely the lighter the density the higher the consciousness. Since the physical world follows this pattern, we looked to see if a similar correlation exists with the evolution of the soul and discovered that it does. The soul's frequency increases as it grows and evolves. We express these growth stages with the familiar terms of Infant, Baby, Young, Mature, and Old Souls. The soul learns and evolves in the physical world with the help of other souls via spiritual agreements known as Soul Contracts. You choose the lesson you want to learn, even ones filled with hardship, suffering, and heartache. You can accelerate spiritual growth by choosing a life of high frequency thoughts and actions.

All the learning activity in the heavy density of the physical world drains the soul, which requires a break to recharge its batteries. The soul relieves itself in the dream state when the physical body is asleep and disconnected from its physical environment. Dreams are as real in the spirit realm as the body's activities are in the physical world and much can be gained from analyzing them. And finally, dream state activity is essential for the soul to continue its lesson in this lifetime.

So, you see, this chapter isn't as scattered as it appears. It all relates to the soul's growth. All these pieces connect to show us a picture of spiritual evolution. We can see through this analysis that we are here in a physical body to learn for the growth and evolution of your soul.

It's time to bring the investigation into the purpose of life to an end and wrap up the case with final closing arguments. In this case I'd like you to act as a member of the jury, weighing all of the evidence with an open and unbiased mind, and drawing a logical conclusion. So, let's present the findings and see how the jury deliberates…

Ch. 12: Your Purpose Revealed

"We have taken birth to evolve; but we are so allured by the worldly desires that we forget the real purpose of life."
- Dada J. P. Vaswani

Closing Arguments

Well, it's been quite a journey! Eleven rock'em, sock'em chapters of thought-provoking insights on the physical and spiritual properties of the Universe. We set out to ask nontraditional provocative questions, and did we? *"Yes, we did!"* We said we'd look at alternative perspectives of reality, and did we? *"Yes, we did!"* We committed to investigate the issues relating to the purpose of life, and did we? *"Yes, we did!"* And we pledged to compile all of our findings into a summarizing conclusion, and did we? *"Yes, we did!"* ...Oh wait, sorry, getting a little ahead of myself there. *"No, we haven't!"* However, that's exactly what we'll be doing in this last and final summary chapter. Which means our time together is coming to a close. But rather than a tearful goodbye, let's focus on all the good times shared! Think back to when we first met, some 400 pages ago, when we were just beginning our spiritual journey. Let's reflect on the good ole days with a nostalgic review of the many fascinating and life-altering things we've learned. And as we piece together this collection of knowledge, I'd like you to recall the challenge I posed in which I asked you to read and digest the contents of this book with openness and desire.

Before you close the covers for good, think through the contents and decide where you stand on the evidence presented. Don't simply read these pages and go on with life without making a definitive choice about your beliefs. If you choose to accept the information I've presented, then apply it to your life. Use it to grow, to make a difference, to attract and manifest the life of your desires, to improve upon your life and to better the world at large. However, if you still have reservations after all the corroborating information I've provided, then I want to express my sincere gratitude for spending the time together and giving me an opportunity to share the understandings of spirituality I've come to believe.

The very first sentence of the book is a quote from Albert Einstein, *"There are only two ways to live your life; One is as though nothing is a miracle. The other is as if everything is. I believe in the latter*." Eleven chapters later you now have an understanding of the Universe that is much closer to Einstein's, so you too can begin to live your life as though everything truly is a miracle.

We first plunged into our investigation of life by discovering a genetic code forming by random chance boils down to a mathematical impossibility, even for the simplest lifeform. This gave rise to the theory of intelligent design as a force behind the creation of life on this planet, which is supported by many of the most brilliant scientific minds of the past century who have advanced understandings of quantum physics and cellular biology. This discovery furthered our investigation to other natural phenomenon guided by a higher intelligence. We saw it in the atomic structure of the elements, the migratory pattern of Monarch butterflies, the molecular assembly of apple and orange trees, and as a mathematical constant in the design of the universe.

With various examples of a higher intelligence, we then uncovered the secret behind its ability to govern the physical world - energy. Yep, our old friend E=MC². Putting energy under the microscope brought us down to the quantum depths of the atom where we discovered the brick and mortar, flesh and blood world of solid structures isn't very solid at all. The solidity of the physical world is nothing more than vibrating bits of energy forming atoms that are close to being 100% empty space. This unveiled an unequivocal picture of an energy-based world operating at different vibrational frequencies, including the matter making up the cells of our bodies. We too are nothing more than vibrating energy.

Deductive reasoning compelled us to ask, *"If all matter is made of the same subatomic particles, why does some matter have consciousness, free-will, and emotions (humans), while other matter doesn't (minerals and elements)?"* Exploring this conundrum led to the revelation that humans are comprised of two components, a physical body and an energy body. Our energy body is an immortal soul requiring a vessel to experience the heavy energy density of the physical world. This redefined our understanding of the human body, showing it as a bridge connecting the physical world with the spiritual dimension. We learned the fascinating reality that all we see, touch, taste, smell, and hear plays out in the inner recesses of the mind. The five senses are tools for our immortal soul to experience the physical world...but why?

Investigating this provocative question pushed us to study the soul's intent for incarnating in a physical body. Our analysis revealed evidence of the physical world being a school for the soul. We questioned how any soul could squeeze an entire curriculum of life lessons into just one lifetime, forcing us to confront the stark reality of death. It opened our eyes to observe death from a different perspective, that of the soul. This

**Purpose of existence is to fully accept and give gratitude for
your incredible present life -- and to bring forth more love,
acceptance, and positive energy into this world
in spite of your current difficult life situations.**

You have lived many, many other lifetimes on this Earth School.

You will have played every characters and roles in this Earth School.

**Playing the role of a poor person in this lifetime would means that you
have had also played the role of a rich person in another lifetime(s).**

**We express our thanks to you for playing the tough role of a "poor"
person now in order for us to be able to give and help others in need.**

The loving Universe will always help, support, and guide you.

We ask the Universe to bless you always!!

You are not alone in this Universe!

You are always one with the All That Is.

Everyone including you is truly worthy in this Universe.

**Every person on this Earth has a purpose for their existence.   **

You are not your present or past life stories or situations.

**You are truly an eternal soul/spirit inhabiting this body, on
this Earth School to have life experiences to learn and evolve.**

**You are not your body. Your body is like a pet or animal (pet-body)
that you inhabit and control. Respect and help your body and take
very good care of it to the best of your ability.**

**It is you, yourself, that have chosen this current difficult Earth
life lessons for your own learning and spiritual growth.**

**These hardships are your own personal lessons on this
Earth school to help you evolve spiritually.**

allowed us to realized death for the immortal soul is simply a transition from one state of consciousness to another state of higher consciousness. Research stepped us through the process of the soul's assimilation to its spiritual home upon death of the physical body. In the spiritual dimension the soul reviews and evaluates all it has learned and areas of future growth. The soul then chooses the body and life that will provide the lessons it wants to experience in its next lifetime. Our skeptical investigative minds demanded credibility to what seemed like fanciful tales of the afterlife, so we dug into the marvels of reincarnation.

The details of five true past-life cases were examined including the Dali Llama and one of my personal experiences. Facts and evidence presented forced us to recognize the undeniable realities that souls do incarnate in different lives and different eras. With convincing evidence of an afterlife, we needed to understand the rules by which it functions. We learned the spiritual dimension is governed by its own set of rules and laws. The two powerhouses are the Law of Attraction and the Law of Karma. Studying these laws helped us to realize the frequency of our thoughts and actions attract our reality, which was supported by the scientific principle of harmonic resonance. We learned that you can accelerate spiritual growth by choosing high frequency thoughts and actions. Controlling our thoughts to manifest our desires led to practices that help achieve mastery of the mind. Powerful techniques such as visualization, meditation, and the Mind-Body Refresher were learned.

Accumulating all this information reinforces that you, and you alone, determine the outcome of your life. Advanced knowledge of the spiritual body offers a powerful gift to guide and control your life. With all that you've uncovered, I'd like you to take another look in the mirror…this time, what do you see? Take a deeper look with your new spiritual perspective, is the image in the mirror any different? Do you see nothing more than a biological organism composed of 30 Trillion cells staring back at you? Or do you see a beautiful spiritual being? An immortal soul? The real YOU? What about God? Do you see God reflecting back to you?

Never lose sight of the fact that you are a spiritual fragment of the higher intelligence that governs the Universe. You are a portion of the divine creator. You are not made in God's likeness, you ARE a part of God. This is the most life affirming secret known by the sages, shamans, and prophets throughout the ages. We are all fragments God. The realization of this my dear friends IS the purpose of life. You are a spiritual being having a human experience for the evolution of your soul. The reason you are here today, in the body that's holding and reading this book, is to learn life lessons that bring you closer to uniting with your true self, God.

And with that, jury of my peers, I ask you for your verdict. What does all this evidence mean for you? The choice is entirely under your control. The knowledge you've gained affords you the gift to question all the false notions about the realities of the world. Knowledge of your spiritual body provides perspective of the world most are blind to. As you grow in your understanding of the powerful spiritual forces and accept it was you who chose to incarnate in this life, you begin to recognize how much of a blessing life truly is. All life!

Life doesn't happen TO you, it happens FOR you. Show gratitude and appreciation for the opportunity you've been given to experience life's miracles. Look beyond the challenges and hardships you may face and stand in awe and gratitude of life. Enjoy your physical experience, show gratitude for your opportunity to grow, and radiate the full loving spectrum of your spiritual being. The acknowledgement that your immortal soul will return to Earth's school builds a profound level of respect for all lifeforms and natural resources on the planet. Begin here and now to enjoy the powerful forces within. Choose unconditional happiness regardless of the ups and downs, the pros and cons, and the joys and the heartaches.

Every soul is here to accomplish its destiny. We are here to experience the deception of separation from God and to understand how we are both independently unique and collectively one. We must exert compassion for one another, support for one another, and strive towards loving one another. All souls are fragments of God trying to find their way home. It's the one common thing we all share. You are a spiritual being having a human experience for the purpose of spiritual evolution to become one with God. So, let's end our time together with some thoughts on a subject that has been debated, contemplated, coveted, worshipped, denounced, praised, cursed, honored and vilified more than any other in the history of mankind…God!

The Divinity

I'd like to conclude the book in a symbolic way by defining God as I've come to accept. After all, I've presented considerable evidence supporting the extraordinary case that the soul's purpose is spiritual growth to achieve oneness with God. What better way to end the book than with the final destination of the soul. But what exactly is God? What are we all trying to return to? What are we striving to unite with? It raises a rather perplexing conundrum…how do you define something that's undefinable? The totality of God is something that can't be defined in written word or spoken language. The human mind is finite and simply unable to comprehend the infinite as it pertains to God.

As advanced as modern science has become, it is still in an extremely limited infancy in scope and technology to understand the universe and the mysterious meaning of its existence. Contemporary science defines the universe as an immense collection of interstellar material originating some 14 billion years ago from a primordial expansion known as the "Big Bang." From this event, all time, space, matter, energy, and life originated. But how did the Big Bang form? Where did it come from? Why did it occur? What existed prior to the Big Bang? We currently have no answers to these questions.

Rather than make futile attempts to explain why the universe exists, I'll present beliefs and descriptions that approach a concept of God that I've come to understand. I've defined the universe as energy-based. All things from the physical to the spiritual are energy. Many cultures throughout time reference an omnipresent, ubiquitous, unseen primordial energy that expands the depths of the Universe. It is not air, nor is it the empty space of a vacuum, but rather an energy of higher consciousness that permeates and animates the entire Universe. It is recognized as the energy of life itself. God is that energy.

All the vibrating and pulsing energies we learned of collectively constitute God. God is the original source of the Big Bang that now provides life and structure to the universe, the source of creation itself. God is the singular consciousness that encompasses all consciousness. God is omnipresent on all planes and dimensions. God is everything and everyone, the totality of everything. Try to perceive God as an energy, rather than an entity. Think of God as a verb, the energy, not as a noun, a person, place, or thing. Once your perception of God becomes a noun you separate yourself from God and become confined to the deception of that separation. This separation from God is what differentiates spiritual beliefs from many religious beliefs.

You are not separate from God, you are a fragment of God. God is not independent of you, God is a part of you. We are all composed of energy that originated from the Big Bang. There is no separation. You are an independent person with free will, independent thoughts and emotions, unique in your own way. However, the biological reality is you are composed of 30 trillion cells, each of which are separate and independent of one another. Every cell in your body lives, functions, and reproduces independently. Collectively they become you! Extend this to the concept of God. Independently there are billions of people on this planet, and an unknown number of lifeforms throughout the universe. The energies of all these independent individuals, both physical and spiritual energies, collectively become God.

But what about God's disposition? Are we judged, admonished, and persecuted by God? Not the loving God of my beliefs. God is not a wrathful God depicted by some religions, but rather an omnipresent, all-knowing consciousness of pure, unconditional love. God's love radiates unconditionally throughout all of the universe, not just Earth. You can think of God's unconditional love as you would the sun's rays. The sun radiates its life-giving energy on everything and everyone throughout our solar system without judgment. Man, animals, plants, and all the planets and moons in the entire solar system. The rich and poor, innocent and offender, honest and criminal, moral and immoral, cosmopolitan and primitive, advanced lifeforms and unicellular organisms. Its rays are unconditional and never ending. God's energy radiates in the same unconditional manner.

The description of the afterlife from individuals who have had near death experiences approach the realities of being in God's loving presence. The presence of God is like being engulfed in a brilliant enlightened white light of pure unconditional love and awareness more powerful than the greatest human nirvana. A place of expanded awareness, a loving realm of an all-knowing spiritual power, filled with joy, peace, acceptance, harmony, and universal love. A heavenly experience of such profound bliss, glory, and enlightenment that all souls yearn for this Godly union.

And now, it's time for you to take what you've learned and apply it to your life. You now have the keys to unlock your spiritual superpowers. You alone are the master of your destiny. Your thoughts, your beliefs, your emotions, and your actions are all powerful factors in manifesting your reality. If your mind becomes dominated with negative thoughts of hatred, envy, disdain, fear, vengeance, violence, and greed, then negative energy will be drawn into your life. However, fill your mind with positive thoughts of love, affection, joy, caring, and compassion, and you will draw positive energy into your life. What you think and believe is the reality you live. It's as basic and simple as that! The choice truly is yours to make. Use all your God-given free will to fill your life with positive, loving, prosperous, and grateful thoughts. Force them into your life. Whatever you hold within your soul's mind will manifest in your life. It is spiritual law.

Start today. Begin making conscientious efforts to control how you think. Look for the beauty in life instead of focusing on the doom and gloom. Be grateful for what you have and not envious of what you don't. Quit bitching about all that's wrong with your life and replace those thoughts with ones of love and appreciation. Make the conscious determination to magnetize your mind with intense thoughts and desires for all the positive things you want – health, happiness, loving relationships, prosperity, adventure, friendship, etc.

Love yourself for who you are as you are. Love others for who they are as they are, without judgment or criticism and you'll be on your way to peaceful positive mental energies. Look for ways to be grateful even when there's nothing to be thankful for. As you proactively engage in positive thoughts, the Law of Attraction and harmonic resonance will pull positive energies into your life like a powerful magnet. Day by day, you'll begin to experience your life consumed with joy, love, prosperity, and happiness. Little by little your blessings will grow and build upon themselves until your life is filled with such beauty and abundance you won't have any problem finding gratitude.

Never lose sight of the fact that YOU ARE a tiny fraction of God. Believe in yourself as an immortal spiritual fragment of God and life becomes a miracle to cherish. All that occurs in your life are great blessings. The good, the bad, the triumphs and the hardships. They are all lessons offering your soul opportunity to grow. Seize them! Show appreciation for them.

As you experience adversities, remember the universe only gives that which the soul is capable of enduring. Great tests are only given to great souls. When you release the need to know why things happen and accept them for what they are, you begin to master spiritual growth. Trust the reason behind your experiences is part of a higher purpose designed to benefit you, and life will flow with much less resistance.

Well, there you have it. Earth is a school for the soul. Your purpose is to learn this life's curriculum. Welcome to class!

I feel love,

I am Love.

Love is God.

God is Love.

I feel God. I am God

I'm an expression of God.

I'm God's loving consciousness.

I feel love. I am Love.

Love is the consciousness of God.

God is the consciousness of love.

I feel God. I am God

I am an expression of God,

I am God's loving consciousness.

INDEX

A

Akashic Records, 297
algor mortis, 187
alpha State, 137
amino acids, 12-28, 309, 372, 373
Arnold Schwarzenegger, 153
astral projection, 402
astral travel, 402
aura, 90, 101, 107

B

baby stage, 385
basic-consciousness, 376
belly chakra, 96
beta state, 136
Big Bang, 27, 412, 413
bi-location, 70
bio-plasma, 89, 108, 113, 114
body memories, 152
brain wave, 26
brain waves, 26, 105, 186, 266, 397, 400
Buddha, 377, 378

C

cellular memories, 152, 166, 168, 169, 236
chakras, 93-101, 113, 145, 163, 168, 254, 293, 344, 354
Chi, 86-101, 109, 112, 145, 189, 328, 344, 369
communication chakra, 99
companion soulmate, 254
conscious mind, 137-140, 145, 191, 313, 314, 326, 402
Creator, 27, 157, 158, 176, 207, 309, 366, 390, 391
crown chakra, 100

D

Dalai Lama, 153, 228-235, 279
dark energy, 85
delta state, 137
diaphragmatic breathing, 337-340
dream state, 196, 398-405

E

Einstein, 1, 3, 5, 29, 30, 67, 79, 80, 130, 148, 180, 264, 396, 407
elixir of life, 302-304

F

Fibonacci Sequence, 55, 56, 58, 59, 63
Fibonacci Spiral, 59, 60
first chakra, 95
flutter, 47
forgiveness, 356-359
frequency, 26, 27, 73-75, 89, 105-108, 136, 137, 160-170, 185, 190, 207, 250-254, 262, 267, 272-280, 285, 308, 309, 320, 345, 346, 375-382, 387, 389, 404, 409

G

genetic code, 14, 20-22, 27, 372, 407
genome, 13-14, 20-24, 35, 104, 166, 398
Golden Ratio, 55-61, 64

H

harmonic resonance, 272-279, 285, 307, 409, 415
heart chakra, 98, 101
hertz, 26, 73, 136, 137
higher intelligence, 2, 26, 29, 34-37, 42, 44, 54, 64, 65, 71, 83, 145, 176, 286, 309, 404, 407-410
higher-self, 162, 307, 320, 334, 347, 348, 355, 362, 387, 403
human energy field, 89, 90, 101, 108, 113

I

infant souls, 174
infant stage, 385
interbrain, 181
irreducible complexity, 18

J

Jesus, 378, 384

K

karma, 202-206, 210, 218, 251, 287-298, 312
kinetic energy, 72

L

Law of Abundance, 263
Law of Attraction, 262-298, 307, 310, 312, 319, 320, 345, 346, 363, 409, 415
Law of Balance and Polarity, 262
Law of Chaos and Order, 263
Law of Circulation, 259
Law of Conservation of Energy, 80, 260
Law of Gender, 263
Law of Growth and Abundance, 259
Law of Harmonic Resonance, 272
Law of Karma, 262-264, 286-298, 409
Law of Rhythm, 263
Law of Universal Life, 263
Law of Vibration, 262
life between lives, 159, 161, 198-208, 210, 213, 228
life review, 209
light being, 160
livor mortis, 187
lucid dreaming, 403

M

Magnificent Seven, 93-95, 102, 163
Master Zhou, 109-111
mature stage, 386
Max Planck, 180
meditation, 26, 105, 137, 140, 162, 169, 189, 230, 254, 288, 303, 321-349, 354, 358-360, 381, 402, 409
meridians, 90-92, 113
Michio Kaku, 29

microtubules, 180
Mind-Body Primer, 346-350, 358, 359
Mind-Body Refresher, 335-338, 346, 347
mind chakra, 99
Monarch Miracle, 47

N

Near Death Experiences, 190
Newton, 69, 79, 260, 264, 301, 302
nucleotide, 13

O

old soul, 174, 221, 386, 404
organelle, 12
over-soul, 162-165, 169, 170, 179, 192, 198, 203, 212, 401-403

P

pallor mortis, 187
panpsychism, 68, 368
pantheism, 64
pareidolia, 64
past lives, 216-227, 244, 245, 251-257, 293, 395
Periodic Table, 39, 40, 44, 396
Philosopher's Stone, 301-306
placebo effect, 351
Planck, 30, 35, 180
plasma, 107, 150
Plato, 68, 150, 368
potential energy, 72
prayer, 162, 269, 270, 298, 349, 350
primary flaccidity, 187
primary soulmate, 254
pronoia, 362

Q

quantum entanglement, 70

R

rigor mortis, 187
root chakra, 95

S

sacral chakra, 96
self-consciousness, 376
self-healing, 269, 328, 345-354
singularity, 365-374, 377, 386, 404
Sir Francis Crick, 30
Socrates, 7, 68, 86, 150, 382
solar plexus chakra, 97
soul contract, 176, 390-394, 404
soul family, 196, 198, 253-255, 394, 395
soul group, 196, 207-213, 393
soulmate, 252-254
sound waves, 72, 123, 124, 275
spirit guides, 194
subconscious mind, 137-147, 199, 222, 235, 266, 313, 320, 321, 335, 346, 356, 403
super-conscious mind, 138-141, 145, 313
superposition, 70
synchronicities, 320, 326, 360, 361, 401

T

theta state, 137
third eye, 99
throat charka, 99

U

Universal Consciousness, 91, 377, 380
Universal Intelligence, 35-37, 65-71, 158, 297, 363, 374
Universal Laws, 259

V

visualization, 105, 313-335, 345-350, 409
Vital Life Energy, 86-93, 112, 149, 337

W

willful amnesia, 395

Y

young souls, 174
young stage, 385